A GENERAL HISTORY OF EUROPE

EDITED BY DENYS HAY

EUROPE IN
THE FOURTEENTH
AND FIFTEENTH CENTURIES

DENYS HAY

LONGMAN

LONGMAN GROUP LIMITED
London

*Associated companies, branches and representatives
throughout the world*

First published 1966
Third impression and first paperback edition 1970
Sixth impression 1976

ISBN 0 582 48213 5 cased
ISBN 0 582 48343 3 paper

*Printed in Hong Kong by
Commonwealth Printing Press Ltd*

Contents

Maps

Acknowledgement

We are grateful to Böhlau Verlag-Köln for permission to reproduce a table from 'Der Binnenhandel des Deutschen Ordens in Preussen' by W. Böhnke, published in *Hansische Geschichtsblätter*, No. 80 for 1962.

Preface

I undertook to edit this series in 1955 and at the same time I agreed with
Reginald Betts that we should be jointly responsible for a volume on
Europe in the fourteenth and fifteenth centuries. That the editor's own
volume should only appear in 1966, eleven years later, is an indication
(I hope) of other pressing business and not least the absorbing business
of teaching the period itself. That the volume should come out under
one name instead of two accounts for further delay, occasioned by the
premature death of Betts in 1961. Betts, who was Masaryk professor of
East European history at London University, had never enjoyed good
health. His death nevertheless came as a shock, depriving his many
friends of a generous and sympathetic spirit and this volume of an
expert hand. He had completed two chapters when he died. Chapter II
below was drafted by him and revised and recast by me. Chapter IX,
slightly revised, is as he wrote it. I also benefited from his shrewd comments on early drafts of the first and fifth chapters.

I have often regretted the absence of Reginald Betts, but I have been
frequently helped by other friends and colleagues. Besides the individuals whom I have pestered on particular points (Dom David Knowles
has suffered more than most) I must particularly thank Dr K. A.
Fowler, Dr A. T. Luttrell, Mr A. Malkiewicz, Dr S. Oakley, and Professor H. S. Offler who have all read portions of the book and given me
their advice. Dr Roger Highfield kindly read a version of the book in
typescript and was good enough to show me page proofs of the volume,
referred to at p. 399 below, of which he was editor. I must also
record my sense of obligation to the late Mr Cyprian Blagden of Long-
mans, whose idea this History of Europe was, and to Mr Christopher
Newsom of the same firm. Both have given me (and other contributors)
encouragement, support and sound advice.

I hope the design of this volume is self-evident. It represents an
attempt, in early chapters, to display the main social groups; then to
outline the main changes in political life; finally, after the necessarily
diverse patterns of politics, to survey the unifying forces, religious,
cultural and commercial. The political ideas and the political practice

of the period, which are thus sandwiched between the treatment of more general social themes, occupy a substantial amount of space. This seems to me to be defensible in a book of this kind which deals with a long period. The desire for political power is the motor which drives men to public action. And power tends to spread over ever larger areas and ever longer times since it always seeks both to extend the area of its efficacy and to make itself permanent. It is also the politically dominant, a small fraction of the total population at most times and a very small fraction in these centuries, who are largely responsible for the cultural qualities of an age.

These cultural characteristics are often chosen to represent the total life of a period by providing its name. This particular era was called by Huizinga 'The Waning of the Middle Ages'. It covers the lifetime of Petrarch and the flowering of letters and art in fifteenth-century Italy, and many academics, perhaps all historians in America, would regard it as constituting part of the 'Renaissance'. Yet the men and women who at this time were coping with their day-to-day problems were not conscious that they were living under such labels. The handful of intellectuals in northern Europe were not aware that there had been a Middle Age or that it was waning. Another handful of intellectuals in Italy had, it is true, discerned a Middle Age and were engaged in defining a Renaissance. Their activities were soon to colour the whole of European civilization and I was tempted to adopt the title 'Europe in the Early Renaissance', naming the whole from one of its parts in what is a reasonable enough way. In the end I have chosen a neutral and chronological term, leaving the reader to determine the name he finds most appropriate for these centuries. May I remind him that *centuria* meaning a hundred years is neither a classical nor a medieval Latin word? We owe it, along with many other useful expressions, to the inventive genius of the humanist pedants of the Renaissance.

Edinburgh, July 1965   Denys Hay

I have now to thank Dr Fowler and Dr Luttrell for reading the proofs. Neither they nor the other scholars I have named are responsible for the views expressed in what follows.
January 1966

Reprints enable me to correct a number of errors which have been courteously pointed out by Dr D. M. Nicol, Dr Elizabeth Ratcliff, Dr S. H. Steinberg and Professor Donald W. Sutherland.
May 1967, December 1969

I

The Sources

A historian depends on the evidence of every kind left by earlier ages. Buildings, tools, clothing, works of art and works of utility are all grist to his mill. His prime source of information is, however, the words of the period with which he is concerned—literary works, including contemporary histories, and administrative records of all sorts, from the official accounts of governments to the ledgers and letters of private persons and corporations. These written records are usually more

BIBLIOGRAPHY. The sources of European history for this period are very unevenly treated in existing bibliographies and there are no general surveys other than those provided by A. Potthast, *Bibliotheca historica medii aevi*, 2nd edn., 2 vols. (Berlin, 1896), which lists narrative sources and U. Chevallier, *Répertoire des sources historiques du moyen âge: Bio-bibliographie*, 2 vols. (2nd edn., Paris, 1905–7) and *Topo-bibliographie*, 2 vols. (Paris, 1894–1903). These works have to be used with extreme caution and are hardly to be recommended to a beginner. They are also fuller and more reliable for the centuries before 1300 and this is also true of L. J. Paetow (ed.), *A Guide to the Study of Medieval History*, rev. edn. (New York, 1931). All in all the best general survey of the sources will still be found in the various bibliographies in vols. VII and VIII of the *Cambridge Medieval History* and in the other works listed in App. I (see below, p. 399). For France there is A. Molinier, *Les sources de l'histoire de France: moyen âge*, 6 vols. (Paris, 1901–6), excellently conceived and executed but by now out of date; the same remarks apply to the manual on German sources by O. Lorenz, *Deutschlands Geschichtsquellen . . . seit der Mitte des dreizehnten Jahrhunderts*, 2 vols. (3rd edn., Berlin, 1886–87), though it may be supplemented by Dahlmann-Waitz, *Quellenkunde der deutschen Geschichte*, 2 vols. (9th edn., Leipzig, 1931–32). By comparison C. Gross's *Sources and Literature of English History* (2nd edn., London, 1915) is a mere list of titles and also badly in need of revision; for the fifteenth century, however, there is the useful survey by C. L. Kingsford, *English Historical Literature in the Fifteenth Century* (Oxford, 1913). There is unfortunately nothing worthwhile for Italy, though for Italy and for other countries the standard literary histories (below p. 333) are often useful guides to chronicles and other narrative sources. Record materials are best discussed in works devoted to administrative and legal history (below, pp. 78–9).

I

informative than the silent witness of bricks and paint, and in any
brief account of the sources they take pride of place.

In the course of the period here discussed the sources of this type
changed very considerably in most regions of Europe. Earlier the bulk
of writing had been in Latin; now it was often in the vernacular, a
trend which by the late fifteenth century had become dominant, despite
a remarkable and important revival of writing in 'classical' Latin.
Earlier the record keepers had been mainly clergy, the clerks who acted
for king and magnate, and whose own records, for church or monastery,
have been better preserved than lay documents; now the king's officials
were often laymen, and laymen themselves began to keep more documents, because they were frequently literate, exchanging letters with one
another. These were perhaps the most important changes but many
others followed on the king's securing (as we shall see that he did) a
greater power in most countries, for this affected the administrative
records which are usually our most continuous source of information
about public life. We now begin to find secretarial records, for example,
and a new type of diplomatic agent with a growing range of reports and
detailed negotiations. The very changes in the documentation are thus
frequently a valuable guide to what people were doing and what they
said they were trying to do, which is what the historian wants to find
out.

For the plain narrative of events—the kind of material one can nowadays accumulate by keeping a file of newspapers—one must at this
time turn to the historians, the men who were chronicling their own day
for themselves and their contemporaries. Here, too, we shall find
changes indicative of new needs: the old chronicle, annalistic and largely
the product of monasteries, was going out; annals of a quite novel type
began to be compiled; and fresh varieties of narrative made their
appearance. These developments in narrative sources will first be
considered.

Narrative sources

One has to remember the great number of chronicles composed and
'continued' in the twelfth and thirteenth centuries to view in perspective
the output of the monastic annalist in the later Middle Ages. At first
sight the work of the monastic historian seems considerable. In France
the great house of St Denis, north of Paris, maintained its 'Great
Chronicles' in both Latin and the vernacular, and the Latin narrative
of the anonymous monk covering the years 1380–1422 (ed. Bellaguet,

1839–52) is, if the last important contribution to the series, by no means the least impressive. Similarly at St Albans, north of London, the house that had produced the splendid chronicles of Roger of Wendover and Matthew Paris could still muster a Thomas Walsingham, several of whose works and notably the *Historia Anglicana* 1406–20 (ed. V. H. Galbraith, 1937) are significant sources. But after the early years of the fifteenth century the monastic chronicle dried up, even in France and England; elsewhere it had become parochial long before.

This decline in historical writing by members of religious communities is of interest for the light it throws on the intellectual life of the religious themselves, as well as on the broader topic of what was of interest to other sections of the reading public. There is no overall decline in historical composition; rather the contrary, for several new types of narration appeared to compensate for the failure of the traditional genre. There is, first, a curiously shortlived burst of what must be termed 'chivalric' history; secular chronicles begin to be plentiful in towns; and, in Italy, original forms of sustained and mature historical composition were evolved.

A knightly way of life had been the accepted social norm in western Europe for many centuries. This had certain literary consequences (the romance epics, for instance) but it was not until the fourteenth century that historiography was markedly affected. One important reason for the timelag undoubtedly lay in the illiteracy of the laity—or at any rate of the landed laity—who earlier had of necessity to listen to bard or storyteller, but who could now often read for themselves. To them the subject of war was particularly congenial and to them were addressed the chronicles of Jean le Bel and his great successor, Jean Froissart (d. *c.* 1404). The success of Froissart's *Chronicle*, which in its various recensions covers the years 1327–1400, is to be measured by the large number of manuscripts which have survived—so numerous are they that to this day there is no complete and adequate edition. (What will be the best, that published by the Société de l'histoire de France, began to come out in 1869 (ed. Luce) and has not got beyond the year 1388 in the fourteen volumes which have so far appeared.) Froissart's success was undoubtedly due in part to the way he coincided with a period of Anglo-French rivalry which subsumed the history of Scotland, the Low Countries and Spain: his canvas covered Europe. In part it was due to his brilliance as an author, for it is hard even today to put him down once one has begun to read his stately and colourful prose. But equally important are the long lists of lords, knights and gentlemen

3

who throng his pages; for many readers his story had all the charm which later notables were to find in the *Almanach de Gotha* or *Who's Who*. Le Bel and Froissart were clerks in orders. Their successors in this type of contemporary history were often laymen: Enguerrand de Monstrelet (d. 1453) and Georges Chastellain (d. 1475), who between them cover the first three-quarters of the fifteenth century from a European viewpoint somewhat similar to Froissart's, were gentlemen in the service of the dukes of Burgundy.

This chivalrous history, concentrating on wars and tournaments, is of the first importance to the historian but, as the authors gathered much of their material from the parties whose actions they were describing, the authority of any single episode as recounted even by Froissart or Chastellain has to be controlled by other sources. There is also the danger that these literary men might have coloured their pages in a way favourable to the patron of the moment: it is this which has led some critics to identify and disparage the so-called 'Burgundian School'. Yet the greatest literary champion of a prince had a detachment which gives his pages the very highest authority: Philippe Commynes, former servant of Charles the Bold who became adviser and man of affairs to Louis XI of France, wrote in his *Mémoires* (conveniently edited by Calmette and Durville, 3 vols., Paris, 1924–25) an astonishingly cool analysis of the reigns of Louis XI and Charles VIII, when he had been at the centre of political life. But with Commynes we have left the chivalric narrative and entered a world which Froissart would have hardly recognized: the *Mémoires* have more in common with the new diplomatic despatch than the old chronicle.

In these years a new type of chronicle made rapid strides all over Europe. It was composed by townsmen for their fellow townsmen and it is evidence both of the growth of urban importance in society at large and of the literacy of yet another group of men and women. Not surprisingly the town chronicle is found most often in areas where towns were large and politically important: in Italy, in parts of Germany. No collection of Italian town chronicles has ever been made, though a great many are now in print, not least in both the old and the new 'Muratori'—the Rerum Italicarum Scriptores published by L. A. Muratori in twenty-eight folio volumes (Milan, 1723–51) which has been slowly appearing, newly edited, since 1900. In Italian civic histories one series stands apart, the chronicle composed by three members of the Villani family of Florence (ed. Magheri, 8 vols., 1923; *Cronisti del Trecento*, ed. R. Palmarocchi, 1935). Giovanni's work ran from the creation to 1348; his brother Matteo continued this to 1363; and Matteo's son Filippo added a further section. For German town chronicles we have the great work, known by the name of its first editor C. Hegel, *Die Chroniken der deutschen Städte von 14 bis 16 Jahrhundert*: this began to appear in 1862 and vol. 36 was published in 1931. The narrative of events in great cities like Hamburg, Augsburg, Florence or Milan naturally embraced much general history. In France or England urban chronicles were both rarer and more parochial. London was really the only English town to develop a flourishing tradition; in France even Paris failed to provide a proper civic chronicle, though it had in the so-called 'Bourgeois' a diarist whose work is a vital source of French history for the period 1405–49 (ed. Tuetey, 1881). It should be noted that this urban historiography contributed greatly to more ambitious works of the late fifteenth century—for example Fabyan's *Chronicle* in England (London, 1516) and in Germany the *Liber Chronicarum* of Hartman Schedel (Nuremberg, 1493) which, with its illustrations, was to prove an influential work, although in itself an uncritical compilation. It will be noted that we have now moved into the era of print (see below, p. 356); with Schedel we have also moved into a literary tradition where the new historiographical methods of Italy are beginning to be influential.

The nature and stages of the 'Renaissance' in Italy form the subject of a later section of this book (below, p. 347). One of its characteristic fields was historical composition. The turning point in this was the close identification of literary culture with civic politics in the writings of Leonardo Bruni. Florence had in Bruni a chancellor who aided with his pen the diplomacy of the town and who presented to his fellow citizens a rational picture of Florentine history designed to fortify Florentine sentiments of primacy and independence and to win respect by its polished presentation. Bruni's *Historiarum Florentini Populi libri xii* (1415–29, best ed. by Santini in the new Rerum Italicarum Scriptores, 1914–26) was soon emulated all over Italy. Even the popes had such a survey of their past in B. Platina's *Lives* (ed. Gaida, Rer. Ital. Script., 1912–32), though this could naturally not be made, as other histories were, to serve the interests of a dynasty. The classical Latin historians were regarded as models and, though the directness and charm of the old civic chronicle was lost and a polemical aim often distorted the facts, much was gained in clarity of exposition, analysis of motive and concentration on significant events. At this stage history became 'past politics' and frequently—as in the vernacular writings of

Machiavelli and Guicciardini in the early sixteenth century—maintained a function in present politics as well. Another strand in Italian culture was an interest in the past for its own sake. This is best seen in the works of Flavio Biondo, a papal servant who wrote a number of influential works on Roman antiquities and who broke new ground by his description of Italy (*Italia Illustrata*, 1448–53) and his survey of history, the *Decades* (1439–50) which cover the period from A.D. 412 to 1442: with him the concept of the 'Middle Ages' effectively takes form; the phrase *media tempestas* is found in 1469.

By the end of the fifteenth century Italian writers were for the most part in the service not of republican towns but of increasingly autocratic princes and this was to facilitate the acceptance of the new Italian styles in northern Europe in the course of the sixteenth century. But even before then some traces of a new interest in antiquity and a new analysis of politics can be discerned north of the Alps. In France one must note the remarkable works of Thomas Basin (1412–91) in Latin (C. Samaran published an edition and translation of the *Histoire de Charles VII* in 1933 and the first volumes of his edition of the *Histoire de Louis XI* appeared in 1963–6), and the Latin *Compendium* of Robert Gaguin (Lyons, 1497). In Germany Schedel has been mentioned. To his name we should add the more important writers Johannes Nauclerus who published in 1504 a chronicle in which Italian influences are evident; and Jacob Wimpheling who at about the same date published his *Epitome rerum Germanicarum*. Yet these men were clerks of an old-fashioned kind and their works are often almost indistinguishable from medieval writings on similar themes. Only in Wimpheling, with his deliberate attempt to bolster German prestige, do we encounter a genuine Italian element and that in its most crude and chauvinistic form. In fact the most sophisticated northern historian was Commynes, writing not in Latin but in the vernacular. But even in Renaissance Italy the vernacular was about to be used for mature historical and political analysis by Machiavelli and Guicciardini.

It will be apparent that, apart from Italy, the new types of narrative history found in the later Middle Ages compensate only in part for the absence of the great church chronicles of an earlier epoch.[1] That the history of the fourteenth and fifteenth centuries can none the less be written with a new richness and precision is due to the much greater

[1] For a note on the remarkable Byzantine historians of the later Middle Ages, see below, p. 252.

bulk of record material and of what may loosely be described as private papers.

Public records and private papers

Government at every level in the Middle Ages depended on written documents. As government became more ambitious and effective in the thirteenth and later centuries this documentation becomes more abundant.

In great kingdoms—in Iberia, France, England—the central machinery was now more prolific than ever before. Acting on instructions from prince or council, the old departments of state issued executive directions. The very deliberations of the intimate councillors were often minuted. Formal charters were issued by the chancery under the great seal of the realm and the chancery also issued a host of directives less solemn (letters patent) or more *ad hoc* (letters close) as well as even more casual writs and injunctions. Of these copies were carefully registered. Likewise careful records of the prince's financial rights in his land were kept by the exchequer or treasury which, like the chancery, had an executive side. Equally it had a judicial side, though in all kingdoms there now existed a hierarchy of courts of law operating from the local level with appeals upwards to the centre of political power. Here too litigants demanded and judges imposed the maintenance of full records of proceedings. Finally there were everywhere bodies of a consultative or legislative or legal character—parliament, estates, *cortes*—whose deliberations and decisions were sometimes enrolled either because this was the wish of the representatives present or because their decisions affected public administration or finance.

To these steadily accumulating 'public records' this period was to add new categories. Here again the innovations are first encountered in Italy. The Italian princes and republics began to employ 'secretaries': the word itself suggests the familiar and confidential nature of the work. By the mid-fifteenth century we encounter secretaries in the entourage of the prince in France and England. The office was destined to have a future of importance, for as the prince began to govern more and more personally he found the secretary a more adaptable instrument than the cumbersome chancery; the secretary was his *alter ego*, his pen, his ear—his master at times, and frequently his scapegoat. Masses of papers came to this influential factotum—notes from his sovereign, reports from underlings, endless requests for favour and intervention from even the greatest in the land. By the end of the fifteenth century we can discern some of the functions of the future 'secretary of state'.

Another official was likewise born in Italy at this time: the permanent diplomatic agent. This development, and the secretary, will be briefly mentioned later (p. 115). Here must be noted the emergence of his records—formal instructions, formal despatches, and the multiplying papers of his daily inquisitiveness, as he retailed to his government the comings and goings of the court to which he was attached and estimated the significance of gossip and rumour. Again, by the end of the century, northern princes are falling into line, not least in maintaining agents at the court of the pope.

The *curia Romana* merits a word to itself in connection with record sources for, as we shall see, the administration of the church *qua* government was elaborate and up-to-date. Here we find not only the chancery and treasury (the latter called the *camera apostolica*) and law courts (notably the *Rota*) all with elaborate registries, but from the fifteenth century, a secretarial staff both numerous and influential. The resulting records, dealing as they do with Christendom at large, are one of the prime sources of European history and as such are being exploited by scholars of every country. French, German and Belgian scholars have over the years made available vast quantities of the papal registers of the fourteenth century; in the *Calendars of Papal Letters* and *Papal Petitions* we have volumes throwing light on many aspects of public and ecclesiastical life in the countries of Britain. An admirable survey of this material has been recently published by Mr Leslie Macfarlane (*Archives*, vol. IV, 1959). Church history also witnesses attempts at conciliar government at Constance (1414-18) and Basle (1431-47). These assemblies resulted in a mountain of documentation which represents every type of historical source—narrative (including the important accounts by Aeneas Sylvius Piccolomini and John of Ragusa), documents of all sorts and diaries, letters, sermons and debates. There have been many collections of this of which the most notable are volumes XXVII-XXXV of J. D. Mansi, *Sacrorum Conciliorum Collectio* (1759-98, reprinted 1901 ff.), E. H. von der Hardt, *Magnum Oecumenicum Constantiense Concilium* (Frankfort, 1696-1717), *Monumenta Conciliorum generalium saec.XV: scriptores*, ed. O. Richter and others (Vienna, 1857-95); and the more recent collections by H. Finke, *Acta Concilii Constanciensis*, 4 vols. (1896-1928) and J. Haller and others, *Concilium Basiliense*, 7 vols. (1896-1926). Translations by Louise R. Loomis of some of the Constance materials are contained in *The Council of Constance*, edited by J. H. Mundy and K. M. Woody (1961).

Preceding paragraphs have been devoted to the archives of central government. But this is only part of the story. At a regional or local level in great kingdoms the administrative controls were only in part to be found in royal officials: prévòts, sheriffs and other magistrates. Much law and administration was still seignorial—in the hands of the lord of land—or municipal. And there were large areas in Europe, notably in Germany and Italy, where at the start of the period the only government that mattered was seignorial and municipal. In the case of a great lord, whether in France or Italy or Germany or England, the machinery he employed was not so very different from that of the king, though it was much more rudimentary. The great man—and the great independent city—had a treasury and a chancery. If the lord's private affairs were inextricably intertwined in his public duties, let it be remembered that even in large and relatively centralized kingdoms the king's household, his 'family' in its widest sense, was also confused by the king and his contemporaries with what would today be called 'the state'.

Besides his official records, so to speak, the landed magnate of the later Middle Ages aped monarchy also in his increasing use of intimate clerical assistants and thus from the highest (like a duke of Burgundy) to the least (like the Paston family) accumulated a collection of family papers more intimate and, in a sense, ephemeral than anything surviving from earlier ages. With the survival of the laundry list and the love letter, of estate documents and contracts for craftsmen and artists, social history on a new scale becomes possible.

Within this category of 'private' papers we should perhaps link those of the church in the provinces. In theory ecclesiastical bodies were required to keep very elaborate records. The bishop's register should have documented the enormous range of his duties—ordinations and inductions, visitations of his diocese, appointment of his officers and so forth. The bishop, like the abbot, also had lands to administer. That all this record-making was often imperfectly done is part of the history of the church in this period; what was recorded is accordingly the more valuable. Within the church we must also reckon the archives (at this date they are all more or less regional) of the great religious orders. And likewise clerical in the technical sense are the records of the universities, at this time maintained systematically better in Italy and Germany than elsewhere.

Broadly speaking we may say that the narrative sources discussed in the first pages of this chapter are all nowadays available in print. This is not true of the records and semi-public or private papers of which we have just spoken. To begin with many have perished. Against the incomparable collections of papal documents in the Vatican Archives and the equally complete series of administrative records preserved in the Public Record Office in London, we must set the lamentably disjointed and dispersed records of the French crown—victims not only of time but of revolution and reform. In particular, French financial documents of the medieval period (including material bearing on the pay and recruitment of the army) were largely destroyed by fire in 1737 and by decision of the Convention in 1794. The records of the principal Hanseatic towns are for the most part preserved; many Italian cities have incredibly rich archives; but in many a great town the story has to be pieced together from fragments which have survived war and fire. No country (for instance) can boast the rich series of bishops' registers which have survived in England, but English university and municipal archives are poor before the sixteenth century.

Where records have survived their publication presents serious problems. The great series of *Patent Rolls* and *Close Rolls* in England have been printed in summary form for this period, and so have extensive ranges of other materials; but enormous areas of documentation remain buried in manuscript—most notably the records of royal courts. The administrative records of the Vatican, despite the publications noted above, are still largely unpublished. In these instances fairly accurate indexes and other aids enable the student to explore the documents *in situ* or by way of photographs: access to these repositories is easy, and this is true of all the state archives of Europe, as far as medieval documents are concerned. But there are still papers in the custody of families and ecclesiastical corporations all over Europe to which access is either not granted or is given so whimsically that it is useless to depend on it. The missing decades of Livy or the missing books of Chastellain may yet be found in some Spanish library.

Involuntary evidence

The men who kept official records did not always tell the truth about the events they described. Many conventions had grown up which made fiction rather than fact a convenient way of speeding business. Any historian must therefore take the precaution to verify if he can the lists of witnesses, the ages recorded, the places and the times where and when documents purported to have emanated. Likewise in formal chronicles or narratives he must be alert to the danger of his source being ignorant, inventive or malicious. For these reasons the involuntary information yielded by a record or a contemporary historian—what we learn (so to speak) despite the author—is often of particular value. It is (for example) not what the Emperor Charles IV sets out to tell us in his brief autobiography (a revised text of this was published at Heidelberg in 1950) but what it reveals unconsciously of the mentality of the sponsor of the Golden Bull of 1356; the process condemning Joan of Arc and the process of rehabilitation have been a quarry for all manner of information (the best edition is still that of J. Quicherat, 5 vols., 1841–49, but a number of recent translations and summaries are available). A final instance is the unreliable but immensely readable history of his own day composed by Pope Pius II (ed. and trans. Gragg and Gabel, 5 parts 1936–57; and, somewhat abbreviated in one vol., 1960): here it is the extraordinary display of the pope's vanities and ambitions, his conviction of human immortality and reflection of contemporary love of display, which impresses a reader no longer prepared to accept his violent diatribes against Venice or the Malatesta of Rimini.

If the clerks in their registries and the historians in their studies are thus despite themselves capable of yielding unvarnished pictures of attitudes and assumptions, this is true to an even greater extent of the artistic literature of the period. This is a period of very considerable artistic creation in both prose and poetry, and many works illuminate the general history of the age. Some writings are particularly rewarding. Giovanni Boccaccio and other 'novellists' frequently gave their stories actuality by casting contemporaries or near-contemporaries for leading roles in traditional tales (see V. Branca's ed. of the *Decameron*, 2 vols., Florence, 1951–52). The two parts of the *Roman de la Rose*, the *Canterbury Tales*, the *Cent Nouvelles Nouvelles* and other imaginative books reveal changing attitudes to public and private morality. Such unconscious testimony is in some ways the best entry of all into the underlying convictions of an age, but it is hard to interpret. Here the danger lies in choosing the correct emphasis to lay on an individual author or work. It is all too easy to make all English parsons at the end of the fourteenth century like the author of *Piers Plowman*, all students in mid-fifteenth-century Paris like François Villon; both are significant precisely because they were so exceptional. A different hazard is presented by the tendency of writers who may resurrect and embellish older or alien ideas and whose books may thus be exotic and untypical. Nor does the existence of one manuscript make a public opinion, although editors have been known to argue that such bare survival in the days before printing implies a public so hungry for the work that other copies have been literally worn away. We are on safer ground making inferences regarding popularity from the hundreds of manuscript and printed copies which have survived from the fifteenth century of the *Imitatio Christi* of Thomas à Kempis, of the scores of manuscript Wycliffite translations of the Bible or of the English chronicle called *The Brut*.

Literature at large thus comes to the aid of the modern student of the past. So do all the material remains—the buildings, furnishings, clothes, weapons and pictures which have survived. Some of this material, which is more plentiful for these centuries than for earlier times, contributes mainly to the history of style pure and simple: clothes and furnishings, for example. But much can be learned about later medieval war from the collections of armour in museums and from changing ways of building. Church architecture can reveal a good deal about ecclesiastical economics and religious sentiment. Painting enables one to visualize with the eyes of contemporaries the vanished world of the later Middle Ages. That the period saw several great schools of artists— in France and Burgundy, in Italy and in Flanders—makes this exercise particularly enjoyable. The painters also display the preferences of their patrons in both subject and execution and, from time to time, popular reactions to art can be followed in the great pageants and processions of the period.

Much of the delicacy in approach needed to interpret the poet and storyteller is equally called for in handling the artist, for by the end of this period the time is close at hand when artists began to claim a measure of autonomy. By accepting the architect and the painter as a genius, his contemporaries in effect dissociated him from the common conscience of mankind. Yet for practically the whole of the period this had not happened and it is proper, within limits, to accept Giotto and Ghiberti, the Van Eycks and Van der Weyden as fair witnesses to the decorative impulses and religious tastes of the fourteenth and fifteenth centuries. From the great galleries of Europe not a few sidelights may be gained on the social groups which are discussed in subsequent chapters. Moreover the portrait had arrived. The student of the fourteenth and fifteenth centuries can look upon the faces of many of the great men and their intimates whose public activities constitute the politics of the age.

II

Europe at the Beginning of the Fourteenth Century[1]

By the end of the thirteenth century European man had not yet made enough progress as a civil engineer to diminish much the control exercised by physical geography over his activities and communications. The most powerful factor was still what it had been since the Iron Age, the division of the European continent into two physically different halves by the diagonal which runs from the Rhine delta to the Bosphorus. To the north-east of that line lies the triangle of the great European plain with its apex in Belgium and its base on the Urals; south-west of it is the hilly and mountainous triangle which includes the northern half of the Mediterranean basin, with its base on the Atlantic seaboard and its apex where Europe ends and Asia begins at the Straits of Constantinople. The British Isles and the mountainous Scandinavian peninsula lie outside this scheme.

The economic geography of Europe at the beginning of the fourteenth century

Much of fourteenth-century Europe was still as nature had made it. Its vast mountain forests for the most part remained intact. The wide grass lands of central and eastern Europe had not yet been ploughed up for agriculture or mined for minerals. Except in the Mediterranean area the great European rivers meandered shallow, broad, unbanked and unbridged through wide tracts of marsh where only a few fowlers and fishermen could live. Its mineral wealth, especially that of Scandinavia, the Ukraine and Great Britain, was still largely undiscovered. The farmers and civil engineers of the Roman empire had indeed done much in southern and western Europe to control and exploit natural resources, but during the period of the wandering of the nations and of the bar-

[1] See Appendix I for general books and atlases relevant to the later Middle Ages.

barian invasions the forest and the swamp had resumed much of their primeval domain. Only slowly was the agelong struggle with nature turning again to man's advantage. In southern England, in France, Germany, Bohemia, Poland and Hungary farmers were still, as they had been for centuries, cutting their way into the forest, 'assarting' it for agriculture. The Netherlanders were building dykes against the sea and confining the mouths and tributaries of the Rhine delta between dams and polders. A beginning had been made in the confinement of the lower Thames within a bridgeable channel. Monks and municipalities were building causeways and embankments in the English Fens and in the marshy estuaries of the Po and the Rhône. But this taming of the rivers was still only in its beginning. The mazy channels of the Danube and the Tisza in Hungary still made a quarter of that country useless. The enormous marsh of the river Pripet in western Russia was an obstacle to the economic and political exploitation of the no-man's-land between Poland and Russia.

Every stage of economic development, from primitive food gathering to capitalist production, was represented in fourteenth-century Europe. Specialization was still far from complete: farmers and shepherds supplemented their livelihood by hunting, fowling and bee-keeping, craftsmen by working in the fields, monks by agriculture, stock-raising and pisciculture, professional soldiers by brigandage. Nevertheless it is possible to define certain areas where one or another economic activity was predominant. In Iceland, around the coasts of the North Sea, and in the southern Baltic fishing was important. The profitable herring shoals of the North Sea were still making their annual migration into the Baltic and the people of Norway were beginning to exploit cod fishing. In an age when there was no fresh meat from Michaelmas to Easter and when the Church strictly enjoined the Lenten fast, fish was so valuable a commodity that landowners were making artificial lakes for fish breeding, especially in Bohemia where there are no natural lakes.

For another large minority of Europeans the chief source of livelihood was the breeding and nurture of animals: pigs, goats, poultry, cattle, horses and above all sheep, for there was then virtually no rival to wool as a textile except the scarcer and more costly linen; cotton was unknown except in Sicily and the Levant; though a little silk was already being manufactured in Naples and Tuscany, most of it had to be imported from Asia. Most sheep and cattle breeders, however, did not produce for the market but merely to provide themselves with clothing, meat, milk, butter and cheese. A great many of the pastoralists were semi-nomadic, moving with their flocks and herds from the valleys where they wintered to their summer pastures in the mountains. Such communities were to be found wherever there were alpine conditions, as in the Abruzzi or the central Apennines, in the forest cantons of Switzerland, on both sides of the Pyrenees and in Castile, in the mountains and valleys of Serbia and Greece and in the Carpathians, where the immigrant Vlach shepherds were finding new pastures throughout this period. Not only mountain pastures are suitable for sheep and cattle rearing, but also steppe and downland. At opposite ends of Europe the Tatars in southern Russia and the Cistercian monks in Yorkshire and the south-western shires were exploiting the natural grass, one of the most valuable and least troublesome of all raw materials. The production of wool for the market was increasing in value proportionately with the growth of a class of urban folk who kept no animals.

At the beginning of the fourteenth century most people in Europe still grew or bred or caught their own food. Agriculture was still primitive. In eastern Europe the hook plough, which could do little more than scratch the lighter soils, was still almost universal. The cultivation of the fields had indeed become nearly everywhere intensive. But though the farmers now tilled the same patch of cleared land year after year, they still left a third or a half of that patch fallow each year. The more economical three-field system and the heavy plough with its iron share had only reached those areas east of the Elbe where German colonists had already settled. The land was tilled by peasants who usually cultivated the two or three large, unenclosed fields as a community, though each peasant had the right to the crops from assigned strips of land. There were also some peasant freeholders and some landless farm labourers who worked for wages. The great majority of the peasants however paid rent for their holdings in money, produce or services to a landlord. The landlords usually kept part of their estates as 'demesne' to be cultivated by their serfs to supply the lords' household needs or to produce commodities which they could sell in the market. The most fundamental factor making for the increasing differentiation of the two halves of Europe at this time was the decrease of demesne farming in the west and its increase in the east; intimately connected with this change was the consequent decline of serfdom in the west and its growth in the east.

Though land was still the chief source of wealth and though animal and field husbandry was still the occupation of the vast majority of

Europeans, the localization and specialization of production and the exchange of goods produced by industry for the products of field and forest was rapidly developing. The craftsmen and merchants were indeed only a small minority, but because the profits of industry and commerce were proportionately far higher than those of unspecialized and often self-sufficing agriculture, the craftsmen and merchants exercised a much greater influence in politics and society than their numbers warranted. There was one really large city in Europe, Constantinople, but even that was now much reduced as a result of the Latin conquest. The number of places where the majority of the inhabitants spent most of their time in industry or trade had been increasing; the population of such places was usually only a few thousands but they were given and deserved the name of town or city. As trade extended further west and north so urbanization was spreading to eastern Spain, the Languedoc, Champagne, southern England, Belgium, the valleys of the Rhine and upper Danube, to northern Germany and the Baltic coast, to Bohemia, southern Poland, northern Hungary and Transylvania. With the advance of the Seljuk Turks in the Levant and the decline of Byzantium the economic centre of gravity in Europe had shifted from the Bosphorus to the cities of Venetia, Lombardy and Tuscany. The world of Byzantium became a 'colonial' area for western merchants to exploit.

The increase in specialization was not merely a matter of individuals devoting themselves to particular crafts; large regions were ceasing to be self-sufficing and were specializing in the production and export of commodities for whose production they were particularly well fitted by their convenient geographical situation or by the possession of raw materials. England was beginning to realize the value of its grass lands and the sheep they nourished. German merchants in the Baltic were exploiting the wide market for fish. North-west Russia was sending furs to clothe the wealthy merchants and their wives in western Europe. The Flemish towns had used their favourable geographical situation to become the centre for the manufacture of good quality woollen textiles; The Czechs in Bohemia and the German immigrants in northern Hungary and Transylvania were producing silver and iron to supply the needs of European mints and metal workers.

The most grievous obstacle to the development of international trade was still the absence of roads good enough to carry wheeled traffic. Nor were there any canals. The rivers however were being used more and more, especially for the carriage of bulky goods on rafts of timber,

which themselves were broken up for sale at the ports. But what contributed most to the growth of international commerce in the later
Middle Ages was the extension of maritime trade. Venice, which had
been the greatest beneficiary from the Latin conquest of Constantinople,
had eliminated Slav pirate bases on the Dalmatian coast and had made
of the Adriatic, the eastern Mediterranean, the Aegean and the Black
Sea a network of maritime trade routes. The only serious rival to Venice
in this area was Genoa. The sea also provided a link between the older
commercial area of the Mediterranean lands and the newly developing
commerce of northern Europe. In the more hazardous waters of the
Atlantic, the Bay of Biscay, the Channel, the North Sea and the Baltic
the small northern sailing ships, with their high freeboard and broad
beam, were beginning to play an increasingly important part in exchanging the cloth, hardware, salt and luxury goods made in the west for the
fish, corn, furs and forest products which the Hanseatic merchants
were collecting from the countries of north-eastern Europe.

The clearing of the forests, the eastward extension of more advanced
methods of cultivation of the soil, the renewed exploitation of mineral
wealth, the development of specialized crafts and of international trade,
all suggest that the economic condition of Europe as a whole was still
improving at the end of the thirteenth century. It was a moment when
the burden of serfdom was disappearing from western Europe and when
it had not yet fallen heavily on the countries of the north-eastern plain.
It is possible that the lot of the peasants was never happier than it was
at this time. There was a blessed surcease from barbarian invasions after
those of the Mongols in the mid-thirteenth century. Wars were still local
and short and Europe in the thirteenth century enjoyed relative peace
and prosperity. Soon economic regression was to come. The great
famine of 1317, the Hundred Years War, the Turks and the Black
Death arrived to put an end to what had been a halcyon time.

The peoples of Europe in the later Middle Ages

By 1300 the ethnographical map of Europe was more or less what it is
today. The wandering of the nations had ceased three hundred years
earlier. The last incursion of the nomads from central Asia was that of
the Mongols. It only remained for the invasion of south-eastern Europe
by the Ottoman Turks to complete the modern picture.

Since the collapse of the Roman Empire the peoples of Europe had
been so mobile and there had been so much mingling of the blood of
conquerors and conquered, of migrants and their hosts, that already by

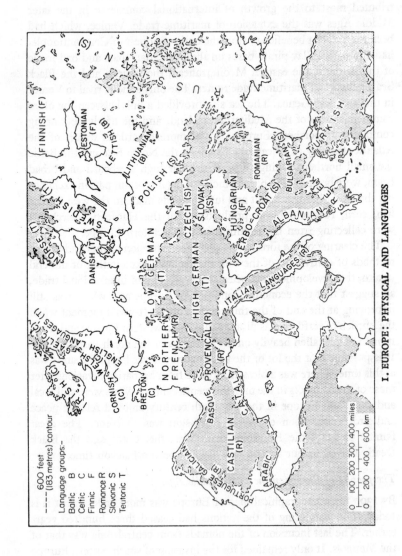

I. EUROPE: PHYSICAL AND LANGUAGES

---- 600 feet
---- (183 metres) contour

Language groups:-
Baltic B
Celtic C
Finnic F
Romance R
Slavonic S
Teutonic T

0	100	200 300	400 miles	
0	200	400	600 km	

the fourteenth century it is both difficult and unhistorical to talk of the races of Europe. The only safe and practical approach is to describe the main language groups, for it was community of language which often became the basis of the formation of political and cultural units.

In 1300, as at the beginning of the Christian era and as today, the great majority of the inhabitants of Europe spoke languages of the Indo-European group. Spanish, Welsh, Dutch, Lithuanian, Serbian and Greek, different as they may seem, are all of this family. The languages of the Romance peoples, of the Celts, Teutons, Balts, Slavs, Albanians and Greeks have a common basic accidence and syntax, and a vocabulary which in its essentials has a common origin.

One of the oldest of Indo-European languages is Albanian, the direct descendant of ancient Illyrian. Though Albania did not exist as a state in 1300 the language was spoken over a wide area in the south-western Balkans by descendants of the Illyrians who had survived Roman, Slav and Byzantine conquests in the precipitous valleys of the rivers which flow into the southern Adriatic. They were nominally subject to Serbian, Bulgarian or Greek rulers, but in fact lived a life of primitive independence. The Greek-speaking peoples also had lived in their present home for well over two thousand years and at the beginning of this period Greek was spoken and written all round the coasts and in the islands of the Aegean Sea, in Greece, southern Macedonia and Thrace, in Crete and Cyprus as well as in the coastal parts of Asia Minor, and in parts of southern Italy. Closely allied philologically within the Indo-European family was the group of languages derived from Latin, the Romance languages, which were spoken in those parts of the former Roman empire which had been thoroughly Romanized: Italy, Sicily, Spain, Portugal and France. There had survived too in south-eastern Europe among the peoples who had adopted Latin or who were descended from Roman colonists and legionaries, pockets of pastoral people commonly known as Vlachs who still spoke dialects that were basically Latin. The Vlachs constituted considerable groups in Macedonia, Croatia, Serbia and Bulgaria. Being shepherds they were mobile and were already migrating across the Danube into Transylvania, Walachia (to which they gave their name) and Moldavia, where, it may well be, they found descendants of the Romanized Dacians who also had preserved their Vlach or Rumanian language.

The westernmost of the Indo-European groups was that of the Celts. The Celtic languages, which on the eve of the Christian era had extended over nearly half Europe, had been swamped in large areas of

Spain, Switzerland, the Rhineland, France and the British Isles by the invasion of Latin and Teutonic speech, but Celtic was still the living language of Brittany, Cornwall, Wales, Ireland, the Isle of Man and the western parts of Scotland.

In the north-eastern half of Europe also the Indo-European element predominated. In this area there were three important branches of the family: Teutonic, Baltic and Slavonic, all fairly closely akin. The Teutonic languages were spread over a wide area and had assumed a variety of local forms: Icelandic, English, Norwegian, Swedish and Danish, low German (including Flemish and Dutch), southern or 'high' German, and various German dialects spoken in Luxemburg, Alsace and Switzerland. The Baltic language group is one of the oldest branches of the Indo-Germanic family. Its members were Old Prussian, Lithuanian and Latvian. The first was already being suppressed by the German speech of the Teutonic knights who had conquered Prussia in the thirteenth century, but it did not finally disappear until the seventeenth. The Slavonic group of languages covered a larger part of Europe than any other, though by 1300 the eastward flowing tide of German conquest and colonization was already killing Slavonic speech in northeast Germany, in Pomerania and in the towns of Silesia. Nevertheless Slavonic was still dominant in the kingdoms of Poland and Bohemia (where it is called Czech), in Lusatia and northern Hungary (Slovak), in Volhynia, Podlesia and Galicia and in the Russian principalities. Southern forms of Slavonic were the speech of the Slovenes of Carniola, of the Croats, Serbs, Bosnians, Montenegrins, Bulgarians and of most of the inhabitants of Macedonia.

Though most of Europe in the later Middle Ages was inhabited by people enjoying a common Indo-European kinship of language and to some indefinable extent of race, a large part of it was already the home of peoples of very different origin and speech. These had all come, some perhaps ten thousand years earlier, some very recently, from that part of Asia which lies between the Ural and Altai mountains. The oldest inhabitants of Europe stemming from this Uro-Altaic origin are the so-called Finno-Ugrians. It seems that their remote ancestors had crossed into eastern and northern Europe soon after the land had become habitable after the last retreat of the ice, some 11,000 years before Christ. They had settled, very sparsely, in eastern, northern and central Russia and in Lapland and northern Scandinavia. In the early Middle Ages the east-Slavonic tribes had diminished Finnish territory by their settlement in central and eastern Russia so that by 1300 the Finnish peoples were confined to the east-Baltic areas of Finland, Estonia and Livonia, and to large ethnic islands in northern and eastern Russia. Early in the ninth century a group of Finno-Ugrian tribes, later known as the Magyars, had wandered off from their home in eastern Russia, stayed for a time on the north coast of the Black Sea and thence had crossed the Carpathians into the Hungarian plain, where they ultimately settled down amid the Slavonic peoples they found there. These Magyars, speaking their Finno-Ugrian language, retained their identity in the multiracial Hungarian state which they built up in the eleventh and twelfth centuries.

Also ultimately of Uro-Altaic origin, and therefore very remotely akin to the Finns and Magyars, were the Turkish-speaking inhabitants of southern Russia, the accumulation of many layers of invading Turkic nomads: Huns, Khazars, Pechenegs, Cumans (whom the Russians called Polovtsians) and on the top of them the latest arrivals from Asia, the Mongols of the Golden Horde, who in 1300 were directly or indirectly the overlords of most of Russia. On the doorstep of Europe in Asia Minor were other Turkish tribes under the upstart chief Osman who were soon to renew that Asiatic assault on Europe from which the Arabs had desisted in the eighth century.

Three smaller ethnic groups remain to be mentioned to complete the picture. First, everywhere in the Spanish peninsula but dominating the south-east corner were the Muslim descendants of the successive waves of invaders from Africa: the Semitic Arabs, the Berbers and the Moors. Secondly, over a large area on both sides of the western Pyrenees, much more extensive than it is today, dwelt the Basques, whose language is pre-Indo-European, and is therefore the most ancient in Europe. Thirdly, and of great importance were the Semitic, Hebrew-speaking Jews, of whom there were two distinct branches: the Sephardic Jews of Hebrew descent living in all the countries of western and central Europe except England, whence Edward I had recently expelled them, and the east European Jews, the Ashkenazi, of mixed Hebrew, Khazar and Slav descent, whose homes were mostly in southern and western Russia.

Linguistic boundaries corresponded even less precisely with political boundaries at this time than they do today. There were many isolated pockets of alien speech, such as those of Germans in northern Italy, Transylvania, Slovakia and Little Poland, of Cumans in central Hungary, of Armenians in Galicia in southern Poland, and the Finnish speaking Mordvinians and Cheremesh in Russia.

It has also to be remembered that almost no European vernacular language was yet standardized. Northern, southern and south-western Englishmen still spoke dialects which could be mutually unintelligible. In France the Langue d'Oil and the Langue d'Oc were as different as High and Low German; the varieties of Italian and Sicilian were (and are still) numerous, and none had the precedence until Dante gave it to Tuscan. It was to be one of the most important features of the centuries discussed in this book that in England, France and Italy one of the dialects was emerging as the national language.

Against the multiplicity of vernaculars it is necessary to set the existence of Latin. Latin was still a living language in western Europe. The language of the Bible and of the ritual of the Church, Latin was learned by all clergy and was currently written and spoken by all educated men. It was the language of much administration, of practically all high-level diplomacy, as well as of serious literary composition. Since it was a living language it had departed considerably from classical norms and, when spoken, it varied somewhat in pronunciation from one area to another. But, unlike the vernaculars, it was systematically taught and bound the literate together. In similar fashion, though on a smaller scale, Greek acted as a link in eastern Europe.

The political scene

Two great empires and two great branches of the Christian religion were bequeathed by the early and central Middle Ages to later times. The Eastern Empire, based on Constantinople, was a shadow of what it had formerly been. Broken by the Latins in the Fourth Crusade but re-established (again by Latin intervention) in 1261, the power of the Palaeologi emperors was diminished, their lands largely under alien control. The Holy Roman Empire had lapsed for a time after the death of Frederick II. When the interregnum ended in 1273 the emperors were far less powerful than they had been both inside Germany and in the Italian lands they still nominally ruled. Curiously enough the Orthodox Church in Greek lands and, in the Latin West, the Roman Church were both vigorous, and neither shared the debility of the empires with which they were associated. Indeed, the Roman Church had been in large part responsible for the declining authority of the German empire. In the thirteenth century, fortified by the evangelism of the friars and the intellectual and artistic achievements of great architects and university-trained philosophers and theologians, it had reached the height of its public influence.

Popes had been successful in curbing the power of the emperors, especially in Italy. They had done less to contain the ambitions of kings. In France, in England and in the kingdoms of Spain, western Europe witnessed in the twelfth and thirteenth centuries a growth of stronger royal administration and a general acceptance that hereditary monarchy was an unavoidable part of the political life of the great magnates, hitherto content to turn their backs on the crown. This pattern of emergent monarchy was far from universal. The kings of Scandinavia were not powerful, and princes in eastern and central Europe, busily importing administrative institutions from the west, were already encountering resistance among their more influential subjects. Even in the west of the continent government depended still to a great extent on the personal qualities of the king. In every part of Europe public order was precariously preserved and, even under strong kings like Edward I of England or Philip IV of France, banditry and ineffective justice could make whole regions miserable for years at a time.

Nor must the historian see too clearly prefigured the vaster unities of later national states. In 1300 it might have seemed that the English king was predestined to dominate the British Isles, the king of Aragon his equally diverse inheritance. Independent Ireland, and a Catalonia still stubbornly resisting Castilian pressure, are today vivid reminders that forces were at work which in the end were to offer effective opposition to governments much more powerful than those of the later Middle Ages.

At the end of the thirteenth century the towns of Europe had become important, as observed above. In monarchies the burgess had, in effect, become identified with the 'third estate', especially in the representative assemblies which by then were a feature of monarchical administration. In certain parts of Europe the town had gained more than recognition as a source of royal finance. In north and central Italy towns had enjoyed, especially in the generation after Hohenstauffen power collapsed in 1250, their greatest period of independent development. The inherited tensions of earlier struggles in Italy carried with them the danger of tyrants who would sweep away communal liberty; before 1300 Milan had experienced a period of Visconti rule. Yet the temptation to regard the urban republic as foredoomed to collapse before the rising duke or king must be avoided. Many German cities retained their independence for centuries, and even in Italy Lucca and, more impressively, Venice survived the later Middle Ages and the early modern period as republics.

The frontiers of the European countries at the start of our period were mainly the product of earlier dynastic politics. The Norman duke who became king of England regarded himself as entitled to claim the country he conquered so easily in 1066; a century later his successor Henry II added to Normandy vast territories in France—Anjou, Maine and Aquitaine. Much of this was lost by King John by 1214, yet the rights he could not lose, nor were French kings ready ruthlessly to expropriate; their vassal of England thus still held Gascony at the beginning of the fourteenth century. Just as wars were occasioned by disputes over inherited or acquired territorial rights, so they could only be permanently ended by marriage treaties which aimed to transcend through dowry and progeny the dilemmas of sovereignty which could not otherwise be resolved. The thirteenth century had not evolved even an elementary system of international law: in place of this there was the Law of Arms and princely matrimony. Any maps of the Middle Ages thus catch Europe at a moment of royal relationships which may or may not be of much significance.

On the other hand earlier centuries had seen the development of some larger loyalties. The widest (and vaguest) of these notions was Christendom, which had crystallized in the eleventh century but which was to be eroded in the later Middle Ages. More immediately relevant were regional affiliations, often (it may be suspected) the reflection of deep cultural and linguistic experience. The king of England and the king of France could depend on an extraordinarily diffuse if ill-defined support, which only declined if and when traditional institutions or sentiments were tactlessly offended. Edward I was accepted by the Scots as, in some sense, their king's superior—so long as this superiority was not effectively asserted. Part of the secret of successful Aragonese expansion was the willingness of the kings to tolerate wide divergences in their Mediterranean empire, already in existence by 1300, in return for loyalty to the 'Crown of Aragon'. No stronger indication of this profound respect for public authority can be found than in the re-established Roman Empire of the West: Germans—magnates, clergy and townsmen—were not prepared to jettison an institution which represented their awareness of cohesion, even if they were not prepared to tolerate a powerful emperor.

The play of politics bequeathed to the fourteenth and fifteenth centuries was thus between local affinities, inescapable but often tongue-tied, and the bigger programme, of which kings were the principal exponents, though they too, one guesses, were not always conscious of the degree to which they were innovating. The actors in this European drama were seldom in possession of the plot and indeed there was not one plot but many. The broadest pattern of action one can discern— the prince against the great landed magnates—had already begun, as can be seen in the England of John, Henry III and Edward I, the France of St Louis and the Castile of Alfonso X. The future fortunes of the crown and the nobility in central and eastern Europe had been hinted at in the concessions to magnates and clergy extracted from Casimir II of Poland (d. 1194) and in the Golden Bull (1222) in which Andrew II of Hungary granted away massive privileges to the same groups; but in eastern Europe these developments were obscured for a while by the Mongol invasions of the mid-thirteenth century, which also overwhelmed Kievan Russia.

Properly to understand the varieties of political activity in the later Middle Ages these earlier experiences should be studied and remembered. It is also necessary to examine the main social groups whose ambitions conditioned public life. They are the subject of the next two chapters.

III

Society and Its Structure
1. The Peasants: Population Trends

Late in the thirteenth century a priest at Zurich wrote down a list of the component parts of the social scene as he knew it. His analysis was, of course, that of a townsman, and a country gentleman would have had a rather different scale of values. The priest called his hierarchy a

BIBLIOGRAPHY. Agrarian society in the Middle Ages is the subject of the *Cambridge Economic History*, I (Cambridge, 1941), ed. by J. H. Clapham and Eileen Power, with full bibliographies; a revised edition of this is in the press. A recent review of the later Middle Ages is provided by Jacques Heers, *L'occident aux XIVe et XVe siècles: aspects économiques et sociaux* (Paris, 1963), which also has good bibliographies; see also G. Duby, *L'économie rurale et la vie des campagnes dans l'Occident médiévale*, 2 vols. (Paris, 1962), vol. II, pp. 541–634; there is now an English trans. (London, 1968). Regional studies are numerous and basic. Many are listed in the above books. The following are significant examples of the very active research in this sector: R. Boutruche, *La crise d'une société: seigneurs et paysans du Bordelais pendant la guerre de Cent Ans* (Paris, 1947); R. H. Hilton, *The Economic Development of some Leicestershire Estates in the XIV and XV Centuries* (London, 1947); W. G. Hoskins, *The Midland Peasant* (London, 1957). A useful survey of developments in Central and East Europe is provided by Jerome Blum, 'The Rise of Serfdom in Eastern Europe', *Amer. Hist. Rev.*, 62 (1956–57), pp. 807–36.

Population Trends. J. C. Russell provides a general conspectus in 'Late Ancient and Medieval Population', *Transactions* of the American Philosophical Society, n.s., vol. 48, pt. 3 (1958) and deals with one region in *British Medieval Population* (Albuquerque, 1948); a review-article by Professor Russell, *Speculum* 40 (1965), 84–101 surveys recent literature. A general discussion is contained in the *Rapports* of the IX Congrès international des sciences historiques (Paris, 1950), pp. 55–80. Related matters are discussed in H. S. Lucas, 'The Great European Famine of 1315–17', *Speculum* 5 (1930); M. W. Beresford, *The Lost Villages of England* (London, 1954). There is no complete general study of the Black Death, but see a sound popular survey, with useful bibliogs., P. Ziegler, *The Black Death* (London, 1969). Plague and population are both subjects dealt with in a large number of local studies.

divisio personarum, and this might fairly be regarded as the equivalent of another Latin expression, *dramatis personae*, the actors on the stage of life. He begins with Great Personages, the emperor, kings, dukes, nobles and so on, down to the magistrates of towns. His next category is Small Personages and this includes lawyers, town councillors, justices. Lesser Personages are 'mere knights', stewards and managers, merchants and shopkeepers. Finally there is a fourth element in society: all men of servile status (peasants), all who practice 'mechanical arts' (artisans).[1] We shall have occasion in the next chapter to examine further the first three of these groups. In any consideration of the structure of society it is, however, necessary to begin with the peasants. Their place was regarded as humble, as is evident from the foregoing, but they formed the largest single element in society and their activity provided far and away the most important support for all other groups.

The eve of the fourteenth century

It will be noted that the *divisio personarum* mentioned above stressed the servile character of the peasantry. This had been for centuries a basic social distinction between the majority of those who laboured on the land and the rest of European society. The noble, whether rich or poor, sometimes possessed land absolutely, but more commonly owed his acres to his tenure obliging him to produce the gentlemanly service of arms; the townsman often had property as well as an income from commerce or business, but his houses and shops were burdened with few if any obligations, at any rate in the larger towns. The serf, on the other hand, held his share of land in the village in return for labouring for the lord of the manor. He was subject to certain additional demands by the local seigneur for money and service; he was tried in the manorial court; and on a number of occasions he had to demean himself by asking permission to marry or give in marriage, or to absent himself from the village. The very fact that he held a servile tenure involved a man in servile status.

This, however, is a somewhat abstract picture. Far from the whole of rural society being composed of peasants holding their land by labour services, there were many wage labourers who worked both for the lord of the land and for wealthier peasants. And there were, most numerous in the south of France and in other Mediterranean lands, peasants who had absolute possession of their lands, whose tenure was allodial. Even

[1] Quoted by S. Stelling-Michaud, *L'université de Bologne et la pénétration des droits . . . en Suisse aux XIII et XIV siècles* (Geneva, 1955), pp. 116–17.

in regions where servitude prevailed for hundreds of years there had been in western Europe a fairly general trend towards the commutation of labour services for rent. Instead of providing the lord the sweat of his brow the peasant paid cash. The lord became a rentier and the serf became a tenant. This was, it must be stressed, not a uniformly consistent development. Servile tenure persisted in many places, and serfs lived in some communities alongside rent-paying tenants. Nor did these social and legal changes necessarily affect the patterns of agriculture themselves: the 'open fields' were in a few regions to survive much more radical innovations than the shift from labour services to rent and were sometimes to survive into relatively recent times; the evolution of agrarian society followed a very different course in eastern Europe. There were in nearly all countries large tracts where, though important locally, agriculture in the narrow sense, the ploughing of the soil, occupied quite literally a marginal amount of rural activity.

It may be best to deal briefly with this last point first of all. In al really poor land—hill, mountain and fen—the population was compelled to stretch its meagre resources to the limit. A sufficiency of food was often attained only by efforts and sacrifices of a heroic kind and chiefly by exploiting piecemeal the surrounding countryside. The villagers would till for a season one or two freshly opened fields, sometimes many miles from their settlement; and then, when the fertility of the patch was exhausted, cut fresh fields elsewhere. Likewise the poor grass of the moor and mountain, which made it impossible both to harvest hay and to graze sheep and cattle in the area round the settlement, involved the community in driving flocks long distances in spring and only bringing the beasts back in the autumn. The high pastures and fields of spring and summer, the seasonal movement which this involved for both men and animals, were found all over Europe wherever there was high ground. Such a rural economy was more or less indifferent to outside pressure, and remained largely unchanged almost to our own day in parts of Europe—the Highlands of Scotland, the Pyrenees, parts of France, Spain and Italy. The Swiss, of course, were involved in just such a situation but, straddling international routes and near the important urban centres of north Italy, they could afford to develop their dairy farming and rely on imported cereals. It was significant that in mountain and hill areas there was plenty of land, even if it was of bad quality.

Since fields were small and shifting in such highlands and moors, and since hunting was very difficult there and the rights that went with it were not jealously preserved, conflicts of lordship and 'frontier disputes' were not common save in the areas (like the Anglo-Scottish border) where sheep might wander from one kingdom into another. What did characterize this semi-pastoral life was a barbaric code of customary law, designed to mete out rough justice to the cattle thief. And even in more developed regions the seasonal movement of flocks to and from high land (transhumance) led to bitter hostility between the mountain and the plain. In the Abruzzi such quarrels (together with disputes over tolls and taxation) frequently disturbed the political relations of the popes and the kings of Naples. In Spain there was great tension between shepherds and peasants arising from the privileges accorded to the graziers' guild, the *Mesta*. The traveller in Italy, in Spain, in France, whose path crossed stretches of moor or high hill went in fear of the wild, independent and lawless folk who were not averse to augmenting their slender income with money extorted by terror or worse. All through the Middle Ages and well on into the eighteenth century there were pockets of land where no government could be sure of being effective, even in territories otherwise under relatively firm control. In the later Middle Ages the townsman and the lowland farmer had not yet endowed the mountain dweller with the romantic aura of 'freedom': he was usually regarded as a natural enemy.

The peasant farmer on the good land in northern Europe had inherited from a distant past the open-field farming which was the main, though not the only, way in which agriculture was organized.[1] The fields had been notably increased in number and size in earlier centuries, by extending existing settlements through taking in adjoining waste, by clearing forests and by draining marsh land. The land in each field was allocated to the peasant farmer in the community in parcels, often in strips scattered over the field, each section separated from its neighbours only by a low baulk; the land directly under the lord, the demesne, was likewise distributed. In addition the community had a meadow which produced hay and where cattle were grazed in proportion to the holding of the individual in the open fields. Members of the community had the right to gather firewood and pasture swine in the forest and waste. The fields surrounded the village and were worked according to a

---

[1] Enclosures, both by peasants and lords, were already by the end of the thirteenth century affecting the open-field farming described in what follows. There were also a number of arable areas where the peasant's house stood among his small enclosed fields: e.g. in Maine and in Cornwall. Many small holdings, especially near the bigger towns, were devoted to market gardening.

cooperative plan so that a portion of the land lay under crops, and each year a different part lay fallow. The crops consisted of cereals and 'pulse' (peas and beans) in proportions which varied according to soil and climate. The cereals—wheat, rye, barley and oats—were sown either in autumn or spring and the villagers' cattle were driven on to the fallow field. It is customary to refer to the rotation achieved in this way as the 'two-field system' or the 'three-field system', on the assumption that roughly a half or a third of the arable land lay fallow each year. In fact the arrangements in many settlements were much more flexible than this would suggest. The 'three-field system' was perhaps common to the point of being typical, but communities were not bound to it and we sometimes find for a series of years that there are four or more fields.

A large part of western Europe fed itself in the Middle Ages in this way, and for centuries surpluses of grain had usually been sufficient both to support a rising population and to provide the cash necessary to turn labour dues over to rents. But there are notable exceptions, areas where specialized farming was the basic pattern.

First in order of importance was the production of cereal crops in the Mediterranean area. In Roman times grain had come from intensive cultivation in North Africa and Sicily: such 'granaries' remained essential to supply the needs of the towns of Italy which were often entirely unable to obtain adequate supplies locally. Genoa ringed by inhospitable mountains, Venice on its marshy islands are two extreme cases of urban development which would have been impossible without imported food. This still came in part from the ancient fields of Sicily and the south of Italy. But production was not equal to the growing demand and remained a serious problem for all Mediterranean town governments.

Another specialized crop was found in both the Mediterranean and other lands, the vine. The cultivation of the vine had even taken over former ploughland in parts of France, where the area round Bordeaux was one of the great centres of wine production. Here and elsewhere the population depended on selling wine in return for imported cereals. It has been pointed out more than once that the tending of the vine— compatible as it was with the successful operation of relatively small holdings of land—involved an individual initiative on the part of the cultivator which contrasts with the organized team work of open-field farming.

Within this ancient framework of rural society the lord of land played a dominant role. Something will be said in the next chapter concerning the social status of the proprietors. Here they figure as the beneficiaries of the agricultural system. As such they shared in the wealth of their tenants, whether servile or rent-paying, and they or their stewards had much influence in the management of communal agriculture. Above all they had the choice of encouraging or resisting the trend from services to rent.

This change was, on balance, accepted by the seigneurs although when lordship lay in the hands of a corporate ecclesiastical body—a cathedral chapter or a monastery—more conservative policies often prevailed. The change, it must be insisted, was primarily of juridical importance. The rent-paying tenant was free of servile obligations but he was not necessarily better off. He paid rent in money instead of rent in services, but he was far less firmly wedded to his acres than he had been as serf, more liable to encounter difficulties if times were bad. On the other hand the successful tenant farmer could now readily acquire more land. So, even among the new tenantry, there were extremes of wealth and poverty, the poorer tenants sometimes competing as day labourers with the unlanded poor who had always hired themselves out and who presumably had always lived on a very narrow margin.

Among the rural population by the early days of the fourteenth century there was therefore a new uncertainty. Freedom in the legal sense could mean greater prosperity or greater poverty than had been likely in earlier days when servitude predominated. This situation had been developing during the thirteenth century; its dangers were only to be revealed on a large scale when the thirteenth-century boom was followed by a fourteenth-century slump.

The economic crisis of the fourteenth century

Precarious as life was for most men before 1300 it was rare to have serious and prolonged famine, widespread plague and peasant risings. After 1300 these phenomena all occur repeatedly. Why does the period witness this marked deterioration in the tone of economic life and in social relations?

The brief answer is that population, which had been rising for centuries, declined sharply. This, however, merely restates the question. Population rises or declines because of a variety of pressures.

There is now no doubt that by the end of the thirteenth century the boundary of productive land in western Europe had been pushed to its limit. Earlier increases in cultivated land doubtless go far to explain the steady growth of population. But much of the land taken in was marginal, and the moment its productivity declined men went hungry. The big urban centres had also absorbed many unemployed rural labourers, but they likewise absorbed much food, depending, especially in the case of seaboard towns, on the import of grain by sea. If there was any local shortage Bruges, London or Bordeaux could step up imports from regions where there was a surplus; as well as Mediterranean granaries, certain northern areas were now specializing in grain production for export, notably Prussia. What could now make for disaster was a general failure, when rural areas could not help one another nor the bigger and richer towns purchase their supplies from more distant producers. Such general failures occurred several times in the early fourteenth century, affecting big areas. Most notable was the great famine of 1315–17 in which mortality increased alarmingly in the towns, where its incidence can sometimes be measured (Bruges lost over 5 per cent of its population in six months of 1316, Ypres 10 per cent), and doubtless reached even higher figures in rural areas. What is most striking is the persistence of famine and near famine for nearly a generation; so unrelieved a picture of gloom invites an underlying explanation beyond the processes of overproduction and overpopulation. Such a basic influence may have been a deterioration in climate. The study of climatic change in the Middle Ages has only just begun, but there seems to be reason to think that early in the fourteenth century a change for the worse of a cyclical kind did occur. Winters were longer and colder, summers colder and wetter. Crops failed, men went hungry and many died.

It is this background of fifty years when many, perhaps most men lacked adequate food that explains the intensity with which the bubonic plague struck Europe in and after 1348. The etiology of the Black Death was not, of course, understood. The bacillus carried by the fleas on black rats spread the disease which became pandemic (and also assumed a pneumonic form) as it strengthened its hold. As in the East five hundred years later[1] famine and undernourishment prepared the way. Hence the spread of the plague is itself a commentary on the stark conditions prevailing in Europe for at least a generation. Carried from the Middle East it first struck the Mediterranean lands, including Italy, France and

[1] 'According to the Plague Research Committee of Bombay, the predisposing causes are "those leading to a lower state of vitality", of which insufficient food is probably the most important.' *Encyclopaedia Britannica*, 11th edn., XXI (1911), 701 b (s.v. Plague).

Spain. In 1349 it ravaged Germany and England; next year Scotland and the Baltic countries suffered; it was not until 1402 that Iceland suffered.

The effects of the plague are more easily measured in towns (below, pp. 76-7) and religious communities than among the rural population. From its economic consequences, however, it is clear that the peasantry suffered terribly and occasionally this can be illustrated with figures. Deaths on the Taunton estates of the bishop of Winchester were recorded as follows: 23 in 1346, 54 in 1347, and 707 in 1349;[1] in the Burgundian village of Givry, where in normal years deaths ranged between 14 and 43, in 1348 the parish register recorded 649 deaths. Nor were the years 1347–50 the end of the story. The Black Death not only lingered on as it spread to remoter communities, in this way becoming endemic; it returned in epidemic proportions again and again, as in 1361–62. After this and before 1500 epidemics occurred in Italy in 1371–74, 1381–84, 1400, 1422–25, 1436–39, 1447–51, 1447–79, 1485–87; in England there were eleven other 'national' epidemics between 1362 and the end of the fifteenth century.

Yet the plague itself would presumably have died out but for continuing scarcity, just as a natural buoyancy would have redressed the loss of population. At Givry the register shows that, whereas marriages had averaged twenty-five in the years before 1348, they rose to eighty-six in 1349; a birth rate of 60 per cent is recorded for a country district to the north of Milan in the post-plague period. But there was no lengthy respite. Famine and death from plague continued to haunt the countryside well into the fifteenth century, even though by the end of the period the worst effects of the pestilence were to be seen in towns.

To these grim spectres the fourteenth century added a further scourge, one which was fiercer in the countryside than in the towns of the territories it afflicted. This was war, waged now to a greater extent than earlier by mercenary troops. The Hundred Years War may not have involved continuous hostilities between England and France, but the intervals of peace between the main protagonists were filled with related campaigns in Brittany, Flanders and Spain. The Free Companies, when they had exhausted the north, moved into Italy where the *condottiere* armies battened on the land. The *plat pays*, the open country, was the scene of the ravaging marches (*chevauchées*) of the armies of

[1] M. M. Postan and J. Titow in *Econ. Hist. Rev.*, ser. 2, 11 (1959), pp. 392–410, table 1.

Edward III and the Black Prince; the successful defence offered by the French under Bertrand du Guesclin, a scorched-earth policy which aimed at depriving the invader of his subsistence, did equal damage to crops and buildings in the French countryside. Bandits, recruited from nobles as well as peasants, preyed on the population from castles in Germany, Italy and France.

The result of prolonged scarcity, endemic and pandemic plague, the intermittent but catastrophic invasions of ruthless armies, and the constant threat in many areas from well-organized robber bands, was seen not only in a dwindling population but in roads abandoned to brambles and briars, in arable land out of cultivation and in deserted villages. Contraction in the area of cultivation in its turn made dearth the more likely. There was in every sense a vicious circle. A sober estimate suggests that 'in 1470 the number of households was halved in most European villages compared with the start of the fourteenth century'; the reconquest by forest and waste of the arable is 'an episode equal in importance to the drama of the earlier clearings'.[1]

The effects of regression on rural economy were far-reaching. Labour was scarce and prices rose rapidly. In England (Statute of Labourers, 1349), in Castile (*Cortes* of 1351) and elsewhere legislation was attempted to fix wages, but without success. Services continued to be commuted for cash rents and at an accelerated pace, lords of land being ill placed to resist the demand for legal freedom. Likewise lords increasingly farmed out the demesne land—often having to break it up into modest-sized units before they found tenants. The lord's strong attachment to his inheritance combined with a fear of starvation to make him often insist on a proportion of rents being rendered in kind, especially in grain; similar anxieties presumably lay behind the rapid development in this period, especially in southern France and Mediterranean countries, of *métayage* or share-cropping—contracts of various kinds which ensured that the tenant gave the landlord all or part of the produce of the farm in return for the use of the land, the house, the equipment and the seed. The price of land dropped; labour was difficult to get; and the enclosure of land for sheep in England may at any rate sometimes have occurred only after it had proved impossible to cultivate it in traditional ways.

These harsh changes were, in the main, likely to give some economic improvement to the peasantry of western Europe. In the boom condition

[1] Duby, *op. cit.*, II, pp. 556, 558. See below, p. 387, for further discussion of regression.

of the thirteenth century there had been in rural areas a degree of over-population which made many peasants—day labourers, poor serfs—very vulnerable. Now the countryside was more sparsely occupied and a better living was possible for those who remained. The changes also had direct consequences for the lords of land. Though some undoubtedly suffered, the situation was by no means unpropitious for those able to buy land when the price was low, for those able to organize big estates on up-to-date and efficient lines. What was new in the slump conditions of the fourteenth century was a bitterness in the lord's relations with the villagers.

The peasants' revolts

During earlier centuries there was a relative absence of sustained and widespread hostility between peasants and the lords of land. This is presumably because in most areas increasing productivity and increasing population were giving a sensibly improved position to each succeeding generation. The adventurous and discontented could without much difficulty either improve their position at home (by securing amelioration in the conditions of servile tenure or obtaining its cancellation) or could strike off to new settlements anxious to recruit labour and willing to offer favourable terms to incomers. In the regression after about 1300 such openings no longer existed, nor were the stagnant towns anxious as they had once been to encourage immigrants. But what, at any rate in certain regions like England, most irritated the peasant was the survival of serfdom alongside liberty. Lords had indeed gone far in abandoning their ancient rights, but very many sought to ensure basic services by retaining the old status in certain tenements. The old thus lingered on with the new, and the stronger central governments of the later Middle Ages added a further grievance through more rigorous and general taxation. Taxation had often sparked off the isolated demonstrations of earlier days. Now that war was expensive and continuous, taxation was proportionately heavier, falling often on social groups which had earlier escaped direct contact with the fiscality of kings.

Three major upheavals occurred: in Flanders from 1323 to 1328, in northern France in 1358 (the Jacquerie) and the Peasants' Revolt in England in 1381. The explosion in the coastal region of Flanders had as its leader a prosperous farmer called Nicholas Zannekin and the kernel of his support came from solid peasantry. These men resisted seignorial taxation and then refused to pay the tithe; the aim was to deny to the rentier, gentleman or clerk, his former income and the gentry rallied in self-defence. The ensuing struggle was violent, marked by social hatred and acts of cruelty, and rapidly became involved in the social tensions of the neighbouring towns. This indeed goes far to explain the duration of the conflict. Fortified by the rebellious members of underprivileged guilds in Bruges, Ypres and other towns (though not Ghent), the revolt survived an attempted pacification in 1326 and it was not until 23 August 1328 that a French royal army defeated the insurgents at Cassel; harsh repression then followed.

The French rising was provoked by the presence of troops, English and French, battening on the Île de France, the rich agricultural region round Paris. The early demonstrations by the peasantry in May 1358 were spontaneous protests against the local lords who had, it was felt, exposed the land to the horror of war. Many nobles were murdered, many castles were destroyed and, as in Flanders, artisans from the towns joined in the rebellion. Attempts to use it for their own ends were also made by Etienne Marcel, leader of the Paris burgesses who aimed at a reformed administration, and Charles king of Navarre, whose aims were higher—the domination and perhaps the acquisition of the throne. The revolution was short-lived. In violent reaction the nobles destroyed the peasants who had caught them off their guard. 20,000 peasants and their supporters had been killed by the end of June 1358 and resistance was at an end.

The English troubles were precipitated by the imposition of a series of unpopular taxes. The first, in 1377, was at the rate of a groat (4d) a head; the second (1379) related the tax to income and ran from a groat from the poor to ten marks (the mark was 13s 4d) from the rich; the third (1380) was again in strict terms a poll tax, demanding a shilling from all men and women over the age of fifteen, modified by the provision that within each district the better-off should help the poor. It was the evasions provoked by this last poll tax and government attempts to screw out the money that set off the Revolt of 1381. Isolated rioting in the Thames valley spread to Essex and Kent, and it was from the Home Counties, the rural areas round London, that the rebels drew most of their strength. The principal leader, Wat Tyler, possibly of gentry stock, had the Kent men behind him and was responsible for the march on London in June 1381. Some Londoners were not unsympathetic and the rebels entered the city. Much rough justice was then done; a number of lawyers and officials were attacked and killed; property was destroyed. A terrified government gave in to the peasants' demands at a parley during which Tyler was killed and the fifteen-year-old Richard II displayed great coolness (15 June). Their leader dead but their aims apparently achieved, the rebels dispersed; all the royal promises were revoked. The main danger was over, but the demonstrations continued throughout June and July, gradually spreading to counties further from the capital. Repressive measures were only called off at the end of August.

What makes the English rising of great interest is the clarity with which the peasantry expressed their policies. Basically they asked for the abolition of serfdom and the commutation of services for rent at 4d an acre; the abolition of the poll taxes was another demand put forward; and John Ball, who claimed to be a priest, expressed anticlerical and egalitarian sentiments. The Statute of Labourers (also violently denounced by the rebels) and the poll tax were presumably the immediate causes of the rising. Its long-term causes are more probably to be found in the illogical and irregular development of peasant society (the demand for the ending of villeinage is probably the clue here), and in a deep-rooted antagonism to authority.

The three risings briefly described above are by no means the only peasant rebellions of the later Middle Ages. A whole series of risings are found in rural France, especially in Normandy (associated with the later stages of the Anglo-French war) and in the south (the 'Tuchins'). In Catalonia there were risings in 1409–13 and from 1462 onwards; Jutland had disturbances in 1411, Finland in 1438. In Germany the culmination of lesser troubles came in the Peasants' War of 1524.

There is no doubt that these movements represented a new awareness of social differences. Important as it is in discussing revolutionary movements in the fourteenth and fifteenth centuries (as indeed in the eighteenth and the twentieth) to scrutinize carefully the precise local occasions of conflict and to avoid generalizations which obscure the multiplicity of irritations and vested interests involved in each moment of crisis, there are nevertheless certain common features to be discerned. First, it is evident that these agrarian risings mainly originated in the richer lands and that the leaders were the prosperous rather than the poorer elements in rural society. Questions of status, the dislike of the juridical nature of villeinage and envy of the privileged quality of the gentleman and the priest, were likely to weigh most heavily with the richer peasants. Second, an anticlerical sentiment existed throughout Europe, fortified by dislike of paying tithes and by the poor quality of the average parish priest, which was touched off by the heretical and near-heretical doctrines of the Lollards and field preachers now commonly to be found throughout western Europe.[1] Third, it is to be noted that in the case of the major upheavals each was associated with a great urban centre. Flanders was the seat of the most precocious town development in northern Europe; the Jacquerie took place round Paris; the Peasants' Revolt round London. This, as we have seen, gave the peasants in revolt urban allies. Beyond that one is tempted to argue that the precise privileges of the townsman, his 'liberties', were becoming a larger liberty for which his country cousins were prepared to fight and die.

One cannot regard these violent episodes as doing much to affect the course of economic or social change. The movement towards a rent-paying tenantry continued. By the end of the fifteenth century there are few serfs to be found in western Europe.

Recovery and change

Even in the darkest days of the fourteenth century there are regions where a steady agricultural improvement can be noticed and others where traditional lord–peasant relations survived. In Italy the rural areas round the towns in Tuscany and Lombardy seem to have witnessed improved farming methods. The association of the bourgeoisie with land in the *contado* had always been close; now, perhaps because famine was a more oppressive danger, the citizen took a greater interest in improving the returns from his country property, not least by the use of contracts of *mezzadria* (*métayage*); while lords of land, particularly churches, found it easy to set tenants leases of 'emphyteusis', varieties of long term or perpetual tenure involving improvement of the land (*livellum*). As for the survival of serfdom, this is to be seen often in hill areas. The small lords of the Genoese hinterland or in the area of Nice continued to exact the old services and the peasantry continued to render them.

Elsewhere in western Europe recovery, and the changes that went with it, were seen very generally as the fifteenth century went on and became most marked after about 1450. Much of the work of earlier centuries had to be done again: the waste had to be cleared. Often the only way this could be done was by employing peasants from far away and by offering them favourable terms. Some peasant enterprise there was in this, for there were lands where lordship had virtually perished and where squatters' rights in the end prevailed. But most of the

[1] See below, Chap. XII.

initiative was taken by lords who thus encouraged considerable migrations from hills and moors into the good land, and who had to abandon their old rights in the process.

The principal change which reconstruction brought in its train, apart from a rise in the peasants' social status, was more specialized farming. The later fifteenth century saw a great increase in the cultivation of the vine, above all in Italy, in Spain and in France, but also in south-west Germany. On the other hand grain production in the vicinity of towns was undertaken more systematically and led, for example in north-west Germany, to new villages being carved out of the forests: the local towns took the timber for building and fuel and then they took the corn. Likewise the countryside was called on to produce more meat, both beef and mutton. In the later Middle Ages we find in all parts of Europe the beginnings of the drove roads which were to link the producers of cattle with the urban consumer of meat until the coming of the railway train in the nineteenth century.

Sheep were raised for their wool as well as for their carcases, and in all areas of hill and plain transhumance greatly increased at this time. The most remarkable result of the demand (largely Italian, see below, p. 383) for fine wool was the development of the Castilian drovers' guild which has already been mentioned, the *Mesta*. This guild of graziers, which went back in origin to the thirteenth century, had steadily grown, helped by the royal protection it enjoyed, especially on the drove routes which ran from the north of Castile down to the south, to Estremadura and Andalusia. By the end of the fifteenth century there were about 3,000 members, mostly small men, though their policies were often dominated by the handful of very rich proprietors. The duke of Béjar with a flock of 25,000, the monastery of the Escorial with a flock of 40,000 had a big stake in the business, and the treasurer of the *Mesta* was the Grand Master of the Order of Santiago. The *Mesta* had regular meetings, usually attended by several hundred graziers (including women). These meetings laid down the duties of the shepherds who accompanied the flocks, made arrangements for privileges for its members, and organized fairs. This monopolizing of the Castilian countryside by the *Mesta* irreparably damaged agriculture as such.

In England fine wool had been a major export during the thirteenth century; in the fourteenth the looms of Flanders and Florence were often cut off by war or policy; and heavy taxes on the export of wool, known to be desired by foreign manufacturers of high grade cloths, encouraged the development of a native cloth industry which, by the end of the fifteenth century, was beginning to export woollens and worsteds to the Continent. Sheep had always been kept, sometimes in surprising numbers, by lowland peasants, though the sheep runs of the great proprietors like the Cistercian abbeys of Yorkshire had been the main source of exported wool. Now the manufacture of cloth gravitated to areas where water power made fulling mills easy to operate, and dearth of labour or a desire to make more regular profits led many lords to enclose arable and turn it over to grazing. The result was the transformation of the countryside in the Cotswolds, the Mendips, in Shropshire and Herefordshire, and in the south-west, which is marked to this day by placid country towns with solid houses and large village churches. The peasant in these areas was now frequently not only a shepherd but a domestic manufacturer of woollen thread.

East–west contrasts

Islands of serfdom and traditional seignorial rights survived in France, Italy and elsewhere in western Europe, as we have seen. Nevertheless the overall picture of the peasantry in this region was one in which the juridical status of unfreedom, of servitude, was rapidly disappearing. The peasant was, by the end of the period, probably better off economically as well, though he had passed desperate days during the prolonged slump, and by becoming a tenant he was to be exposed to the vicissitudes of landlordism. In eastern Europe a very different evolution took place in the later Middle Ages.

Faced with crisis the lords of western Europe had in general chosen to abandon seignorial rights and lease or sell their demesne lands. East of the Elbe they chose to organize their estates as economic units. In north-east Germany—Brandenburg, Holstein, Pomerania and Prussia —the existence of flat arable land excellently suited for grain production offered a staple crop to the enterprising lord. Brandenburg and Prussia had been colonial lands and there, although earlier there had been remarkable peasant freedom, bondage now increased. The Junker emerged as the resident and active proprietor. He exploited his demesne land (in any case larger than the peasant holdings and enlarged by expropriation of the latter) by servile workers, no longer with any rights to the land; public rights of jurisdiction were invoked to bolster economic controls. A region which had once been marked by the large number of its free tenant farmers now displayed a contrary aspect. This would have come about with difficulty if the export of grain had not made large-scale farming profitable.

This German development is characteristic also of the Slav lands of eastern Europe, for (with certain modifications) what was true of east Germany was also true of Silesia, Bohemia, Poland and Russia, as also of Hungary and Romania. There too the period saw peasant burdens increasing. Labour dues which had often been no more than one day a year became by the end of the fifteenth century one day a week—a figure which was to rise much higher in the sixteenth and seventeenth centuries. The liberty of movement of the peasant was severely restricted, and elaborate precautions were taken to prevent serfs escaping to the towns or across frontiers into neighbouring kingdoms. The precise occasions for this development were many: peasants became indebted to lords during the depression of the fourteenth century and were compelled by financial obligations to accept greater dependence; depopulation enabled lords to occupy vacant holdings and so to extend the demesne; purchase, often forced, gave the lord a further means of increasing his lands. Here, as in east Germany, the direct control of land and production of grain for the market made such a course of action attractive to lords. But the ultimate explanation for these changes is to be found in the political field.

The weakening monarchy of east and central Europe is discussed below.[1] Rival claimants and civil wars played into the hands of the nobility, especially the lesser nobility. Already in the thirteenth century many lords had secured immunities which excluded royal power from interposing itself between them and their tenants. Such grants became widespread, indeed normal, as weak kings strove to buy support from the nobility. By the fifteenth century the king had no longer any ability to intervene between a lord and his peasants. The result was a vast and unchecked increase in seignorial jurisdiction. Not merely did lords prevent the monarch from treating their serfs as in some sense his subjects, but they forced him to declare positively that the servitude they were imposing had state sanction. Thus in 1496 Polish peasants were formally tied to the soil. Beyond that the towns were compelled to surrender their ancient rights of harbouring serfs; they were compelled to abandon leagues with other towns; and the lords were even able to avoid using the towns as markets for their grain by selling it direct to exporters. Here too a further political factor was influential in north-east Germany; the defeat of the Teutonic Knights and the contracting activity of the Hanseatic League had already led many towns to decline in this area.[2] In Russia stronger monarchy did in fact develop by the end of the

[1] Chap. IX. [2] Below, pp. 204–5.

fifteenth century,[1] but by that time the boyars had secured massive rights over the men who worked on their lands.

In this way one of the profoundest differences between eastern and western Europe arose. A result of the political dominance of lords and of their success in farming the demesne for profit, it had in its turn far-reaching social and political consequences, lasting almost to our own day. It is important to note that, while the recession of the fourteenth and fifteenth centuries did not prevent, and may possibly have accelerated, the steady trend towards peasant liberty in the west of Europe, similar conditions in eastern Europe contributed to the growth of servitude.

Population trends in the later Middle Ages

The ups and downs in population can only be guessed at for periods before European governments embarked on accurate counting of heads. But the absence of censuses such as began to be compiled everywhere after 1800 does not entirely preclude the study of what has been called the 'prehistory of demography'. There is no doubt that much of value to the general historian will in future be contributed by the scientific study of demography.

The type of evidence used in estimating population in this period varies from one region to another and has only one basic characteristic: the data on which it is based was not originally recorded with the intention of counting all the persons in any community. The commonest type of material is that which arises from taxation. Here the historian of population must arrive at a figure, representing the non-taxpaying population, with which to multiply the number of tax payers. Commonly this involves computing how many members of a family should be reckoned for every 'hearth' or household. To get at this factor other material is scrutinized. A handful of registers of births have survived; the families of nobles have often been the subject of intense research by antiquaries, so that the average number and age of their children can be calculated. Wills, recording the members of a family among whom bequests were made, have survived; many court proceedings give details of a litigant's or an accused's relatives. By careful analysis of this type of material a factor is arrived at by which returns of persons paying taxes can be multiplied in order to arrive at a global figure. Such information is often tolerably plentiful for towns in continental Europe. It is often totally inadequate for the rural populations;

[1] Below, p. 264.

many of the hill and moor farmers escaped taxes; and we know far too little as yet of the way of life even of the relatively prosperous peasant let alone the luckless day labourer, or the gypsies who make their appearance in western Europe in the fifteenth century. With towns a further, but much cruder, method is also available in the study of the superficial area occupied by the town from time to time, as measured by the known area enclosed by the city walls. Successive enlargements of town walls undoubtedly reflect a growing population, though often not much more than that, for the density of population frequently did not justify the enlargement. The area within the last wall at Florence (1284–1328) was not completely used for human occupation until the middle of the nineteenth century.

Such assessments have survived, more often than not, for a single town or village, and refer to disparate dates which (in view of migration and pestilence) make comparison hazardous with other areas and other times. Taxation returns do not frequently cover a large territorial area such as a kingdom. Such relatively complete coverage is provided most fully for England where there have survived: the Domesday Book (1086), the poll tax returns of 1377 and later, and the chantry return of 1545.[1] For France, although taxation was much more intense than in England, no comparable general figures exist, but there is a famous hearth tax list of 1328, covering about two-thirds of the country as it was at that time. General returns from the provinces of Italy and the kingdoms of Spain mostly date from the sixteenth century.[2]

It would be satisfactory if we could with confidence state approximate totals for the various countries of Europe, if we could accept that the France of 1328 contained about $13\frac{1}{2}$ million souls, the England of 1377 about $2\frac{1}{2}$ million (with 125,000 in Wales, 50,000 in Ireland and 348,000 in Scotland).[3] But such figures depend on coefficients per hearth or home or head of family about which doubt and debate is continuous. It can be shown that a factor of between three and four is probably too low for some rural areas; that in some families there were nine or ten or (in certain Italian centres) as many as twenty or more persons. Precise totals or even approximate totals are probably to be avoided at present.

[1] Which reveal, *inter alia*, the number of communicants. See Russell, *British Medieval Population*, pp. 19–22.
[2] A mass of statistics covering the whole of Europe in Russell, *Ancient and Medieval Population*.
[3] These are Professor Russell's estimates.

What can be stated with a fair degree of conviction is the overall change in broad terms in Europe as a whole. Population began generally to decline in the early years of the fourteenth century and fell even more steeply during the second half of the century as a result of the plague. The second half of the fifteenth century saw a slow recovery and by the early sixteenth century it is probable that numbers had reached something like the level they had attained by about 1300. Within this framework there are endless variations, not so much country by country as region by region. Decline may well have begun before 1300 in some areas of Italy and France; recovery probably began sooner than elsewhere in favoured parts of Italy, Spain and Portugal. Decline and recovery can be estimated with greater precision for the towns[1] than for the countryside.

In these changes the principal victim and the principal beneficiary was the peasant, the countryman who directly cultivated the soil and watched the flocks. He was usually a silent witness of the public events of his day. The great peasant risings mentioned above are an indication that under provocation he was capable of violent and effective action, but not of sustained and organized pressure. It was a world organized in the interests not of all men but of small privileged groups. To these, the social and political pacemakers of the period, we must now turn our attention.

[1] Below, p. 76.

IV

Society and Its Structure
2. Clergy, Nobility, Townsmen

From a very early date in the Middle Ages it pleased the socially prominent groups to distinguish three components in the community: those who fought, those who prayed and those who worked, i.e. knights, clergy and peasants. In the later Middle Ages a good deal of embroidery

BIBLIOGRAPHY. Little has been written explicitly on the social groups here discussed. There is a valuable discussion for Spain in *Historia social y económica de España y América*, ed. J. Vicens Vives, II. *Patriciado urbano, reyes católicos, descubrimento de América*, by S. Sobrequés Vidal and G. Céspedes del Castillo (Barcelona, 1957), a short but useful chapter (part I, chap. v) in Piero Pieri, *Il Rinascimento e la crisi militare Italiana* (Turin, 1952), and some hints in P. Imbart de la Tour, *Les Origines de la Réforme*, I, 2nd edn. (Melun, 1948). For the clergy: R. Aubenas and R. Ricard, *L'église et la Renaissance* (in Fliche and Martin, *Histoire de l'église*, 15, Paris, 1951); M. D. Knowles, *The Religious Orders in England*, 3 vols. (Cambridge, 1948–59); G. Mollat, *Institutions ecclésiastiques*, in Lot and Fawtier, *Histoire des institutions françaises au moyen âge*, III (Paris, 1962). See also general histories of the Church, below, p. 267. Eileen Power, *Medieval English Nunneries, c. 1275–1535* (Cambridge, 1922) is the only scholarly work on the nuns of a large country.

Nobility and Gentry. Maurice Keen, *The Laws of War in the Late Middle Ages* (London, 1965); A. R. Wagner, *English Genealogy* (Oxford, 1960); many books dealing with agrarian history are relevant, e.g. Boutruche (above, p. 26); G. A. Holmes, *Estates of the Higher Nobility in XIV Century England* (Cambridge, 1957). E. M. Fernandez, *Evolucion de la nobleza en Castilla bajo Enrique III* (Valladolid, 1968); R. Highfield, 'The Catholic kings and the titled nobility of Castile', in *Europe in the Late Middle Ages* (below, p. 399). Cf. Frances E. Baldwin, *Sumptuary Legislation and Personal Regulations in England* (Baltimore, 1926).

Townsmen. J. Lestocquoy, *Les villes de Flandre et d'Italie sous le gouvernement des patriciens* (Paris, 1952); S. Thrupp, *The Merchant Class of Medieval London* (Chicago, 1948); see also bibliography to chap. XIV (below, p. 359).

Slavery. C. Verlinden, *L'esclavage dans l'Europe médiévale*, I (Bruges, 1955); Iris Origo, 'The Domestic Enemy: the Eastern Slaves in Tuscany in the XIV and XV Centuries', *Speculum*, 30 (1955), pp. 321–66.

of this motif took place and its general propriety was accepted by the literate. On the practical level it was, of course, shot through with inconsistencies, and it was unable to accommodate a minority of townsmen and merchants whose public influence was considerable. It has, however, one considerable merit. It is a division of society which ignores the modern word 'class' and all that it stands for. That is not to deny that there are occasions when antagonisms analogous to those of our own day are seen. The peasants' risings described in the previous chapter have a striking similarity to certain proletarian movements of the nineteenth century. And in the medieval town there is a better case than anywhere else in medieval history for a fruitful employment of Marxist terminology. Something like a middle class is to be observed in fourteenth-century Florence and Bruges, and something like a working class and an upper class. But it cannot be too firmly stated that contemporaries did not themselves divide social groups in this way.

A popular picture of society is provided by the characters depicted and described in pictures and verses dealing with the 'Dance of Death'. One such *Danse Macabre* of the late fifteenth century[1] gives us the following pairs of dancers:

Pope	Emperor
Cardinal	King
Patriarch	Constable
Archbishop	Knight
Bishop	Squire
Abbot	Bailiff
Astrologer	Burgess
Canon	Merchant
Carthusian	Sergeant
Monk	Usurer
Doctor	Lover
Advocate	Minstrel
Curé	Peasant
Friar	Child
Clerk	Hermit

Here are two hierarchies. The great division is between the clergy and the laity. Other assumptions beside this basic one lie behind the two

[1] Guy Marchant's edition (1485) of the *Danse Macabre*, quoted by E. F. Chaney, *La Danse Macabre* (Manchester, 1945), p. 9. For the *danse macabre*, cf. also below, p. 307.

parallel lists, some sly satire and yet another antithesis, that between grand and humble. But the list does not reveal a contrast as such between rich and poor; it does reveal a fundamental concern with a man's function in society, with his *status* or role.

The most generally used distinction was, in fact, between one 'estate' and another. The 'estates' were the categories in which all society was divided. The 'first estate' comprised the whole body of clergy; the 'second estate' comprised the whole body of nobles and gentlemen; the 'third estate' covered everybody else—the peasants and the townsmen. The expression is, however, equivocal, for estate can also mean a unit in a representative assembly. The Estates in France, for example, meant not only the elements of French society, but their members or deputies gathered together from time to time in an organized meeting. It is for this reason that it is preferable to use another word equivalent in meaning, *ordo* or 'order'; we preserve the meaning in the fast-dying phrases 'lower orders' and 'clerical orders'. What follows will be a discussion of the clerical order,[1] the noble order and that part of the 'lower orders', the townsmen, not covered in chapter III.

The clergy

The clerical order or estate must be treated first for several reasons. At the time no one would have questioned that clergy—monks, friars and secular priests—did come first. They were holy in that they participated, as no layman could, in the mysteries of the sacrament; by now this uniqueness was reflected in the ritual itself, for only the clergy communicated in both kinds. The literate added to this instinctive reverence for the clergy a theoretical justification: in the Great Chain of Being, the hierarchy of divinely appointed relationships in the world, the clergy came nearer to God. Reverence was thus accorded, but by no means an automatic respect, for we are in the first great age of anti-clericalism.

A second and perhaps to us a more compelling reason for giving prior consideration to the clergy is that they were members of the only estate to which entry was more or less clearly defined. One was usually born into other orders of society: the clerical order was entered by the consenting adult man—or such at any rate was the theory. This order, in short, involved for most of its members 'ordination'; one was 'ordained' or made part of the order in a formal ceremony; and in principle membership involved the wearing of uniform, laid down in the law of the Church and in the traditions of the clergy. In actual practice no

[1] 'Order' as applied to clergy has other meanings: see below, p. 49.

such rigid separation between clergy and laity is possible. Since legal protection of an enviable kind was afforded by the 'cloth', many laymen tried, sometimes successfully, to obtain recognition as clerks. Thus the servants of a great church, the cathedral at Noyon, viz. the bailiff, proctor, four guards, and two ringers, claimed in 1478 to be ecclesiastics; and about the same time a similar claim was advanced by the four churchwardens of Notre Dame at Paris. Even more notably, the undergraduate students at northern universities, many of whom in the fourteenth and fifteenth centuries had no intention of following a career in the Church or even of obtaining a bachelor's degree[1] and who were usually boys in their teens, were also regarded technically as clergy, a matter which explains much of the town and gown bitterness of the period. For the majority of students such clerical status did not involve ordination, but only the tonsure and the observance of celibacy. In Italy, where students were older, the privileges of the university scholar in a town depended hardly at all on his clerical status, almost entirely on local arrangements between the municipal authorities and the university.

Finally, measured by its control of land, the Church in many parts of Europe was extraordinarily rich and powerful. Estimates of church lands must be regarded with caution, although legislation everywhere against mortmain suggests contemporary awareness among jealous laymen of the vastness of the territorial endowment of the Church. Some conservative calculations suggest that in Catalonia about a quarter of the land was under the lordship of great clerical corporations, and in Castile the proportion was probably higher; the military orders in Spain alone held something like one-tenth of the land. In Italy, where in the north much land passed out of the control of the Church in the later Middle Ages, by the early sixteenth century clerical property varied from about 65 per cent in the south to 10 per cent in Lombardy. In England calculations have varied between a sixth and a quarter; in Bohemia we are told that the Church owned a third of the land.

Within the clergy there were two great branches, as there had been for hundreds of years. The regular clergy were those monks and friars who lived according to a rule (*regula*), who were normally cloistered or at any rate cut off from the world by vows of a more compelling kind than those taken by the secular clergy (*saeculum* = the world), the clergy whose ministry as priests lay among the laity. Here, too, confusion could arise. Nearly all monks were now ordained priests; a number were given 'faculties' enabling them to hold secular benefices; while a

[1] Below, p. 337.

number of important secular clerks held monasteries and priories *in commendam* (i.e. enjoyed the income of the abbot or prior but exercised the office only through deputies).

As noted above, one could be regarded—perhaps for many years or even a lifetime—as a clerk without taking orders, but ordination was the inevitable way into the ranks of the secular clergy as such. Orders were by now of two kinds, minor and major (or holy). Minor orders consisted in ascending rank of the 'door keeper' (*ostiarius*, which went with first tonsure), 'reader', exorcist and acolyte. There were three holy orders: subdeacon, deacon and priest. These orders had all to be conferred by a bishop,[1] to whom discretion was left as to the intervals between minor orders; in practice all were normally conferred at the same time as the ordinand was made an acolyte. In principle a year elapsed before the subdiaconate was conferred, and after that three months between that and the diaconate and between the diaconate and priesthood. The subdeacon had theoretically to be twenty-two years old, the deacon twenty-three and the priest twenty-five. Many examples occur of ordination of youths below canonical age, but it is likely that the majority were older than the minimum laid down. The ceremonies of ordination were public and in those creating deacons and priests the bishop laid his hands on the ordinands; this was the moment of full entry into the clerical order as far as secular clergy were concerned.

Regular clergy (monks and friars) often, even perhaps normally at this time, also became priests but their membership of the estate of clergy was essentially a domestic matter for their house or their 'order' —for this word is also used to cover the great communities of religious —Cluny, Cîteaux, Chartreux and other monastic groups, Franciscans, Dominicans and other families of friars. Into such groups of 'religious', as the regular clergy were and are termed, it was by now rare for an adult layman to be recruited. The monastery in the later Middle Ages usually recruited its novices in their late teens; the boys could not make final profession (solemn or perpetual profession) before the age of twenty-one. Much the same rule covered the friars, though they were more attractive to younger boys through their close connections with universities. The nuns, though certain social pressures made recruitment different in their case, were governed by similar rules for profession. Nuns, though religious were not regarded as clergy, and, though members of an order, could not, of course, be ordained.

[1] Despite his unique position the bishop was not regarded as belonging to a separate order (and is not today in the Roman Catholic Church).

Certain features of Church government are discussed in chapter XI and the problem of religious sentiment in chapter XII. The questions dealt with there are not unrelated to the social structure and social activities of the clergy which are our concern here. Who were the clergy, secular and regular? What were their relations with one another? How many were there? Answers to these questions are by no means easily found. Information on the clergy is less plentiful for the fourteenth and fifteenth centuries than for earlier periods and has been less fully studied. One must also, as with all material of this kind, be chary of generalizing what may be purely local in significance.

The secular clergy

The secular clergy, ranging down from some twenty or thirty cardinals, through hundreds of archbishops and bishops, to thousands of priests, in many ways offered a cross section of the whole population. Within the secular clergy there were very rich and very poor; many a humble curate must have felt his bishop infinitely more remote than the local squire, and felt it hard to accept that he belonged to the same order. Not that all bishops enjoyed rich sees, for many did not. In the south of Italy, in the Mediterranean islands, in parts of Spain, in Wales and Ireland, there were sees whose bishops had smaller incomes than the rectors of many a fat living in rich lands, let alone the splendid income of a potentate like the bishop of Winchester. In the standard list of bishops the see of Rouen's assessment in the papal camera at this time is given as 12,000 florins; it is flanked by the sees of Ross in Ireland and Ruvo (near Bari) in Italy, both assessed at 33 florins.[1] It is, therefore, a mistake to regard the episcopate as socially homogeneous. The bishop of Ross earned an honest penny, as like as not, acting as a dogsbody for some greater prelate, absent from his diocese, performing for him those acts which only a bishop could perform, the ordination of priests in particular.

It is easy to see reasons why an ambitious clerk should try to become one of the princes of the Church, quite aside from vocation. Who became pastors in the underprivileged sees? It is no accident that many such bishops were friars, who also filled a majority of the titular sees, bishoprics *in partibus infidelium*, whose holders were intended to provide a pool of suffragan and auxiliary bishops for diocesan work. It should also be remembered that such *ad hoc* posts were the only way the Church

[1] C. Eubel, *Hierarchia catholica*, II, pp. 225–6. Winchester is also assessed at 12,000 florins.

responded in our period to changes in population: new sees were usually created in Europe at this time only in converted or reconverted territory.[1] A bishop was, nevertheless, a key figure in his locality, even if the locality was poor and the bishop relatively humble. There never seems to have been a shortage of recruits even for the most thankless and ill-rewarded bishoprics.

The reverse of the medal might be expected to show the monopolizing of the greater and richer sees by nobles and members of princely houses, for in general it was the case that princes everywhere had the last word in appointments to prelacies. Many of the German sees were from time to time the battleground of rival noble and princely families, who regarded the local bishopric as a legitimate prize of social pre-eminence. A celebrated case is that of the family of Mörs. Dietrich von Mörs, archbishop of Cologne from 1414 to 1463, obtained another see for himself (Paderborn 1415), one for his brother Henry (Münster 1424 and in 1442 Osnabrück), and partial enjoyment of another for his brother Walram (Utrecht 1433). For a generation Dietrich von Mörs used his ecclesiastical position to keep north-west Germany in bloody ferment. Another grim episode was the struggle between two members of the noble chapter of Mainz, Dietrich of Isenburg and Adolph of Nassau, who, with their allies, disturbed the area, sometimes to the point of actual war, between 1459 and 1463. Not many areas display ecclesiastical politics in such stark fashion, but princely nepotism is found elsewhere: the Stewart kings of Scotland obtained many bishoprics for their issue, legitimate and illegitimate; Burgundian dukes used bishoprics as essential elements in their state-building; and—on a very different level—we find Venetian patricians (Dandolo, Barbo, Zeno, Foscari) occupying the see of Padua in the fifteenth century; at Milan the fifteenth-century archbishops include a Visconti and a Sforza.

Yet it would be wrong to regard the majority of bishops as the near kinsmen of the princes who had so great a control over 'election'. No son of a Valois king became a bishop in France. In England the nearest we get to a royal bishop is Cardinal Beaufort, issue of John of Gaunt's irregular association with Catherine Swynford, who became bishop of Lincoln in 1398 and was translated to Winchester in 1404; and he was a man who might have earned these high rewards by his brilliant and loyal service of the crown. For that was without question the normal

[1] Cf. below, p. 300; John XXII created 16 new bishoprics in the south of France (1317-8) but these, and Pienza (1462, below, p. 352) were not in response to changes in population.

route to the highest preferment in England and France. Many magnates did secure bishoprics for their children; it has been said of fifteenth-century France that the 'nobility took possession of the episcopate'.[1] But one suspects that a high proportion of these noble bishops were, like their counterparts in England, men of ability, university trained (above all in law), and that they were used by the crown.[2] Scandalous appointments there were; the vain and ignorant Louis de Beaumont, cousin of Queen Isabella, held the see of Durham from 1317 to 1333; Charles of Bourbon was given the income of the see of Lyons at the age of thirteen in 1446. And there seems little doubt that, once appointed, most bishops who had secured wealthy sees lived like lords, provoking much adverse comment from reformers (below, p. 311). It is, however, salutary to note that the kings of France and England were not tempted to deflect the wealth of the Church to their own children: the plums in the lay pie were bigger and, equally important, they were heritable.

At a level below the episcopate the secular clergy numbered many substantial and well remunerated posts. These were partly attractive because of the power and wealth that went with them (such as many of the archdeaconries) and partly because they involved no ministerial functions (canonries in cathedrals are the best and most numerous example of this type of preferment). To consult the lists of archdeacons and deans of any cathedral is to have before one's eyes the élite of the clergy at a professional level. It was this type of preferment which came to the rising administrator, in Church or State, who hoped to become a bishop; here were the curial officials whom popes, kings and cities had rewarded for their services. As for the prebendaries or canons, the large majority were university doctors—doctors of civil law, of canon law, of theology, busy teachers in their universities, men of letters, civil servants, whose endowments from a great church were part of the perquisites of solid success in the groves of Academe and in the chanceries of princes, popes and prelates. Who were they? In Germany chapters were noble to a notorious extent; in a city like Florence patricians filled the cathedral stalls. In France, we are told, canons were recruited 'from the educated bourgeoisie, sometimes from the gentry'.[3] It was probably no different elsewhere.

At the foot of the secular ladder came the vast mass of priests—some

[1] G. Mollat in Lot and Fawtier, III, p. 372.
[2] Cf. J. R. L. Highfield, 'English Hierarchy in the Reign of Edward III', *Trans. R. Hist. Soc.*, 5th ser., 6 (1956), pp. 115–38.
[3] Aubenas, *op. cit.*, p. 318.

with rich livings, some perpetual curates with a meagre stipend, some the personal clerks of nobles and gentlemen. Of the latter group, assuredly large, very little is known, save that they ranged from the humble domestic dominies kept by country gentry—to write their letters and teach their children as well as serve in chapel—to the ambitious clerks in the entourage of a great man, for whom high preferment in the Church might be a reward. There is, however, a good deal of scattered information about the parochial clergy.

By the later Middle Ages two important changes had occurred in parochial arrangements: to some extent in England but to an even greater extent in most continental countries, a large number of benefices had left the hands of lay patrons and come into the gift of ecclesiastical bodies; and, facilitated by this development, great churches, monasteries and colleges had successfully applied to have the bulk of the income from parishes in their gift transferred to themselves, leaving only a small stipend to cover the living expenses of the vicars or curates who performed the church services. The result of this, of the absenteeism which was created by rich livings being given to administrators or used to finance young men at universities, and of the devastations of war in France, the north of England and in many other parts of Europe, was a steady decline in the financial value of a great many parish livings; revenue from land was in any case smaller than it had been in the thirteenth century. The clerk personally known to the majority of rural parishioners was normally a man paid very little, compelled to eke out his income with school teaching and farming of the glebe. He was in all probability of the same social class as the bulk of his parishioners, whose humble and sometimes unedifying pleasures he frequently shared. The unfortunate moral results of this situation attracted much attention at this time.[1] What drew men into the ministry when its rewards were so low?

Undoubtedly we must place first a sense of calling. Chaucer's poor parson was 'rich . . . of holy thought and work', willingly caught in the toils of an apostolic Christianity; and there are others like him in the records, though they are dimmer figures than the rogues, who secured the immortality of court proceedings or public scandal, as they still do. Yet for Chaucer the poor parson is an exceptional man. Not only, Chaucer tells us, was he a virtuous, hard-working and inspired pastor, but he did not desert his flock while they had to put up with a substitute; he did not try to get the less onerous and better paid work

[1] Below, pp. 302, 311.

of a chantry priest: 'He was a shepherd and not mercenary'. Many mercenary priests existed: who tried to raise money by exchanging a good benefice for a less good one ('chop-churches' they are called in a censorious late fourteenth-century English document); or whose interest in their parishes ended with the collection. But these were the men who had secured the better livings.

The pool of talent from which the humble curates were drawn was, it seems, the rural population, the peasantry. The normal pattern was doubtless the training by the incumbent of a parish of one or two boys to act as choristers or servers. This involved letters being learned by the children and little more than that was required by the law of the Church for its priests. A council at Paris in 1429 reminded bishops that they were not to ordain anyone who did not know 'the epistles and gospels, who could not read and adequately comprehend the rest of the office'.[1] It is, however, clear that in every part of Europe this modest standard was often not attained. Visitations tell again and again of priests who are ignorant and illiterate: a Burgundian priest, we are told, 'when he said mass made nonsensical noises' (si dicat officium, dicit titinellando).[2] It was the job of the bishop before ordination to examine priests as to morals and education. Everywhere bishops and the officers to whom they committed this task neglected to do it seriously; when they did the results were lamentable, as when a late fifteenth-century bishop of Utrecht found only three capable candidates out of 103. There also seems to be no doubt that a large number of semi-illiterate peasants secured nomination as curates and by-passed even perfunctory examination.

The serf was precluded by canon law from being ordained. By now, as we have seen, the number of bondmen in western Europe had markedly declined so that relatively few were held back from a career as a priest on account of their birth. Moreover to have a priest in the family conveyed enhanced status, and many poor folk must have encouraged their children to learn their letters as a way of avoiding a miserable life as a labourer. Poor as the parish priest often was he was probably better off than many of his parishioners. He had also a position in the community which made him important. Something of all this can be glimpsed in the early pages of Thomas Platter's *Autobiography*, where the orphan from the Valais, who had been a shepherd boy, was at the age of nine taken to his cousin 'Mr Anthony Platter', a priest, in order to learn writing. His subsequent miseries and adventures were to lead him

[1] Below, p. 304.   [2] G. Mollat, in Lot and Fawtier, III, p. 384.

to acquire higher education and his mother despaired of him: 'I am not so fortunate that I should bring up a priest.'[1]

Two further substantial inducements must have encouraged men to take orders: the priest, like all clergy, was protected by his cloth from prosecution in civil courts; and he was in many places exempted from the taxation of the state.

Benefit of clergy was being whittled away in the later Middle Ages, but in terms of broad theory a clerk could not be tried save by the courts of the Church. Church courts imposed mainly spiritual penalties and, as they never imposed the penalty of death, a clerical malefactor was better off than an ordinary criminal. This was a distinctly attractive aspect of holy orders in a violent age. Moreover, studying the accounts that have survived of organized crime in the fourteenth and fifteenth centuries, one is tempted to think that gangs of desperadoes positively recruited clerics because of the value of their immunity as well, perhaps, as their sophistication in guile. As for direct taxation, it is true that in France and Spain the clergy were in the end more or less successful in securing technical exemption. The price they paid, however, was that they might not traffic on their own account; and the simple mercantile activity which elsewhere helped priests to turn an honest penny may have been an equally valuable perquisite. In any event, the clergy were taxed by the Church on behalf of the State in all parts of Christendom and were peculiarly vulnerable—whether in England or Florence— when war involved hostilities with the Roman curia. The priest had many privileges, but he was exposed to lay pressures of all kinds as well as to the fiscal appetite of governments.

The regular clergy

Monks, whose convents depended directly on endowments from land, suffered materially in this period as did other lords. A number of smaller houses disappeared, or were merged with larger and wealthier communities; many survived but were in considerable financial difficulties; a few weathered the storm and were, at any rate relatively, extremely prosperous. The state of a monastery's finances directly affected recruitment, for a poor house was unwilling to admit new members unless they could add to its resources; and a rich house sought to limit recruitment

---

[1] The autobiography of Platter (1499–1582) is translated in P. Monroe, *Thomas Platter and the Educational Renaissance of the Sixteenth Century* (New York, 1904); see pp. 80–120.

by charging heavy entrance fees. The charging of such fines was prohibited by canon law, but the practice is legislated against everywhere
with such regularity that it seems to have been all but universal.

The result of this was the tendency for monks in all the older communities—Benedictine houses, Cluniac, Cistercian, Carthusian and the
houses of regular canons[1]—to be drawn pretty exclusively from social
levels which could afford to pay the entry fine and to continue to supply
a relative in the convent with a few luxuries and pocket money additional
to that often handed out to its members by the convent itself. In most
houses the lay brothers were now non-existent; the choir monks were
nearly all priests; the illiterate layman thus was very nearly excluded,
except as a boy in his teens who could be taught the liturgy as a matter
of rote.

The provenance of the English monks in this period, we have been
told by the historian of English monasticism, was mainly from localities
where the convent was known:

> . . . the vast majority of recruits came from the manor and estates
> owned by the monastery and (in the case of urban sites) from the
> town or city and its environs. . . . The number of recruits of standing
> from distant and even from foreign parts, which was appreciable
> in the century after the Conquest, was negligible in the fifteenth
> century . . .
> The social status of these recruits is less easy to discover, but it is
> probably safe to say that a majority were sons of burgesses or of the
> middle and lower ranks of rural landowners and freemen.[2]

With suitable adjustments this statement probably applies also to the
continent: in Germany there seem to have been more 'nobles', that is
sons of knightly families; in urban areas of Italy and Flanders the
bourgeoisie predominated. In Germany and France rather grander
families interested themselves in the higher monastic offices and above
all in that of abbot; this was facilitated by the practice of holding *in
commendam*, almost unknown in England before the sixteenth-century
case of Cardinal Wolsey, which enabled ambitious seculars to line their
pockets at the expense of the regulars. Certainly the disorders in certain
continental monasteries, which were also almost unknown in England,
suggest a marked degree of aristocratic licence. The offences for which

---

[1] Augustinian and Premonstratensian canons were by now generally leading
claustral lives like ordinary monks.
[2] Knowles, *Religious Orders in England*, II, p. 229.

monks are most often censured in England—hunting and fishing—reflect the avocations of the society from which they were drawn.

If monasteries were in the main recruited from relatively well-to-do families, nunneries were almost exclusively populated by the daughters of the wealthy. This was partly because the only permanent alternatives before the womenfolk of the landowners and the bourgeosie were matrimony and conventual life. Many girls had, of course, a genuine vocation —the list of women mystics and zealots is so long that we may be confident that many nuns took the veil because they desired ardently to lead a religious life. Other women, while lacking a vocation for religion, also lacked a vocation for marriage, even although their families were rich enough to provide the necessary dowry. Yet it remains the case that it was often cheaper to pay the dowry (as the entrance fee to a nunnery was also called) of a nun than find the money to secure the girl a husband of suitable status. The father who had a great many daughters cannot have been sorry to see one or two of his children in a fashionable convent, mixing with highborn ladies. In England well-known families, who had apparently little interest in monasteries, placed their daughters in nunneries; there are hardly any noble abbots in later medieval England but there are a number of noble abbesses and prioresses. That this was even truer in many parts of the continent may be seen, as with the monasteries, in the disorders there associated with nuns.[1] But often the life of the nunnery led to no worse activities than those of young ladies in the castle or the town house: gossiping with the young men from the university, like the nuns of Godstow near Oxford; dancing on the eve of the Ascension, like the nuns of the abbey of the Paraclete in Champagne; both activities were thundered against by the bishops concerned.

Of the social background of the friars in this age we know little. In all the established Orders literacy was now practically essential and a majority of the brothers became ordained priests. Newly developed Orders (like the Minims at the end of the fifteenth century) or fresh branches of existing Orders (like the Observant Franciscans at the end of the fourteenth century) undoubtedly for a time recruited humble and illiterate adults, but soon began to insist, as St Bernardino did for the Observants, on a high degree of training. After all the friars were anxious to compete with parish priests, or at any rate to be a model to the secular clergy in education as well as in virtue. Many of the friars of whom something is known were the sons of citizens—St Bernardino

[1] Below, pp. 302, 319.

57

himself, for example, came from a prominent Sienese family; two other Observant saints of the mid-fifteenth century, Giovanni Capistrano and James of the March, were well-known and successful lawyers before they joined the order. This suggests, of course, an Italian pattern of recruitment, going back to the *poverello* of Assisi. In the north many friars came from country villages as well as from the towns: William of Ockam, the most famous English Franciscan of the later Middle Ages, probably came from a Surrey village; John Baconthorp (d. 1348), the greatest Carmelite doctor, came from the Norfolk countryside. All in all it seems likely that the social background of the friars was much less exalted than that of the monks. Some slight confirmation of this can be found in England in the assessments for the poll tax of 1377 where monks and nuns had each to pay a shilling, along with other wealthy members of the community.

How numerous were the clergy? The question is hard to answer with confidence for any country save England, where, as already mentioned, statistical information is more complete than for continental countries and where Dom Knowles and Mr Hadcock have made a detailed study of the regular clergy from precisely this point of view.[1] English evidence suggests that at the end of the fourteenth century the proportion of clergy to laity in counties in which there was a cathedral or university was about 1 to 50; in the country as a whole the proportion was of the order of 1 to 70; that is, there were something like 33,000 clergy in a total population of 2·2 million.[2] Of these 33,000 some 11,000 were regulars (about 6,400 monks and regular canons, 2,500 friars and 2,000 nuns); there were some 4,500 parishes with incumbents of one sort or another and a great number of chantries with one or more priests; the remainder—numbering many thousands—were unbeneficed clerks, clerks in minor orders, university students. The fluctuations in the clerical population as a whole cannot be computed, but so far as the regulars are concerned the findings of Dom Knowles and Mr Hadcock can be summarized as follows:

	Monks and canons	Friars	Nuns	Total
c. 1350	9,148	5,016	3,247	17,411
c. 1422	6,494	2,564	2,030	11,088
c. 1500	7,070	3,050	2,116	12,236

[1] D. Knowles and R. N. Hadcock, *Medieval Religious Houses: England and Wales* (1953).
[2] Russell, *British Medieval Population*, pp. 144–6.

The changes down and up seem to be confirmed by Dom P. Schmitz's researches on the Benedictine Order, by M. G. de Valous for the Order of Cluny and by Richard W. Emery for the French friars.[1] The pattern, it will be observed, follows more or less the general population trend.[2]

Failing similar studies for other countries we must assume that the clerical population of Europe was of about the same order of magnitude; if some countries (Italy, perhaps, with its hundreds of bishoprics) were higher, others (like the Scandinavian countries) were probably lower. A famous passage in Giovanni Villani's *Chronicle* (xi, p. 93) suggests that at Florence before the Black Death the clergy numbered about 3 per cent of the population; in smaller towns with universities and cathedrals the proportion of clergy might rise, as it apparently did at Toulouse by the end of the fourteenth century, to as much as 15 per cent. The clergy were thus a much more numerous group in the community than they are today, especially in towns of any size. Even if by dressing like the laity (and all the records suggest that the more prosperous clerks did this and that the rules for tonsure were often broken) the clerk went unnoticed in the streets, the numbers of friars, whose mendicant garb was less easily disposed of, must have been striking. On the other hand, there were great areas of Europe where parishes were big and incumbents scattered; in Northumberland, in the Cevennes, let alone in the Alps or the Pyrenees, country dwellers must often have not seen a priest for months on end.

If the clergy numbered 1·5 per cent of a population which totalled for Europe in 1340 something like 46 million, there would have been about 700,000 of them: a formidable pressure group, if the estate had been united. Such unity was, however, not forthcoming. We have seen that social differences permeated the estate, that there were rich and poor bishops and monks and priests. Beyond that, the secular clergy, depending on patronage (lay patronage for most of the greatest offices, the bishoprics), had always been involved in the public life of their age and had mostly remained enmeshed in the private politics of their families. Selected more often than not because of their administrative ability or family fortune, the bishops of the later Middle Ages not only played an

[1] P. Schmitz, *Histoire de l'ordre de S. Benoît*, III (Maredsous, 1948); G. de Valous, *Le monachisme clunisien des origines au XVe siècle* (Paris, 1935). Mr Emery summarized his findings for foundations of new houses thus: to 1275: 423; from 1276 to 1350: 215; 1351–1450: 110; 1451–1550: 134, *The Friars in Medieval France* (London and New York, 1962), p. 3. Though new houses are founded the total number of friars fell, *ibid.*, p. 5.

[2] Above, p. 44.

active part in managing the State, but also naturally found time to help their kinsmen and dependants. An abbot, however good and upright, would have been regarded as odd if he had not used his influence to appoint nephews and cousins to livings in his gift, if he had not made his father and brothers lay farmers and custodians of the lands, the forests, the hospitals and granges of the convent. Such family connections were increased in this period, for it was accepted that entry into a monastery no longer cut a man off from kith and kin; it was, for instance, common for monks to have holidays with their families. Nobles, gentry and burghers with relatives in religious orders now could feel even more than before that their kinsmen in religion were still members of the household. At a lower level it is clear that many simple priests shared the interests of their peasant neighbours from whose ranks so many of them were drawn: the anticlerical sentiment of the risings described in the previous chapter was often formulated and fanned by priests.

It is, moreover, pretty evident that the estate of the clergy in these centuries had no programme of its own. In the eleventh and twelfth centuries the Church had campaigned for a position *vis-à-vis* the laity which in many respects conflicted with the interests of kings and magnates. The acceptance of the clerical estate as a separate entity was perhaps the only solid result of these conflicts. Borderlands of dispute there still were: benefit of clergy, mortmain legislation, fiscal immunities. But they were no longer being made the centre of concerted activity by the Church, which had in practice admitted provincial and partial solutions and accommodations. We shall therefore not expect to find the Church in the fourteenth and fifteenth centuries emerging as a protagonist in the public sector. The clergy were regarded, by themselves and by society at large, as a separate and distinct order or estate. That order or estate was, however, active through individuals and in an uncoordinated way. And these individual priests, monks and friars reflected in the main the interests not of their cloth but of the social background from which they came. This meant that the influential clergy were often those who stemmed from the influential group in lay society or who, as bishops and abbots, became members of it. The people who mattered were the nobles and gentlemen.

The military orders

Before turning to secular society as such it is necessary to consider a group of men who, in a sense, formed part of both the clergy and the laity. The members of the military Orders were technically clergy (and some of them were ordained priests) but lived lives which could be described broadly as knightly. All full members were subject to the monastic vows of obedience, chastity and poverty, yet they were necessarily involved in the world.

The military Orders originated in the early crusades. The Templars and the Teutonic Knights were fighting orders. The Order of the Knights of St John of Jerusalem (Hospitallers) was originally particularly devoted to the provision of a hospice at Jerusalem and this remained a minor side of their work when they too became a fighting Order. With the thirteenth-century decline in the crusade many changes occurred. Possessed of vast landed wealth, with territories and buildings not only in the Levant but in every part of Christendom, the Templars became more concerned with international finance than with supporting attacks on the infidel, and their inactivity following the expulsion of the Latins from Syria in 1291 was particularly noteworthy. Their headquarters in Paris, the Temple, acted like a bank, providing loans not least to the French crown. This was to lead to their fall. Philip IV of France, pursuing a ruthless financial policy to which the Italian bankers and the Jews had already fallen victims, turned on the Templars and secured their destruction. In 1307 they were arrested in France on charges of gross blasphemy and immorality. Torture secured many confessions and Pope Clement V was ultimately persuaded to dissolve the Order. This was accomplished, with the help of royal pressure, at the Council of Vienne in 1312. The property of the Templars was transferred to the Hospitallers, save in the kingdoms of Spain where some of it went to other military Orders. The destruction of the Templars was undertaken, with much less enthusiasm than in France, in other parts of Europe.

In the fourteenth century the international character of the military Orders was further weakened. The Teutonic Knights were in any case now concentrated in north-eastern Germany.[1] In Spain there were several Orders which were more or less restricted to the peninsula: the old and mainly Castilian Orders of Calatrava, Santiago and Alcántara, and the newer Orders of Montesa (1317) in Valencia, and Christ (1319) in Portugal. Even the Hospitallers, whose wealth was vastly extended by the dissolution of the Templars, had already divided up into 'languages', that is into regional groups. The high officials were associated with these separate provinces so that the Order became a kind of

[1] Below, p. 204.

federation and sometimes the preceptories in England and on the continent were only nominally under the direction of the grand master, established from 1310 in Rhodes.[1] This divisive trend (common to all the religious orders) was seen also in the Iberian peninsula. The Knights of Calatrava in Portugal were by the thirteenth century virtually separated off as the Order of Avis.

Finally, all military Orders became increasingly the preserve of good families. There were three categories of full members, knights, chaplains and serjeants, and the knights were in the end required to prove their gentility before admission, as were members of probationary or associated grades. This meant that the Hospitallers, the Teutonic Knights and the Orders in Spain recruited from the landed nobility and gentry. By the end of the fifteenth century the Orders of Christ and of Avis had received papal permission for their members to marry while remaining entitled to their clerical rights. The Hospitallers maintained a certain activity in the defence of Christendom in the Middle East, and the Teutonic Knights were heavily involved in the crusade and the commerce of the Baltic area. But the Orders in Spain became the preserve of the younger sons of important families and the senior positions and especially the masterships of the orders entered into the field of high politics: the master of Avis became king of Portugal in 1385 and Henry the Navigator used the resources of the same Order to promote his Moroccan and Atlantic expeditions. The Knights were thus a peculiarly privileged section of the community, vastly endowed, especially in Prussia and in the kingdoms of Spain, but their organizations were now mainly geared to estate management, a congenial occupation for their members.

The nobility and gentry

This subtitle needs a word of justification for it has become one of the English-speaking world's assumptions that the gentry are a phenomenon (like the word itself) of the sixteenth century and after. Even in English, however, the word 'gentleman' in its later social connotation has reached the point of being committed to paper by the mid-fifteenth century, after a long period when 'gentle' had been an adjective referring to character rather than birth. How long before then the word had been spoken in its social sense cannot be told; one of the difficulties is that some of the earlier sources are not in the spoken language but in the French and Latin of the records. For example an Act of Parliament

[1] Below, p. 260.

of 1363 contains the phrase 'esquieres et toutesmaneres. de gentils gentz', a phrase which, as it was spoken in the Commons, must have been 'squires and all kinds of gentlefolk' (*Statutes of the Realm*, I, pp. 380-1). At any rate 'gentleman' and 'gentlefolk' certainly met a need which had long existed in England for suitably ambiguous terms to describe persons who were higher in status than the free farmer (yeoman or franklin) and yet lower than the 'squire' or 'knight', whose titles reflected an older world of military tenure. *La chevalerie* had been, indeed, the general term used for the landed classes of an earlier day. For long enough, however, the knight and his warhorse had parted company, or at least a knight was no longer regarded as automatically constituting a mounted warrior. In France the *chevalier* held, like the English knight, a rank in society rather than the office of a soldier. On the continent, but not in England, the knight and the squire were technically nobles. It is therefore more difficult, at first sight, to distinguish the German, Spanish or French gentleman from the nobleman.

The older explanation for this was the greater social mobility in England. There it was supposed to be easier to rise, and easier to fall: 'ploughboy to ploughboy in three generations'. It now seems unlikely that there was any sharp difference between England and other countries in this regard, save that the strict primogeniture of England meant that a peer's children were not legally peers themselves. On the continent the gradual emergence of fiscal immunity for the nobility as a whole led the rest of society (and the governments whose revenues suffered) to scrutinize sharply attempts to enter the magic circle of the privileged. This immunity was, however, only just crystallizing by the end of the fourteenth century.[1] In England, on the other hand, entry to the narrow nobility of the peerage was by the end of the period very jealously guarded, and membership of the Lords had become closely defined. It is probably fair to say that the titled peerage (counts, earls, dukes and so on) was everywhere a relatively small body to which entry was difficult and in practice dependent on the will of the prince; and that everywhere there was a much larger class of landowners in which social distinctions were much vaguer.

The bulk of the land held by the nobility at all levels was feudal as far as tenure was concerned. That is to say that in theory the land was held of a superior on terms of military service. In practice the link was tenuous between tenure and service in war. Princes still summoned their vassals to perform military service, but this was usually a mere

[1] Below, p. 104.

device to secure cash instead. Feudal tenure was still important financially and in other ways since it enabled the lord to insist on his right
to a relief when the estate of a 'vassal' passed to an heir, and to those
other rights of wardship and marriage which were to linger on for centuries as 'fiscal feudalism'. Subject to these dues and privileges land
owners had in effect the entire use of their lands; they were in effect
proprietors.

In addition to land held in this way there were considerable areas
where non-feudal, or allodial, land was relatively common (Friesland,
Saxony and other parts of Germany, the south of France, the north of
Italy and Castile); in a few areas (England was one) it was by now
unknown. Such allodial land was free of feudal service; its possessors
(many of whom were small men, some peasants) had a more or less
absolute right to dispose of it. The greatest magnates normally held of
the Crown the fiefs from which they drew their titles, but might also, in
their own right, possess territories not feudally subject to the prince.

The higher nobility

At the start of the fourteenth century the great nobles of western European countries were already playing a highly significant part in public
affairs in every country. The reasons for this lie in the principal aim of
the great landowner: more land. Undoubtedly the main way in which
land was sought was by marriage. Except on troubled borderlands
war, spoliation of the Church, pressure on weaker neighbours, were
generally speaking insignificant means of augmenting one's domains;
heiresses were in every region a safer and more profitable investment.
The pages of the *Complete Peerage* tell in detail the story of the marriage
market for England; similar works of aristocratic piety commemorate
matrimonial activities in other parts of Europe. It is an extraordinary
story in which great dynasties were built up and, usually by natural
causes (infertility or a large number of daughters), disintegrated. English
evidence suggests that a third of the peerage tended to die out in peacetime every two generations, a rate which could be sharply accelerated in
time of war, especially of civil war.

If marriage was the main preoccupation of the landed magnate it was
not the sole way in which land could be obtained. It could be bought
with money and, in the later Middle Ages, with depression and depopulation weakening the smaller proprietor, the great man was favourably
placed. Evidence from Spain, France and England suggests that great
estates became greater at this time. For some, on the other hand,

extravagant building and imprudent management brought ruin. The ruined peer was still free to fall, the doctrine that a peerage could not be lost through poverty not yet having been evolved.

Along with his desire to be better endowed, the grandee wanted more grandeur. Titles proliferated at this time, spreading out from the French court, which in the fourteenth century exemplified the chivalric notions of western aristocratic society. The first English duke appeared in 1337, taking precedence over earls; in 1385 the title marquis was imported (a 'strange' or foreign word, as one of its earliest beneficiaries described it); the marquis took precedence over an earl too, but not over a viscount, this foreign title coming in England in 1440, and giving its possessor seniority over the simple baron or Lord. A very similar story is found in Spain. In Italy the Visconti lord of Milan became a duke in 1395, the first of many such in northern Italy. With this should perhaps be linked the multiplication of Orders of chivalry. Edward III's Order of the Garter was the first (1348) and remained one of the most coveted. Others in plenty followed: the French Order of the Étoile (1351) and the Burgundian Golden Fleece (1430) were two of the most celebrated. These are very different organizations from the military Orders founded before this period and mentioned on a previous page. Whatever the original intentions behind the Garter may have been it soon became the preserve of princes and great nobles, and the other Orders of chivalry were no different.

Outward magnificence was also aimed at by the magnate. Huge retinues, elaborate feasts, picturesque jousting, hunting over well-stocked land, these were his amusements and he indulged in them lavishly. Above all, and in this period for the first time, the great lord began to build on a massive scale. The castles of the later Middle Ages still had defensive purposes wherever there was danger: in Scotland, in the Italian mountains, in Spain. But where good order was more regular the castles of the great nobles became more luxurious and comfortable than they had ever been before. Although machicolation and other traces of military tradition are found on most of the fifteenth-century châteaux, this is no more bellicose than the elaborate engraved armour of the joust. The châteaux of the Loire valley date in many cases from the period after the Hundred Years War; in England buildings like Lord Cromwell's Tattershall, the palace of the dukes of Medinaceli at Cogolludo in Castile, represent the same trend to both improvements and comfort. Building at this rate not only cut a noble off as never before from the lower orders, it was prodigiously expensive.

To secure each of his ambitions—heiresses, cash and honour—the magnate had to turn to the Crown. Hence a further characteristic of the great men of the period is that they were physically drawn to the king's court whence flowed so many of the good things of life, rich brides, valuable offices to shore up empty treasuries or produce ready money, titles and respect. The great man's pleasures were largely rural still and his estates with their game took up much of his time. But he had to be sure of his fair share and this often meant that he had to dance attendance on the prince; the magnate with an itch to get on in the world simply could not afford to neglect politics. By the end of the fifteenth century the wealthiest English and French peers were beginning to maintain their town homes in London and Paris.

Recruitment to the territorial aristocracy (to use a later term) was, for the most part, from the lower ranks of the landowners by way of crown service or by marriage to the daughter of a magnate. In the western kingdoms a merchant could scarcely become a peer; although the son of a Hull war profiteer, Michael de la Pole, became earl of Suffolk in 1385, his like is not found in France or Spain, or even again in England, for centuries. A peer, on the other hand, could, and occasionally by the fifteenth century did, refresh his fortunes by marrying a son to a merchant's heiress. Yet, since the landowners below the peerage often had connections with townsmen and commerce, and since they were the main source for new aristocratic families, we should not make too absolute the separation of the magnate from mercantile wealth; in north and central Italy and in Spain the highest nobility were more closely involved in towns than elsewhere.

Lesser nobility and gentry

The lesser nobility are harder to define, since they ranged from knights and men of knightly rank, some of whom had fortunes greater than the lords who were their social superiors, down to farmers, humble perhaps in status but legally independent and capable of rising. English terminology was no clearer than that found in many other parts of Europe: the yeoman, the franklin, the gentleman, the squire and the knight constituted an ascending order of vague ranks in society. In Turin early fifteenth-century sumptuary laws recognized not only *baroni cavalieri* and *baroni sardieri* (that is knights and squires) but also *bannereti cavalieri*, *valvassori* and *dottori cavalieri*. In the kingdoms of Spain the general word for knights was *caballeros*. Below the knight came a bewildering variety of names for squires: *donzells* in Catalonia, *infanzones* in Aragon, *escuderos* in Castile. Below the squires there were a host of solid peasants, living like the squirearchy, Catalan *generosos*, Castilian *caballeros villanos*. In France a similar imprecision reigned: *barons*, *chevaliers*, *écuyers*, *gentils* was the contemporary description of those giving homage to the Black Prince in 1363. *Gentilhomme*, imported into English, Catalan and Castilian, was a French expression designed to cover the lower ranks of the nobility. It was destined to be the generic term for those who had once been included in *la chevalerie*.

The aim of the lesser noble, like that of the magnate, was land, and marriage was his chief means of acquiring it. He was, however, more vulnerable than greater men to the economic pressures of the age and although many prospered, many also got into difficulties. This undoubtedly helped to make military service attractive in an age when armies were everywhere offering paid and almost permanent employment. Penury also drove many a petty lord into brigandage and banditry, or the near-banditry of exacting numerous tolls from the traffickers passing his castle. On the other hand inheritance and purchase of land provoked endless litigation: this made a career in the law increasingly attractive to families anxious to push themselves up in the world.

The recruitment of the lesser nobles, the men of knightly status descending to the *gentils*, was much more diverse than that of the higher nobility. Many rose from a peasantry which was rapidly losing its attributes of servitude. Others came from merchants and their families, investing in land in the countryside near the towns and thus willy nilly beginning to climb the social ladder. Others again earned their gentility in the field of battle, like the English soldiers at Agincourt. Formal knighthood might, at any rate in theory, only be conferred by the prince or his lieutenant; the style and title of knight and squire might be inherited; but anyone could hope to become a gentleman merely by acquiring landed wealth.

A further complication arose from the existence of considerable numbers of officials who, being exempt from certain direct forms of taxation or sharing other privileges of a nobility, began to constitute themselves a kind of caste with social pretensions. The high officials of French legal and financial administration, the personal officers of the French king and queen and the dauphin, the household of a duke of Milan—in these groups can be seen the start of an administrative nobility, of a *noblesse de robe*. It was, moreover, becoming common in France for office-holders (especially in legal administration) to resign their posts in favour of a relative, usually a son. In this way the notion of office as possession or property gained ground, and this process was found generally at work as the states of Europe employed more laymen in place of celibate clergy.

Just as English kings were now conferring peerages by patent, so on the continent nobility could be conveyed by formal documents. Normally this was the prerogative of the Crown, and the charges levied could make it a profitable business for the prince and his officials; but a Castilian or French duke in the fifteenth century also sometimes issued letters conferring noble status. Many ambitious men tried to by-pass the expense or the embarrassment of securing legal recognition in order to obtain exemption from taxes and social recognition. From 1460 in France lists of such attempted evasions had to be submitted to the financial officers of the Crown. In England, where gentility did not involve fiscal privileges, neighbours could only complain of a family's origins, as an anonymous enemy claimed that the Pastons were descended from serfs. In France a countryman near Auxerre had his hopes of advancement ruined in 1460 because it was proved in court that he had been a ploughman (*homme de labour*) and at Chaumont in Champagne another in 1467 came to grief because the court found that he was 'a serf, son of a serf, grandson of a serf'. In Spain by the end of the fifteenth century, and as a result of anti-Jewish activity, we meet the notion of *limpieza de sangre* (purity of blood) as a *sine qua non* for social promotion, though it had not yet acquired all of its later importance.[1]

Servitude was, as we have seen, becoming rarer, and there is not much doubt that the prosperous peasant everywhere was attracted by social preferment; in any case if he throve a peasant had to invest in land and thus inevitably began to climb up towards gentility. In England, where nobility as such was restricted to the peerage, coats of arms were a significant sign of gentle status and there the scrutiny and authentication of the right to be a gentleman came, by the end of the fifteenth century, to be a matter for the College of Heralds, who were perhaps less strict in their exclusion of undesirable elements than administrative courts on the continent. There, at the time when in England heraldry was becoming closely linked with the public recognition of gentle birth, the importance of the coat of arms may have declined. The French nobleman liked to have his *armoirée*, but laid much more stress on his right to have a weathercock on the roof of his home; what he cherished above all were his rights of hunting and avoiding taxes.

Attempts have been made to calculate how large a group in the com-

[1] Below, p. 331.

munity was formed by the nobility. For Spain it has been estimated by Professor Sobrequés that at the end of the fifteenth century there were some 5,000 members of magnate families who, together with the great prelates, constituted the minute proportion of ·07 per cent of the population; and that the 'nobility' below that level (50,000 of them) added another ·72 per cent; which, if we add the prosperous and independent peasantry (25,000 or ·35 per cent), totals 80,000 souls and 1·14 per cent of the total 6½ million.[1] The so-called income tax of 1436[2] enables some guesses to be made for England which would suggest that about 1,000 persons belonged to the baronial class (i.e. members of the peerage or their families); that knights and men of knightly rank together with their families numbered about 5,000, 'squires' about 6,000 and 'gentry' 22,000. This gives a percentage of 1·7 per cent of the population, with rather fewer *potentes* and rather more 'middle ranks' than in Spain. These figures are, of course, highly speculative; they do no more than suggest an order of magnitude.

It is tempting to try to go further (as has sometimes been done) and guess at the wealth and power possessed by the various strata in the nobility. Given the unreliability of tax returns and the complication that in many continental countries the jurisdictional rights of magnates by no means corresponded with their holdings of land, this is a fruitless exercise. It is safe to say that the tiny handful of dukes and counts possessed a colossal proportion of the landed resources of every country. But it is equally true that in wide areas the dominant social figure was a lesser nobleman. Indeed the aggregate wealth of the lesser nobility and gentry may well have equalled or exceeded the total of the magnates.

Chivalry and war

For later ages the most attractive aspect of the nobility and gentry of this period has been the code of conduct summarized in the word 'chivalry'. This was in essence a doctrine of knightly service to the community and of equality between knights; it assumed both a military basis for the life of the landed classes and an exalted reverence for personal honour. The origins of chivalric ideas belong to an earlier age, when only the knight was a fully-fledged member of lay society and where knights were practically all men of war. By the fourteenth century the reality was different, but the old ideals coloured literature and to

[1] Sobrequés, *op. cit.*, pp. 417–18.
[2] The returns are analysed, though not from this point of view, by H. L. Gray in *Eng. Hist. Rev.*, 49 (1934), pp. 607–39.

some extent affected practical affairs. Some knights did seek adventures in perilous places; some did make extravagant vows; and on the whole they treated each other humanely when they fought on the battlefield. Yet we can often find adventure developing into banditry or membership of a mercenary company, while humanity in warfare must be translated into stiff ransoms.

The norm of an international knightly order was reflected in the general acceptance of the 'Law of Arms'. This was derived from ancient feudal practice and the Law of Nations which had been evolved earlier by canonists and civilians from Natural Law. The Law of Arms laid down the precise obligations of a soldier in public and private warfare, assuming a reasonableness which in practice was often absent. The real sanction was a fear of acting, not illegally, but dishonourably. Just as the violence of conflicts which were increasingly patriotic in time strained the doctrine of the Law of Arms, so the nature of warfare reduced the significance of the knight. The battles of the later Middle Ages were largely fought by infantrymen. Heavy cavalry played a small part in the major battles and men at arms and archers, though frequently mounted, fought on foot, as did knights. The most interesting examples of this trend were the successes of the Swiss against Austrian and Burgundian armies. Gunpowder came to add a further hazard for the knightly soldier, just as it made his castle vulnerable to an enemy with artillery.

It was, of course, still open to the resolute to embark on a crusade in the Levant or (until the end of the fourteenth century) in Prussia.[1] But mostly those gentlemen and nobles who hankered after the chivalrous way of life had to play it out in make believe. The tournament, in which knights fought with blunted spears, often now resembled a ballet more than mimic warfare. Moreover the joust and tournament involved elaborate armour for both horse and man, which was extremely expensive to have made and which was treasured as a work of art; most of the early armour in European collections dates from this period and it is easy to appreciate from it how graceful and unwarlike the grandee had now become. Chivalric display thus needed uncommonly large resources and it was natural that its main patrons were great princes—Edward III of England, John II of France, Dukes Philip the Good and Charles the Bold of Burgundy—and that the most sumptuous examples of chivalric activity occurred when there was a meeting of princes in connection with diplomacy or marriage.

[1] Cf. below, pp. 258–62.

Townsmen

Information about the town and its inhabitants is so comparatively plentiful, and the ultimate influence of the bourgeoisie in European life and values so pronounced, that it is tempting to give urban problems an exaggerated place in the general picture. This would be a distortion. Save for parts of Italy, Germany, Catalonia and the Low Countries, towns and townsmen were relatively less important in public life than the nobles and gentlemen. On the other hand, although they constituted a minute proportion of the population, they were by now an indispensable ingredient of western society. Commerce, local and long distance, was now essential to the organization of daily life; seigneurs and peasants were profoundly affected by it; commercial wealth had come to be a supplement to agrarian wealth. And the key points for trade and commerce were the towns.

In advanced countries in the modern world there is an opposition between town and country which would have seemed strange to the men and women of the later Middle Ages. Many towns were so small that nowadays they would be regarded as villages. Even larger towns had big gardens inside them and extensive fields immediately outside so that a high proportion of the town dwellers in fact pursued rural occupations. This was strikingly the case with many small towns in the Mediterranean area. There was a certain hostility in some areas between the townsman and the rural landowner and of this something will shortly be said; but it was an antagonism of a social kind, not one necessarily based on different economic functions. Nor was the contrast supported as much as it was to be later by the different origins of the townsman and the rural population. It seems likely that the towns were constantly recruiting from the neighbouring countryside. The patrician group had its origins in many places, so it seems, not so much in the handful of pedlars and pirates of earlier days as in the adventurous possessors of land, capable of turning their capital into new activities in the eleventh and twelfth centuries. Such rural sources of capital seem to have continued to reinforce urban resources throughout the later Middle Ages.

The term 'patrician' has no contemporary justification. It was used by the Belgian scholar Henri Pirenne to describe the socially and economically dominant groups which had emerged in larger towns by the end of the thirteenth century. As such the term is extremely useful. We should, however, guard against treating the patricians of the fourteenth century towns as being everywhere similar in background and

ambitions. In many cities of the Mediterranean world, especially perhaps those away from the sea, the local nobility and the town patricians
were often closely connected. Yet even in the Mediterranean towns and
generally in those of the North the patricians were men who, whatever
their origin, were now opposed to the nobility. In Florence for instance
there was political tension between the *grandi* or nobles and the *haute
bourgeoisie*, the patrician *grassi*. This is particularly true of the larger,
commercially more significant centres.

What gave the patrician his social eminence was partly his connection
with long distance trade, partly his possession of property in the town,
partly his control over town government. The aristocracy of the town
was composed of families used to the monopoly of power, accustomed
to the enjoyment of greater wealth than other townsmen. In important
towns the patricians formed a coterie or caste, intermarrying within
themselves, jealous of newcomers to fortune, anxious to manipulate
town government, and above all town taxation, in their own interest.

The patrician dynasties of the larger towns also, and especially in
this period, acquired much property in the countryside round the
towns. They did this partly because land was the only secure investment, and partly because it gave them control over a regular supply of
provisions. Acquisition of rural property (especially in the north) tended
to make the purchasers become founders of families of the lesser
nobility. There were also many nobles who married their sons to wealthy
bourgeois heiresses. Other connections with the nobility offered themselves: the law might lead a merchant's son to court; an ecclesiastical
career enabled a townsman to rise in the social hierarchy; and in
England service as an M.P. for a borough could from time to time give
citizens a chance to oblige a magnate. In Italy, apart perhaps from the
kingdom of Naples, there was virtually no impediment to the ambitions
of a rich bourgeois. There even the nobility was town-based and in
every large town save Venice (where the large patriciate was regarded
as noble) there were nobles as well as rich merchants in the town. This
produced queasy political situations but made it much easier for the
merchant class to share the patterns of life of their rivals, with whom in
any case they frequently intermarried.

Below the level of the patricians came the respectable, though often
politically underprivileged, guildsmen whose activities were largely
concerned with local produce and local services. And below them came
a mass of workers and artisans, ill-organized and entirely deprived of
any say in the management of the town. These two groups were able to

exert political influence more than once in some of the bigger manufacturing cities[1] and from the resulting disturbance the circle of the
governing class of many towns was significantly enlarged by the triumph,
permanent or temporary, of the craft guilds. Yet overall what is impressive is the total failure of the urban worker to improve his political
status and the tenacity with which the patricians so often retained power,
even when they had to admit new families to the governing circles. The
tumults of fourteenth-century Florence leave the oligarchs with even
greater power in the town; in London the aldermanic families, the rich
members of the great guilds, never really lose their commanding
positions.

Outside Italy the townsman was looked down on by the nobleman. For a fifteenth-century Burgundian gentleman like the historian
Chastellain a bourgeois of Ghent was, however rich, however useful, a
mere *vilain*, a contemptible member of the third estate. The marquis
of Berkeley disinherited his younger brother when he married the
daughter of the mayor of Bristol in 1465. For the townsman completely
to escape this pervasive sense of social inferiority he had to acquire
noble lands. The rest then followed in time: coats of arms, employment
by the Crown, marriage with the nobility. It would, however, be mistaken to see citizens as crippled by inadequate recognition, ostracized
by a harsh feudal world. Not only were they often indispensable to the
nobility and the crown, as money-lenders, as purveyors of luxuries, as
tax-payers, but they had their own internal grades and honours which
were more important to them than any attitude of the outside world.
The rich patrician of London or Florence was addressed by his social
inferiors as if he were a lord. The minor guildsman addressed his superior
as *Messer* or *seigneur* or 'master'; and the patrician's wife was a lady,
with all the priorities and privileges within the town that the *grande
dame* was accorded in her castle. Moreover we find in many a town the
development which was carried furthest and earliest at Venice: the
attributes of nobility at large were given to the rich patrician; he had
his coat of arms, his sword, even sometimes his formal knighthood.
Thus it was at Augsburg and Milan; and elsewhere there is plenty of
evidence that the society of the town tacitly emulated the values of the
nobility at large.

There are also indications that the great landowners in practice
accepted the rich or important townsman as deserving of honour and
regard. In the late thirteenth-century Zurich list of important ranks

[1] Below, pp. 118–23.

(quoted above, pp. 25-6) we find that the first group, which includes the emperor, kings, dukes, marquises—the cream of society—concludes with 'magistrates of famous towns and cities'. The next group consists of stewards, town councillors (*sarlteti*) and judges, who are thus placed above the 'lesser personages' of the third group—simple knights, household officials, businessmen and shopkeepers. And, as we have seen, the peasants and the artisans come after that. Even more telling, as early as 1363 an English sumptuary law treated merchants and citizens with goods worth £500 as entitled to eat and dress like landed gentry with up to £100 of rents; merchants with property valued at £1,000 enjoyed like privileges with knights of £200 per annum. The poet Geoffrey Chaucer, who rose in his middle years to be an important figure in the royal administration, began his career in a noble household (he was a page of the duchess of Clarence) although he was the son of a London vintner. Two Marseilles brothers, the merchants Jean and Palamède Forbin at the end of the fifteenth century became high officials, one an ambassador, the other the king's lieutenant in Provence. The successful merchant and the citizen might often (as in France) be deprived of direct political influence in the country as a whole, but they could usually secure social advancement if they wished it both inside the town and outside it.

No single group within the town had more persistent influence in public life than the lawyers. Trained in civil law at a university in Italy or elsewhere on the continent, or in the common law at the Inns o Court in London, and then given experience in the office of a practitioner, the lawyers of the later Middle Ages were much sought after. There was much for them to do. The extraordinarily elaborate commercial exchanges of this period, discussed below in chapter XIV, produced a great deal of legal work both in framing contracts and in enforcing them. In Mediterranean lands such contracts were normally drawn up by notaries, appointed by the emperor or his nominee. Their records have sometimes survived to afford valuable evidence for economic and social historians. Likewise the landed magnate and gentleman had invented trusts and other methods for evading the residual embarrassments of the feudal relationship; other ingenious devices had been formulated to make (and to break) the entailed descent of land; all of this was meat and drink for the lawyer. An able advocate could make a fortune from wealthy and litigious clients; the sire d'Albret in 1500 was involved in no fewer than seventy legal actions. But a lawyer was not only employed in his professional capacity. He could often expect high promotion in civic government—as *podestà* or chancellor in an Italian city, as a councillor to princes in the kingdoms of Spain, England and France, let alone in less exalted but more numerous public offices. On the other hand in many Mediterranean cities the easy multiplication of notaries produced numbers far in excess of demand, and many of them, ignorant of the law yet possessing a diploma purchased from a complaisant official, resorted to dubious devices to make ends meet. The later Middle Ages were responsible for many stories about the lawyer whose name was Necessity.

Slavery in Mediterranean towns

If the successful town magnate could regard himself and be regarded by his neighbour as a gentleman, the poor town worker might be grateful that he was not a landless peasant. In Mediterranean lands there was a further compensation for the porters and day labourers whose lives were precarious enough: below them there were slaves.[1] Virtually unknown in the north of Europe at this stage, slavery was an important feature of the Italian and the Spanish city from the thirteenth century onwards. There were doubtless more slaves in the Muslim parts of the Mediterranean littoral but in Christian towns on or near the Mediterranean slaves were a significant group. They had originally been obtained by warfare, especially in the Spanish peninsula. This source of supply remained important in Castile and to some extent in Portugal into the fifteenth century; Castile continued to have a frontier with Moorish Granada and Portuguese crusades were used to recruit slaves. Elsewhere they were the objects of trade, and the Genoese were particularly active in importing slaves from the Levant and from the region of the Black Sea. Children of slaves were a further source of supply and in Iberia slavery was frequently imposed on rebellious Moors; after 1306 the Aragonese punished recalcitrant inhabitants of Sardinia with *servitus poenae*. Trade was, however, supplemented by raids on Muslim territory and by the pirates and corsairs of the western Mediterranean.

In the towns of Catalonia M. Charles Verlinden shows that down to the mid-fifteenth century there were many Russians, Tatars, and people from the Balkans, including Greeks; thereafter Turks are found and a few Negroes; but the Moors were throughout the most numerous. It can be proved that in 1431 the number of slaves in Catalonia was a multiple, probably a high multiple, of a minimum of 4,375. In Castile and in Portugal Negroes also make their appearance in significant

[1] See also below, p. 374.

numbers by the later fifteenth century, but the trade in Negro slaves was almost from the start directed towards colonial territory in the Atlantic islands during the fifteenth century. A list of slaves sold in Florence between 1366 and 1397 gives some idea of numbers and origins: of the total of 357, women and girls accounted for 329; 274 of the total were Tatars, 30 Greeks, 13 Russians, 8 Turks, 4 Circassians, 5 Bosnians or Slavs, one Cretan and the rest 'Arabs' or 'Saracens'.[1]

In these slave-owning communities of the Christian Mediterranean there is not much evidence that slaves were used in agriculture. The bulk of the slaves were women, in roughly the proportion of two to one, and the main employment of the female slaves was in domestic service. The rich had many such slaves, but even relatively modest Catalan and Italian families possessed one, and there were many in Marseilles and other towns in the south of France. Their exotic faces figure in many Italian paintings; their treacheries form material for many of the later Italian novelists. The official policy of the Church was on the whole humanitarian. In Iberia the slave had a right to baptism and the baptized slave was supposed to be treated more leniently by his master. In Italy all who were not Christian on arrival were baptized. The learned casuistry of the clergy was, however, able to defend the anomalous position. St Antonino of Florence allowed a Christian to keep a Christian slave provided the wretch had been pagan at the time of purchase.

The size of towns

The numbers of burgesses and their general political significance are not directly related. Town population fluctuated in the same way as the general population, though the movement of decline in the fourteenth century was probably severer in towns than in the countryside. This is not only because in crowded and insanitary conditions the urban dweller suffered more from plague, but also because plague frequently led to sizeable emigration from the town. Albi seems to have had its population nearly halved between 1343 and 1357 (9,341 to 5,712); Bézier's dropped from 14,476 in 1304 to 4,280 a century later. These figures are, of course, estimates.

From these figures it will be evident that the largest of medieval towns would today be regarded as small. Some of the smaller towns, significant as they were at the time, were tiny: Toulon numbered 2,800 souls in 1332; Canterbury had 3,861 and Newcastle upon Tyne 3,970 in 1377; Leipzig and Meissen had just over 2,000 at the end of the

[1] Iris Origo, *op. cit.*, p. 336.

fifteenth century. When one is dealing with 'towns' as small as modest villages (and some English boroughs returned M.P.s although their size was minute: Hedon in Holderness, a borough after 1348, had a population of 482 in 1372) it may seem unreal to guess at the total size of the 'urban' population.

Yet even allowing such small places to qualify the number of town dwellers is small. For Spain in 1500 it has been reckoned that 15.3 per cent of the total population was town based. The English proportion is very much lower: about 8 or 9 per cent.[1] There is no doubt that in Mediterranean lands towns were more numerous, bigger and more important than in northern Europe. In parts of central and northern Italy and Flanders the proportion of town dwellers may well have been higher than it seems to have been in Spain.

Regarded sometimes with contempt by the magnates and gentry, the townsman was nevertheless a recognized part not only of the economic world of the later Middle Ages, but also of the political world. Towns, as has just been observed, predominated in many parts of Italy. Elsewhere the citizen was accepted as representing the third estate in political assemblies. His direct effect on politics might seem to have been weak. Only in England and Catalonia did the burgesses come by the end of the period to form an essential part of the machinery of royal government. In England this was because they were linked in the Commons with the 'knights of the shire', representatives of what on the continent was regarded as the lesser nobility. In Catalonia their importance derived from the outstanding wealth and influence of Barcelona. Yet everywhere the bourgeoisie was slowly acting as a leaven in society. It was by the activity of the merchants that the economic patterns of an earlier day had been changed. It was through the pervasive penetration of new commercial facilities that the landed classes had come to change their way of life. It was from the privileges or liberties of the towns that the peasantry and artisans had acquired that more general notion of liberty which, though illusory in the fourteenth and fifteenth centuries, was later to grow into the basic political aim of western Europe.

[1] Sobrequés, *op. cit.*, pp. 417–18; Russell, *Brit. Med. Pop.*, pp. 142–4.

V

The Theory and Practice of Government

Political speculation

Political thought in this period, as in others, is in many ways irrelevant to the general historian's main concern—the practical programmes and the actions of the influential individuals and groups of the society he is studying. The irrelevance springs from two causes. First, there is usually a curious time-lag in the formulation of theory, so that doctrines emerge

BIBLIOGRAPHY. *Political Thought.* The standard study of medieval political thought is by R. W. and A. J. Carlyle, *A History of Medieval Political Thought in the West*, 6 vols. (London, 1909–36). A shorter but very stimulating account is C. H. McIlwain, *The Growth of Political Thought in the West from the Greeks to the End of the Middle Ages* (London, 1932), and there is a good essay by A. P. D'Entrèves, *The Medieval Contribution to Political Thought* (Oxford, 1939). For English theory see S. B. Chrimes, *English Constitutional Ideas in the Fifteenth Century* (Cambridge, 1936). For Italy and the civilians see F. Ercole, *Dal comune al principato* (Florence, 1929); C. N. S. Woolf, *Bartolus of Sassoferrato* (Cambridge, 1913); W. Ullmann, *Medieval Idea of Law as Represented by Lucas de Penna* (London, 1946). On Commynes see W. J. Bouwsma, 'The Politics of Commynes', *Journ. Mod. Hist.*, 23 (1951). Brian Tierney, *Foundations of the Conciliar Theory* (Cambridge, 1955) examines the background to conciliar thought and J. N. Figgis's *From Gerson to Grotius* (Cambridge, 1907) remains still a valuable exposition of conciliar speculation and one of the most exciting books on the history of ideas ever written. The main texts are fairly accessible; Woolf and Ullmann provide many extracts from the Post-glossators; Fortescue's *Governance*, ed. by C. Plummer (Oxford, 1885) and the *De Laudibus* by S. B. Chrimes (Cambridge, 1942); Marsilio of Padua, *Defensor Pacis*, ed. C. W. Previté-Orton (1928), trans. with a commentary by A. Gewirth, 2 vols. (New York, 1951–56); Commynes several edns. and trans. (see above, p. 4).

Administration. This is discussed in most of the national histories (cf. below, p. 126). The following are some useful specialized studies: T. F. Tout, *Chapters in the Administrative History of Medieval England*, 6 vols. (Manchester, 1923–35) and *The English Government at Work 1327–36*, 3 vols., ed. J. F. Willard and others (Cambridge, Mass., 1940–50) are two major works for the country which has been most fully studied and which has the best sources; a shorter book by S. B. Chrimes, *Introduction to the Administrative History of Medieval England* (Oxford, 1952), has good references to recent work. The *Histoire des institutions françaises au moyen âge*, ed. F. Lot and R. Fawtier, so far covers *Institutions seig-*

later than the social and political situations to which they apply. Second, it is a fact that governments and pressure groups act without being fortified by abstract principles; they try to get what they want without being at pains to relate it to the ultimate ends of mankind.

Yet there are telling reasons for beginning any discussion of government with a short examination of contemporary speculation about the purpose of society. To start with it has often occupied the acutest minds of an age and from their reflections we can judge the tensions which affect the intellectual in his period, and observe what at any rate some of the trained minds regarded as desirable forms of political activity and acceptable ways of fitting government into the larger schemes of philosophy or theology. More than that, the jargon of everyday politics is usually based on earlier abstract doctrines and (as we shall see) men still in the fourteenth century accepted the crusade and Christendom, chivalry and the fief as viable concepts. And finally there are moments of

neuriales (Paris, 1957), *Institutions royales* (1958) and the Church (above, p. 45); a remarkable earlier work is G. Dupont Ferrier, *Études sur les institutions financières de la France à la fin du moyen âge*, 2 vols. (Paris, 1930–32). For representative institutions see C. H. McIlwain's chapter in *Cambridge Medieval History*, VII; A. Marongiu, *Il parlamento in Italia nel medio evo e nell'età moderna* (Milan, 1962), surveys Europe at large in the thirteenth and fourteenth centuries in chap. III of part I, trans. and ed. Woolf (1968); further comparative study is badly needed.

Towns. La Ville, 3 vols. (Société Jean Bodin, 1954–57) is the best collection of studies; it is also useful to consult M. V. Clarke, *The Medieval City State* (London, 1926) and F. Rörig, *Die europäische Stadt im Mittelalter* (3rd ed., Göttingen 1958), now available in English (London, 1967). The bibliography of Italian towns is vast and the following works are only illustrative of the wealth of material now available in secondary works: J. Luchaire, *Les démocraties italiennes* (Paris, 1915); R. Caggese, *Firenze dalla decadenza di Roma al Risorgimento*, II (Florence, 1912); Gene A. Brucker, *Florentine Politics and Society 1343–1378* (Princeton, 1962); D. Marzi, *La cancelleria fiorentina* (Rocca S. Casciano, 1910); Fondazione Treccani degli Alfieri, *Storia di Milano*, vols. V–VII (Milan, 1955–56); *Storia di Roma*, vols. XI and XII—E. D. Theseider, *Roma ... 1252–1377* and P. Paschini, *Roma nel Rinascimento* (Bologna, 1952, 1940); F. Thiriet, *Histoire de Venise* (Paris, 1952). In general see publications of the 'Commission international pour l'histoire des villes' since 1960. For the Low Countries see H. Pirenne *Les villes du moyen age* (Brussels, 1927) and *Histoire de Belgique*, II (Brussels, 1922); for Germany, H. Planitz, *Die deutsche Stadt im Mittelalter* (Cologne, 1954) and P. Sander, *Geschichte des deutschen Städtewesens* (Bonn, 1922). For the Swiss confederation, E. Bonjour, H. S. Offler and G. R. Potter, *History of Switzerland* (Oxford, 1952). For the Hanseatic League, P. Dollinger, *La Hanse* (Paris, 1964) and in English (London, 1969).

crisis when the embattled groups seek to defend their position by general arguments involving a radical redefinition of public obligation which, even if they prove not to be germane at the time, form the basis of future assumptions.

The way in which men viewed their political purposes at the beginning of our period had been determined by both scholarly reflection and by moments of polemical crisis in previous centuries. The speculation had a history going back to the Fathers of the Church, behind them to Rome and Greece. For centuries social structure had been explained by what are often termed 'Augustinian' principles. St Augustine, writing at the moment when Rome fell to the barbarians in A.D. 410, viewed the earthly life of man as a pilgrimage towards the Heavenly City. For him, and for many succeeding generations, political institutions, the organized life of society, was the price man paid for the corruption of his nature: authority, law, magistrates, servitude, were the product of man's Fall. It was not until the thirteenth century that a more optimistic attitude gradually grew up in the wake of the rediscoveries then made of Greek philosophy. Aristotle gradually edged into the academic world and his *Politics* slowly began to affect the scholars who speculated about government. For Aristotle the machinery of government was not a by-product of man's essentially sinful nature. It was a direct fulfilment of man's social nature; man without politics would not have been man. In the course of the later thirteenth century a kind of reconciliation took place in these conflicting attitudes and the great scholastics accepted and taught that, in the hierarchy of created nature, a series of laws determined the rights and wrongs of day-to-day government. All authority had to conform to divine law, and in natural law was expressed that part of God's plan common to all society; from natural law flowed the conventions of the *jus gentium*, the law of nations, i.e. the social practices observed in all civilized communities. Nevertheless an enormous range of discretion was left to the *ad hoc* arrangements of governments, the field of positive or coercive law, of rules and regulations with their accompanying sanctions.

These abstractions had occasionally been jostled and excited by events. In the eleventh and twelfth centuries the sluggish relations of emperor and pope, both with an authority extensive and vague over the welfare of large areas, and both with more precise rights in parts of northern and central Italy, came into open conflict. The details of the ensuing struggle for mastery do not here concern us. What is important is that in the course of it a number of important steps were taken. The popes advanced the theory that human authority was exercised at their discretion. A pope crowned an emperor; therefore a pope transmitted to the emperor his powers, and could if need be take them back. From this it followed logically that the pope was the immediate source of all government. If they were to preserve their liberty of action, emperors and other princes were left with no alternative but to assert that God had conveyed authority to them directly; the mystique of coronation fortified this view. These developments were on the whole favourable to the popes; the theorists on both sides were clergy; theology as well as popular opinion accepted that the priest had a rank in earthly society nearer to God than the layman. Moreover it was during the eleventh century that a gradual awareness revealed itself that the society within which these conflicts arose had only its religion as a common denominator and that this religion had external foes. Both the notion of Christendom and the activity of the crusade further confirmed the pope as the only possible head of the Christian peoples. By the early thirteenth century the papacy had achieved an acknowledged leadership in society as a whole.

Yet in practical matters things were different. Popes, like other princes, had territories to defend which were theirs in a peculiar way, and through which they came into conflict with princes even more extensively endowed. Innocent III and his successors might succeed in weakening the king of Germany who as emperor stood in the way of their Italian policy. But they found recalcitrant towns and princes in Italy itself, and outside Italy governments which refused to accept, or accepted only fitfully and reluctantly, the doctrine of papal supremacy in practical politics. The culmination of these trends came at the end of the thirteenth century when Boniface VIII tried to impose his will on the powerful kings of France and England. On the level of administrative action it was clear who would win. When the pope forbade the taxation of the clergy by kings, Philip IV of France prohibited the export of money to the papal curia and Edward I of England outlawed those English clergy who obeyed the pope. Boniface had to retreat. As he was told by the emissary of the French king, his power was theoretical, the French king's power was practical. Nevertheless, in one grand and, as it proved, final gesture Boniface returned to the attack. In the bull *Unam Sanctam* (1302) he laid down that it was necessary for his salvation that every person should be subject to the Roman pontiff. 'He that is spiritual', he quoted from Corinthians, 'judgeth all things, yet he himself is judged of no man'.

The place of the king

Unam Sanctam in more than one way sets the scene for the period discussed in this book. It was to lead, for example, to the attack on the pope by Philip IV and, indirectly, to the establishment of the papacy at Avignon during the fourteenth century. But from the point of view of political thought it represents a definition of sovereignty and as such was to influence other thinkers, not least those bitterly opposed to papal claims. As a statement of these claims *Unam Sanctam* was important, for in the fourteenth and fifteenth centuries there were a number of respectable clergymen who continued to advocate papal primacy, thankless though the job was. The Augustinian canon Agostino Trionfo wrote (1324–28) a scholastic *Summa de potestate ecclesiastica* and John XXII's penitentiary, the Portuguese Franciscan Alvaro Pelayo, issued several versions of his *De planctu ecclesiae* between 1330 and 1340. Even a century later there were still advocates of papal omnipotence. The Sicilian canonist Niccolò de Tudeschis (called Siculus, or Panormitanus from his being archbishop of Palermo) was a vehement defender of papal rights who died in 1453, and so was the Spanish cardinal Juan de Turrecremata (the elder Torquemada), whose *Summa de ecclesia* was written in the aftermath of the conciliar movement.

These continuing arguments for papal sovereignty were not paralleled by like arguments for kings, whose actual authority greatly exceeded the pope's. A few apologists were found for the emperor's claims to an overriding position. The most significant of these was the Florentine poet Dante, but his *De Monarchia* (completed by 1313) was written in the framework of Italian politics and was intended to justify the intervention in Italy of the Emperor Henry VII. Dante in any case did not envisage an emperor who would have ruled in Italy in an arbitrary or effective way. The cities of Italy were self-sufficient politically and a doctrine explaining their independence in terms of loyalty to the emperor was being adumbrated, as will shortly appear. Even in kingdoms princes were faced with powerful groups which could appeal to immemorial tradition and to documents for their right to independent authority. The feudal lords of France and England had a recognized right to political influence. The big towns were protected by charters which recognized their juridical integrity, a process which went perhaps furthest in Catalonia, where some modern historians have discerned a *pactisme*, a mutual limitation by contract of powers as between crown and ruling urban oligarchy, in the relationship of the kings of Aragon and Barcelona.

In view of these built-in limitations to monarchy, the tradition of 'king and people', of feudal consent, of respect for public bargains between crown and corporation, we should not be surprised at the relative absence of theorists explicitly justifying the growing power of the kings of France and England, and indeed of other princes. We know that round the French king were civilian lawyers who were ready to prompt him with the autocratic aphorisms of Roman law (*princeps legibus solutus, rex in regno suo imperator*); and the common lawyers in England were proud that their system was independent of the compromising canon law which looked to the pope and of the civil law which looked to the emperor. But in the fourteenth and fifteenth centuries we find no doctrines evolved which could positively explain or defend the enormous increase in the power of the prince. His place is certainly important in Ockham's cautious speculation, as it is in that curiously irrelevant essay on lordship the *De dominio civili* (*c*. 1366) where Wycliffe, employing feudal terminology and developing further ideas expressed in the *De pauperie salvatoris* of Richard FitzRalph (archbishop of Armagh, d. 1360), advanced the notion of power founded on grace and argued that 'every righteous man is lord over the whole earth'. The very doctrine of Divine Right is only hesitatingly hinted at by the end of our period and the two great theorists —Fortescue in England and Commynes in France—are singularly unlike the doctrinaires who had earlier battled for and against emperors and popes. Consequently the evidence they offer for the central position of the king in both kingdoms is all the more telling.

Fortescue and Commynes differ from earlier writers on politics in being men of affairs. An empirical attitude is thus to be expected of them and is not concealed even in the formal categories in which Sir John Fortescue, a royal judge, wrapped up his thought in the *De laudibus legum Anglie* written for the benefit of the exiled court of Henry VI about 1470, and in the shorter *Governance of England* composed a little later. Fortescue's analysis rests on the distinction between absolute and limited or mixed monarchy; of the former he instanced France, of the latter England. The English constitution was a combination of king and parliament, a partnership in which neither side was shackled by prescription.[1] Fortescue's purpose in writing the dialogue *De laudibus* was the instruction of the future king, but in this work and in the *Governance* we have something very different from the traditional *de regimine prin-*

[1] There has been, and doubtless will be, debate on Fortescue's views. The above follows R. W. K. Hinton in *Eng. Hist. Rev.*, 75 (1960), 410–18, who disputes the opinions expressed in the books of McIlwain and Chrimes.

cipum, such as that begun by Aquinas. Fortescue's analysis is based more on observation than on abstract principles and his aim is not the instruction of a ruler concerning his place in the divine scheme but the instruction of a ruler in the art of government; in the *Governance* he has a series of practical proposals such as the resumption of crown lands and a reformed council.

Across the Channel the government of what the English judge regarded as an absolute king was scrutinized by Philippe Commynes, whose reflections are no longer couched even in the form of a treatise, but are presented as the garnered observations and reflections of one who has seen much of politics at close quarters. The *Mémoires,*[1] his own title for the work, were written in two stages. The first and biggest section covers the reign of Louis XI and was composed between 1489 and 1491; the rest of the work, dealing with Charles VIII and the invasion of Italy, was probably written between 1495 and 1498. It is despite his avowed intention (to provide Angelo Cato with material for a projected Latin history) that Commynes is treated here and elsewhere as a political theorist—one, moreover, who challenges comparison with the Machiavelli of both the *Prince* and the *Discourses.* For in Commynes effective government is an end in itself, despite his conventional and doubtless sincere remarks on Providence and virtue. The good king for him as for Fortescue is the king who is successful. Success for a monarch is partly dependent on advisers who are themselves expert, experienced and wise. If the *Mémoires* have in them guidance for princes they are also full of counsel for councillors; Commynes had after all suffered under a stormy Charles the Bold and he had been imprisoned by the regents who governed France after the death of Louis XI. It is therefore not in the bold sweep of his vision of society, nor in the profundity of his understanding of man that Commynes is revealing, but in his practical interest in day-to-day administration and negotiation, in his undisguised admiration of the shrewd, calculating, harsh but intelligent Louis as against the brash Burgundian or the stupid Charles VIII. When he does touch on principle he is conventional enough: *quod omnes tangit ab omnibus approbetur* —he would have echoed the thirteenth-century tag, as we may see from his condemnation of direct taxation at the will of the prince and his admiration (almost as great as Fortescue's) of the English parliament. But even here he admits that a king's arbitrary act may save the people from pernicious bullying and extortion.

Fortescue and Commynes thus approach the king as a ruler in a way

[1] Above, p. 4.

new in France and England, and both do so from a pragmatic stand-point. Their writings are based on observation and they have no grand design, no basic philosophy into which monarchy must be fitted. The later Middle Ages do, however, see some occasions for a more doctrin-aire approach. In 1324 there was published in Paris a book called *Defensor Pacis* and in the years from 1378 to 1417 the schism provoked among the clergy a fresh attempt to define the nature of the church as a corporate entity.

Marsilio of Padua's *Defensor Pacis* is a thoroughly Italian work[1], des-pite its composition in Paris where the author was a prominent member of the University. In Italy, as in England and elsewhere, lawyers had speculated much on government for in their profession they were called upon to apply the civil law, which tended to exalt the emperor, in a land much of which was legally imperial[2] but where the reality of power ex-cluded the emperor and often, even in his own states, the pope, from any genuine participation in government. The jurists who commented on legal texts, known in legal history as the 'Post-glossators' in distinc-tion to the earlier commentators, were practical men, who reveal their views on society and its government while discussing a text, delivering a judgment in the courts, or composing an opinion for a litigant. They were thus forced to keep their feet on the ground. It is this which makes their views so interesting, for in their very different ways they were as empirical as Fortescue and Commynes. Of the three great names in the civil jurisprudence of Italy in the fourteenth century, Cino da Pistoia (d. 1336), Bartolo da Sassoferrato, and Baldo degli Ubaldi (d. 1400), it is Bartolo, pupil of Cino and master of Baldo, who is the most impressive, not least because he expressed his views in some treatises as well as in his commentaries; he lectured and practised at Perugia from 1343 to his death in 1357. To him is ascribed the final form of the doctrine giving real independence to the Italian town—whether its ultimate lord was emperor or pope: the city, he consistently argued, was *sibi princeps*, its own master, a corporation with omnicompetent jurisdiction. It was an achievement on a par with that which had been independently ham-mered out in the thirteenth century in France, where the 'king in his kingdom is as an emperor'. Richard II of England was accused of be-lieving that 'His laws were in his mouth, sometimes in his breast, that he alone could change or establish the laws of the land'. Roman law is here seen again. We are approaching a doctrine of sovereignty.

[1] Cf. now N. Rubinstein in *Europe in the Late Middle Ages* (below, p. 399).
[2] Below, p. 165.

Marsilio's great originality was to expound such a view of sovereignty. For him there is only one law that matters: positive, coercive law. And this is applied in any community by one executive instrument —the 'ruling part', *pars principans*. The *pars principans* in a city is chosen by the citizen body as a whole, 'having regard to their quality', i.e. it was based on the restricted franchise common in Italian republics, and was not the 'one man, one vote' of modern democracy. This executive or governing element was responsible for the control of all other groups in the community, including the clergy. Much of this is Aristotelian, much of it derives from the civilian tradition, all of it is hard to understand, for Marsilio was groping for a new terminology to describe the realities of power and he was inflamed by a polemical hatred of the papacy which it was his aim to expose as the destroyer of political stability in Italy. It is tempting to elaborate the doctrines of the *Defensor Pacis* at greater length than its influence would justify. For Marsilio, proscribed by the popes, was not influential, even when he accompanied his protector the Emperor Lewis of Bavaria to Italy; he died in obscurity in 1342 or 1343 and it is not easy to find true disciples before the sixteenth century. In Italy itself Marsilio's book was translated into Tuscan, but the most politically conscious of the Italians, the Florentines, were too preoccupied with the ethics of republicanism to find his teaching relevant; though it chimed in with the general Italian dislike of papal power, it suffered from two defects—it was neither practical jurisprudence nor good literature. William of Ockham, the most original philosopher of the later Middle Ages, was not uninfluenced by his Italian contemporary, · but basically he accepted a strong Church. He argued, especially in the *Dialogus* (1333–38), that, faced with a heretic pope, the whole body of the Church, or a general council (which might be summoned by bishops or princes) was the repository of truth and authority. It will be evident in a moment why Ockham rather than Marsilio was useful in the crisis which overtook the Church in and after 1378; it was only with difficulty that Marsilio adapted his ideas to the old ecumenical Church, which was accepted as axiomatic by his contemporaries.

Conciliar thought

The ecumenical Church in 1378 acquired two heads; when the Council of Pisa tried to end this schism in 1409 it succeeded only in adding a third head. It was not until the end of the Council of Constance that one pope again emerged as the titular master of the Church. These events are discussed below in connection with the constitutional history of the papal monarchy[1]. Here they must occupy us for the effect they had on political thought.

For centuries clergy and laity had been accustomed to papal control over the Church as an institution. Popes confirmed the appointment of all prelates and (through reservation) nominated many of them; they defined doctrine and they summoned councils of the Church which embodied papally conceived directives in canons which were papally confirmed. Now with the Schism of 1378 this unique headship was disputed and little experience or theory was available to meet the position, though there had been a few sober canonists who, like Ockham, accepted a council as the ultimate source of authority in certain cases, for example, if the pope were a heretic. The theologians were in fact driven more or less to accept such a solution: the Church was in the last resort a corporation formed by all the faithful, a general council being the nearest practical equivalent to this totality. Such a council might—in default of the pope's being willing or able to act—be summoned by others. These and consequential views were hammered out in the home of theology—the University of Paris—and the greatest of the doctors who devoted themselves to the question was Jean Gerson, who will appear later in this book in other connections. It was on these grounds that the Council of Constance was summoned and many of the Fathers were already virtually committed in principle to those great attempts to preclude any further schism which were the Council's principal contribution to the theory of government: the declaration that all men, including the pope, were subject to the Council; and the formulation of a regular conciliar machinery which would function independently of the pope. These will be discussed in their proper place in so far as they form a turning point in Church history (below, p. 287). Why should they be introduced here? Because, in the words of Figgis, the theologians at Paris and the Fathers at Constance had determined 'the depositary, the function and the limits of sovereign power in a perfect society'; what was found good for the Church as a body politic would, *a fortiori*, be true of all governments on earth. This is what makes the so-called decree *Sacrosancta* of 1415 a 'revolutionary' document, for it firmly stated that the pope was a limited monarch, responsible in the last resort to his subjects. Thus was the bull *Unam Sanctam* reversed and the principle of autocracy formally denied. But only on paper. As we shall see, the machinery devised at Constance slowly ground to a stop and the

[1] Below, pp. 279–88.

theory on which it was based was repudiated by the popes of the mid-fifteenth century. Yet it was not this papal resistance to conciliar ideas which led to their being for long uninfluential in western Europe, for the limited monarchy advocated at Constance would have encouraged a similar trend in secular principalities if there had been any general sympathy at the time for constitutional checks on princes. In central and eastern Europe at this time the sovereign's powers were being constricted by magnates and gentry,[1] but this development owed little to the constitutionalism of Constance.

That there was no general anxiety to have written constitutions and limited monarchy, that the prince was steadily coming to be the pivot for political doctrine are perhaps the only inferences we can make from this short survey of the theorists of government. This is true even of the civilians who accept a popular origin for monarchy (the *lex regia*), even of Fortescue and Commynes when they urge the king to avoid arbitrary taxation and to 'live of his own'. Fortescue was a supporter of 'mixed monarchy' but his analysis of the English situation led him to urge his king to put himself above the 'overmighty subject'; it was the road to Henry VIII. And when Commynes admitted that Louis XI's tyranny precluded the tyranny of lesser men he was anticipating the *politiques* of a century later and paving the way for Louis XIV.

In the course of this period the prince's powers in most western countries largely explain this implied recognition of his commanding place in government. In most of the rest of this chapter we shall be concerned with the machinery by which kings controlled or tried to control their subjects. In Italy and elsewhere there were communities in which government was not as yet princely but urban; their administration will be discussed at the end of the chapter.

Kings and administration in western Europe:[2] France and England

In the early fourteenth century when our period begins there were some informative parallels and contrasts in the position of the Crown and the character of the administration in the main countries of western Europe. While kings were personally responsible for day-to-day government the

[1] Below, pp. 238–40.
[2] What follows is concerned largely with England and France. The administrative history of the kingdoms of Spain is not given adequate attention partly because of the author's ignorance and partly because it has as yet not been adequately discussed in the secondary literature. See works (below, p. 127) by Merriman, Soldevila (esp. II, 51–139) and Elliott. For a note on the problem in Germany, see below, chapter VIII.

older machinery, devised and perfected from the tenth century to the thirteenth, had begun to exist almost independently of the Crown and was capable of obstructing even the clear will of the king, who was therefore compelled to develop fresh ways of running his affairs. The great officers of state of an earlier day—steward, constable, justiciar—were often now holders of grandiose sinecures, working, if at all, through deputies.

The king, surrounded by panoply and riches, regarded as peculiarly exalted by reason of the coronation ceremony when he was anointed like a bishop, had moved far from the earlier days when his power had derived from his descent from a god and had depended on his military following. His rise had owed a good deal to his function as custodian and mouthpiece of tribal or regional custom, for this gave him from the start a public role independent of his might. But the chief cause of his success was the identification of land with office and the prevailing method of maintaining supporters by grants of fiefs. There were two reasons for this. As feudal superior the king was naturally elevated above other lords; even when he was unable to make good his pre-eminence it was admitted grudgingly by men who depended on it for the titles to their own lands. In the second place the hereditary principle (which so soon made nonsense of the fief as a military device) confirmed the king as it confirmed all lords in the possession of land. When Edward I succeeded unopposed and in his absence to the English crown in 1272, this was a victory for the feudal king; the transmission of the French Crown from Capetians to Valois in 1328 is likewise due to the acceptance of a feudal principle. 'Le roi est mort! Vive le roi' would not have been shouted if monarchy had adhered to its original popular or elective nature. Nonetheless the popular element had its part to play: it was not as feudal superiors that kings extended their legal administration and their fiscal demands; and in most monarchies there were substantial areas of allodial, non-feudal, land which might have escaped the control of a purely feudal monarch.

For weeks, sometimes months, at a time kings avoided all but the most pressing business. They were travelling, or hunting, and only when a weary embassy or worried minister caught up with the royal entourage might a few hours or days have to be spent on matters of state. A great deal of business could, indeed, be transacted in the king's name and without his personal knowledge, for the king was himself an institution as well as a man, and the chancery and the treasury worked for him and in his interests, and so did the courts of law. Yet no country could survive happily even a few years of inept monarchy. Edward II, Richard II, Henry VI in England point this moral; in France it finds illustration in the reign of Charles VI and the early years of Charles VII. Even if he ruled positively only from time to time, an early fourteenth-century king had to rule if he was to survive. It is significant how hesitantly the English magnates in opposition to Edward II distinguished between the individual and the Crown, and how little the distinction availed them.

Every king had, of course, a small group of intimates whose advice he naturally sought when faced with decisions. These men were his counsellors, chosen by him because they were his ministers and servants, because he respected their judgment or enjoyed their company. This was his council—his small, privy or secret council in distinction to the great council, intermittently summoned, of the great men, great tenants-in-chief, great prelates. With the small council the king's future as a resourceful administrator was intimately bound up. There were tensions between the two bodies—not least because the king tended to choose for the small, effective council men of lesser rank, and because this small group tried to act as a leaven when the meetings of the larger, more imposing and less effective body were held. In France and in England there was trouble in the thirteenth century and a lasting animosity in our period, which led to attempts to 'reform' the council.

The old departments, once part of the royal household, moving round with the king, were now in England and France more or less fixed in London and Paris respectively: the chancery, the treasury and the superior courts of law.

The chancery was responsible for the issue of the king's instructions to his officers and grants to his subjects and was headed by the chancellor, in charge of the Great Seal, which was used for the most solemn authentication of formal documents and which was made afresh at the start of every reign. The chancery clerks, who were paid out of the charges levied by the department on those who sought documents, were maintained as part of the household and could in England expect promotion in the Church; in France they were more frequently notaries and had a bigger remuneration direct from the Crown. The Exchequer in England, headed by the treasurer, was both a central accounting department for the king's revenues, a court and an instrument which could be used for other miscellaneous administrative purposes. In France the *chambre des comptes* and the *trésor*, the one an accounting, the other a receiving and spending department, had emerged—a significant difference from England being that there was no one responsible officer like the English treasurer.

The immediate household of the king (*hôtel du roi*) still had important administrative functions—so important that English historians have sometimes argued that the 'household departments'—the wardrobe (a kind of treasury) and the chamber (a kind of chancery)—offered a challenge, even an alternative administration, to the older bodies. This is to press the matter too far, for the thirteenth-century kings, and especially Edward I, had developed such domestic offices as a necessity of war and diplomacy—using often the same personnel as that staffing Chancery and Exchequer. As the older departments tended to be stationary, so the officials of the household grew more important—the privy seal was used more frequently, the wardrobe received moneys which might otherwise have gone to, or stayed in, the Exchequer. And as the actual activity of the Crown increased—in extraordinary war or ordinary administration —so the officials near the king became more important. In a sense the *hôtel du roi* in France likewise grew in importance with the efficacy and range of royal administration. But in France the *chancelier* retained a general control over all royal clerks and officers which precluded sharp separation and which enabled more effective supervision even of old and conservative officials.

Royal justice was now only exceptionally dispensed by the king in person and had for long become formalized in a series of courts. In England the central courts were the King's Bench and Common Pleas. The latter was now fixed in London and was much busier than King's Bench, still itinerant, still close to king and council whence it had sprung and continuing in cases of great difficulty to act as a court. King's Bench's jurisdiction consisted mainly in correcting errors in Common Pleas, and in hearing pleas of the Crown (very serious crimes). There were also specially commissioned justices who regularly took central justice to the regions of the land in assizes. The scheme of courts in France was, in a sense, simpler, for the thirteenth century saw the appellate jurisdiction of the *curia regis* gradually handled by experts in sessions called *parlement*. By the beginning of the fourteenth century the sessions were continuous: the *parlement* of Paris had emerged. In 1307 an *ordonnance* laid down the composition of the *Grande Chambre*, where pleading took place and which issued definitive *arrêts*, the court of inquiry (*Enquêtes*) where the substance of the appeal was determined, as was the court of Requests (*Requêtes*) where the appeal was lodged and which occasionally directed the case to be heard not in *parlement* but before a local tribunal. *Parlement* became one of the most powerful corporations in French history.

One other element in central administration had also made an appearance by the beginning of this period: the assembly called in England 'parliament'. The word had the same meaning at the start as the French *parlement*. It was used in the thirteenth century to cover meetings of important people who deliberated on important business. Attached in France to that aspect of the *curia regis* which in the end became almost entirely judicial, the word in England covered those extraordinary convocations of magnates, representatives of the shires, representatives of the lesser clergy, officials of the crown and councillors, gatherings which had been provoked by the stormy reign of Henry III and utilized as an instrument of royal government by Edward I. At this stage parliament was fluid in composition and had not settled down into rigid procedures. It was the council enlarged; it acted like a court of law—transcending all other courts; it was the vehicle for presenting requests to the Crown, and for hearing and dealing with problems presented to it by the king and his ministers. It could make 'law' but nothing that it did could not also be done by the king and his council without its assistance, save for authorizing 'extraordinary' taxation. It could be everything, it could have become nothing. That it was to grow into the basic constitutional check on the Crown and the supreme legislative body must not lead us to give it undue prominence at the beginning of the fourteenth century. Such solemn assemblies were, after all, common enough everywhere at the time. In France their small importance is revealed by their poor documentation; all one can say is that there are no estates-general even by the end of Philip IV's reign, though there are many meetings of an *ad hoc* character—in connection with the king's conflict with Boniface VIII and in connection with currency questions. The other region where one can talk with confidence of representative institutions is Spain, referred to shortly.

Local government

Thus far the central government of France and England at the start of the fourteenth century has been outlined. Government at the regional level must now be considered. This order, giving pride of place to the king's headquarters administration rather than to the authorities who ran local regions, seems to reflect the true position in both kingdoms by about 1300. (The reverse would have been true two centuries earlier and was still true of certain other parts of Europe.)

One must nevertheless begin by making a sharp distinction between seignorial and royal government, between areas where a lord exercised a few or many public functions by virtue of his land and title, and areas which were directly under the control of the king's officers. The distinction is less important in England than in France, for the king's deputy in each English county, the sheriff (*vice-comes*), had by the end of the thirteenth century become again a relatively humble officer. The sheriff still accounted twice yearly at the Exchequer for royal lands in his county, and other jobs had come his way, such as finding juries for various purposes and returning representatives of the shire to parliament, but the king had other regional officials who were making the sheriff a less important though not a less busy person; the coroner presided over the legal activity of the county court and the feudal rights of the crown were looked after by two escheators, one north and one south of the Trent. Above all the keeper or justice of the peace had made his appearance and had already begun to act locally as the enforcer of government policy. As for the seignorial administration, there were a few franchises, the greatest being the county of Durham, where the bishop had extensive privileges. Broadly speaking big landowners exercised minor public jurisdiction in only those hundred courts which had become private property in an earlier age. Such courts were called courts leet or courts baron and had merged with the manorial courts; the relative unimportance of their jurisdiction (they were important enough in the day-to-day life of the community, for they punished petty crime and enforced contracts) was indicative of the popularity and leading place of royal courts and officials. In the growing towns the king also played a predominant part, for as a town reached maturity it sought increasing privileges which only a king could grant, notably 'incorporation', the right to exist as a corporate personality. The first incorporation of a borough was Coventry in 1345, but already London had liberties which brought it into relation with the Crown as if it had been an independent shire.

Across the Channel private jurisdiction was much more important and, though royal officials had made much progress, their ultimate victory was by no means assured. Great men—the counts of Flanders or Armagnac, dukes of Brittany or Burgundy and many less exalted nobles —had rights and powers subject only in the most distant way to the king of France, the feudal superior. But that superiority, tenuous though it was, gave the king not only the ability to absorb even great fiefs when they lacked heirs, but a kind of moral or political ascendancy. The result in the administrative field was that—broadly speaking—the quasi-independent magnate aped the government of the master whom he defied or disdained. In any event all lords—the king as well as his tenants-in-chief—were faced with similar problems: they all needed local agents to secure their rights and their revenues. As a result there was considerable uniformity even within the framework of a country which lacked the impetus to centralization which England had been given by the Conquest of 1066.

In the lands directly in the control of the French king, the royal domain, the early officers or stewards called *prévots* (*praepositi*) had by the start of our period sunk to be mere deputies of the thirteenth-century *baillis* or *sénéchaux*.[1] The *bailli*, like his predecessor, was a maid of all work—financial, administrative and military—with a series of officers (notably the hated *sergents*) to execute his orders and subject, when complaints became clamorous, to the supervision of *ad hoc* commissions of inquiry. The little tenants-in-chief forming enclaves in the royal domain, or with lands adjacent to it, soon succumbed to the acquisitiveness of the king and his local officers. In great honours the count and the duke were less vulnerable to such pressure, though appeals from their courts to the *parlement* were now regularly entertained; and in their lands we find not only an apparatus for local government of *baillis* of *sénéchaux*, but a machine modelled on the central offices of the French Crown—a chancellor, treasurer, council.

One must be careful to remember how confused were all the territorial arrangements in both England and France briefly described above. The *bailliage* had no defined territorial frontiers and was usually riddled with contradictory and conflicting rights and jurisdiction. Even the English county was anything but a tidy area; in the county of Northumberland (for example) two sizable areas were technically part of the palatinate of Durham and one was governed by the archbishop of York. The way men saw administration was in controls over men, not in control over tidily divided up regions.

Royal administration in other parts of western Europe

The apparatus of administration available by the early fourteenth century to the rulers of England and France was commonly found in all countries of western Europe, though it admitted of infinite variation in detail. Even in the British Isles there were important differences. The kingdom of Scotland, at this very moment engaged in the conflict with

---

[1] Broadly speaking *bailli* (with a *bailliage*) is the term used in the north, *sénéchal* (*sénéchaussée*) in the south.

England which did so much to clarify its institutions, had a government more rudimentary than that south of the border. Feudalism had hardly penetrated into the highland area, and in the counties the earls still had military responsibilities they had long lost in England. And in Ireland, though the English king was represented by a justiciar, and a skeleton apparatus of exchequer, courts and assemblies existed, there was in most of the country a state of almost continuous war, with real power in the hands of the Norman-Irish grandees and the survivors of the native Irish kinglets. In North Wales, recently conquered by Edward I, the new castles and the new sheriffs stood as symbols of an alien tradition. In the end these parts of what was centuries later to be the United Kingdom were more or less to fall into step with the patterns hammered out in England and France; some developments in this direction will be recorded later in this book. Other differences in the kingdoms of western Europe were to prove more pertinacious.

So far as the kingdoms of Spain are concerned the long reconquest from the Muslims had produced societies in which the central government tended to be relatively weak. This is reflected in several institutional developments not found elsewhere. The united kingdom of Leon and Castile acquired in the thirteenth century a local administration in which the provinces (*adelantamientos*) bordering on Granada were somewhat differently managed from the rest. Legal systematization under the influence of Roman Law, had produced, also in the thirteenth century, the code known as the *Siete Partidas* (Seven Books). In the Iberian lands of the Crown of Aragon (Aragon itself, Catalonia and Valencia) one of the most interesting features of government arose from the prosperity and importance of the mercantile centres, and notably of Barcelona.[1] However the institutions which chiefly distinguish the kingdoms of Spain are the representative assemblies or *cortes*. These developed differently in the constituent parts of the Crown of Aragon, in Castile, Navarre and Portugal. Generalization about the 'Spanish *cortes*' is therefore hazardous; there was as yet no 'Spain'. Nevertheless one can regard the *cortes* in all the kingdoms as evidence of a remarkably sophisticated attitude to government. This is particularly notable in the Aragonese lands and there Catalonia has an easy pre-eminence as pacemaker and protector of constitutional assemblies.

By the end of the thirteenth century *cortes* are found in each of the lands of the Crown of Aragon—in Aragon itself, in Catalonia and in Valencia. There were also *cortes* occasionally for the three together,

[1] See below, p. 148.

though these were not normally of much significance. Each *cortes* was composed of three estates (*brazos*) the clergy (all prelates and representatives of cathedral clergy but not of parochial clergy), the magnates (*ricoshombres*) and knights, and representatives (proctors, *procuradores* of *personeros*) of certain towns. (In Aragon proper there were four estates, the powerful magnates, *ricoshombres*, being separated from the lesser nobles who formed a *brazo de caballeros*.) With the origins of these remarkable assemblies we cannot here concern ourselves. They are to be sought in a much earlier period, but the very term used to describe them suggests parallels with other countries where the curia, the king's court in its largest and most solemn sense, formed the centre of not dissimilar bodies. Yet the differences are already profound by the early fourteenth century between the royally inspired and directed assemblies of France or England and these *cortes* of the Aragonese lands, where the rights of the estates were jealously preserved against royal interference; where grants of money were the function only of the estates of the towns; where regular meetings were in theory, and usually in practice, accepted by the Crown; and where in the intervals between meetings a permanent committee supervised the execution of the decisions resolved on in the previous *cortes*. The most striking similarity between the English parliament and the *cortes* was, perhaps, the existence in both of machinery for the presentation of petitions to the king and the acknowledgement that the assemblies and the king jointly legislated; the most significant difference was the success with which the estates of the Crown of Aragon in some ways succeeded in making themselves independent of the king,[1] for this (it could be argued) was to prove their undoing, though in the period dealt with in this book this was not evident.

In Castile the *cortes* were far less powerful, their rights far more precarious. Though they had to be asked to vote exceptional taxation (*servicio*), they had no claim to be summoned at regular intervals and the king was not even limited in the particular nobles, prelates and towns he might invite to attend. As and when the Crown found alternative means of financing itself, the *cortes* could not fail to have diminished importance. In any case the legislative process was entirely in the hands of the king (as it was in France). In broad terms the Castilian situation was also reproduced in Portugal.

The rulers of the larger German states had most of the administrative machinery outlined above: a chancery, an exchequer of some sort,

---

[1] Below, p. 112.

courts of law. But it is impossible to generalize about an area which was so large, so diverse politically and so markedly lacking in effective central institutions. One point is clear. As a model to the princes who disputed the emperors' authority the Empire itself offered less than a kingdom such as France or the papacy. The emperor might have an apparatus of government as a prince in his own dynastic lands; as an emperor his resources were in the main illusory.[1] It is hardly surprising, at this time when power in Germany had left the emperors and had not yet been recreated by the princes, that German Estates were found displaying some of the aggressiveness of the Aragonese *cortes*.

Innovations of the later Middle Ages

The previous pages have provided a summary account of the constitutional and administrative machinery of western European kingdoms at the start of the period. It is necessary now to turn to survey the changing patterns in government during the fourteenth and fifteenth centuries. Attention will first be drawn to certain general political trends and then to particular developments in France, England and Spain; a discussion of a few innovations common to all areas will follow.

The internal tensions and conflicts in western kingdoms are discussed in a later chapter. In surveying administrative history it should be remembered that often the politics of the region directly influence its institutions. Yet at this time the action of the central government was still not the main concern of the community. Most men were content to manage their own affairs and intervened in public issues only intermittently. Thus kings and princes made their stealthy advances to ever greater power without being regularly challenged by their subjects. Moreover, the prince was by no means consciously furthering his public control. For him, as for other great men, the land he ruled was principally of dynastic importance. The king's family came before his country. It was only with difficulty that kings and peoples began to draw a distinction and assert that a ruler was responsible for more than the welfare of his own house.

The apanage

This is sharply underlined by a fourteenth-century development common to France and England, and not entirely absent in Spain: the granting to members of the royal family of extensive lands on terms of relative independence. These grants may best be referred to by the

[1] Below, p. 194.

French term *apanage*. In a sense there was nothing very new about this: it was natural that in days of personal government kings should entrust great areas to relatives whose loyalty might be depended on. In the fourteenth century the process has nevertheless an anachronistic air about it, for the French or English ruler had by then at his disposal an apparatus of central and local administration which might have seemed better adapted for government—not least because some earlier examples of devolution (the sons of Henry II of England come to mind) had proved that proximity to the Crown did not prevent a man from being a traitor. The desire to endow the royal family, even to the ultimate impoverishment of the Crown, was still dominant, especially in France; and, as the preamble of many charters creating *apanages* stated, the king 'desired that our children, after our death, should live in love and peace and that any occasion for discord should be taken from them'. How far this policy succeeded in contenting princes of the blood royal and avoiding strife will emerge later where certain of these *apanages* enter the field of politics, notably Philip III's gift of Valois to his second son Charles in 1285, Philip IV's creation for the benefit of his half-brother Louis of the county of Evreux which was to descend to Louis's grandson Charles of Navarre, and the group of creations of John II for his sons: Louis was given Orleans and John was given Berry in 1360, while Philip was given Burgundy in 1363. King Charles V seems to have been doubtful of the wisdom of this policy, but other kings accepted it until the mid-sixteenth century.

The count or duke thus endowed remained, of course, the vassal of the sovereign; it came to be stipulated that the territory should revert to the Crown in default of heirs male; and the royal *baillis* whose area was curtailed by such a creation often fought a successful rearguard action against the officials of the new *apanagiste*. But the intention was to provide the duke with large revenue and the tradition in France was to allow a duke to be master of his duchy. Hence the Crown's rights in the *apanage* were strictly limited. In certain circumstances (the dukes of Burgundy in the fifteenth century are the most notable example) the duke could pursue policies at variance with those of the king and it was luck rather than good management that brought the great *apanages* back at the end of the fifteenth century—lack of heirs (Berry), the inheritance of the Crown by successive holders of *apanages* (Orleans and Angoulême), and the death of Charles of Burgundy in battle; part of Burgundian territory on this occasion escaped the clutches of Louis XI. These accidents restored to the royal domain the bulk of what had been so carelessly handed away in the previous two centuries. Yet it was not an accident that these territories reverted to the Crown in good working order, but rather that the great men who had held them deliberately copied the machinery of the king of France. In the fourteenth century we find the ducal household, the council, chancery, *chambre des comptes*, even judicial arrangements to impede appeals to the *parlement*; in the fifteenth century the Burgundians even added Estates, a *parlement* and an army copied from France. When Louis XI made his brother Charles duke of Guyenne in 1469 'he was in truth king in his *apanage*'.[1]

Nothing so wholesale occurred in England, if only because titles and territories there had for long been divorced. As puzzled foreigners found out, an earl had no necessary connection with the county from which he derived his title; a noble might be duke of Norfolk but draw much of his income from lands in Sussex or, like Clarence, enjoy a title which was not that of a place. Dukes, indeed, first appear in connection with Edward III's endowment of his family. Edward was made duke of Cornwall in 1337; Lionel, duke of Clarence, and John of Gaunt, duke of Lancaster, were given their titles in 1362; the other two surviving sons were mere earls during their father's lifetime. There is, however, a striking difference between the endowments Edward III gave his children and the French *apanages*. The royal domain was not dismembered save for the enrichment of his eldest son, the Black Prince, who got the earldom of Chester, the earldom (later the duchy) of Cornwall, and the principalities of Wales and Aquitaine. The king gave his other sons titles but their wealth came from the heiresses to whom the king married them. Nor was there ever any moment, as there was in France, when the Crown failed to insist on its rights to the reversion of the fiefs in default of heirs male. Above all the royal dukes and earls were not allowed regalian rights. Indeed the closest parallel to the French *apanage* found in England is the grant made to the king's distant kinsman and close comrade-in-arms Henry Grosmont whose many promotions culminated in the title duke of Lancaster in 1351—the county being given to him with palatinate rights which made him virtually independent of the Crown. The grant was, however, for the duke's life only; his heiress married John of Gaunt who succeeded to much of his father-in-law's wealth and in particular to the duchy of Lancaster in 1362, which thus re-entered the royal patrimony.

As in France, so in England, the great men followed in their administration the pattern of royal government; it is noteworthy how many

[1] Lot and Fawtier, *op. cit.*, II, p. 137.

men moved from the service of the Black Prince or the duke of Lancaster into the king's employment. It is true that the wealthy sons of Edward III were a problem to his grandson, Richard II; and one of them—John of Gaunt—was the father of Richard's successful rival, Henry IV. But this would presumably all have happened without the generosity of the old king, and without that generosity the troubles might conceivably have been worse.

If the *apanage* (in either its French or English form) influenced government so did another feature of the political life of the fourteenth and fifteenth centuries: the long-drawn-out war between England and France, the course of which is summarized below,[1] and which also touched at many points the history of Scotland, Spain and western Germany. Some social consequences of the Hundred Years War have already come before us.[2] Here we must observe that it imposed on these countries financial burdens greater than ever before. The solutions of the problems thus presented were, however, so different and their consequences so far-reaching that they must be considered separately for each country.

War and finance in France

The war went badly for France during much of the fourteenth century, the first period culminating in the capture of John II and the treaty of Brétigny of 1360. It is perhaps fair to say that the main reason for this was the failure of the French government to develop new resources to meet what was a very new type of attack. The machinery we have described certainly continued to function. *Parlement* grew slowly more influential and, where they were not excluded from operating by new *apanages*, the *baillis* and *sénéchaux* were effective as watchdogs for the Crown in the domain. Yet financially France was weak. The feudal revenue of the Crown was enough only to pay for the court and the expenses of running the domain. Custom's revenue—levied on exports—was intermittent and unimportant. Exploitation of Jews and other moneylenders (Lombards and Cahorsins) yielded small sums, and profits from the frequent manipulations of the currency could only be short term. All these sources of revenue could be and often were anticipated by loans from Italian bankers, who recovered their capital by collecting the king's revenues; and further sums were raised by loans from individuals and towns. But none of this could stand the expense of

[1] p. 153.
[2] pp. 65–70.

war. Only taxation could do that and steps towards systematic taxation were taken only with hesitation.

Already under Philip IV, however, we can see the line of future advance. The king regularly called on the clergy to contribute tenths of their income; a sales tax (the *maltôte*) was occasionally levied on sale and purchase of commodities and a hearth tax was locally collected from time to time. These expedients were all directly associated with the war and with the royal right in an emergency to the service in the army of all men—the *arrière-ban*—which could be compounded for in money. With these resources the crown struggled through the early disasters of the war with England. The capture of John in 1356 and the enormous ransom written into the treaty of Brétigny (1360) forced a radical extension of taxation. Earlier essays had invariably provoked resistance, or had been made acceptable by sharing the proceeds with the lords of lands. Now—from 1356 onwards—the French people grew accustomed to the regular payment of taxes. The taxes involved were those which had been developed in the early fourteenth century: the sales tax or *maltôte* which was gradually termed an *aide*; the hearth tax or *fouage*, commonly termed the *taille*; and the royal monopoly on salt, the *gabelle* (the Crown had cast envious eyes on salt in 1315 and it had been taxed experimentally from 1341 to 1346). The *aides*, *tailles* and the *gabelle* were to form the financial basis of fifteenth-century French government and, indeed, of the *ancien régime* itself. Other sources of revenue continued: customs duties, clerical tenths, and loans; new devices were invented, notably the sale of titles and of offices in the royal administration. But the taxes first mentioned maintained their primacy. Abolished by Charles V on his deathbed in 1380, the taxes were for a good many years imposed only intermittently. In the 1430s and 1440s, however, they reappeared and for the same reason that had led to their original emergence: the war with England. 1453 saw all English territory lost save Calais, but no peace treaty was signed. The state of war therefore continued, and so did the taxes.

Extraordinary revenue needed the consent of those who had to pay it. Early occasions when the *aides* or the *taille* were imposed had followed meetings on a regional basis of the clergy, nobles and towns, who had voted a sum and provided for the means to collect it. Gradually this process of prior consultation and consent was avoided by the councillors of Charles VII—faced as they were with the crises of war with Burgundy and war with England. At first the Crown levied the *taille* and this was retrospectively approved by an assembly: this happened, for instance, in

1425. But attendance at such meetings was unwelcome. The king in 1441 and 1442 explained that his taxation without prior consultation was due to the desire of sparing his lieges the expense of coming to a gathering of Estates, and to the urgency of his needs. 'From 1451 he levied *taille* and *aide* on his sole authority.'[1] It is hard to exaggerate the importance of this. One consequence was the progressive irrelevance of Estates; another was the possession by the Crown of a source of revenue much greater than a king of England would dispose of. Each of these two factors has a part to play in accounting for the emergence centuries later of absolute monarchy in France and limited monarchy in England. More immediately it provided the king with a means of reforming the army, and extended a new network of royal officials over the country.

The complexity of French financial organization is hard to convey in a few words but since so much else depended on royal revenue a brief description must be attempted. The administration distinguished between the ordinary and the extraordinary sources of income. The ordinary revenue, the traditional feudal income of the Crown, was in the control of four *trésoriers*, one for each of the four areas into which the domain was divided; these were called *charges*. In each *charge* income and expenditure were in the hands of *receveurs ordinaires* and *contreroleurs des finances*. These officials accounted to the *changeur du trésor* in Paris, and had subordinate officers in each *bailliage* or *sénéchaussée*. The expenditure was largely devoted to fixed local charges; the surplus was absorbed by the Crown's granting its creditors *décharges* or quittances which were directed to a particular *charge* and which the creditor had the responsibility of cashing. Much of this revenue was farmed, i.e. sold to the highest bidder for a sum of money, which enabled the Crown to anticipate its revenue and know in advance what it would receive.

Extraordinary revenue was controlled by a separate organization, which grew up haphazardly during the fourteenth century. The assessment of taxes was placed in the hands of men at first chosen in the Estates. They were called the *élus* (elected men); they retained this name even when—after about 1360—they became Crown nominees. After a time the area in which the *élus* operated, which often corresponded to a bishopric, was called an *élection*; these fluctuated in size and in number, rising from a total of thirty-one in 1380 to eighty-five at the end of the fifteenth century. The *élection* was far from being a tidy self-contained area. Villages and towns in one *élection* were often separated from the

[1] Lot and Fawtier, *op. cit.*, II, p. 264.

central town by settlements in the area of another *élection*. The *élus* (there were usually two in each *élection*) and their officers (chiefly the *receveurs des tailles* and the *receveurs des aides*) were constantly quarrelling with other jurisdictions. It is wise not to try to see in our period the later distinction drawn between *pays d'états* and *pays d'élections*; there were *pays d'états* where *élections* are also found (e.g. Brittany) and there were *pays d'élections* where there was intermittently consultation with the Estates. The division is essentially a rationalization by sixteenth- and seventeenth-century lawyers. At the head of the extraordinary revenue were officers who, like the *élus*, were at first *ad hoc*, called *généraux des finances*. By the end of the fourteenth and the start of the fifteenth century the *général des finances* had given his name to his office. Between 1372 and 1449 the number of *généralités* fluctuated between two and three; from 1449 there were four and from 1477 there were five.[1] The *généralités* had a rough correspondence with the *charges* of the *trésor* mentioned above, but it is important to remember that they fluctuated and increased with the variations in the controls of the king. Acting collectively and in consultation with the council, the *généraux* were responsible for the division of the total *taille* among the regions under their charge. The sums raised by the other forms of extraordinary revenue, *aides*, *gabelle*, and customs duty (*imposition foraine* or *traites*), were less amenable to alteration and the *aides* and the customs were regularly farmed. The *aides* were controlled by the same officers who dealt with the *taille*; the *gabelle* had its own hierarchy in local areas; the customs were also under separate local officers, headed at the centre by a *maître général des ports et passages*.

Since the *taille* produced the bulk of the money for the Crown it is worth considering how it was collected. The total prescribed by royal order was divided between the *généralités*; the ratio tended to be constant, but there were some major and many minor adjustments. Each *général* was responsible for the further division among *élections* which was done as a result partly of personal inspection of the region, partly from reports by *élus*. The allocation of an *élection* varied widely. Paris within a few years paid 7 per cent and 40 per cent of the *taille* in the *généralité* of Outre Seine et Yonne. Such variations were due to allowing for the variations of harvests, the ravages of war—and also influence and intrigue. The sum for the *élection* having been determined (and in the so-called *pays d'états* this was usually done by the Estates) the *élus* met

[1] Languedoc, Languedoil, Outre-Seine, Normandy (lost in 1420, recovered 1449), Picardy.

their 'council', which consisted of their officers and a few local men of importance, and, on the basis of their annual inspection, they decided on the further division (*département*) of the *taille*, between rural parishes or by towns (which then corporately divided the total between the urban parishes). At the level of the parish the community met and elected assessors (*asséeurs*), in theory representing rich, middling and poor folk, who proceeded with the final assessment (*assiette*) by hearths. The money was collected by an official also elected by the parish.

It will be obvious how much contention and prevarication was invited by this machinery. To settle disputes the *élus* had a court. Appeal from that lay to the *cour des aides* at Paris; in the fifteenth century similar courts were established at Toulouse, Montpellier and Rouen. In order to meet constant complaints of corruption the Crown, particularly in the fifteenth century, frequently appointed commissioners to 'reform' the administration of the finances, with sovereign powers to reward and punish royal officials. The accounting processes (and disputes in connection with accounting) were still the province of the old *chambre des comptes*, which maintained its supremacy in this against the claims of *parlement* on the legal side but which, on the financial side, was by the fifteenth century a somewhat remote and uninfluential body.

Just as the final accounting for all revenue, ordinary and extraordinary, was in the hands of one office, so the initial budget was unified in the *état général des finances*. Some sort of forward planning existed at an earlier date, but from the 1430s we see distinctly the *trésoriers* and *généraux* forming a financial council and preparing an overall estimate, the *état général*. When this had been approved by the king it was broken up into *états particuliers* and formed the basis of the taxation described above. Something like a budget was thus available to kings and administrators in France by the mid-fifteenth century; and through the direct tax (*taille*) and the indirect taxes (*aides*, *gabelle* and customs) every man in France was in direct contact with *le roi*—either as an involuntary contributor or as belonging or claiming to belong to groups exempt from the royal fisc.[1] It must always be remembered that in this period the royal power depended not only on the ability to levy money but also on the power to excuse payment. Taxes made a king rich, but he could also buy loyalty and service by waiving his rights.

This astonishing financial apparatus—so casually invented, so empirical in its forms, so hateful to the people who none the less put up with it, is the chief symbol of growing royal power in our period but the

[1] Public opinion reluctantly accepted noble immunity from about 1400.

slow process of centralization is found elsewhere in the royal administration: in the army, in legal administration and in local government.

The army was transformed. Attempts were made to secure a rational and up-to-date army of paid specialists by both John II and Charles V (*ordonnance* of 1374).[1] The first sustained acceptance of the principle comes in the *ordonnance* of 1439, and the *ordonnance* of 1445 was the turning point. This established an army composed of fifteen companies of cavalry, each composed of 100 lances; a lance was a battle-unit of six men—a man-at-arms, a *coutillier*, a page, two archers and either a second page or a third archer. In 1446 this arrangement was extended to Languedoc and a grand total of 1,500 lances or 12,000 mounted men was the result; Louis XI raised this total to 2,636 lances (15,816 men). These are the *gens d'ordonnance*, the first standing army in western Europe, paid by *trésoriers de guerre* and a first charge on the augmented income of the Crown. Against this achievement must be set the modest navy; for long the French government relied on Catalan mercenaries and on the Castilian fleet. And likewise it relied on foreign infantry. The *ordonnance* of 1448 to establish one archer in each parish never really came to much. The archer was *franc*, free of taxes, and the *francs-archers* were soon little more than another class seeking to avoid the *taille*. These military developments had direct political repercussions.

Law and representation in France

The law, as represented by the *parlement* at Paris, continued its majestic course in the fourteenth century. The establishment of its courts was laid down by royal ordinance in 1345. *La grande chambre*, the heart of *parlement*, was staffed by three presidents and thirty masters and was the supreme general tribunal of the kingdom. The forty masters of the *chambre des enquêtes* heard cases, remitted to it from the *grande chambre*, which depended on written documents and especially on previous decisions of *parlement*. The jurisdiction of the *chambre des requêtes* lay largely over persons and bodies exempt from other tribunals; it had eight masters and appeal lay from it to the *grande chambre*. In these courts, as in lower courts, there were royal *procureurs* and *avocats*, though even in the fifteenth century the latter could still undertake private work so long as it did not conflict with the interests of the crown. By now the courts of the *bailli* or *sénéchal* were in practice presided over by deputies: the *lieutenant général* and by the fifteenth century the

[1] I am obliged to Dr K. A. Fowler for information concerning the reform of the French army in the fourteenth centuyy.

lieutenant criminel. By about 1400 such courts were in fixed *chefs-lieux* and virtually in permanent session.

The uniformity of legal administration was, however, modified during the fifteenth century. After the English occupied Paris in 1420 the 'roi de Bourges' established a *parlement* at Toulouse; this became permanent in 1443—the first of the provincial *parlements*. Despite the bitter resistance of the *parlement* at Paris—which had previously carried its sovereign jurisdiction to the provinces in assizes or *grands jours*—the great provinces reacquired by the Crown usually retained as a separate tribunal or *parlement* the body which had existed before their union with the Crown. Thus Grenoble became the seat of the *parlement* for the Dauphiné in 1456; Bordeaux (Guienne), 1462; Dijon (Burgundy), 1476; in Normandy the tribunal was not given sovereign jurisdiction till 1515. Yet the king could and did act as of grace to suspend the decisions of these 'sovereign' bodies; as the fifteenth century wore on there were more appeals direct to the royal council. At the same time the law of France grew more homogeneous. Roman law penetrated the north, just as customary law had penetrated seignorial administration in the south; the king multiplied his *ordonnances* and thus added to the volume of written law. In any case local custom was being written down on a regional basis especially after the *ordonnance* of Montils-les-Tours of 1454, which prescribed the compilation of 'customs' for '*tous les pays de France*'.

With this phrase we are brought back again to two final points in the administrative machine: regional government and representative assemblies. We should now know better than to talk of French 'provinces', let alone provincial governors, in this period. But already the demands of war and the nature of the great liberties or *apanages* accruing to the king in the fifteenth century, were compelling him to devolve on lieutenants the supervision of the entire administration of large areas. Under Charles VII and increasingly later in the century we find *grands gouvernements* and a distinction between the *lieutenant* (mainly military government) and the *gouverneur* (civil). There is no 'system', and there are even dangers analogous to those of the old *apanages*: the officers were often grandees in their own right; there were Bourbon *gouverneurs* of Languedoc from 1461 to 1523. But they were the king's men in theory.

To discuss the Estates in France during the later Middle Ages is to enter on a field singularly ill-cultivated by French historians. English parliamentary institutions of a later date have bedevilled the constitutional history of France almost as much as they have that of England. There seems to be no truth in the view that the Estates General, developed by Philip IV at the same moment that Edward I was experimenting with parliament, was neglected or sabotaged by later French kings, or deflected into innocuous 'provincial' channels.[1] Philip IV undoubtedly held in 1302 a large and representative assembly in order to enlist public support during his quarrel with Boniface VIII; Commynes calls the meeting of 1484 'les trois Estatz tenuz à Tours', but it is the only assembly he so characterizes, and it is significant that the use of the term 'Estates General' occurs first in 1461 but is very rare before 1484. Kings, in fact, preferred to treat with more manageable groups and consequently preferred the *bailliage* as a unit. At crises the Crown tried to assemble larger bodies and used the *pays* for this. These so-called 'provincial' estates are more important in the fourteenth than in the fifteenth century. Yet even the largest of these meetings was usually very incomplete—partly because of the inexplicable absence of representatives of certain towns and partly because of refusal to comply with the summons, usually because of hostility to the Crown. For example the Estates of 1468 were not attended by Dauphiné, Provence and Brittany, nor by Burgundy, Flanders and Picardy. There is much to commend the view that the first real Estates General in France was the meeting of 1484, which was extraordinary in all ways and not least because—unlike all previous large assemblies—it was fairly well documented, though not in official records.

When estates were held on a regional basis magnates and prelates were at first summoned by name, but often from the early fifteenth century they attended only by proxy; the 'third estate' was represented by the proctors of the corporations of towns. Such meetings were, in a sense, not intended to be representative, but to put the Crown in touch with the notables in an area; many such meetings of notables were held without the estates as such being summoned. Other matters than finance were occasionally discussed at such meetings, and at the larger assemblies such as the 'Estates of Languedoc or Langue d'Oui'. The main aim of the Crown was, however, the grant of money and, though grievances were sometimes submitted, any action on them took the form not of legislation by the estates, but of a royal charter or an *ordonnance*. Supply, then, is the occasion for the so-called 'provincial' assemblies: the Estates voted taxes either prospectively or retrospectively. And since in the mid-fifteenth century the Crown secured in practice the

[1] What follows is mainly based on Dupont-Ferrier, II, pp. 24-33.

right of levying 'extraordinary' taxes without prior assent, the Estates dwindled into formal parts of the financial machine—a relic of the doctrine that such taxes *were* extraordinary. 'Provided taxes were paid the king was willing to allow that in principle they need not be paid.'[1]

The Crown's preference for small and manageable bodies was reinforced by two occasions when the Estates, convoked on a wide basis for an emergency, proved difficult: in 1355 and in 1484. On the first occasion the Estates of Langue d'Oui made a large grant in return for concessions of 'reform'; but all that remained of the gesture was the creation of offices elected by the Estates to supervise collection, the *élus*, who retained the name even when they became royal nominees. In 1484 recrimination against the harsh policy of Louis XI was expressed at a meeting which can genuinely be called an Estates General of France as a whole. The Estates on this occasion were also truly representative, for proctors from each Estate were chosen in all *bailliages* by a general meeting of all adult males. Two main reforms were demanded: representation of the Estates, including the Third Estate (*Tiers État* now so named), in the royal council; and a further meeting two years later. Neither demand succeeded. The Crown continued the consultation of notables as before. The Estates were too feeble and divided to be an efficient instrument of government.

England: taxation and parliament

In most respects changes in English government and administration are less adventurous than those we have sketched for France. English kings had also to finance a major and prolonged war and under Edward III the army, which was a paid one, undoubtedly stimulated constitutional change. Under Edward I and perhaps earlier, the king had contracted with captains to provide him with a given force of soldiers for a prescribed period and for an agreed payment. From this grew the contract or 'indentured' army of the fourteenth century. The old device of the county levy was still used, more particularly for defence at home and in the wars against Scotland. But the French wars were fought by troops who, from the highest commanders downwards, were 'retained' in the service of the Crown. The feudal summons was not quite dead: the last occasion on which it was used was in 1385; but the feudal host was a thing of the past. It is important to note that the adoption of 'indentured retainers' for life by the English magnates went some way to

[1] Dupont-Ferrier, II, p. 33.

providing, and at no cost to the Crown, the nucleus of a permanent army. Such men were paid by the magnates in time of peace. In time of war they and their masters became the king's paid soldiers.

Payment of the army was the chief problem for, as in France, the king's 'ordinary' revenue in England sufficed only to maintain his peacetime activities. The sources of additional money were various and had in common only that they were granted to the king by the consent of those who were asked to contribute—the clergy, the towns, the magnates, who were consulted separately or jointly in the Great Council or parliament. Such were the customs (the 'ancient' and the 'new') levied on exports, especially of raw materials, the grant of subsidies on movable wealth (tenths and fifteenths), and money voted by the clergy. The king could, of course, anticipate this—by assignment to creditors of 'tallies' (which gave him the money at once and left the creditor with the job of collecting from the sheriff of a county or the local customs official at a port), and by loans from financiers, foreign or domestic, secured on a specific source of revenue. He was, however, naturally tempted to get more money from the one great staple export, wool. Here there was certainly a decisive development in Edward III's reign, for the parliament of 1362 succeeded in extracting a promise from the king, which was gradually honoured, that he should not levy taxes on wool without the consent of parliament. The bodies of townsmen and merchants, from whom the king had earlier secured agreement for levies on wool, fade away, parliament remaining the sole source of authority for new revenue. In the fifteenth century, with the stabilization of existing 'extraordinary' revenue at relatively low figures, a few striking attempts are made to impose a regular and graduated income tax. But in the event the Crown's main solution of its financial problems was to keep out of war and make the domain revenues as productive as possible. There is, therefore, in England no extension over the whole country of the financial officers of the Crown. The Exchequer remains the ultimate accounting body and, although under Edward II there is dispute over the royal household's finances, the main spending department is the wardrobe. Taxes, when granted, were collected by *ad hoc* commissioners or were farmed to groups of financiers.

What is impressive in the administration of England during this period is the steady development of local magistrates—the justices of the peace, who were responsible for an ever larger share of law enforcement. The title is first formally used in 1361, but before that local gentlemen, 'two or three for each county', had been commissioned with powers wider than that of the old keepers of the peace; by the end of the fourteenth century there were usually eight in each county. Practically every statute dealing with domestic affairs laid fresh duties on the justices, and in particular they were required to operate the labour legislation of the later fourteenth century. In their purely judicial capacity they met either in 'petty sessions', when two or more sat for minor offences, or four times a year in the more impressive 'quarter sessions', when all the J.P.s of a county were present and serious crimes were tried. From all these local courts appeal lay to the King's Bench.

At the centre of the legal structure King's Bench and Common Pleas maintained the primacy of the common law, more jealously now that Englishmen had had some experience of the insidious doctrines of the civilians on the continent. The price of this was a rigidity in procedure in both courts, and a specialization in each, which went far to denying judges their earlier discretion. Judges tended to refuse a reasonable decision and demand a new statute. Even without enacting a new statute parliament could and did intervene to direct the affairs of lesser courts. And so did the council. It was, in fact, as the agent of the council that the chancellor began to act as a kind of judge in equity, the council directing to him petitions for redress, mainly in civil actions and in particular those arising from recent social developments (trusts, partnerships and corporations) for which the common law afforded no remedy. In the second half of the fifteenth century the council itself, sitting often in the Star Chamber, became a court in criminal matters where the rules and limitations of precedent, so carefully cherished in the common law courts, did not apply.

In the previous paragraphs the word parliament has occurred several times. Parliament had secured the right to approve all extraordinary taxes; judges refused to act without a statute in cases outside existing law. It was, in fact, during this period that parliament changed from the improvised institution of the thirteenth century—a kind of enlarged Great Council—and became firmly associated with certain types of public action. Its form hardened. The 'lords' consisted of those magnates, lay and ecclesiastical, summoned to attend in their own name; the 'commons' consisted of two 'knights' for each shire,[1] two burgesses from a steadily lengthening list of towns. The proctors of the cathedral and diocesan clergy ceased to appear after the 1340s; after that they

[1] From the beginning many county representatives were not knights, but men of knightly status.

taxed themselves in the two convocations of Canterbury and York, while the prelates (by virtue of being great landholders) also sat in parliament. After 1327 the Commons were present at every parliament and from 1376 they elected their own speaker. Parliament was so immensely convenient that king and council used it continuously—for taxation, for sifting petitions and drafting legislation, for securing publicity and public support. The spring behind it was the king's council, which acted discreetly in managing parliamentary business, save when parliament functioned as a court of law, when the royal judges, councillors and the chancellor were naturally prominent. On its judicial side the work of parliament tended to contract, save, of course, in the making of statutes and in the trial of persons accused by the commons: 'impeachment'. It is not easy to describe parliament at this stage, when its composition was fluid, its duties ill-defined. But it steadily occupied a focal point in English politics.

Scotland

England's near neighbour Scotland had a markedly less developed type of government. It is, perhaps, proper again to stress the military and financial aspect of the matter, for Scotland too was embroiled in foreign war. Save for a handful of foreign mercenaries the Scottish army, unlike the armies of England and France, was unpaid in this period and indeed much later. As a result the Crown was able to survive on its feudal and domain revenues and the customs. The financial demands following the capture by England of David II (1346) and James I (1406), with the consequential payment of big ransoms, were mainly financed by the customs duties.[1] These two calamities also did much to complicate the emergence of effective centralized institutions, and the scope of the departments under the chancellor and the chamberlain (the exchequer) was accordingly affected. James I divided up financial responsibility between a comptroller (crown lands, farms of the burghs, customs) and a treasurer (feudal incidents and other casual income). The weakness of the Crown also favoured peculiar representative machinery. In some ways the parliament of Scotland followed English practice; the representatives of burghs gradually established themselves as a necessary element in parliament by the second half of the fifteenth century. But Scottish kings were unable to ensure the attendance of lesser lairds and

[1] David II's ransom was fixed at 100,000 merks (Scottish marks); of this 76,000 merks were paid by 1377; James I's ransom was 60,000 merks of which only 9,500 was paid. Dickinson, *op. cit.* (below, p. 126), pp. 184–5, 206–7.

even among the greater men who attended few were prepared to wait long. Hence another device emerged—the Lords of the Articles. First in 1367 and repeatedly thereafter the Scottish Estates elected a committee to 'hold parliament' while the majority went home.

Spain

All the kingdoms of Spain had, like Scotland, suffered from civil war and had been embroiled in Franco-English fighting. The result was central institutions weaker than those found in England and France. On the other hand there were aspects of government which had originality and performed remarkably useful functions.

The fourteenth century was the time when the *justicia* was most influential in the kingdom of Aragon. Appointed by the Crown from the lesser nobility (*caballeros*), the *justicia* was charged with the tasks of ensuring the observance of the laws and of protecting individuals from the abuse of power on the part of royal officials; beyond that the *justicia* frequently arbitrated in quarrels between the magnates. In this way the *justicia* became a kind of supreme judge in traditional law, while the Roman law began to be applied in the *audiencia*, the royal council in its judicial aspect. The office of *justicia* did not really establish itself in Valencia, and it was unknown in Catalonia. In Aragon proper it was in decline by the end of the fifteenth century.

Much more impressive were the *cortes* of Catalonia which were at the height of their power from the middle years of the fourteenth century, when there was established on a regular basis the standing committee of the *cortes* which operated during intervals between sessions of the full body. Consisting of a representative of each of the three Catalan Estates nominated for a three-year term, each with an auditor of accounts (*oidor*), this committee was known as the *Diputació del general de Catalunya* or *generalitat*; from 1365 the *generalitat* had permanent quarters in Barcelona and it employed a staff of subordinate officials. Originally the *generalitat* had a financial or fiscal role, to assure collection and correct appropriation of sums voted by the *cortes*. But to these tasks it added judicial and military responsibilities and above all acted as the custodian of Catalan privileges as against the officers of the Aragonese Crown. The institution was copied in Aragon proper and in Valencia by the beginning of the fifteenth century and it is even found in Navarre at the end of the century; but it had no place in Castilian arrangements. The *cortes* themselves flourished at this time and were exported by the Aragonese to their Mediterranean lands. Another invention of the

Crown of Aragon, even more pregnant for the future, was the occasional appointment of viceroys to represent the crown in the royal absence. This provided an extraordinarily flexible constitution for the Aragonese 'empire'; something of Catalan independence was carried to Sicily, Sardinia and the other overseas territories.

In Castile this 'Catalano-Aragonese' constitutionalism was largely absent. The Castilian king was thus not constricted by the representative assemblies, which he continued to summon as he pleased. This basic difference between Castile and Aragon was to be important for the future development of the peninsula, and already in the fourteenth and early fifteenth centuries it is possible to see Castilian kings advancing their powers and seizing opportunities to build up existing institutions in the interests of the Crown. In this they had the support of many groups in the community which were wearied of disorder. Provincial royal government had weakened as the *adelantados* became hereditary, but in the *hermandad* there was a counterweight to noble disobedience. In the thirteenth century the brotherhood or *hermandad* between Castilian towns had been primarily designed to resist all powers, noble or royal, which threatened urban privilege and urban communications. In the fourteenth century the associations between towns ceased to be so hostile to the Crown; the groups of towns linked together tended to be larger. In decline by the end of the fourteenth century, the *hermandad* was revived in 1465 with a general committee or *junta* and four regional groups of towns. Security of roads was the main aim and the institution was greatly developed under royal impulse from 1476. Similarly the local magistrates called *corregidores*, first found in the mid-fourteenth century, survived to become all-important agents of the strong monarchy of the later fifteenth century. The royal finances were fortified by the sales tax (*alcabala*). At first fixed at a twentieth, it later rose to a tenth, and was permanent by the end of the fourteenth century. Financial administration at the centre, the *hacienda*, began to develop; there are rudimentary budgets from 1429. Above all there was steady development in the courts. The *audiencia* or *cancilleria* in 1433 split into two sections, a civil court (with auditors, *oidores*) and a criminal court (*alcaldes*). Here again was a structure on which Ferdinand and Isabella could build.

No such simplification can help us in dealing with Germany in our period. The fruitless attempts to rationalize the position of the emperor belong to political and not to administrative history.[1] Problems of

[1] Below, p. 195.

taxation and representation were tackled in Germany but at the level of the great magnates and the important towns.

Councils and administration

In the foregoing account pride of place has been given to institutions which were not common to all the monarchies, and particular stress has been laid on the French financial machine, for it is, in all probability, the most significant administrative innovation of the later Middle Ages. We must now turn to certain developments common to a greater or less degree to all the countries concerned: the use of councils of a new type in government, the emergence of a novel type of secretariat and the recruitment to government service of a new kind of public servant. We must also consider royal control over the Church and the increasing influence on the continent of Roman law.

The king always had his advisers. Some of these had been great officials who became over the centuries purely honorific, or mere holders of valuable sinecures, for instance the butler. Some were ancient officials who retained important bureaucratic functions, like the chancellor. The great vassals of a feudal king had formed his 'natural' advisers, and felt their exclusion acutely when, in the thirteenth century, kings began to rely more on the advice of less exalted men. An almost universal trend of the period was the rise in importance in the councils of kings of these humble men chosen for their training in affairs, for their expertise in managing finance or domestic intelligence, above all for their skill in managing men. The old council gave place to a new body, not 'natural' in that the king summoned to it whom he would, but swifter and surer in advising him, and disinterested in carrying out his policies—which were, after all, often hammered out by the councillors themselves. These councillors encountered criticism from the magnates. This did not prevent their survival. Often in the end they were rewarded by promotion to the nobility, but others were ready to step into their shoes.

The councillor in France and England was by the end of the fourteenth century a paid adviser, under oath to his master. Great men were still councillors, and particularly great ecclesiastics, for the prelate of the later Middle Ages was often a well-trained lawyer. There were times when nobles were even predominant—as in the France of Charles VI. But much of the detailed work was necessarily in the hands of lesser men and it is remarkable how many councillors survive political upheavals. Twenty-six men were in both Edward IV's council and in

Richard III's; twenty men were in Richard III's council and after Bosworth continued to serve the Tudor usurper; fourteen councillors served both Edward IV and his brother and Henry VII.[1] How much work was done by the council it is hard to say, for in England there are gaps in its records and in France its records have all but perished. But it is clear that the council was omnicompetent—so much so that a tendency to specialization is evident, notably in France where financial matters tended to be settled separately. In both countries the chancellor was the executive officer of the council. These tendencies are also to be seen in the kingdom of Castile. This tendency of the council to ramify offered kings an admirable way of delegating power by creating subsidiary councils of a specialist or regional character. This was to be one of the ways in which Ferdinand and Isabella strengthened their government; other countries began to follow suit in the sixteenth century; and it is tempting to see a rudimentary Council of the North at work in England as early as the end of the Yorkist period.

In line with the importance attached to conciliar administration is the advent of the secretary. Some clerks had clearly to be with the king's household as he moved about, and had therefore to be detached from the chancery, now a fixed department. In France the notaries thus attached to the king are called *clercs du secret* from the early fourteenth century, and their steady rise in the administrative world was linked, one need hardly say, with the ever-growing complexity of financial administration. By the end of the fourteenth century there are between four and a dozen *secrétaires des finances*; a century later they have become responsible for financial administration and are recognizable as the prototype of the sixteenth-century minister. The process of evolution was much the same in England, but had added formality through the king's use of the signet ring to move other departments of state, and through the secretary's control of the signet office. The reign of Edward IV seems critical in this matter, as in other administrative developments; in England as in France we can see the shape of the future secretary of state. With this innovation (paralleled in Spain also by the end of the period) we should perhaps link a new type of diplomacy. There were Italian models for this, and Italian influence may perhaps be suspected. In all courts the grand and ponderous embassy, the formal exchange of heralds, were supplemented now by the use of experts who

[1] See J. R. Lander, *Bull. Inst. Hist. Res.*, 32 (1959), pp. 179–80: these different figures often refer, of course, to the same man. Forty-two councillors in all overlapped two or three reigns.

had or acquired some degree of specialist knowledge of the countries involved. We have entered the world of Louis XI, Commynes and Ferdinand of Aragon. We are close to the permanent diplomatic agents of the sixteenth century.

These changes gave additional power to western monarchy at the end of the Middle Ages. So did the king's control over the clergy.[1] The Church of earlier ages had been in every country the greatest of the 'liberties', the most significant exception to the rights claimed by the king. In the fifteenth century this immunity appreciably dwindled, lasting longest in the protection of clerks before civil magistrates, 'benefit of clergy', though by the end of century even that was a shadow of its former self. Above all, kings in every country taxed the clergy and controlled all senior appointments. In France this was, through the notion of the 'Gallican' church, a matter which came within the purview of *parlement*; in England the statutes of Provisors and Praemunire, especially as re-enacted in the reign of Richard II, virtually made the Crown supreme over the Church by law. Matters fluctuated more in Spain but there was no doubt about the royal mastery of the Church—even of the great crusading Orders and the Inquisition—by the end of the fifteenth century.

The rise of the prince's power was, on the continent, reinforced by the progressive acceptance of the precepts of Roman law. We have noted its influence in France and Spain; it was becoming influential by the late fifteenth century also in Scotland and in Germany, where the lord substituted for his declining feudal controls the new civilian doctrines. From this development England stood apart. The Crown in England had its civilians (Roman lawyers) and its notaries-public; law was civil law in international issues, and it was canon law in matrimonial or testamentary issues. Yet the common law as such was never under any serious danger from the Roman law, nor the king's ministers less ambitious and effective because they were not civilian-trained.

The lawyers were ubiquitous in administration in these last centuries of the Middle Ages. They were found in the households of great rulers and prelates, and in the councils of kings. They were often the lay *clercs* who were the French king's secretaries and notaries; they were the *letrados* of Castile. In France, as has been noted, a new type of entrenched class emerged through the king's administration, the *noblesse de robe* (above, p. 67). Here again England developed somewhat differently. The J.P. was not a *bailli*. Even when the *bailli* became largely

[1] Below, pp. 295–8.

honorific, the title was worth having because of its perquisites, and no one could have claimed that the small remuneration of the J.P. made his heavy duties worth while financially. All over Europe the clerk and the lawyer were climbing into positions of importance. But in England alone the Crown succeeded in enlisting the cooperation in royal government of the gentry, perhaps the most influential single group in later medieval society.[1] In later centuries this was to put English political development on lines distinct from those of other regions of western Europe.

Government in urban areas

There were towns everywhere in Europe by the start of the fourteenth century. The larger towns for the most part faced common administrative problems and often met them in similar ways. In towns situated where there was strong royal or seignorial control the ultimate authority lay with king or lord and the institutions of the town could not develop as they did in those parts of Europe where towns for long formed the dominant element in public life: Italy, the Low Countries and parts of Germany. In what follows consideration is given to Italian and Low Country towns. But it should be remembered that Paris and London, Bristol and Lyons all have histories which can be fitted into the general pattern of urban development.

There were striking similarities in the machinery of government found in most towns. There were two reasons for this. Towns had usually gone through the same stages of development, whether they were in Italy or Flanders, in France, England or Spain. And the ultimate problem facing the government of the town was everywhere the same: the collection of taxes for itself or for its sovereign.

The three social layers in most towns have been mentioned[2] and their existence was reflected in town government. At the start of the fourteenth century the group in control of the town's administration was generally either 'patrician'—in the sense the term has been already used—or else composed of a mixture of patrician and guild elements (by guild is meant the full members of the craft guilds, whose 'masters' represented broadly speaking a middle-class section of the urban population). Competing as they often were for power, the patricians and the guildsmen were of one mind about the exclusion from influence of the third component: the porters, labourers, unskilled workers. In surveying the history of towns in the fourteenth century, we are thus dealing with

[1] Above, p. 69.   [2] Above, pp. 71–3.

something like a class struggle in the Marxist sense, especially in those few centres where the unskilled workers were sufficiently numerous and vocal to come forward as a political proletariat.

The patricians had secured their dominant position, and perhaps some of their wealth, from possession of land in the early days of the town's self-conscious existence. They had framed the demands put to the local lord—bishop, baron or king—for independence, an independence secured by written documents in which urban 'liberties' or privileges were recorded. In Italy feudal lords were also an internal as well as an external threat, the *grandi* of earlier Guelf-Ghibelline rivalries, who were often in theory entirely excluded from office (as at Florence) or kept in uneasy and somewhat ineffective subjection (as at Siena). The patricians (*grassi, poorterie*) had in the beginning organized the town in its new role: a corporate body responsible for its own defence against foes within and without; where money had to be collected to build and maintain defences; where policy had to be hammered out to ensure that trade and trade routes were protected and a steady supply of food and raw materials ensured.

The central device for performing these functions was a council. Naturally the rich group, whose interests were on the whole in long-distance rather than in local trade, formed the council, and in their subsequent government of the town, above all in raising money, the patrician councillors sought to protect their own interests. From the thirteenth century this had made for trouble, especially in the larger and more flourishing communities. Some of these troubles continued in this period and were intensified at two or three places by proletarian gestures; these turmoils, the political history of the towns, will be mentioned later. In the course of them many towns not only changed their constitutional arrangements but ceased to operate in any meaningful sense as towns, either becoming themselves principalities or becoming submerged as mere subordinate units in existing monarchies.

The council or committee (*consiglio, Rat*, and many local names) was, of course, a body which was easily remodelled from time to time to reflect changes in the political power of the various groups in the town. In the parlance of several Flemish cities there were 'members' of the council corresponding with the influence of socially identifiable blocks of citizens. Thus at Bruges there were nine 'members' or groups with equal representation in the council: 1. the *poorterie* (the old patrician element); 2. drapery crafts (weavers, fullers, shearers, dyers); 3. butchers and fishmongers; 4. metal-working crafts; 5. leather-working crafts; 6. crafts connected with the making up of cloth; 7. bakers; 9. seventeen less important crafts. At Ypres the members were much simpler: 1. the *poorterie*; 2. weavers; 3. fullers; 4. other crafts. The importance here given to the guilds as against the patricians is evident and the great authority of the wool manufacturer is seen if we compare either town with arrangements at Liège, where all thirty-two guilds had equal membership in the council. The ultimate stage was reached at Ghent, where from 1304 there were three members, and there we can see the arrangements being varied as each member struggled to have its own way: thus in 1343 the fullers lost their share in government, to recover it in 1349 at the expense of the weavers. From 1359 the town was governed by the patrician *poorterie*, the weavers and a third member representing all the other craft guilds.

Not dissimilar shifts in the balance of power were reflected in the Florentine constitution, where the guilds were divided into the seven which had predominantly capitalist and wholesale interests (the *arti maggiore*, greater guilds) and the rest, though some of the remaining fourteen were for certain purposes regarded as 'middle'.[1] The nine magistrates, eight *Priori* and the *gonfaloniere* (standard-bearer) *di giustizia*, who were called collectively the 'lordship' (*signoria*), were elected by citizens who were full members of guilds. Until 1329 only membership of the greater and the middle guilds qualified; thereafter membership of the lesser guilds was also accepted. In 1378 when the Ciompi seized power their political aims were reflected in this guild structure; three new guilds emerged, the dyers, the needleworkers and the Ciompi—this last soon being destroyed.[2] For a time five *Priori* were allocated to the lesser guilds, four only to the greater. But in January 1382 the greater guilds acquired five *Priori*, in the next month six, and in 1387 seven. Power was now entirely in the hands of the merchant oligarchy.

Restriction of the franchise (to use modern terms) to full guild membership was a feature common to many other Italian and Flemish

[1] The greater guilds were: 1. judges and notaries; 2. dealers in imported cloth (Calimala); 3. money changers (i.e. the bankers); 4. cloth manufacturers (*arte della lana*); 5. leading retailers and silk merchants (Por Santa Maria); 6. physicians and spice dealers; 7. furriers. The middle guilds were: 8. butchers; 9. shoemakers; 10. blacksmiths; 11. builders; 12. secondhand dealers. The lesser guilds were: 13. wine merchants; 14. innkeepers; 15. olive oil dealers; 16. tanners; 17. armourers; 18. locksmiths; 19. harnessmakers; 20. timber merchants; 21. bakers. Cf. below, pp. 383-4.
[2] See below, p. 175.

towns; the patricians acted together and sometimes indeed (as at Florence) remained effectively in control most of the time. What was important in any event, whether government was patrician-controlled or in the hands of the 'middle class' of the town, was to prevent executive power being monopolized by one small section of the dominant group. To this end elaborate precautions were taken. Short-term magistracies were the main device at Florence, where the *signoria* in these centuries held office for only two months at a time and where the outgoing *Priori* were not eligible for re-election for two years. The deans of guilds, who represented their members on the large council (*Collace*) at Ghent, were usually chosen by lot every year. But the most elaborate elections were those in Venice.

Venice was to survive as a republic until the end of the eighteenth century, a fate very different from that of most European towns. Among many reasons for this some importance attaches to the characteristic features of Venetian government. The patrician oligarchy, a large body, was in complete control of the city long before this period begins and the Venetian merchants were already emerging as 'nobles' *vis-à-vis* the full citizens (who were largely employed in the Venetian administration) and the rest of the population. By the end of the thirteenth century the great council (*Maggior Consiglio*) elected a doge for life by a complicated alternation of vote and lot; and the great council was 'closed'—only those families which had been in it prior to 1297 were to be members in future. This closed great council chose the doge as follows. First the entire body chose thirty of its members by lot. The thirty were then reduced, by lot, to nine who elected a body of forty. The forty were reduced by lot to twelve who elected a group of twenty-five, this in turn being brought down to nine by lot. The nine elected forty-five, the forty-five were reduced by lot to eleven, and this eleven elected a committee of forty-one; it was this forty-one which elected the Doge. This convoluted procedure did not entirely avoid (as it was intended to do) the emergence of a doge with active political aspirations and, in effect, real power from 1310 was in the hands of an executive of ten men (the *Dieci*). The *Dieci* were chosen for a year at a time by a group of twenty, ten being the nominees of doge and officials, ten being elected by the *Maggior Consiglio*. Day to day consultation on public affairs was through a senate of 160 members of the patrician class, the 'nobles'.

These examples must suffice to illustrate the infinitely varied representative machinery of the late medieval town. Government was conducted by the *échevinage* or *signoria* through a multitude of different agencies, the majority of which were *ad hoc* or at any rate voluntary. One exception to this was the small writing office or chancery, staffed by clerks and legists; though usually subject to annual election these officers were often more or less permanent. Another exception was the legal administration—judges in Flanders were appointed by the territorial prince, and the *podestà* of the Italian city was, though chosen by the city administration, almost invariably a jurist from another town. The bulk of the work of running the town, however, lay with small, unpaid groups of citizens. Arrangements at Liège may serve as an example. There there were two *maîtres* (prototypes of the later burgermaster) who were responsible for controlling the soldiers and police in the pay of the town and for settling day-to-day problems, assisted by the councillors. Taxation was in the hands of twelve men, *Les douze de la fermeté*. Six men were in charge of the fairs; six men were responsible for discipline in the drapers' market. Separate commissions were appointed to supervise streets and water-mills. Another commission supervised elections in the guilds. All of these bodies were appointed annually.

So far only the similarities between the governments in civic areas have been touched on. There were also differences. Venice, governing an extensive colonial empire and (by the mid-fifteenth century) a great domain on the Italian *terra firma*, needed and developed administrative machinery more complex than that of any other medieval town; the management of the Arsenal, mentioned elsewhere,[1] illustrates the point. Another urban community falls outside the normal categories—Barcelona. As with Venice, here was a patrician-dominated city with vast commercial interests in the Mediterranean, and with institutions which ensured it considerable independence. The municipality not only had its own council, but in the *cortes* of Catalonia the citizens of Barcelona (and of the other towns which followed in its wake) were the vital force in securing the entrenched constitutional position noticed above. Yet Barcelona was not a republic; it was part of the lands of the Crown of Aragon. What chiefly was to distinguish one town from another was the degree to which constitutional and administrative processes survived the threats to municipal independence. By the end of the fifteenth century the only great and genuinely republican cities were a few in Germany and Venice in Italy. The rest had more or less succumbed to the prince from without or had (as in Italy) produced a tyrant from within. These developments, which were to bring the towns of Italy and Flanders more or less into line with the towns of England and France, which

[1] Below, p. 385.

had never for long asserted a genuine independence, are essentially political in their nature and will be mentioned later.[1]

German towns: the Hanseatic League

German towns were numerous and many were large and imperially privileged. Their internal evolution was in most ways comparable to that elsewhere in the north and may be summarized by saying that in general patrician control was maintained or was shared with the guilds. Two towns displayed interesting variations. Cologne, the only German city with a large manufacturing population, experienced proletarian troubles (similar to those in Flanders and at Florence) in 1370, when the weavers evicted the members of the small patrician council. The patricians soon regained power but in 1396 a guild-dominated *Rat* was peaceably established. At Nuremberg, where the patrician *Geschlechter* behaved like nobles, the guilds challenged their authority in 1348 but the revolt was shortlived and the city prospered thereafter under its old masters.

German cities were frequently leagued in defensive associations. For the most part these were of small moment in the fourteenth and fifteenth centuries. Those in south Germany were mainly directed against the territorial lords and to protect trade routes. In 1349 twenty-five cities were organized in a temporary federation by Ulm and Augsburg. In 1376 the Swabian League was formed which nominally linked together more than thirty towns; in 1381 this group allied with another composed of cities on the Rhine; and a treaty in 1385 brought in some of the Swiss cantons. The towns thus associated were, however, unwilling to tax themselves for war, and suspected their allies of profiting from the situation. The League had no organization, no officers and no real economic cohesion. It was typical that the Swiss cantons were left to fight on their own in 1395. In the fifteenth century these associations of towns are even less significant.

There was one league of German towns which had a strikingly different history. The Hansa originated in the common trading policies of the patricians who monopolized political and economic power in the Wend cities of the southern Baltic coast in the thirteenth century. The strength of the Hanseatic League remained commercial and its longevity owed relatively little to its constitutional arrangements. By the mid-fourteenth century the alliance was no longer between the merchants as such but between the towns,[2] and fairly elaborate machinery for joint

[1] Below, pp. 165–76, 198–202.
[2] The Grand Master of the Teutonic Order was a member.

action was devised. Regular assemblies began to be held (*Hansetage*). These met on the average every eighteen months in the last three decades of the fourteenth century, and there were attempts to subdivide the League into regional groupings, 'thirds' and 'sixths'. Yet there were curious weaknesses. There was no common seal; usually only twenty towns sent delegates, many smaller towns giving proxies to Hamburg, Bremen, Lübeck or one of the other big centres; there was no common treasury; and there were no regular contributions. The effectiveness of the Hansa therefore consisted of the sum of the resources of a few individually important towns and the threat of·expulsion. The only sanction against towns which defied the decisions (*Rezesse*) of the assembly, was in practice largely unenforceable in the case of the larger towns, which found it easy to secure readmission. In the second half of the fifteenth century the *Hansetage* met on average only every six or seven years.

The machinery doubtless creaked badly by then, but the habit of consultation was engrained and the economic and political pressures which threatened Hanseatic prosperity continued to hold together the sixty or seventy towns which formed the heart of the confederation. Of these Lübeck was incontestably the most important. *Hansetage* were summoned by Lübeck, they normally met there and that city's seal was commonly used on Hanseatic documents. The other large towns resented this management and leadership, but necessarily tended to accept the situation. In any event there was a further, and political, reason behind the League. It was a condition of membership that all attempts to upset the political power of the patricians in Hanseatic towns should be repressed. This did not prevent the patricians being challenged—at Lübeck the guilds succeeded in sharing power in 1408—but it contributed to the survival of the old burger oligarchies in many towns of north Germany.

The Swiss

To the princes of northern Europe in 1500 the Hansa still seemed a formidable power bloc. No such respect was paid to the Swiss. From small beginnings at this time and a little earlier, and with infinite slowness and hesitation, they were nevertheless to hammer out a political association which was to defy powerful neighbours and internal dissension until it finally reached maturity in the nineteenth century. The Swiss provide, in fact, the only example of moderately successful federation in the medieval period. One may well ask if this success (which should be compared with the shortlived alliances of German and Italian cities) lay in the rural nature of the earliest contracting cantons. For at the heart of the confederation were the forest cantons of Uri, Schwyz and Unterwalden, where free communal institutions had survived. In the desire to resist the bailiffs of their Habsburg masters, the three cantons had a common cause which produced the first loose *Confederatio* of 1291 and its subsequent strengthening in the pact of Brunnen in 1315. But in a sense the kind of tough association produced by the forest cantons was urban or communal in spirit; it was not for nothing that the routes between the towns of Germany and the towns of Italy crossed these mountain areas. And soon towns were associated with the rural cantons: Lucerne (1332), Zurich (1351), Berne (1353); two other forest areas, Glarus and Zug, were incorporated in 1352. These were the eight *alten Orte*, the original cantons which for long were the only full members of the association. Expansion continued, at the expense of Savoy, Austria and Milanese territory, but this added territories which were usually not given full rights, though they were protected by or allied to the confederation as a whole or individual members of it. In 1481 the *alten Orte* were joined by Freiburg and Soleure (Solothurn). In 1501 Basle and Schaffhausen, and in 1513 Appenzell, were admitted to full membership (see map below, p. 142).

The conjunction of towns, where patrician oligarchies predominated, and rural cantons, with a simpler and more popular government, produced tensions which nearly wrecked the flimsy agreements on which the confederation rested. These were the Priests Charter of 1370, which laid down the ecclesiastical autonomy of the region and provided also for federal action against lawbreakers, particularly on the routes leading to the St Gothard Pass; and the Charter of Sempach (1393) which decided common military discipline for confederate forces. There were moments when the alliance practically collapsed, notably when Schwyz and Zug came into conflict in 1404, and when in 1477 Lucerne, Zurich and Berne threatened to withdraw. After this last episode a further agreement, the Charter of Stanz (1481), was reached. This laid down measures for preventing rebellions within the confederation and limited the unauthorized raising of armed levies or holding of assemblies. These decisions were taken at a Diet, to which each canton sent delegates. The Diet was, in fact, the only federal institution and for long enough individual cantons were able to defy its decisions with impunity. It is significant that records of its early proceedings were poorly kept and have been poorly preserved. Yet any attempt to force on the diverse

associates stronger bonds would have undoubtedly broken the confederation. It survived because it lacked a genuine constitution, and because, with Swiss infantry in demand, better terms could be got by
joint agreements than individual cantons could have secured.

Outside Switzerland the Swiss were regarded in the late fifteenth century with suspicion, for they seemed to be mercenary in every sense of
the word and they were doughty opponents of the princes on their
borders. But hostility to towns was also found generally in a Europe
where—save for Italy and Flanders—they were still a small part of
society and had a reputation for rebellion. One may question how deep-
seated this hostility to towns was. Many a nobleman had a town house
and a few had recouped their fortunes with marriages into mercantile
families. Prudent kings were also alive to their bourgeois allies as may
be seen in the policies of both Louis XI and Edward IV. But apart from
Italy, Flanders and Germany the towns play a minor role in the public
history of the later Middle Ages, as will be seen in subsequent chapters.

VI

Political Development in Western Europe

The public affairs of France, England, Scotland, the Low Countries and the kingdoms of Spain were frequently linked in this period by a series of conflicts to which the misleading title 'Hundred Years War' has been given. In 1337 Edward III claimed the French Crown and from then onwards there was intermittent campaigning by English armies in France; for a time in the early fifteenth century the English occupied considerable areas of northern France. As allies of one or other side in the protracted conflict we find the Scots, the people and the rulers of Flanders, Aragon, Navarre, Portugal and Castile. Yet to make the war itself the main subject of this chapter would give it undue importance. It was not a continuous conflict. To contemporaries it was for long periods of only marginal significance. And to begin an account of the

BIBLIOGRAPHY. The fullest continuous narrative of French political history is still E. Lavisse (ed.), *Histoire de France*, vol. III, pt. 2 (C. V. Langlois), IV. pt. I (A. Coville), IV, pt. 2 (C. Petit-Dutaillis). Fuller accounts in R. Delachenal, *Histoire de Charles V* (5 vols., 1909–31); M. Rey, *Les finances royales sous Charles VI* (Paris, 1965); G. Du Fresne de Beaucourt, *Histoire de Charles VII*, 6 vols. (Paris, 1881–91); P. Champion, *Louis XI*, 2 vols. (Paris, 1927); see F. Lehoux, *Jean de France, duc de Berri* (Paris, 1966–8), and for Burgundy, R. Vaughan, *Philip the Bold, John the Fearless*, and *Philip the Good* (London, 1962–70). For England, J. H. Ramsay, *The Genesis of Lancaster*, 2 vols. (London, 1913) and *Lancaster and York*, 2 vols. (London, 1892) are still not entirely superseded; but see also T. F. Tout, *History of England 1216–1377* (2nd edn., London, 1920); M. McKisack, *The Fourteenth Century* (Oxford, 1959); and E. F. Jacob, *The Fifteenth Century* (Oxford, 1961); the excellent chapter by K. B. McFarlane in *Cambridge Medieval History*, VIII and the bibliographies in VII, VIII should be consulted. There is not much to commend the big books on individual reigns of English kings save their completeness: J. H. Wylie, *Henry IV*, 4 vols. (London, 1884–98), and with W. T. Waugh, *Henry V*, 3 vols. (London, 1914–29); C. L. Scofield, *Edward IV*, 2 vols. (London, 1923). The best history of Scotland is W. Croft Dickinson, *Scotland ... to 1603* (*A New History of Scotland*, vol. 1, Edinburgh, 1961); of Ireland, E. Curtis, *A History of Medieval Ireland* main political events of the period with external war would make it difficult to explain how the wars themselves came to be fought for so long and, in the end, to so little purpose. By itself, indeed, the Hundred Years War is a paradoxical episode. It must properly be regarded as part of the long-drawn-out consequences of the duke of Normandy becoming king of England in 1066 and of the French inheritance of Henry II which added Aquitaine to the fiefs of the English king. French sovereigns faced with this situation had no alternative but to fight their powerful vassal. Having in John's reign deprived the English king of Normandy, later kings tried to deprive England also of Aquitaine, and this was accomplished in 1453. The French had, therefore, every inducement to be aggressive against England. Yet in fact it was Edward III and Henry V who were the aggressive parties in the fourteenth and fifteenth centuries. To understand this it is necessary to consider the main internal events in both countries.

England in the fourteenth century

The masterful Edward I was succeeded by his unimpressive son in 1307. Edward II inherited (besides personal anxieties at which we can only guess) an empty treasury, a war with Scotland and a magnate class restive and resentful. It was no wonder that his reign consisted of a series of defeats for royal policy culminating in the king's own deposition and murder. Lacking authority, Edward II was at the mercy of his intimates; lacking discrimination, he promoted men who were self-seeking and uninterested in anything save the pickings which came their way. But there was little of principle in the king's critics, who could see their way to frustrating the court but could not find any sure solution of

1110–1513 (London, 1923). For the Low Countries, H. Pirenne, *Histoire de Belgique*, II, 3rd edn. (Brussels, 1922). For the kingdoms of Spain, F. Soldevila, *Historia de España* (Castilian version), II (Barcelona, 1952); P. Vilar, *La Catalogne dans l'Espagne moderne*, I (Paris, 1962); R. B. Merriman, *Rise of the Spanish Empire*, vols. I, II (New York, 1918); recent work on the fifteenth century is reflected in J. H. Elliott, *Imperial Spain, 1469–1716* (London, 1963) and in the chapter by J. M. Batista i Roca in *New Cambridge Modern History*, I. For Portugal, H. C. Livermore, *A History of Portugal* (Cambridge, 1947). The wars of the period are the subject of E. Perroy, *La guerre de Cent Ans* (Paris, 1945; Eng. trans., London, 1951); K. Fowler, *The Age of Plantagenet and Valois* (London, 1967); H. S. Lucas, *Low Countries and the 100 Years War* (Ann Arbor, 1929) and P. E. Russell, *English Intervention in Spain and Portugal in the Time of Edward III and Richard II* (Oxford, 1955). A very good account of a peace conference is J. G. Dickinson, *The Congress of Arras* (Oxford, 1955).

their main problem: how to control the king's resources in the interests of their class as a whole.

Piers Gaveston, the frivolous Gascon whom Edward made successively earl of Cornwall and lieutenant in Ireland, had already been sent out of the country by the king's father; he was expelled again in 1308 and 1311 but only ceased to offend when he was judicially murdered by the earl of Warwick in 1312. After an interval, he was to be succeeded in Edward II's counsels by a much abler man, Hugh Despenser, who used his influence to build up great power in the south of Wales. Expelled in 1321, he celebrated his return the next year by securing the promotion of his father, the elder Hugh, as earl of Winchester. Despenser was no fool and stood to gain from stronger royal government. But he alienated Queen Isabella who, when in France to negotiate with her brother Charles IV, formed an alliance, of sentiment as well as of interest, with Roger Mortimer, a magnate from the march of Wales who had been persecuted by Despenser. To the queen all the dissidents flocked, and invasion was completely successful; Edward was captured in November 1326 and deposed in favour of his son in January 1327. The absence of a royal policy above faction was still felt, however. Mortimer proved just as voracious as Despenser and less able to manage the government. His title 'earl of March' (1328) suggested to the suspicious magnates an unbridled ambition and in 1330 Edward III condoned a palace revolution which culminated in Mortimer's execution and the exclusion from power of his royal mistress.

Edward II's troubles were of his own making, in the sense that the great men who resented the rule of the king's intimates were able to secure only their overthrow and failed to establish a system which would have put the crown into commission. It was not for want of trying. Between 1309 and 1311 a determined effort was made to give effect to the magnates' aim of making the king's council and administration matters of public concern. The Ordainers, as the lords were called who formed a committee of reform, grudgingly accepted by the king in 1310, published their reform plans in the Ordinances of 1311. These suggested retrenchment as a solution for royal poverty and sought to ensure that the king's appointments to the great departments of state were made by the advice of the barons in parliament, that the king's employment of his household offices (wardrobe and chamber) should be subject to public control. But once their immediate programme had been achieved the magnates as a body lost cohesion and, in particular, failed to carry with them the richest magnate, the king's cousin Thomas earl of Lancaster, even although he was given a specially prominent position in the arrangements made in the parliament of York (1318) to provide the king with a permanent council drawn from the baronage. The first emergence of the Despensers drew Lancaster back into active cooperation with the other disgruntled magnates; but the Despenser victory at court in 1322 was soon followed by vigorous action against Lancaster. Together with the earl of Hereford and a few of the other barons, he was defeated by a royal army at Boroughbridge on 16 March 1322. Hereford died in the battle, Lancaster was executed soon afterwards.

We shall consider later Edward II's unsuccessful war in Scotland and his almost equally unhappy policy in France; but, though the details of Edward III's French wars may wait, any discussion of his reign must begin by stressing how important for domestic history was the conflict with France. The war at first took the king out of the country, it compelled him to seek financial aid on an enormous scale, it led to the frequent use of parliament as an instrument of government, and it fostered new and important legal and social changes.

The paid army was, particularly at the start, augmented by mercenary forces recruited in south-west Germany by the old device of the money-fief. The 'vassal' was paid a salary graded according to the character of the force he provided; such contracts had probably suggested the indentures on which the domestic army was now mainly recruited. Both sorts of soldier needed payment and for this the traditional revenue of the crown was quite inadequate. 'Ordinary' revenue merely kept the king and his household going in peacetime and the extraordinary aids and subsidies were beginning to formalize themselves at low levels: the tenth on movable wealth in the towns and the fifteenth on the counties produced a sum of about £40,000; the tenth on clerical income about £20,000; both sums tended to become smaller until by the end of the fifteenth century the two together produced only £40,000. To these, which needed grant by parliament or convocation, the king added the old and a new customs which became a regular source of income producing about £10,000 a year and was not, like the tonnage and poundage from 1347 onwards, dependent on parliamentary grant. The king, of course, anticipated these revenues by borrowing on their security. Italian bankers lent Edward III money at the start of the reign; later he relied more and more on groups of native financiers and private individuals and corporations. It seems certain that high interest rates were charged by most lenders, as the risk of repudiation was very great. However, all that these bankers could do was to anticipate revenue; to increase his resources the king had to resort to fresh levies.

The one great source of wealth in the country was wool, and Edward III was not the first king to mulct the trade. From early in the reign the king bargained with the merchants for increased taxes on wool, and *maletoltes* (disliked because the merchants passed the tax on to the producer in the form of lower prices) were very frequent at the height of the war effort in the 1340s and 1350s. However Edward found himself compelled to agree that all such grants should be made in parliament and a start was thus made in the tradition that grievances must be remedied before supply was voted. The merchants got a monopoly:

> The price of settlement was compromise. The king was left in possession of a high permanent tax on wool, and parliament was left in possession of the power to control it. As for the wool trade itself, it now became a quasi-monopoly in the English Company of the Staple ... [This] suited the king because he found in this company a body which could lend money on a larger scale than any small group of financiers.[1]

There is some truth in the aphorism that 'wool paid for the Hundred Years War'. What is surprising is that we do not find any successful later device to tap the real wealth of the country. The poll taxes of 1377 ($4d$ per head on all laymen aged fourteen and upwards), of 1379 (graduated) and of 1380 ($1s$) were difficult to collect and bitterly unpopular—after the Revolt of 1381 they were not tried again. Nor was there an immediate future for the attempt to tax landed income in 1435: the tax began at $6d$ in the £ from persons worth £5 a year and rose to $2s$ in the £ for magnates with an income of £400 a year or more; lands in Wales and abroad were not included; and the total produced was £9,000.[2] This last tax was voted after the treasurer Lord Cromwell had produced estimates which showed that in 1433 annual revenue (including customs on wool) more or less balanced normal expenditure. The Crown could manage with this and a few subsidies from time to time, so long as war made no great additional claims. This hand-to-mouth existence, alleviated by a few loans, voluntary or otherwise, lasted throughout the fifteenth and indeed the sixteenth century. It goes far to explain the Crown's continual insistence on its feudal rights of

[1] Eileen Power, *The Wool Trade in English Medieval History* (London, 1941), p. 85.
[2] Cf. above, p. 69, n. 2.

wardship and marriage, for these were ways of tapping the wealth of the rural magnate.

The financial problems were, however, more or less solved for Edward III, and so was the problem of his absence from the country, though this caused a storm in 1340 when Edward returned from Flanders and accused his ministers, judges and officials—partly in order to levy large fines from them. Archbishop Stratford, who had been chancellor, and other episcopal ministers were for a time replaced by laymen, but the magnates in parliament insisted that, as peers, prelates could only be tried in parliament and compelled Edward to agree to auditors of royal accounts being appointed by parliament, and to all royal ministers being answerable for their conduct to the same body. Edward secured the repeal of this in 1343 and for the rest of his reign avoided any further occasion for such statements of principle.

Finance and the crisis of 1340–41 have both shown how king and magnates accepted a central place for parliament as a forum of debate, as a means of securing taxes acceptable to the community. And this reign unquestionably marks a critical stage in parliamentary history. It was through parliament that popular irritation against the papacy was expressed in the Statute of Provisors (1351) and Praemunire (1353); the first prohibited papal provision (below, p. 271) and the second made it an offence to take to the pope's courts any issue within the competence of a royal court. Again it was through parliament that steps were taken to deal with the immediate social consequences of the Black Death of 1348: the Statute of Labourers of 1351 tried to prevent wages rising with the scarcity of labour (cf. above, p. 33). The courts were now beginning to argue that it was parliament's job to make good any defects in the law. And all the evidence suggests that there was less disinclination to attend than used to be thought. The lords attended fitfully but the gentry gradually came to look upon service in parliament as socially and legally advantageous. Not the least impressive evidence of the place of parliament was its use by all parties in the stormy decades which opened in the early 1370s.

Edward, who was sixty in 1372, was disinclined for business and a prey to factious advice. His heir, Edward the Black Prince, was ill; Queen Philippa was dead. The main power at court was John of Gaunt, duke of Lancaster. Financial strains and unsuccessful war led the councillors to realize that peace was desirable; at the same time there arose an anti-court party which clamoured for efficiency and control. The tensions came to a head in the Good Parliament of 1376: the king's mistress, Alice Perrers, was banished, several ministers were punished, and yet again, as in Edward II's reign, an attempt was made to turn the king's council into a public body. In much of this business the Commons played a more prominent part than the Lords.

Likewise in the reign of Richard II, the son of the Black Prince who succeeded in 1377 at the age of ten, the Commons were again active, particularly during the weak conciliar government of the minority which ended in 1389. For the rest Richard's reign, faction-dominated because Richard himself pursued the short-sighted policy of creating a personal following like any other magnate, was notable only for the king's attempt to bolster up his government in Ireland. There English rule had gone steadily down, especially after the terrorist activities (1315–18) in the north of Edward Bruce, brother to Robert I of Scotland. The disorders of Gaelic Ireland were reducing ever further the areas obedient to the king's lieutenant; the Anglo-Irish were becoming increasingly detached from the English at home. Richard's campaign (1394–95) was not unsuccessful but it produced only a temporary revival of obedience and in the fifteenth century the crown fell back on giving authority to one or other of the rival Irish leaders—the Talbots, the Butlers (earls of Ormonde), or the Fitzgeralds (earls of Kildare).

At home Richard's tentative efforts to secure a stronger court party dependent on his will were crushed by the 'appellants', the representatives of the magnates led by the king's uncle Gloucester, in the 'Merciless Parliament' of 1388: in 1397, when Richard felt himself strong enough to turn the tables, it was in parliament that the appellants were in turn attacked and destroyed. Finally it was to parliament, in September 1399, that Richard's abdication was communicated by the triumphant Henry Bolingbroke, the son of Gaunt, who had been deprived by Richard of his duchy of Lancaster in March of the same year. And it was in parliament that Bolingbroke claimed his place as Henry IV. He was descended directly from Edward III,[1] yet his was in a real sense a parliamentary title. The frequent parliaments of the next half-century explain the invention of the term 'the Lancastrian experiment'.

England in the fifteenth century

It was, however, an experiment of a singularly unscientific kind. Henry IV (1399–1413) never mastered the factions which had tolerated his claim to the throne. The deposed Richard was murdered; the revolt of the Welsh under Owen Glyn Dwr (1400–9) was slowly put down; the

See genealogical table, App. II (below, p. 401).

Percy earls of Northumberland and Worcester were defeated but not entirely subdued at Shrewsbury (21 July 1403);[1] for long the king's opponents saw in the Mortimer earl of March, great-grandson of Edward III's second surviving son the duke of Clarence, an alternative claimant who might be more sympathetic to them, and at the end of the reign the deposition of Henry in favour of his heir was being canvassed. In these troubles parliament was no more successful than the king in either promoting good government or securing the old aim of a council and ministers responsible to itself. Even if the baronial discontents declined after Henry V's accession in 1413, the prominence of the council in the ensuing decades was due not to parliamentary pressure but to the absence of Henry V abroad and, on his death in 1422, to the long minority of his heir; Henry VI came to the throne at the age of eight months. Until the late 1430s and early 1440s there was no one outstanding power behind the throne. Henry V's brothers, John duke of Bedford and Humphrey duke of Gloucester, his uncle Henry Beaufort, bishop of Winchester,[2] each had horizons wider than the council where they uneasily collaborated. Gloucester was given some titular precedence at home as Protector and had ambitious schemes abroad; Beaufort, uncommonly wealthy, became richer in manipulating loans to the government and got a cardinal's hat in 1427; there was growing tension between him and Gloucester but this was regularly balanced by the intervention of Bedford, regent in France till his death in 1435. After that the French war began to go steadily against England; Beaufort, more and more the master of the weak and young king, realized the necessity of peace; Gloucester, excluded from influence, could pose as the champion of a war which still commanded popular support. At this point (1447) Gloucester and Beaufort died.

The vacuum at the centre thus created was hardly filled by William de la Pole, earl, marquis (1444) and duke (1448) of Suffolk, who had risen to influence with Beaufort's support and who was convinced of the need for peace. Gloucester's place as opponent of this policy was now taken by Richard, duke of York. York united in his person great landed wealth and ancient hostilities to the Lancastrian kings: his mother was a Mortimer, his father's father had been Edmund, son of

---

[1] The moving spirit was Northumberland's son Henry, 'Hotspur', killed in the battle.

[2] The Beauforts were John of Gaunt's children by his mistress Katharine Swynford, whom he married in 1396; they were legitimized by act of parliament in 1397, though expressly debarred from the succession.

Edward III; were Henry VI to die without heirs, York would become king. This situation made for crisis round the king and encouraged local disorder. Nevertheless a complete breakdown in government did not immediately follow the loss of Normandy and Suffolk's destruction in 1450, though it precipitated Cade's rebellion in Kent and the home counties, a protest by gentry and peasants at taxation and malad-ministration, which was relatively easily suppressed. The Beaufort earl of Somerset maintained an uneasy ascendancy at court.

In 1453, however, three events occurred which proved fatal to domestic peace: on 17 July Talbot was defeated at Castillon and Guienne was lost, so that only Calais remained of recent conquests and the old Angevin inheritance; on 10 August Henry VI for the first time lost his wits; and on 13 October his queen, Margaret of Anjou, gave birth to a son, Edward. Weak government had already encouraged magnates to ignore the law in the provinces. For the next seventeen years such regional rivalries were subsumed under the 'Wars of the Roses', which saw the duke of York killed in 1460, his son proclaimed Edward IV in 1461 and expelled at Henry VI's 'readeption' in 1470, but once again victorious in 1471 when Edward Prince of Wales was killed and his father Henry VI murdered.

The violence of these years used to be attributed to 'bastard feud-alism'. By this was meant the substitution of money for land in the support of the entourage (indentured retainers) of the great and the growth of local influence in ways which contemporaries stigmatized as 'livery and maintenance'—the processes by which a rising magnate acquired locally an irregular and often unreliable clientage.[1] But the formal contracts of indenture probably made for stability; the looser client-'good lord' relationship was not new, nor was it to disappear for centuries. Local disorder was endemic in the Middle Ages and later. In the mid-fifteenth century it was exacerbated by the failure of the war in France, which embittered nobles and gentry who had become used to enjoying the pickings of service overseas.

In all this confusion parliament and council had no independent initiative. Parliament obediently reflected the policy of the triumphant party; its legislation against 'livery and maintenance', its demands that the king should resume crown lands and live off his own were worthless in the divided state of the monarchy. The 'Lancastrian experiment' falls

[1] All previous discussions of this are superseded by K. B. McFarlane, 'Bastard feudalism', *Bulletin of the Inst. of Hist. Research*, 20 (1945) and 'Parliament and bastard feudalism', *Trans. Roy. Historical Soc.*, 4th ser., 26 (1944).

into perspective when we observe paralysis overtaking government in the absence of a strong king. Under Edward IV and Henry VII we do at length witness some at any rate of these lessons being learned: and not least the lesson that only peace could assure the monarch of a means of keeping within his income.

The savagery of the civil war was not quite over in 1471. Edward had provoked his defeat in 1470 by alienating Richard Neville earl of Warwick who had been his ally, almost his patron, in the early '60s. Warwick negotiated a French marriage for the king in 1464 only to find that Edward was secretly married to Lady Grey, widowed daughter of Bedford's steward Sir Richard Woodville, whom Henry VI had made Lord Rivers in 1448. After Warwick's death and Edward's unchallenged rule in 1471 the Woodville family quickly feathered their nests through the king's influence and it was this which precipitated the troubles of 1483–85. On Edward's death his brother, Richard duke of Gloucester, able and ambitious, was faced with a court where the queen's family looked all powerful: from this came his rapid grasping of power, his arrest of the queen and her relatives, his coronation as Richard III and the murder of the royal children, Edward V and the duke of York. That his real resources were pretty slender was soon shown when, in a country apathetic and disinclined for royal adventures, he was defeated by the Lancastrian Henry Tudor whose claim to the throne was even flimsier than Richard's, but who had the luck and the energy to survive long enough to resume the solid policies, unwarlike and economical, of Edward IV.

Scotland

Dramatic as were the dynastic upheavals in England—Edward II, Richard II, Henry VI and Edward V were all deposed and murdered— the descendants of King Robert Bruce (d. 1329) fared little better. Throughout this period Scotland was still effectively two lands, the English-speaking Lowlands and east coast, and the Celtic Highlands. The defeat of the Lord of the Isles at Harlaw in 1411 hardly affected this. Orkney and Shetland did not leave Norwegian suzerainty until 1472.

For two long periods kings of Scots were English captives. David II, taken at Neville's Cross in 1346, was released in 1357 but remained bound by ties of debt to England. After he died in 1371 he was followed by his nephew Robert Stewart (1371–90) whose grandson James I (1406–37) was taken at sea while being sent out of harm's way to France;

he remained in England till 1424 and in his absence his uncle the duke of Albany was regent. The vigorous but erratic attempts of James I on his return to encourage efficient government on the English model were complicated by the vengeance he took against the descendants of Albany; his high-handed treatment of another Stewart magnate, the earl of Atholl, led the latter's grandson to murder the king. James II (1437–60) was also a child when he inherited and, if he had some of his father's energy, he had all and more of his father's ability to provoke hostility. His principal target was the vastly well-endowed house of Douglas. The king condoned the murder of William earl of Douglas in 1440 and murdered the eighth earl Douglas in 1452; expelled and disinherited in 1455, James Douglas, the ninth earl, lived for thirty years to intrigue against and trouble Scotland. The reign of James III (1460–88) also began with a minority and then proceeded ingloriously. The king's brother, Alexander duke of Albany, was in treacherous league with the Yorkists. Berwick finally passed into English hands in 1482 and the king was in the end murdered by a confederacy headed by the border family of Home in 1488 after the battle of Sauchieburn.

The Scottish story is thus a long catalogue of unruly subjects and kings who never quite succeeded in making their authority accepted. There was no direct taxation; there was no centralized church (the first archbishopric was created at St Andrews in 1472); there was no paid army. Involvement in Anglo-French hostilities was, on the other hand, not an unmixed disaster, for if it led to Neville's Cross as later (1513) to Flodden, it gave a career in the French army to many Scots and it drew the main might of England away from the Border. After Edward III's support of the 'Disinherited' (1332–34)[1] the English kings slowly lost interest in their northern neighbour. The English defeat at Otterburn in 1388 was more in the nature of a battle between the two great border houses of Douglas and Percy. Henry IV in 1400 was the last English king to invade Scotland in person. Nor must we forget that James I and James IV both encountered resistance in part because they were attempting the kind of government successfully practised by contemporary kings elsewhere: not the least of the criticisms directed at James IV was provoked by his employment of non-noble administrators. The royal aim of stronger government was not to be realized for centuries, however, and then only as an indirect consequence of the marriage (1503) between James IV (1488–1513) and Margaret Tudor.

[1] The Disinherited, English Lords with lands in Scotland which had not been restored to them by Robert Bruce, established Edward Balliol as 'king' in 1332.

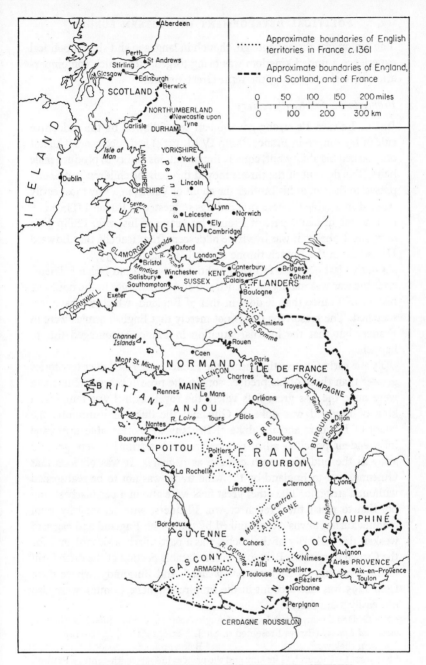

Approximate boundaries of English
territories in France c.1361

Approximate boundaries of England,
and Scotland, and of France

0   50   100   150   200 miles
0   100   200   300 km

IRELAND

Dublin

SCOTLAND

Aberdeen

Perth
St Andrews
Stirling
Glasgow
Edinburgh
Berwick

NORTHUMBERLAND
Newcastle upon
Carlisle   Tyne
DURHAM

Isle of
Man

YORKSHIRE
York Hull
Lincoln

WALES

Pennines

LANCASHIRE
CHESHIRE

Severn R.

ENGLAND

Lynn
Leicester   Norwich
Ely
Cambridge

GLAMORGAN

Cotswolds
Oxford
R. Thames
London

Bristol
Mendips
Salisbury   Winchester
Southampton

CORNWALL

Exeter

KENT
Canterbury
Dover
Calais

SUSSEX

Bruges
Ghent

FLANDERS

Boulogne

Channel
Islands

PICARDY
R. Somme
Amiens

Caen
Rouen

Mont St Michel

NORMANDY

ILE DE FRANCE
Paris

ALENÇON
Chartres

BRITTANY

MAINE

Rennes
Le Mans

Troyes

CHAMPAGNE

R. Seine

ANJOU

Orléans

BURGUNDY

Nantes
R. Loire
Tours
Blois

Dijon

R. Saône

Bourgneuf

POITOU

BERRI

FRANCE

Poitiers
Bourges

BOURBON

La Rochelle

Limoges

Clermont

Lyons

Massif
Central
AUVERGNE

DAUPHINÉ

Bordeaux

GUYENNE

R. Garonne

Cahors

LANGUEDOC

R. Rhône

Avignon
Nîmes
Arles   PROVENCE
Aix-en-Provence

GASCONY

ARMAGNAC

Albi
Toulouse

Montpellier

Toulon

Béziers
Narbonne

Perpignan

CERDAGNE ROUSSILLON

2. FRANCE AND BRITAIN IN THE FIFTEENTH CENTURY

137

The Union was distant enough, though in language and shared political experience a united kingdom was being forged,[1] for which contemporaries were already using the term Great Britain.

France in the fourteenth century

Just as Edward I's strong government was followed by the indecisive rule of his son, so in France Philip IV (d. 1314) had successors who not only lacked his ability but, equally important, his ability to produce male heirs. The descent of the throne moved through his children and finally passed to the son of his brother the count of Valois, in a way most easily studied in a table.[2] These proceedings suggested to Edward II in 1317 that he might claim part of France by virtue of his wife, Philip IV's daughter Isabella; it was by virtue of descent from Isabella that Edward III did claim the French throne in 1328 and again in 1337.

On this last occasion formal hostilities of a new kind began.[3] Thereafter the war was mainly on French soil and bulks larger in the domestic history of France than it does in that of England, which we have just sketched. The reason for this is not merely that English armies were in France, but that the internal situation in France encouraged this to happen.

By the early fourteenth century the French king ruled over territories greater than those of his predecessors in the twelfth century. But there were none the less great fiefs where the royal control was tenuous: a king of England was duke of Guienne; the duke of Burgundy, the count of Flanders and the duke of Brittany were often able to pursue independent policies—all of this before fresh territories were granted away in the mid-fourteenth century as *apanages*. It was obvious that Guienne, tied to England by the wine trade, was not to be reabsorbed without a struggle. The other great fiefs were also in a peculiarly strong position to resist the French crown. Flanders, with its wealthy wool manufacturing towns closely linked by trade with England and eager to weaken the authority of the count, was a particularly awkward unit for the Crown to control; Brittany, with a sizeable portion of the duchy still Celtic speaking, '*la Bretagne bretonnante*', and Burgundy, whose duke from 1295 was also a count in the Empire (Franche Comté), were also not easily assimilated.[4]

[1] See G. Donaldson, 'Foundations of Anglo-Scottish Union', *Elizabeth Government and Society* (Essays Presented to Sir J. Neale, 1961), pp. 282–314.
[2] App. II (below, p. 403).   [3] Below, p. 153.
[4] See John Le Patourel, 'The king and the princes in fourteenth-century France', in *Europe in the Later Middle Ages* (below, p. 399).

Philip VI, the first Valois king (1328–50), a conventional ruler, found his first task the intervention in Flanders at the request of the count against the communes which had risen in rebellion. At Cassel, on 23 August 1328, a French army destroyed the popular forces: the count, and French influence, were dominant. To Edward III Flanders was a useful way of bringing pressure to bear on France and extricating Guienne from French interference. It was not a new policy, but it was energetically performed. Edward III built up alliances in the Rhineland, he forbade (1336) the export of wool to Flanders in order to embarrass the Flemish towns and, when Philip declared Guienne forfeited, he put forward his claim to the throne. In Flanders the popular party under the leadership of the patrician James van Artevelde accepted Edward's new title (1340), although Edward's financial straits did not at this moment enable him to profit by this.

He was soon aided by a disputed succession to Brittany where, when Duke John III died in 1341, his half-brother—supported by England—disputed the inheritance with Charles of Blois, the husband of John's niece—who was favoured by France. Even the Normans seemed ready to join England, according to a disgruntled magnate, Godfrey of Harcourt, who arrived at the English court in 1344. A few years later an even greater French traitor emerged. Charles king of Navarre, descended from Louis X and married to the daughter of King John II, also had enormous Norman lands and a title to the French throne itself.

Granted all this, it is hardly surprising that the French lost many battles and that John II was himself captured in 1356 at Poitiers (below, p. 154). Our concern here is to show how vulnerable in certain ways was the imposing centralized monarchy of France, product as it was of Capetian persistence and the genius of two remarkable if unlovable men, Louis IX and Philip IV. Yet in a sense the fabric of government was strengthened—at the very moment when the royal dukes were being appanaged by John II. The expense of war and the ruinous expense of defeat induced the start of that remarkable taxation system whose structure has already been sketched. And equally significant is the circumstance which provoked this step. 'A reforming' group, associated with the Parisian merchant Étienne Marcel, tried in 1356–57 to make the dauphin Charles, lieutenant and then regent while his father was an English prisoner, subject to the controls of a publicly appointed council and a regularly convoked Estates. The demands were treated equivocally by the dauphin: they were, after all, made by men associated with the treacherous Charles of Navarre; and the bourgeois movement disintegrated in the bloodshed of a peasants' rising, the Jacquerie of 1358 which was indiscriminately aimed at both townsmen and gentlemen.[1] It was repressed; Marcel was killed in Paris, where he had admitted English troops; Charles of Navarre, however, survived to poison French politics until 1387.

The situation in France at John II's death in 1364 was serious: the payments stipulated in the Treaty of Brétigny were heavily in arrears; and mercenary soldiers, French, English, German, continued on French soil where they held up communities and individuals to ransom, waiting till a fresh outbreak of hostilities provided them with regular pay and chances of greater as well as more legitimate plunder. For almost a century the Free Companies were the main social problem in France. To deal with them required more money and the creation of a standing army, disciplined and obedient to the king.

Charles V who reigned from 1364 to 1380 was not oblivious to the problem. An administrative efficiency characterizes his court; something was done to reorganize military service and in Bertrand du Guesclin the king was served by an able general who not only inflicted losses on the English, but carried the war and some of the Companies into Castile (below, p. 154). Flanders was dealt with by marrying its heiress to the duke of Burgundy; Brittany was annexed to the royal domain in 1378— a move frustrated by resistance in the duchy. But royal efforts at re-asserting central authority slackened at the end of the reign, as the war with England quietened down. Enough had, however, been done to provide Charles VI, who came to the throne as a minor in 1380, with a stable administration, staffed by professional experts of modest social rank, and the rudiments of a policy which distinguished to some extent between the kingdom and the interests of the king as a *grand seigneur*. In the early years of the reign there were troubles of a social kind in the Île de France, in Languedoc and in Flanders, but these were on the whole managed not unskilfully by the government. In Flanders Philip van Artevelde (son of James) led a revolution at Ghent which gained the support of the whole of the Low Countries; a French army crushed the revolt at the battle of Roosebeke in 1382; in 1384, when Louis de Male died, his son-in-law duke Philip of Burgundy took over the county. Charles VI in 1388, however, declared his tutelage at an end and resumed his father's councillors and his father's counsels. This did not last long. In 1392 he had the first of a series of seizures which left him for long periods incapable of understanding business.

[1] Above, p. 36.

The madness of the king precluded a continuation of Charles V's *bonne policie*; there followed the decades when the royal dukes monopolized government in their own interests. Broadly speaking it was Burgundian influence which prevailed at court when Charles was insane. In his periods of lucidity he was largely at the disposal of his brother Louis, who in 1392 became duke of Orleans. Orleans, married to an Italian, Valentina Visconti, had great influence over the queen, Isabella of Bavaria, whom Charles VI married in 1385. Such a situation naturally produced rivalry:[1] Burgundy and Orleans pursued incompatible policies in Italy, in Germany, with the divided papacy, and inside France, where Burgundy assumed the role of an ally of the towns; the two dukes were particularly jealous of each other's ruthless handling of the royal finances. In 1407 Duke John the Fearless of Burgundy (who had succeeded his father in 1404) procured the murder in Paris of Louis of Orleans; the Orleanist cause was then championed by the late duke's son and the count of Armagnac. The 'Burgundians and Armagnacs' were to be at each other's throats for more than a quarter of a century. Above all, despite prolonged attempts at patching up a truce, suspicion led both sides to negotiate for the support of England and it is hardly surprising that Henry V invaded France and was remarkably successful there. Nor had the Burgundians for long the monopoly of assassination. At an interview at Montereau designed to end the civil war, supporters of the dauphin Charles murdered John the Fearless in 1419. His successor Philip became an outright ally of England and, by the treaty of Troyes in 1420, co-regent of France with Henry V. When Charles VII acceded in 1422 he was accepted only in the south and centre and was termed the '*roi de Bourges*', which was his principal seat for the next fifteen years.

France after the Treaty of Arras

In 1435 the whole scene was transformed. Bedford died, and Burgundy made his peace with the suzerain whose ties over him were rendered tenuous by the treaty of Arras. Philip was now not only virtually independent; he had still a sense of virtuous innocence as the wronged but forgiving prince. But the treaty marks the start of Charles VII's recovery of France and of a certain amount of power. The next years were the period, decisive in all sorts of ways, when the king imposed taxation without prior consultation, and made permanent the paid army, the

[1] There is a valuable recent study by M. Nordberg, *Les ducs et la royauté* (Uppsala, 1964) dealing with the years 1392–1407.

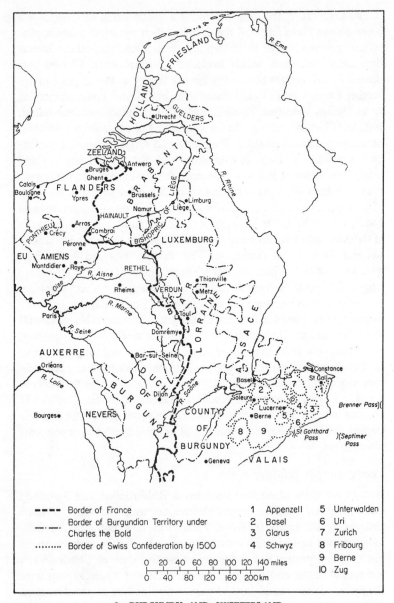

Legend:

- – – – Border of France
- –·–·– Border of Burgundian Territory under Charles the Bold
- ········ Border of Swiss Confederation by 1500

1 Appenzell	5 Unterwalden
2 Basel	6 Uri
3 Glarus	7 Zurich
4 Schwyz	8 Fribourg
	9 Berne
	10 Zug

Map labels: FRIESLAND, R Ems, HOLLAND, GUELDERS, Utrecht, ZEELAND, Antwerp, Bruges, Ghent, BRABANT, FLANDERS, Calais, Boulogne, Ypres, Brussels, Namur, Limburg, BISHOPRIC OF LIÈGE, Liège, HAINAULT, Arras, Cambrai, PONTHIEU, Crécy, Péronne, LUXEMBURG, R. Rhine, EU, AMIENS, Montdidier, Roye, R. Aisne, RETHEL, R. Oise, Rheims, VERDUN, Thionville, Metz, BAR, R. Marne, Paris, Toul, LORRAINE, ALSACE, R. Seine, Domrémy, AUXERRE, Bar-sur-Seine, Orléans, R. Loire, DUCHY OF BURGUNDY, Dijon, R. Saône, Constance, St Gall, Basel, Soleure, COUNTY OF BURGUNDY, Lucerne, Berne, Brenner Pass, Bourges, NEVERS, St Gotthard Pass, Septimer Pass, BURGUNDY, Geneva, VALAIS

Scale: 0 20 40 60 80 100 120 140 miles
0 40 80 120 160 200 km

3. BURGUNDY AND SWITZERLAND

gens d'ordonnance du roi. France was not easily reunited after the long division. But we must recall that family solidarity aided in smoothing over old antagonisms, for all manner of devices had been practised to maintain the unity of inheritances despite the schism in the monarchy. And, as government was localized, so men changed their remoter masters without much regret. No matter of principle had divided Armagnacs and Burgundians; such loyalty as there was the king could recover. Even Philip of Burgundy and Charles the Bold, who succeeded as duke in 1467, could and did claim to be loyal Frenchmen.

Loyal or not, the dukes of Burgundy constituted for Charles VII and, when he followed in 1461, for Louis XI, their main problem. The ducal territories were enormous. The duchy itself and the Free County lay in north-east France and on its borders. The addition of Flanders in the north-west gave the dukes every inducement to join together their divided patrimony. This junction was achieved in the early decades of the fifteenth century: 1421, Namur; 1428, Hainault, Holland, Friesland and Zeeland; 1430, Brabant and Limburg; 1435, Luxemburg. The 'free' bishoprics of Liège, Cambrai and Utrecht were under Burgundian control. Thionville, Rethel, Lower Lorraine and Upper Alsace were linked by subsidiary alliances. The treaty of Arras not only excused the duke for his lifetime from the ties of homage to the king, but added to his territories Auxerre and the 'Somme Towns' (Péronne, Montdidier and Roye) which threatened the Seine valley and Paris; these last places, it was agreed, might be repurchased by the king, a course no one in 1435 could imagine a king affording or a duke conceding. These principalities were heterogeneous; industrial and mercantile Flanders and agrarian Burgundy were at different ends of the economic spectrum. And they were bound to the duke separately and distinctly, for some had come to him by inheritance, some by marriage, some by purchase and some by conquest. None the less for contemporaries the amalgam constituted a 'state', the 'grand duchy of the west' (see map).

Cushioned by English arms from the expenses of war, Philip was wealthy and more or less balanced his budget. The luxury of the ducal court contrasted with Charles VII's threadbare establishment. Art and literature were patronized more at Dijon than at Bourges and ambassadors clustered round a prince who overtly sought to be the leading magnate in Europe. The Order of the Golden Fleece outshone even the Garter in the galaxy of chivalrous orders. In 1454 the 'vow of the pheasant', when Philip ceremonially undertook to champion the crusade, made a great impression. Institutional development reflected these aspirations. All ducal territories in the Low Countries came under one *chambre du conseil* in 1386; a united Estates was summoned occasionally after 1463; in 1473 a *parlement*, on the Paris model, was established at Malines and in the same year an army was constituted like the standing army of France. What was the aim? France was weak and after 1435 the duke's preeminence there was recognized. To the north and east lay Germany where a few counts and dukes were already climbing to a sovereign independence of the emperor. There seems little doubt that the dukes of Burgundy were moving in this last direction; Charles the Bold negotiated with the emperor for a crown.

All other internal problems in France were subordinated to the major rivalry between Charles VII and Louis XI on the one hand, Dukes Philip and Charles on the other, much as in England Yorkist and Lancastrian conflict swept up lesser and local issues. In 1437 Charles VII was faced with rebellious magnates, led by Charles of Bourbon; in 1440 a major rising of grandees (John V of Brittany, the duke of Bourbon, Dunois, and the Dauphin Louis) caused so much disturbance that it was called (from contemporary troubles in Bohemia) the 'Praguerie'. The duke of Alençon was a traitor to both Charles VII and Louis XI (1456, 1474) and so was the count of Armagnac (1455, 1469). There is no doubt that the reason for this was not only the hope of English intervention, but the example of the quasi-independent duke of Burgundy. It was therefore natural that he should take the lead in the most serious noble insurrection, the so-called 'War of the Common Weal'. Charles the Bold led a group which included Duke Francis of Brittany, John of Anjou, the duke of Bourbon and Louis XI's brother Charles of France, as well as many lesser magnates, a few clergy and a few towns; Burgundy stood for an older order, where magnates were left in peace and there was less taxation. The battle of Montlhéry (15 July 1465) was a stalemate and the Peace of Conflans which followed showed how selfish the magnates' aims were, how little they had to do with the Common Weal.

This moment marks the beginning of Louis XI's recovery of authority, though his impetuosity sometimes nearly cancelled out his cunning, as when in 1468 he paid a surprise visit to Charles the Bold at the very moment when the duke learnt that the king had fomented a rising in Liège; he extricated himself by helping to suppress the trouble at Liège and by agreeing that Flanders should be exempt from the jurisdiction of the *parlement* at Paris. But in practice Louis XI avoided the full consequences of this surrender, just as he divided the allied nobles of the Common Weal. England was neutralized by the treaty of Picquigny

(1475); the towns and clergy, and indeed most of the lesser nobles, saw in the king their only saviour from anarchic misgovernment; and the rashness of Charles of Burgundy accomplished his final destruction. In repeated attacks on the Swiss he was repeatedly defeated and at Nancy, on 5 January 1477, he was killed. Louis mishandled this opportunity, which took him by surprise. But if in the end he did not gain the Low Countries, which remained 'Burgundian' to enter the Habsburg principalities, he recovered much. Perhaps the loss of Flanders mattered less than Louis supposed: Ghent, Bruges and Ypres were in full decline commercially (below, p. 389); the new centre of wealth was maritime Antwerp, which lay just outside France. Elsewhere, at any rate, Louis XI was more uniformly successful. The great *apanages* had either fallen back into royal control or were shortly to do so; Roussillon and Cerdagne had been added to France in 1463. When Louis died in 1483 only the duchy of Brittany remained more or less independent.

Louis XI none the less bequeathed serious problems to his successors. His ability and persistence had reinforced the Crown. But he was unloved by the bulk of the population who undoubtedly benefited from his government, and he had been feared and hated by many magnates. His intrigues in Spain and Italy had turned many eyes towards foreign adventure. And, if he had destroyed or immobilized the great dukes, Brittany remained. The minority of Charles VIII, when the council was controlled by Anne, wife of Pierre de Bourbon, count of Beaujeu, saw noble discontent break out in the *guerre folle* of 1485; and it saw the one great representative Estates General assemble in the previous year—a singular example of weakness at the centre and of lack of cohesion in the Estates, whose demands for regular meetings and ultimate financial sanctions were quietly shelved; and it saw a dangerous situation in Brittany. In 1488 Francis II died and, in an attempt to maintain their independence, the Bretons betrothed his heiress Anne to Maximilian. The French invaded in 1491 and Anne was in the end married to Charles VIII. Thereafter Anne de Beaujeu withdrew; the influence of Louis of Orleans, husband of Charles VIII's sister Jeanne and heir presumptive, grew bigger—with the traditional Orleanist interest in Italy. The scene was set for the French invasion of Italy in 1494. Charles VIII's death in 1498 was a mere incident in a new pattern of politics, where for a time foreign war took the place of domestic upheavals as the prime concern of the government of France.

Spain in the later Middle Ages

By comparison with France and England, the Spanish peninsula was a land divided by nature and ethnography as well as by politics. France had, it is true, mountainous areas in the Massif Central and in the Pyrenees, where central government meant next to nothing; and the literary languages of the south (Langue d'Oc) and of the north (Langue d'Oil or Langue d'Oui) covered a multitude of what were only just becoming *patois*. England and Scotland were linguistically divided—the Highlands in Scotland and Wales and Cornwall in England having Celtic speakers. But the multiplicity of cultures in Spain was of a different order.

Ethnically the Latin races predominated, but in the north-west we find Basques, and everywhere there were Jews and converted Moors, or Moriscos. The Moors, still established in the kingdom of Granada, were also numerous elsewhere, especially in the southern half of the peninsula. There was, to a greater extent than elsewhere, a sharp antithesis between pastoralists and agriculturists, and between rural and mercantile activities, the latter being most fully developed in the early fourteenth century in Catalonia. Society had sharper divisions between noble and non-noble, with some peasants more depressed in status than was at this time common in western Europe. Religion reflected and intensified these distinctions. Christians were in the vast majority, but some corrupted by Mozarabic divagations due to the long years when the Church had survived within an Islamic state. There were many Jews, some more or less converted but others still practising their own faith. All of this was marked by short but bitter pogroms and long periods of curious toleration. Linguistically regional speech fell into five main groups: Catalan was spoken in the east and north-east; Castilian in the north, centre and south; Portuguese-Galician covered Portugal, Galicia and part of Leon; Basque was found in the north-west; and in Granada there was Arabic. Granted this, granted the overwhelmingly mountainous nature of the country, it is surprising that there were by our period only five separate kingdoms—Castile (which had absorbed Leon), Aragon (comprising also the principalities of Catalonia and Valencia), Navarre, Portugal and Granada. The peninsula was more or less sealed off from the rest of the continent by the Pyrenees, although Roussillon and Montpellier under the Aragonese Crown remind one that Catalonia at this time was not confined to Iberia. Basque and Catalan made nonsense (as they still do) of the linguistic frontier be-

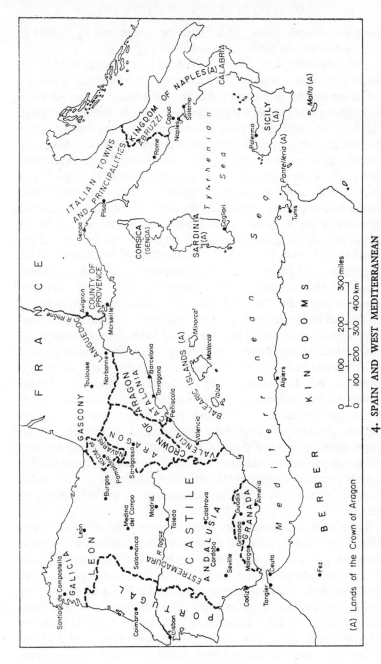

4. SPAIN AND WEST MEDITERRANEAN

(A) Lands of the Crown of Aragon

tween France and 'Spain'. This Roman word was used by Europe at large to describe the peninsula (see map, p. 147).

Aragonese kings in the later Middle Ages were involved in Mediterranean politics as a result of the acquisitions of the thirteenth century and after: the Balearic Islands, Sardinia, and Sicily. These advances were made mainly under Catalan impetus; a more exotic conquest in 1311 was the duchy of Athens which remained with the descendants of the Catalan Company until 1388. Sardinia was not really in Aragonese control until the fifteenth century, thanks to local banditti and a resentful Genoa; the Balearic Islands, where a cadet branch of the royal family was established, were not properly integrated with the Aragonese Crown till the mid-fourteenth century. As for Sicily, the island was ruled by members of the Aragonese royal family. It was incorporated in the Crown in 1409 and Alfonso V made it the base for his conquest of the kingdom of Naples. On his death the kingdom of Naples went to his illegitimate son Ferrante, while Sicily reverted to his brother and heir, Juan II of Aragon. These arrangements were less ramshackle than they appear at first sight. They reflect, of course, the *apanage* mentality of the age, but the Aragonese Crown was familiar with contractual relationships with its territories. The Catalan and Valencian merchants could further their trading interests by having privileges in the main ports of the Aragonese lands overseas and had, indeed, many rights in the mercantile centres. In Barcelona itself the *Consolat de Mar* was a royally recognized corporation with judicial and administrative functions covering commercial and maritime questions. The word 'consuls' was also used for the merchant-magistrates who managed the overseas stations (there were forty-two of them by the end of the fourteenth century) where special facilities had been negotiated. In these ports the Catalan consuls protected trading rights, maintained discipline in the Catalan community and acted also as representatives of the Crown of Aragon.

These overseas commitments help to explain some of the complications of Aragonese politics and in particular they account for the Mediterranean bias of Aragonese kings at a time when the kings of Castile were concentrating on the peninsula. The historian cannot put out of his mind that the later fifteenth century witnessed in Spain the union of the Crowns and the inauguration of a stronger government under Ferdinand and Isabella. Even if it is admitted that the centralization and efficiency achieved under the Catholic sovereigns has been exaggerated, and that on Isabella's death the Union looked as though it might prove ephemeral, there remains an air of paradox about the transformation of a divided into a more or less united land.

It is certainly not easy to identify signs of unification in the fourteenth century. There was, of course, much intra-peninsular trade. There were also many marriages between noble families of the different kingdoms as there were between members of the royal houses themselves.[1] But such royal marriages often tended to exacerbate internal politics by involving each kingdom in the factions of its neighbours. Pedro IV of Aragon (1336–87) was faced by his father's second wife, the Castilian princess Eleanor, and a party of supporting nobles. Pedro himself married Maria of Navarre; he tried in vain to get his daughter by this marriage accepted as his heir, a step which provoked noble resistance round the king's brother James. When Maria died in 1344 the king married Leonora of Portugal. These dynastic disputes gave a chance for the nobles and towns to press further restrictions on the king from which he could not free himself until 1348. Both sides also invoked Castilian help and in this way Pedro was drawn into the civil wars in Castile, where he joined the French in support of Henry of Trastamara against King Pedro the Cruel. Pedro IV of Aragon was in his way an able man; there were moments of strong government. But the ravages of the Free Companies and the dynastic troubles at home and in Castile precluded a settled achievement and after his death matters got worse. Two shorter reigns (Juan I, 1387–95 and Martin I, 1395–1410) culminated in a succession disputed by six claimants. Aragon proper and Valencia were badly disturbed by the ensuing rivalry but Catalonia succeeded in maintaining order by delegating power to commissioners. The final upshot was the famous 'Compromise' of Caspe where in June 1412 nine delegates (three each from Aragon, Catalonia and Valencia) agreed on Ferdinand of Castile, grandson of Pedro IV and called 'of Antequera' from a Moorish fortress he had captured. The peaceful end of this awkward affair was an indication of the political maturity of the Aragonese lands. Ferdinand respected the liberties of his subjects.

The war with Moorish Granada did something to hold Castile together, for it encouraged a lingering respect for an acquisitive and forceful monarchy in distinction to the reiterated limitations placed on the Crown of Aragon, now no longer directly involved in the Reconquest. But even for the Castilians the war against Granada was mainly defensive, as in the reign of Alfonso XI (1312–50), and any attempt at strong government produced reactions from the magnates. Pedro I (1350–69),

[1] See genealogical table, App. II (below, p. 404).

who tried to enforce his will, was promptly faced with opposition rallied round his half-brother Henry of Trastamara. The latter, supported with greater vigour by France and Du Guesclin than Pedro was by England and the Black Prince, finally secured the throne in 1369. Pedro, surnamed 'the Cruel', had married his daughter Constanza to John of Gaunt—but the daughter of this marriage, Catalina, married Henry of Trastamara's grandson who succeeded Juan I (1379–90) as Henry III (1390–1406).

In the fifteenth century, however, both Aragon and Castile enjoyed two long and fairly peaceful reigns. Alfonso V of Aragon (1416–58) was, it is true, involved in the affairs of Castile at the start but spent the bulk of his time in the conquest of Naples and in Italian politics.[1] In Castile Juan II (1406–54) acceded as a child; his uncle Ferdinand proved an able regent before he became king of Aragon; later the reign saw the strong government of the constable Alvaro de Luna—which provoked a feudal reaction.

To both countries, however, the mid-century brought confusion. Alfonso V of Aragon was succeeded in Naples by his bastard Ferrante, in Aragon by his brother Juan II (1458–79), already king of Navarre through his wife Blanche. This led to involvement in Navarrese politics. His second marriage, to Joanna Enriquez of Castile, meant further trouble. There was prolonged Catalan resistance to the king, now no longer a native Catalan speaker; and Roussillon was lost to France. The extraordinary consequences of the marriage of Juan's son Ferdinand to Isabella of Castile (1469) could scarcely have been foreseen—if only because of the Castilian troubles under Henry IV (1454–74). Henry was called 'the Impotent'; his wife's infidelity and the interference of Juan II of Aragon led to continuous disturbances culminating in the 'deposition of Avila' in 1465 when Henry was set aside in favour of his daughter Joanna, 'La Beltraneja' (the name alludes to her reputed father, Beltran de la Cueva). A royalist reaction followed and this was aided by the death of Henry IV's brother Alfonso in 1468, for the next heir (apart from La Beltraneja) was the sister of Henry and Alfonso, Isabella. La Beltraneja was disinherited. Isabella in 1469 became the wife of the Aragonese heir Ferdinand. Isabella succeeded to Castile in 1474 and five years later Ferdinand became king of Aragon. A new chapter of history had begun.

The dynastic tangles, intensified by noble resistance to strong monarchy, which have been inadequately illustrated in the previous paragraphs, could be still further exemplified from the annals of Portugal

[1] See below, p. 180.

and Navarre. Each of these kingdoms had its links with Aragon and Castile and with the wars between England and France.

Portugal in the fourteenth century was divided by factions associated with her two powerful neighbours and by conflicts within the royal family. Alfonso IV (1325–57) quarrelled with his son Pedro, who was married to Constanza of Castile but who had as a mistress Ines de Castro. Alfonso had Ines murdered in 1355. A civil war followed, Ines's brothers and others supporting Pedro. Ines had four children by Pedro and the legitimate line might have been set aside. In fact peace was patched up. Pedro I became king (1357–67) and was followed by his legitimate son Fernando (1367–83). Fernando, however, succeeded in alienating popular support. Castilian pressure had long been feared and was increased when Fernando's daughter and heiress Beatrice was betrothed in 1382 to the son of Juan I of Castile; in the event, and later the same year, she married the Castilian king himself. There was a popular reaction in Lisbon and in 1385 Juan of Avis, Ines's son and Fernando's illegitimate half-brother, was accepted as Juan I (1385–1453). Castile was defeated (with English help) at Aljubarotta in 1385 and peace was made in 1411. The brief reign of Duarte (1433–38) was followed by the long reign of Alfonso V (1438–81). Alfonso came to the throne at the age of six and his early years were troubled by a struggle for power between his mother and his uncle Pedro. But already the first steps had been taken in the Portuguese maritime expansion associated with Juan I's younger son Prince Henry the Navigator (1394–1460), which will be mentioned later.[1] Portugal, like Aragon and Castile, had achieved a certain stability in the later fifteenth century and in Juan II (1481–95) a determined and effective ruler.

Not so Navarre. Perched on the western Pyrenees, with a culture predominantly French and institutions predominantly Spanish, Navarre was bound in the end to succumb to one or other. The French were in the end to be the losers. Ferdinand of Aragon occupied the kingdom in 1485 and in 1512 it was absorbed into Spain.

The reign of Ferdinand and Isabella saw the establishment in Aragon and Castile of sovereigns under whom the two countries made rapid strides towards more efficient government and towards the integration finally accomplished under Charles V and his successor. It is important to realize that the rule of the Catholic sovereigns was, to a large degree, the result of royal inter-marriages common in the history of the peninsula. After all Juan II of Aragon was, and regarded himself as, a Castilian

[1] See below, p. 395.

prince; the Castilian-Portuguese marriage alliance of 1382 was envisaged, at any rate on the Castilian side, as leading to a permanent union. It is equally important neither to neglect earlier progress towards stronger rule in Aragon and Castile nor to exaggerate the achievement of Ferdinand and Isabella. In both Aragon and Castile, but particularly in the latter, fitful but impressive attempts at administrative reform had earlier appeared. In his regency Ferdinand of Antequerra had demonstrated the resources on which intelligent government could depend, and Alvaro de Luna had gone far in subduing by a frontal attack the rebellious magnates. In the *cortes*, too, we see the reiteration of plans for the strengthening of the monarchy: at Madrigal in 1438 a demand for good order and economy; at Olmedo in 1445 a reference to the 'absolute royal power' (*el poder real absoluto*). And in Aragon, Castile and Portugal kings of any character were as much masters of the Church as their contemporaries in France or England. It was on these foundations that Ferdinand and Isabella were to base their government, and on the administrative machinery earlier described. But during their joint reign each kingdom was independently administered and in particular Ferdinand abstained till Isabella's death in 1504 from direct intervention in Castile; there were, after all, good precedents for an almost federal structure in the relationship between the Crown of Aragon and its lands. Such separatism mattered little compared with the length of the period when the two countries were not merely spared the disruptive activities of competing sovereigns, but enjoyed governments which positively collaborated.

The collaboration led to the reduction in the power of the nobility whose factious disobedience had hampered earlier kings. Royal lands and revenues alienated to magnates were partially resumed; private war and unauthorized castles were forbidden; above all the nobility were attracted to court and loaded with honours and honorific but innocuous posts. The *Hermandad* was revived and encouraged to combat local disorder first in Castile and then in Aragon. Ferdinand became grand master of the rich Spanish military orders which enjoyed the immunities of the two privileged groups of nobility and clergy. The Catholic sovereigns insisted to the full on their control of senior Church appointments and in 1478 Sixtus IV established an Inquisition under direct royal control From 1480 it was at work, persecuting converted Jews (*conversos*), whose Christianity was often lightly held, and turning heresy into gold for the royal coffers. All Jews were expelled in 1492.[1]

[1] See below, p. 331.

The chief symbol of the new direction of Spanish affairs was the conquest of Granada. The Moorish kingdom had dwindled by the mid-thirteenth century to a narrow band of territory in south-eastern Spain. Perpetual civil war in which rival Moorish princes allied with Castilian magnates rendered the territory weak, and it could no longer depend in an emergency on alliance with the Berber principalities of North Africa. Technically the king of Castile's suzerainty was recognized from the mid-fifteenth century and it was the defiance of this in 1481 which inaugurated the final campaigns. Even in the last stages the Moors fought with determination and the surrender of Granada itself only came in January 1492. The terms of capitulation were honourable and included the respect of Muslim religion. This was not observed and the chief ecclesiastical adviser of Isabella, Cardinal Jiménez de Cisneros, embarked on a policy of forcible conversion. The resulting Moriscos were, like the *conversos*, subjected to persecution by the Inquisition.

Granada was added to Castile. In 1492 another Castilian advance was presaged by the expedition of Columbus (below, p. 396). The exploitation of Central and South America, which in later centuries was to affect the whole power-structure of Europe, was itself a reason for Castile to become the senior partner in the united kingdoms. But this development falls into the last years of Ferdinand's reign and so outside the scope of this volume. It was, however, already evident that Catalan prosperity was in full decline so that in economic affairs Aragon by the end of the fifteenth century was becoming the junior partner.

The Hundred Years War

The countries discussed above were from time to time brought together as allies or enemies in the war between England and France whose traditional limits are 1337 and 1453. The war was more truly a 'Hundred Years War' for the French, on whose soil it was fought, than for the English. The other countries—Scotland, Burgundy, and the kingdoms of the Spanish peninsula—are involved as allies and stalking horses.

If the 'auld alliance' between France and Scotland goes back to this, the English device of protecting Aquitaine by intervention in Flanders has also a respectable ancestry. Moves along these lines preceded the early hostilities of the English under Edward III. Behind them lies the awkward question of the English king's tenure of his French fief from the king of France, the inability of sovereigns to make concessions to each other, the total absence of any effective international law, public or private. Expelled from Gascony in 1453, bereft of Calais a century later, English kings did not abandon their title as kings of France till the Treaty of Amiens in 1802, though all that then remained of conquest and inheritance was the Channel Islands.

The broad lines of the conflict, the background of which has already been described (above, p. 138), are easily summarized. Under Edward III and the Black Prince great ravaging *chevauchées* were staged in France and two pitched battles were won by the English—Crécy in 1346 and Poitiers in 1356. The French king John II was taken at Poitiers and joined in captivity David II, captured in the Scots' defeat at Neville's Cross in the same year as Crécy. The resulting treaties were determined by the possession of these two royal prisoners and, in effect, were based on ransoms. In October 1357 David II accepted a treaty at Berwick which encumbered Scotland with the payment of the large sum of 100,000 marks. After much negotiation the Treaty of Brétigny was agreed with France in 1360. By this the French king promised to pay 3,000,000 gold crowns and to grant Edward full sovereignty in Aquitaine, Poitou, Ponthieu, Calais and its neighbourhood, and certain other areas; Edward was to renounce the French throne. In the event both sides were unwilling to abandon their claims and only the ransom provisions were in part carried out. When one of the princes left as a hostage broke parole, John returned to captivity and died in London in 1364.

This first stage in the war had proved inconclusive. The English Crown had gained Calais; the French had learned that they must avoid pitched battles, that Flanders must at all costs be prevented from allying with England, and that sea power in the Channel was important. Under Bertrand du Guesclin the first lesson was applied. The combination of long-bow and dismounted knights, which had been developed under Edward I and put to such good use at Crécy and Poitiers, was simply avoided and the English *chevauchées* of the 1370s and 1380s did no real damage. Du Guesclin was also involved indirectly in the French attempt to secure naval support, for that was what was at stake in the French and English intervention in Castile. When Henry of Trastamara was finally established there as king the Castilian galleys greatly embarrassed the English; an English convoy was defeated off La Rochelle in 1372 and a few years later there were raids on the south coast of England. The English contingent which helped the Portuguese to defeat the Castilian attack at Aljubarotta (1385) fits into this pattern and so does John of Gaunt's expedition of 1386. If the duke of Lancaster regarded his claim to the throne of Castile (through his second wife, Constanza the daughter of Pedro I) solely as a way of bargaining for personal advantage, the English government saw it as a way of depriving France of naval support. After an uncertain campaign Gaunt made peace, getting for his daughter Catalina a marriage to the future Henry III and for himself a huge indemnity and pension. This was in 1388, and in the same year the Scots, in one of a series of raids, decisively beat an English force at Otterburn.

As for the control of Flanders, French anxiety to forestall the English led to the hasty marriage of the count of Flanders's daughter and heiress —for whom the English were angling—to Philip the Bold, duke of Burgundy in 1369. The consequences of this step were far-reaching. At the time, it undoubtedly frustrated the English. It also led to the French king helping to subdue the last great popular movement in the Flemish towns; under Philip van Artevelde there was a rising of Ghent, Bruges and Ypres in 1382 which was defeated by a royal army at Roosebeke. But a further consequence was an increase of Burgundian power which exacerbated political rivalry in France and this directly led to the intervention of Henry V and the second stage of the war.

Peace had been patched up by the war-weary government of Richard II when the king married Isabella, daughter of Charles VI, in 1396. But the old causes of conflict remained. Richard retained France among his titles, and the memories of past victories ensured the existence of a war party. Moreover piracy and naval skirmishes were hard to control even when the governments were prepared to act together and the irritations they produced were serious under Henry IV, leading to raids on both sides of the Channel. This, together with French support for Glyn Dwr and an Orleanist attack on Gascony, brought war in 1403 and succeeding years. But what finally precipitated a major intervention in France was the civil war there which led in 1411 to Burgundian offers of alliance and in the next year to proposals from Orleans. Only Henry IV's feebleness in his last years postponed the invasion of France.

When this occured in 1415 Henry V was allying himself to the duke of Burgundy. Until Duke Philip made his peace with the French crown in 1435 the English armies were successful in France. At Agincourt, at the very outset of the war, the English routed the French army in a battle more brutal than any of Edward III's time. Thereafter the English pursued a policy of piecemeal occupation, in sharp distinction to the raiding strategy of fourteenth-century fighting. This was a potential threat to Burgundy as well as to the Armagnac faction, but when John the Fearless was murdered in 1419 his successor had no alternative but to back the English. Normandy was occupied by the English. The

Anglo-Burgundians dominated the Seine valley, Paris and northern France, and Philip the Good controlled the senile Charles VI and his daughter Catharine. On 21 May 1420 Henry V and Charles VI agreed to the Treaty of Troyes. By it Henry V became Charles VI's heir and married his daughter; the English king was to be regent in conjunction with Burgundy. These dispositions excluded the dauphin, who was not in Burgundy's power, from the succession but they were not seriously upset by the deaths in 1422 of Henry (31 August) and Charles VI (21 October). The infant Henry VI acceded in both kingdoms, though he was of course not recognized in the centre and south of France, where Charles VII (*le roi de Bourges*) was, if not obeyed, at least regarded as the true king. Under the regency of Henry V's brother, John duke of Bedford, the English frontier was slowly pushed south. Maine was added to Normandy and in 1428 Orleans was invested by the English.

The area controlled by the English was by no means uniformly obedient. The Normans disliked the attempts made to tax them to pay for further campaigns. Burgundy was beginning the long-drawn-out negotiations for terms with Charles VII. And in the very heart of the Anglo-Burgundian region there were many men who gave their allegiance to the son of Charles VI. There were even sizeable areas which remained loyal to him, such as that in north-east France from which Joan of Arc emerged in the spring of 1429. The mystery of her origin has for long attracted speculation. For contemporaries her role as the shepherd girl with a divine mission to aid Charles VII to secure his kingdom was marginal, as we may infer from the relatively unimportant place she occupies in the annals of the time. She put fire into the relief of Orleans. She encouraged the vacillating king to march to Rheims where he was crowned with traditional rites on 17 July 1429. But she was no military leader and she was unpopular with Charles's advisers. When she was taken in May 1430 by the Burgundians Charles VII did not attempt to redeem her, and he made no effort to intervene on her behalf when she was convicted as a witch by a pro-English ecclesiastical tribunal at Rouen in the spring of 1431; she at first admitted her errors but later retracted and was burnt as a relapsed heretic on 30 May. It was only when Charles VII's cause was indisputably safe that he lent support to a process of rehabilitation. In 1456 this ended in an authorized statement of Joan's complete orthodoxy.

If Joan was not instrumental in turning the fortunes of France, the turning point came soon after her execution, and as the result of years of secret negotiation between Duke Philip and Charles VII. In 1423 and again in 1429 Burgundian terms were put before the king very similar to those ultimately accepted. But it was not until the congress at Arras in 1435 that the English were brought into the negotiations, as they had to be if Burgundy was even to pretend to an honourable ending of his alliance. As Bedford lay dying at Rouen the delegates at Arras, who had with them cardinals representing both Eugenius IV and the Council of Basle, found it impossible to come to a general agreement. But Burgundy made his peace with Charles and the fate of the English in France was sealed.

The last stages of the war were long-drawn-out. Paris was quickly abandoned by the English (April 1436) and they were forced out of the Seine valley by 1441. Soon after this further reverses strengthened the peace party in England led by Suffolk, who negotiated the betrothal of Henry VI and Margaret of Anjou in 1444. Margaret was Charles VII's niece and her marriage to Henry took place in 1445. The surrender of Maine, secretly agreed at the time of the marriage, provoked local English resistance and was only accomplished in 1448. In 1449 Normandy was attacked and French power was re-established there by the summer of 1450. Thereupon the main attack was directed at Gascony. Here trade and tradition aided the English. Driven out in 1451 by the French they returned in 1452. Only after Talbot was defeated at Castillon on 17 July 1453 was the province finally lost.

The end of the war did not bring peace. The English still held Calais and the Channel Islands. There were still noble dissidents in France, not least the duke of Burgundy. If England had in turn her civil war it was over with Edward IV. This king, Henry VII and Henry VIII knew how to play on French fears. Edward IV's invasion of July 1474, followed by the pensions and pacification of Picquigny in August, was a model way of raising money at home for the war and from France for making peace. It was not lost on the early Tudors. Above all, the army and the taxation for it which Charles VII had set in motion remained in existence against future English aggression and could be used for quite other and more adventurous ends, such as the invasion of Italy.

The prolonged if intermittent war between England and France must be viewed within the general framework of the political developments of the two countries. On the English side we must ask why Edward III found it easy to secure support from nobles and gentry for a cause not dissimilar from that for which his grandfather Edward I was unable to enlist interest. The traditional explanation is to stress the latterday chivalry of the king and the landed classes. It seems more plausible to invoke the general economic regression of the early fourteenth century which made paid service in the king's army, not to speak of the opportunities for booty and ransoms, attractive in the fourteenth century as they had not been in the thirteenth. War with rich France was certainly more popular than war with poor Scotland, though the opportunity for romantic deeds of arms was the same. The two treaties, of Brétigny and Troyes, set the tone for the aims of lesser men: in the first half of the war the chance of spoils; in the second the chance of land and administrative openings. The soldiers in Edward III's armies were men on the make, and military considerations seldom clouded their selfish intentions. Bertrand du Guesclin was captured four times and on each occasion was released by his captors for ransoms which steadily mounted. His last captor was the Black Prince at Nájera in 1367, when Pedro I was briefly restored to the Castilian throne, and Froissart shows us cupidity mastering prudence. Du Guesclin taunted the Prince with not daring to release him.

'Sir,' [the Prince replied] 'then ye think that we keep you for fear of your chivalry? Nay, think it not, for I swear by St George it is not so. Therefore pay for your ransom a hundred thousand franks and ye shall be delivered.' Sir Bertram, who desired greatly to be delivered and heard on what point he might depart, took the prince with that word and said: 'Sir, in the name of God so be it: I will pay no less.' And when the prince heard him say so he would then gladly have repented himself, and also some of his council came to him and said, 'Sir, ye have not done well, so lightly to put him to his ransom.'[1]

This game was played at every level, not only by royal dukes but 'poor knights and squires and archers whose comforts and station in society depend upon war', as Gloucester is supposed to have protested when advocating war in 1390. As for the fifteenth-century invasion, it brought perhaps fewer chances of spoils, but many a man from Bedford downwards enjoyed a good living in France and some began to acquire vested interests there. The English inhabitants of Maine, who had been expelled from there to Normandy and finally to England, in 1452 petitioned the Crown for redress.

... you had given and granted them [the petitioners] many benefices, lands, lordships, heritages and possessions ... which they have enjoyed and possessed, and have employed a great part of their goods and substance in repairing and keeping them in good condition and

[1] Froissart, *Chronicles*, trs. Berners, ed. Macaulay, p. 184; ed. Luce, VII, p. 63.

making them of value. . . . The said petitioners have abandoned all
the benefices, heritages, lordships and possessions; and a large number have given up the inheritances which they had purchased and
acquired with their own money, and such as belonged to their
wives. . . .[1]

Gascony had never absorbed many English, as settlers or officials, but
its loss lingered in memory as the abandonment of a territory rich in
lordships, bishoprics and other openings which had once been the heri-
tage of the ambitious. It is hard not to connect the ending of the English
occupation of France with the beginning of the civil war in England.
The mounting violence in England of the mid 1450s (above, p. 134) was
accounted for in this way by one shrewd contemporary observer.
Commynes in his *Mémoires* writes: 'When they were back in England,
none of them wanted to reduce his standard of living (*son estat*). There
was not enough property in the kingdom of England to satisfy everyone.'[2] And so the English civil war followed. This is not the whole truth,
but it is a part of it.

The French side of the war with England follows a different time
pattern. The civil war in France, without which there would have been
no chance for a successful English attack in 1415, came after the successful campaigns of Edward III and his commanders. That these did
terrible damage there is no doubt. The French archives contain large
numbers of documents illustrating the waste and misery occasioned by
English armies and by mercenary captains left behind at the truces. But
it is mistaken to see a continuous export of spoils from defeated France
to victorious England. Some men were prudent and prospered, like Sir
John Fastolf (d. 1459), but in a great many cases the victors were in debt
before a campaign began to French armourers and horse dealers and
afterwards rid themselves of their gains in riotous living in France. So
far as Frenchmen are concerned it is important to note how seriously the
country's troubles were viewed by the lesser gentry and by the towns.
The great magnates played their own game. But the local estates, the
few larger assemblies and the towns regularly if unwillingly contributed
to the demands of the Crown for money. The *élus* date from the crises
of 1356; the *gens d'ordonnance* and regular taxation from the military
revival of the 1440s. It used to be said that the Wars of the Roses destroyed the unruly baronage and left the field clear for Tudor monarchy.

[1] *Wars of the English in France*, ed. J. Stevenson (Rolls Ser.), II, ii, pp. 599–601.
[2] ed. Calmette, I, p. 53.

It is a much truer statement to say that the Hundred Years War in the end rendered the French kings stronger than their 'overmighty subjects'.

As royal power grew it became increasingly difficult for the grandee to find scope for his ambitions at home and one of the most interesting features of the period is the amount of foreign adventure on a large scale undertaken by magnates. England, being an island, hardly lent itself to this, yet in 1386 John of Gaunt seriously pressed his claim to the throne of Castile and in 1423 Humphrey duke of Gloucester nearly destroyed the Anglo-Burgundian alliance by trying to secure his first wife's county of Hainault. In France such enterprises were more readily organized and the ambitions of successive dukes of Orleans and Anjou involved them in marriages, intrigues and war in Italy. Yet it might be noted here that foreign intervention by the English was only profitable when undertaken by the king and that the period ends with the French crown pressing, as no mere duke could have done, its inherited rights in Milan and Naples.

Finally, in both England and France, the war brought to life national sentiments hitherto dormant. The notion of a 'natural' enemy was developed until by the fifteenth century English commanders in France could not rely on French mercenaries. Language encouraged this: Anglo-Norman ceased to be a spoken language and no longer acted as a cultural bridge; and many French and English knights were tongue-tied at the moment of capture or surrender. Francophobia in England was regularly manifested in parliament in the fourteenth century and lies behind some of the anti-clerical legislation—such as that which culminated in 1414 in the suppression of the 'alien priories' (properties in England belonging to French monasteries). Passions rose particularly high in 1435 when Burgundy was felt to have betrayed his allies. In France the English were associated with blasphemous and brutal soldiery, with exploitation and trickery. By the mid-fifteenth century the mutual hatred of the two peoples was a factor of politics no longer to be ignored, however much traditional dynasticism ruled in high level negotiations.

To a lesser degree the period and the wars contributed to national sentiment developing elsewhere—in Portugal, for example, and in Scotland. Even in Burgundy, tending to separate statehood, the pull of loyalty to France was profoundly felt and when Burgundian apologists asserted that they were also loyal Frenchmen we must not dismiss this as chicanery or an empty formula.

Crown and subject at the end of the fifteenth century

By the end of the fifteenth century European monarchs had progressed far towards greater authority and independence. The secret of their success lay in their resources becoming greater, and in this taxation had a considerable part. Parliamentary reformers in England were at one with Étienne Marcel or Simon Caboche in France in denouncing royal extravagance and urging royal economy. The remedy adopted by Edward IV, Henry VII and the Catholic sovereigns was the same: a wealthy Crown and up-to-date management of royal capital and income. The pervasive influence of national loyalty, to which reference has just been made, greatly aided the kings. Just as money was forthcoming in fourteenth-century England for the war against France, so it was forthcoming in the fifteenth century to enable the French monarchy to expel the English. A greater panoply and public display characterized fifteenth-century princes, canalizing patriotic sentiment towards the Crown and enlisting artists and men of letters in the general demonstrations of loyalty.

The king, with his bodyguard, his courtiers and his protocol, was now both grander and more remote than he had been in the thirteenth century. The older offices of state remained, sometimes (as with the chancellor in France) with their powers little diminished. But a new race of public servants, secretaries and ambassadors, had appeared—the discreet and self-effacing instruments of princely authority, masters in the techniques of management, adept in pressing the legal and traditional powers of the Crown, whose rewards were only in the end promotion and public esteem but who meanwhile enjoyed the satisfactions of power.

The Crown in western Europe by the end of the period was nevertheless far from having acquired absolute authority. Government in England, France or Spain remained essentially local and uncentralized. The grandee was still enormously powerful in his locality and local royal officers, sheriffs or *élus*, moved warily in dealing with a great man. French kings created appanages even in the sixteenth century and the English were to experience a duke of Northumberland and an earl of Leicester who were every bit as rich and politically irresponsible as a fifteenth-century Gloucester or Alençon.

Nor had the progress of monarchy been consistently along the same path. Differences are especially notable in the sphere of representative institutions. The Estates in France had never really become General.

In the fourteenth century, and in the fifteenth and sixteenth, French kings and their ministers preferred to consult smaller, more manageable groups—local estates, bodies of important men, or individual towns and magnates. In England the happy alliance of Crown and parliament was to last for most of the sixteenth century, for parliament proved a willing ally of kings not least, perhaps, because it was normally neglected by the great landowners and became the forum for the gentry who had more to gain from a strong and ambitious monarchy. In the kingdoms of Spain the precocious *cortes* were already losing their real vitality by the end of the fifteenth century; Ferdinand and Isabella summoned no meeting in Castile between 1483 and 1497.

Perhaps the surest indication of a trend towards a country unified under a king was the emergence of recognizable capital cities.[1] This could be illustrated by the growth of Lisbon or—in a much less impressive way—by Edinburgh. The principal examples are, however, Paris and London. Paris had a population of some 70,000[2] in the fifteenth century and was much bigger than London with about 40,000. But each was the seat of government and each had begun to act like a magnet on social, linguistic and cultural life. This was perhaps truer of Paris than of London, for at the former a university was to be found which still had greater renown than any other centre of learning in Europe. At London, on the other hand, if there was no university there were the Inns of Court to which young men were now sometimes coming who had no inclination for the law as a profession. The poets who celebrated Paris and London, the clergy and gentry who gathered there for business and pleasure, the great men who began to build their *hôtels* in the *Marais* beside the Seine or on the Strand beside the Thames, were the unconscious architects of unity under the king.

[1] 'Capital' in this sense seems to be a seventeenth-century word in the vernacular.
[2] The traditional 200,000 has been shown to be mistaken.

VII

Italians and Italy

A realization of national identity was growing in France, England, Scotland and Spain as we have seen in the previous chapter. So it was in Italy as well, but in very different conditions. Geographically the peninsula had a unity imposed by the Alps and the Mediterranean, though the Apennine ranges divided and subdivided it. More serious occasions for division lay in the past history of Italy. The Romans had more or less controlled all the land but after the barbarian invasions there was

BIBLIOGRAPHY. The relevant chapters in *Cambridge Medieval History* VII and VIII are accompanied by full bibliographies. Of Italian manuals the best are the old work of C. Cipolla, *Storia delle signorie italiane dal 1313 al 1529* (Milan, 1881) and the new works of L. Simeoni, *Le signorie* (Milan, 1950) and N. Valeri, *L'Italia nell' età dei principati dal 1343 al 1516* (Verona, 1950). Sismondi's *Republics*, ed. W. Boulting (London, n.d.) is useful still. A valuable general survey of 'The City State in Late-Medieval Italy' by P. J. Jones is in *Trans. Roy. Hist. Soc.*, 5 ser., 15 (1965). There is an enormous literature on regional history of which the following is a selection of accessible books mainly in English. Venice: P. Molmenti, *Venice—The Middle Ages*, 2 vols. (London, 1906). Milan: D. M. Bueno de Mesquita, *Giangaleazzo Visconti* (Cambridge, 1941); C. M. Ady, *Milan under the Sforza* (London, 1907). Pisa: D. Herlihy, *Pisa in the Early Renaissance* (New Haven, 1958). Florence: F. Schevill, *History of Florence* (New York, 1936); R. Caggese and G. A. Brucker, as above, p. 79; C. S. Gutkind, *Cosimo de' Medici* (Oxford, 1938); N. Rubinstein, *The Government of Florence under the Medici* (London, 1966). Rome and the Papal States: F. Gregorovius, *History of the City of Rome in the Middle Ages*, vols. vi–vii, pt. I (London, 1898–1900); P. Partner, *Papal State under Martin V* (London, 1958). Naples: E. Léonard, *Les Angevins de Naples* (Paris, 1954); R. Caggese, *Roberto d'Angiò*, 2 vols. (Florence, 1921–30). A. J. Ryder, 'Evolution of imperial government in Naples under Alfonso V', in *Europe in the Late Middle Ages* (below, p. 399). The following works are also useful: F. Ercole, *Dal comune al principato* (Florence, 1929); P. Pieri, *Il Rinascimento e la crisi militare italiana* (Turin, 1952); G. Mattingly, *Renaissance Diplomacy* (London, 1955). See also bibliographies to chapter IV (works on Italian towns), and to chapter XI (p. 267, works by Pastor and Creighton) and the books referring to Italy in bibliographies to chapters XIII and XIV (pp. 333, 359).

no power dominant for longer than a few decades. At the end of the period of migrations we find the Latinized people of the peninsula sharing their land with Lombards in north and centre, Greeks and Moors in Sicily and the south. At Rome was the headquarters of the western Church, the only solid link with antiquity and fitfully conscious of its mission to organize and direct Christian activity at large. After the intervention of Charlemagne the northern half of the peninsula was part of the Empire, and the papacy became aware of its secular mission: to prevent the German emperor securing effective power in Italy. The price of the popes' success was a heavy one—the absence of any central authority in north and central Italy, the development of a wide band of territory from the Adriatic to the Tyrrhenian Sea as a State of the Church, and the recognition of a kingdom south of Rome—Naples and Sicily which had been conquered by the Normans—held in theory as a fief from the pope.

The thirteenth century witnessed the final stages of this development. The emperors of the Hohenstauffen line in fact became the kings of Naples. To evict them the popes invoked the Angevins who succeeded in destroying the power of Frederick II and his descendants. Their rule was, however, unpopular and Sicily rose in rebellion (1282). This, the Sicilian Vespers, resulted in the establishment there of the Aragonese, a situation recognized by the treaty of Caltabellotta in 1302. In the previous century the history of Lombardy, Tuscany and Emilia largely wrote itself and, freed of the interference of the emperor, a string of small independent states covered north Italy. Though the survival of big non-urban lordships (like those of the Malaspina) should not be forgotten, the states were nearly all urban in their origin and for three or four decades at the end of the thirteenth century we have the high watermark of the 'communal' movement in Italy. But already before 1300 many towns had fallen under *signori*, lords different from those found north of the Alps in that, whether they were nobles or burgesses, they had a civic background. Some few communes survived, but they too were greedy for more territory and swallowed up their neighbours. Those that did survive in independence had been given wealth and influence by the commercial boom of the thirteenth century. The early medieval commercial centres had been mainly in the south. Now Italian trade throve at Pisa, Genoa and Venice, and inland at Siena, Florence and Milan.

Soon after 1300 the popes and the emperors ceased to attempt any general influence over Italian affairs. In the fourteenth and fifteenth centuries the emperors came to accept that Italy was merely a place where they could sell titles and privileges. Henry VII, whom Dante saw as the redeemer of Italy, staged a sterile campaign in 1310–13; Lewis IV was in Italy from 1327 to 1330. Thereafter emperors came, but only to barter their shoddy diplomas for solid cash and to obtain the papal coronation without which they were styled merely kings of the Romans. Nor were popes in a position to take much advantage from this imperial withdrawal. In 1305 a Frenchman was elected as Clement V. In 1309 he set up his curia at Avignon and there the papacy remained almost without a break till 1376. In 1378 occurred the Schism which was to make the 'Roman' pope a cypher until 1417.[1] And when the Schism was over it took time for the re-established papacy to recover authority in the Papal States and a certain diplomatic significance in Italy.

The existence of two competing and universal powers, papacy and empire, was nevertheless a feature of peninsular life that could still not be ignored. A régime, however established, always secured legitimization from pope or emperor by acquiring delegated authority from one of them. This is true of the urban communes and tyrannies and, in a sense, it is equally true of the kingdom of Sicily, for the popes were the feudal suzerains of the ruler at Naples. The existence of *de facto* independence and *de jure* acceptance by Roman pope or German emperor produced a theoretical problem which was resolved, as has been pointed out,[2] by the civilian lawyers who elaborated a doctrine of sovereignty based on the notion of a *civitas* being *sibi princeps*. It was not the least of the services performed at this time by the lawyers who were prominent in all branches of Italian administration, clerical and lay, tyrannical and communal.

For convenience the Italian scene may be considered in four regions: the north, Tuscany, the Papal States, and the south (Naples and 'Trinacria', as the island of Sicily was sometimes officially called).

North Italy: Milan, Genoa, Venice

The north contained very disparate elements. On the foothills of the Alps lay a number of rugged principalities. In the west these were heavily involved in earlier French dynasticism and Savoy was outstandingly the most important. Rather like Navarre on the Pyrenees, Savoy straddled the mountains, her feudal nobility retaining for long a way of life which seemed French to Italians further south. The small com-

[1] Below, p. 279. [2] Above, p. 85.

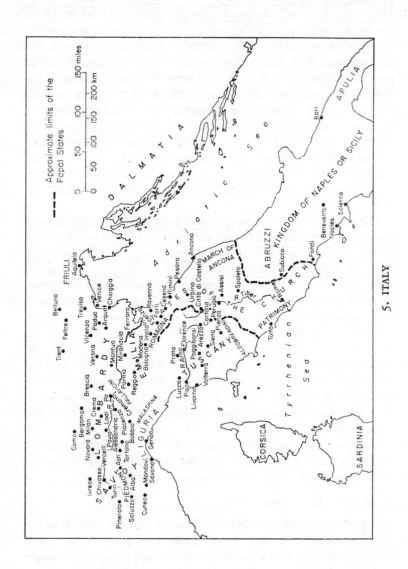

5. ITALY

munes and lordships at the eastern end of the mountains were in the orbit of the German dukes of Austria and counts of Gorizia. In the centre of the plain of the Po Milan was already a powerful city, where nobles and rich merchants struggled for supremacy. From this struggle the family of Visconti emerged supreme under Archbishop Ottone. Before he died in 1295 the archbishop had secured the election of his nephew Matteo as 'captain of the people', and Matteo enjoyed this magistracy for ever longer periods. The rival family of della Torre held power from 1302 to 1310, but they did not reverse the trend towards tyranny, which was intensified when Matteo was re-established in 1311 and under the long line of his Visconti successors.[1] The emergence of Visconti tyranny is a classical example of a process found in many other towns. Factions rallied round a family and its chief who was elected, by 'the people', to public office. The office's duration was extended from a year to five years, to life; the office's powers were enlarged. The 'captain of the people' or 'captain of the merchants' secured a legal 'vicariate'. Matteo Visconti, for example, became Imperial Vicar in 1294 and this was confirmed in 1299. The 'lord' now tried to secure his succession and entered into marriage alliances with the families of other

[1] Visconti and Sforza rulers of Milan:

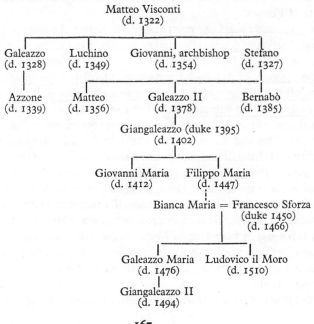

167

'lords'. A principate was thus formed and the process could be illustrated from the della Scala family at Verona, the Carrara family at Padua and many others.

Equally typical of the successful 'states' was the way in which the Visconti extended their dominion in Lombardy. Communes, whether or not under tyrants, often tried to secure the benevolent neutrality of a great neighbour by choosing him as their lord, intending him to be the guarantor of their liberties. But when the lord was a Visconti there was a real danger that the submission of the client town would lead to it positive absorption. By voluntary submission, by intrigue, by marriage, and occasionally by conquest, Visconti controls were steadily extended. When Archbishop Giovanni Visconti died in 1354 the family were masters of Piacenza, Parma, Bologna, Lodi and Bobbio; Cremona, Crema, Brescia, and Bergamo; Como, Novara, Vercelli, Asti, Tortona, and Alessandria. The towns are listed in three sections for they fell in this way to the three nephews of the archbishop. Soon, however, the eldest, Matteo, died and the brothers Bernabò and Galeazzo shared power. When Galeazzo died in 1378 his son Giangaleazzo murdered Bernabò and ruled an undivided territory (1385). In 1395 he purchased the title of duke. Here again one could illustrate the extension of lordship in the case of other tyrannies, such as the Gonzaga of Mantua and the Este of Ferrara.

On the other hand one must exaggerate neither the autocracy nor the centralization of fourteenth-century tyrants. Even under Giangaleazzo, who certainly had grander designs than earlier members of his family, a vast amount of day-to-day power, of a local and non-political kind, was left in the hands of the traditional magistrates and civic councils in Milan and the subject towns. Even at the end of his life, when he ruled not only most of the territories mentioned above but Vicenza, Verona, Pisa and Siena as well, the 'state' was pretty rudimentary. Extensive territorial immunities and a restive feudality (if that word can be used in the north Italian context) make nonsense of any map which tries to show the limits of Giangaleazzo's power inside neatly hatched borders. Nor was Giangaleazzo himself concerned to secure an undivided succession. He died in 1402, bequeathing his vast territories to his two sons; in 1447 Filippo Maria Visconti died making no arrangements for the succession at all—presumably because his only descendant was a bastard daughter, Bianca, married to the *condottiere* general, Francesco Sforza.

Yet when this same Sforza became in 1450 duke of Milan there was much to build on. The cry of 'liberty' which went up in Milan and other Visconti towns in 1447 had been in vain; no profound communal impulse was left in Lombardy. And in Visconti institutions the Sforza dukes had a pattern of government they could develop: a conciliar administration for high policy, for justice, for subject territories, with salaried counsellors and secretaries; a chancery staffed by expert administrators, in which the ubiquitous lawyers predominated; and a treasury or camera to secure and account for the cash. All of this the Sforza encouraged and in particular the financial and military machinery was elaborated. Of his 130 captains of castles Francesco Sforza wrote in 1452, 'on them the safety of our state depends'. The great *castello* built at Milan is another sign of this realistic attitude. Moreover under Francesco and his successors local government came to be increasingly supervised by the duke. The 'Council of 900' at Milan met rarely and merely rubber-stamped ducal policy; the many local commissions to supervise roads and buildings, provisions, local finance, absorbed a good deal of citizen energy, but these bodies were manned by persons favoured by the duke, who recruited into his service (as secretaries, lawyers and agents of all kinds) men of ability as well as men of substance. Only the *podestà*, the senior judge, was in some sense a reminder of older days of liberty, for he was always a 'foreign' jurist, and often a Florentine. Outside Milan itself the duke's power in the subject towns was represented by a lieutenant with full political powers.

The Visconti-Sforza dukes thus represented a tradition of government which was not strikingly dissimilar from that found in northern Europe and which reminds one in particular of contemporary Burgundy. Yet if the Milanese courtier, Milanese court ceremonial and opportunities for advancement in the service of the duke of Milan, all suggest this parallel, the element of genuine allegiance was lacking. The Visconti lands disintegrated on the death of Giangaleazzo in 1402 and again on the death of Filippo Maria in 1447. Likewise they were to fall asunder when Lodovico il Moro, who was the real master of the duchy from 1480, was deposed by the French in 1500. Nor was the name Sforza a sufficient rallying cry in 1512 or 1521. The bloodstained plain of Lombardy had witnessed the rise of a prince, but it had failed to generate a dynasty. Rule was to pass to the Habsburgs.

Neighbouring territories were constantly threatened by the advances of the Visconti dukes and they survived only by vigilance, by luck, or by outside support. Savoy and Piedmont, whose outlying territories had succumbed to Visconti pressure in the mid-fourteenth century, gradually emerged under Amedeo VI (d. 1383) and Amedeo VII (d. 1391) as a coherent block of lands. Under the long and skilful reign of Amedeo VIII (1391–1451) the country developed rapidly into what was in effect a small kingdom on the northern pattern. Amedeo VIII became the first duke in 1416 and his acceptance of the papal dignity from the Fathers of Basle (1439) was perhaps influenced by his desire to control Geneva through its bishop. Savoy was now firmly an Italian state, though French ambitions in Italy were to make its role dangerous for centuries.

Genoa had a less happy fate. Popular government survived there throughout the fourteenth and fifteenth centuries, but at a terrible cost in political instability, foreign domination, and long periods of vicious civil war. Early in the fourteenth century the Genoese introduced the office of doge in imitation of Venice, a rival in the east Mediterranean throughout the period (below, p. 172). But the constitutional change brought no internal peace: there were five doges in July, August and September 1393 and further periods almost as disturbed followed in 1413–21 and 1435. Overseas expansion and the government of the town itself had fallen into the hands of rival cliques of merchants, and the related lords of the surrounding hills took an active part in Genoese politics and commerce. Thus was provided a happy hunting ground for outsiders who wished to establish themselves on the Ligurian coast. Giovanni Visconti forced his lordship on the city in 1353 and held it until 1356; in 1396 the city surrendered to France, freeing itself in 1409 only to fall into the hands of Teodoro di Montoferrato. In 1421 Filippo Maria Visconti became lord; in 1458 it was the turn of the French; in 1464 Sforza got the overlordship from France and, though a successful rebellion occurred in 1478, in 1487 the city was again under Milan. These reversals of fortune continued with the French wars in Italy. They go far to explain why Genoa was so backward in art and letters in the *quattrocento*; but we should remember that some individual Genoese throve in the disturbed conditions and that the Bank of St George was to become by the early sixteenth century one of the great financial powers of the Mediterranean world.

The violence and inconsistency of Genoese politics stand in sharp contrast with the monumental solidity of Venice. There were, certainly, undercurrents in Venetian history which tend to be forgotten: the mysterious conspiracy of the doge Marin Falier in 1354, which was swiftly suppressed; the tendency to strong, almost princely, government under Michele Steno (1400–13), Tommaso Mocenigo (1414–23) and Francesco Foscari (1423–57). Likewise there are odd hesitations and abrupt changes of policy which should not be overlooked. At the start of the fourteenth century an attempt was made at mainland expansion by occupying Ferrara (1308–11)—but the resolute action of the Church and the fear of other Lombard lords that Venice would dominate the mouth of the Po, led to a sharp reaction; the republic of St Mark seemed (1313) to have learned for ever the lesson that she must restrict her expansion to the Gulf, the Adriatic and the Near East. In 1405 Padua, Vicenza and Verona were taken and then in 1425 the Republic, warned by the previous adventures of the Visconti under Giangaleazzo, met the threat of Filippo Maria with the Florentine alliance and a complete reversal of previous policy. From then onwards the Venetians were committed to expansion on *terra ferma*.

Something has been said of the constitution at Venice.[1] The doge, chosen for life by an elaborate alternation of lot and election, was in theory the head of the government of the 'nobles' with whom alone political power lay. But at each election of a doge his real powers were curtailed, his ceremonial grandeur was increased. Real authority lay in the hands of a committee of ten, the *Dieci*, a permanent part of the government after 1335. In the later fifteenth century a further display of prudence was the habit of electing only elderly and mediocre men as doges. Social and political tensions were not entirely avoided; in particular there were difficulties, not so much between the old nobles and those recently elevated, as between the rich families and the many impoverished aristocrats. But as the mainland expansion gained momentum there were plenty of outlets, both administrative and territorial, for ambitious men—outlets which compensated for the decline in Venetian overseas power. The areas of the north of Italy which came under Venetian control were in general content with their new masters. Here again the details of local government were usually left in the hands of the old committees and officials, though a Venetian *podestà*, captain and treasurer effectively secured the ultimate authority of the Republic. These cities were taxed heavily; their lands were confiscated and freely sold to Venetian magnates; but there was a surprising absence of resistance to this Venetian control.

The fortunes of the maritime republics of Genoa and Venice were closely related, and both were affected by the fluctuations in commerce and politics in the Levant. The Palaeologi came to power in 1261, with the help of the Genoese who were rewarded by privileges at Constantinople. The Venetians had, however, made their peace with the

[1] Above, p. 120.

Greek government by the end of the thirteenth century. The trade of the fourteenth century was on a smaller scale than it had been, and in the Levant the aggressions of the Ottoman Turk further reduced mercantile opportunities. The result was fierce competition between Genoa and Venice. Two great wars had taken place in the thirteenth century (1261–70, 1294–99) and these continued in the fourteenth. There was prolonged conflict from 1351 to 1355 but the supreme crisis came in the 'War of Chioggia', 1377–81, so called because the Genoese brilliantly attacked the Lagoon itself in 1379 and were only narrowly defeated by the patriotic energy of the Venetians. In fact this war and the others were essentially maritime, fought over the trade routes of the eastern Mediterranean. Venice was by no means universally successful, but she recovered from her defeats more rapidly than her rival; she made the construction of a war fleet a state responsibility;[1] and she had a strong government and a united people. These resources continued to stand her in good stead when she faced in the fifteenth century the might of Ottoman power and the jealousy of her Italian neighbours.

In the western Mediterranean Genoa clashed with the Catalan subjects of the Crown of Aragon, not only in trade but for control of the island of Sardinia. This rivalry was turned into a more purely Italian issue when Alfonso V of Aragon became king of Naples.[2] Sardinia was lost; but Corsica remained under Genoese tutelage.

Tuscany

Machiavelli stated that republican government was the very lifeblood of Tuscany and the history of the later Middle Ages certainly suggests that communal organization was stronger than in the plains of Lombardy. Even at the end of the fifteenth century we find independent republics at Pisa, Lucca, Siena and Florence; this tradition was still lively in the early sixteenth century and Lucca was to survive as a curious oligarchic republic until the Napoleonic period. Yet almost from the start of the fourteenth century there are hints of the changes which were ultimately to extinguish liberty at Pisa, Siena and Florence. In the economic regression wealth tended to be concentrated in the hands of fewer families. Political survival of prominent families could often only be secured by destroying or exiling their competitors. The military effort to maintain independence or to enlarge the contado offered temptations to adventurers.

Pisa had competed for maritime supremacy against Genoa in the

[1] See below, p. 385. [2] Below, p. 180.

thirteenth century and had lost in the race, partly because of the scourge of malaria. In the fourteenth century the hungry eyes of Florence and of Visconti Milan were cast on her both as a port and as a strategic town at the mouth of the Arno. This competition for control over a town in full economic decline was facilitated by the violent factions within Pisa. These led first to a series of tyrants in the fourteenth century and then to the submission of the town in 1398 to Giangaleazzo Visconti. The control over Pisa by Florence's most feared enemy collapsed with his death in 1402 but it intensified the Florentine desire to occupy the town. There followed the long war and the Florentine capture of Pisa in October 1406. A century of ruinous taxes and a cruel indifference to Pisan interests still further reduced the prosperity of the city, but it did not quench Pisan resolution to be free of foreign domination. The French invasion gave the opportunity. From 1494 to 1509 Pisa was uneasily protected by France, before once again falling under Florentine control—a control which now, however, was less rigorous. Florence herself was abandoning her aggressive aims in Italy.

Florence had always coveted Lucca and in retrospect it seems curious that the city should have escaped, for her resources were small compared with those of her powerful neighbour. All the signs at the start of the fourteenth century were that Lucca was as vulnerable as any other town. From 1316 to 1328 she had a local tyrant, Castruccio Castracani, later to be given a kind of ideal biography by Machiavelli. He exemplified another route to power, the control of a city's armed forces, in his case against Florence; this was legitimized by popular 'election' and an imperial vicariate. Lucca had then a series of remoter 'lords'—protectors from afar like Lewis of Bavaria. For a quarter of a century Pisa dominated Lucca (1342–68). Thereafter there was a long period of more genuine independence and constitutional government in which there came to the fore the Guinigi family, whose members were forced to aggressive leadership to save themselves from rivals. In 1400 Paolo Guinigi became lord of the town. Both the Albizzi and Cosimo de' Medici made unsuccessful attempts to take Lucca yet, although Guinigi power was destroyed in the process, Lucca survived—her territories somewhat reduced, her government in the hands of oligarchs, but technically free and republican.

Siena, bigger than Pisa and Lucca, was no less turbulent. Government in the early fourteenth century was in the hands of the rich merchants, who mainly constituted the Nine, the magistrates (elected for two months at a time) who managed the city. Legally many of the greater nobles were excluded from high office; in practice a few were found in the Nine, along with some lesser nobles, and there seems not to have been so sharp a functional or political antithesis between the two groups as used to be thought. The members of the lesser guilds, more or less excluded previously, in 1368 established a new régime and, after an irruption by woollen workers in 1371, an alliance was established in 1385 between all the main non-noble groups. This survived, in ever more oligarchic form, until the end of the fifteenth century. Hostility to the *gentiluomini*, the magnates, gradually declined; a few were admitted to office (not least during the pontificate of the Sienese Pius II) and this is hardly to be wondered at; since hereditary principles were steadily increasing as a source of political power, the tensions between the 'orders' of an earlier day becoming milder. For all important men, whatever their social party, land was the main source of wealth in *quattrocento* Siena.[1] It was a sign of the times that in 1497 the city came under the control of Pandolfo Petrucci and experienced a 'tyranny' for the next fifteen years.

Florence rightly takes pride of place among the Tuscan communes. The great wealth of her merchant and banking families, which was reflected in a population probably numbering nearly 90,000 at the end of the thirteenth century, had enabled this group, roughly corresponding to the members of the greater guilds, to monopolize power after 1292, though ousted 'Ghibelline' nobles, sadly divided into factions, remained a constant danger to the patricians and had a supreme poet in Dante. Their chances were greatest at the moment of crisis when the government (*signoria*) was put in the hands of Walter de Brienne, titular duke of Athens, in 1342. The failure of the *grandi* was accompanied by so much expense and incompetence that it cured Florentines of seeking a solution in this way; when a one-man *signoria* did emerge with the Medici in the fifteenth century, it was a more gradual and, one might say, a more natural process, for it gave power to the greatest of the surviving patrician families.

The way to the leadership of the Medici was prepared by social disturbances found also in other industrialized areas in the fourteenth century.[2] Proletarian discontents were voiced in 1345 under Ciuto Brandino, but the Black Death of 1348 temporarily stilled the movement. In 1378 a new upheaval occurred, known as the revolt of the

---

[1] See David L. Hicks in *Comparative Studies in Society and History*, 2 (1960), pp. 412–20, and William M. Bowsky in *Speculum*, 37 (1962), pp. 368–81.
[2] Above, pp. 118–19.

Ciompi, a name for the lowest class of day labourers. The immediate result was the creation of three new guilds, for the weavers, dyers and the Ciompi; and a sharing of power between these and the artisan guilds. Such a government was incapable of organizing the conditions necessary for the economic life of the city and within three years the oligarchs were back in control. The struggle between the rival families was now fiercer; the penalty of exile and confiscation was ruthlessly used by the dominant clique to ruin its rivals; the Alberti were expelled by the Albizzi who in 1433 banished Cosimo de' Medici; and Cosimo's return in 1434 was prepared for by the expulsion of Rinaldo degli Albizzi and his associates.

Florence had meanwhile gone through the ordeal of a massive Visconti threat, which was lessened, but only temporarily, by the death of Giangaleazzo in 1402; and she had, at great cost, succeeded in acquiring Pisa in 1406. Wars such as these put a great strain on republican machinery, for they were expensive, involved negotiations with mercenary captains, and provoked endless mutual suspicions in the ruling faction. The crisis paid cultural dividends,[1] but to avoid such a situation became Cosimo's aim; and to govern without subverting the republican forms. In many ways he succeeded remarkably well. The puzzled Florentines found themselves in virtual alliance with their former enemy, the duke of Milan, and later writers such as Francesco Guicciardini looked back to Cosimo's day as an enviable time of successful republicanism. The realities were not so rosy. The celebrated graded income tax (*catasto*) which Cosimo and his supporters took over from the previous government may sometimes have been used to damage potential enemies in Florence, as forced loans certainly were,[2] and there is no doubt that indebtedness to Cosimo and his bank kept many a family in leading-strings. And the *pater patriae*, as the grateful commune termed him, was capable of savage proscriptions of enemies, such as those of 1458.

Cosimo had been *primus inter pares* for so long that the vested interests he had created made it inevitable that leadership should continue in his family on his death in 1464, and ensured that it should pass to his grandson, despite the lamentable ill-judgment and weakness of Piero (1464–69). With Lorenzo 'the Magnificent' we enter on a new phase, more expressly parallel with the principalities found elsewhere in Italy.

[1] Below, p. 349.
[2] Lauro Martines, *Social World of the Florentine Humanists 1390–1460* (Princeton and London, 1963), pp. 99–104.

He did not claim princely recognition inside Florence but he was accorded it by other powers and even in his domestic policy embarked on innovations tending to autocracy. The *parte Guelfa* was abolished and with it one of the great symbols of earlier bourgeois political aims; in 1490 a council of seventeen bore striking resemblances to the machinery of Sforza government, while in these later years Lorenzo was freely nominating to magistracies. Above all, while Cosimo had always regarded his counting-house as the centre of his affairs and the mercantile interests of the Medici bank[1] as the source of his power, Lorenzo neglected business to play politics on a grand scale: he and others of his family married into noble families and, like other Italian princes, he sought to make the Medici powerful in the Church; his son and his nephew both became cardinals. His policy may be justified. Though it led to the disastrous years which followed his death in 1492 at the age of forty-three, it made the Medici a great Italian, as opposed to a respected Florentine, family. Medici popes in the next century were to secure the government of the city for the family and this time, as dukes of Tuscany, the supremacy was both princely and permanent.[2]

---

[1] Below, p. 376.

[2] The principal members of the Medici family were:

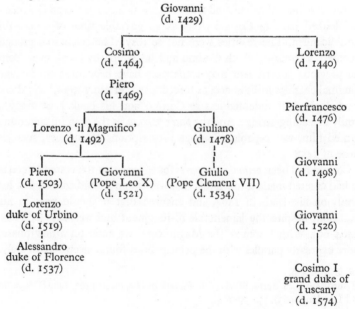

The States of the Church and Rome

Even before the popes took up their residence at Avignon disruptive tendencies were at work in the vast territories which formed the feudal principality of the Vicar of Christ. In Emilia and Romagna communes experienced republican moments and longer periods of tyranny. In the area nearer to Rome the great families of the City sought to entrench themselves in landed power. Already popes had used their office, as Boniface VIII did, to make territorial gains for their families, thus anticipating the excesses of the late fifteenth century. These trends were encouraged by the absence of the popes at Avignon, by the Schism and by the emergence of ambitious rulers in Milan and Naples, for whom the domains of the Church were tempting prizes. They were tempting for several reasons: their divisions rendered it easy to find an excuse for intervention; they were a source of military manpower; they offered a way of moving up and down the peninsula without confronting the forces of the Tuscan communes; and they bred no major and permanently powerful families.

This last was hardly due to the popes of the fourteenth century, though the French pontiffs were desperately anxious to maintain their rights in Italy. In this they had some slight success, particularly as a result of the legateships of the noble Castilian, Cardinal Gil Albornoz (1353–65). But the money extracted (often by French clerks) from the States of the Church was consumed in paying for mercenaries to control it and foreign troops gave much offence. Florence in 1378 could pose as the defender of Italian values in her attempt to rally resistance to the pope. And even a strong lieutenant like Albornoz had to recognize the facts of the case. His famous Constitutions (1357) in fact allowed many towns to run their own affairs, and a big town like Bologna was only different from other independent communes in having to accept the residual lordship of a distant master. For most of the fourteenth and fifteenth centuries papal authority mainly consisted in accepting the communal magistracy and local dynasties of the regions under Rome.

These dynasties produced some impressive leaders but no one who attempted to found a large principality at the expense of the pope. The Malatesta family, established in many towns of the Romagna and the March of Ancona, were important as allies and *condottieri* of greater powers, but made no attempt to organize a state, hostile as they were in general to the popes, not least in the person of Sigismondo Pandolfo Malatesta (d. 1468) at Rimini. Equally content with quick profits and limited territories were the Montefeltro family, whose little hill-top capital at Urbino was one of the centres of fifteenth-century art and literature. Bologna, rent by family feuds, enjoyed a virtual autonomy and saw the emergence of indigenous *signori* like many a commune in Lombardy. In 1401 lordship was seized by the Bentivogli; during the fifteenth century it suited both Milan and Florence to support the Bentivogli and thus ensure a kind of buffer state. Further north still, Ferrara, which was technically papal territory, lay under the lordship of the Este family; by the end of the fifteenth century the duchy, as it became in 1471, was virtually detached from the Papal States. It is, indeed, impossible in the fifteenth century to trace in a meaningful way the northern limits of the pope's domains.

Rome itself suffered terribly during the Avignon period and the ensuing Schism. The town, consisting of detached settlements—notably round St Peter's, near the Capitol, at the Lateran—was not of commercial importance and lacked a thriving bourgeoisie. It depended for its prosperity on the presence of a host of administrators, lawyers and visiting clergy with business at the curia; and on the throngs of pilgrims who came to the Thresholds of the Apostles and who, especially in a year of jubilee, visited the celebrated shrines in tens of thousands.

The Avignon popes continued to govern the city but their absence weakened the traditional power of the Roman nobility and a popular movement developed, hostile to both pope and magnates. Of this the most celebrated representative was Cola di Rienzo whose imagination had been fired by antiquarian speculation and by the laureation of Petrarch on the Capitol in 1341. Eloquent and dramatic, Cola was chosen as tribune in May 1347, the pope soon recognizing him as rector of the City while Italy at large followed events with sceptical interest. The nobles still resisted him bitterly, the pope feared for his authority and the impending jubilee of 1350 made Romans sensitive to the wishes of their spiritual lord, for the expected pilgrims would relieve the city's chronic poverty. By the end of December 1347 Cola was in flight. He returned in 1353 to help Albornoz in the recovery of papal authority but his harsh government provoked even the classes he had earlier depended on and he was brutally killed in 1354 while trying to escape.

For a century Rome suffered neglect and disturbances, victim of great families like the Colonna and Orsini and of the neighbouring king of Naples. Even after the Schism the mob could drive away Pope Eugenius IV in 1434 and it was not until the pontificate of Nicholas V that something like order returned. At this stage, however, the popes were bent on satisfying family aggrandizement in and around the city. Popular government thus became a thing of the past; the Capitol, where the magistrates resided, became a papal palace, less important than the Vatican and the Lateran. But the Renaissance popes resided in the city; they and their cardinal courtiers built lavishly and Rome became, what it had not been for centuries, one of the great Italian towns in amenities and size.

Naples and Sicily

The only old-established monarchical state in Italy was appropriately called '*il Regno*'. The Angevin kings who ruled in Naples in the fourteenth century were, however, in practice not much more influential than the communes and tyrants of the centre and the north. The reasons for this were: the Aragonese kingdom in Sicily, which was regarded as a perpetual menace; the unbridled nobility, whose opportunities for self-interested action were greater than in other feudal areas of Europe; and the weak, impoverished but numerous towns. Of these last only Naples itself was commercially important and it was disturbed by rivalry between bourgeoisie and minor nobility. The only royal machinery which was fostered was financial and even here revenues were squandered and anticipated, the domain of the Crown dispersed.

Robert of Anjou (d. 1343) had every inducement to neglect his inheritance save as a source of cash. His family connections[1] involved him in

[1] The following is a very simplified table showing some of the descendants of Charles of Anjou and illustrating the succession to the kingdom of Naples:

Charles II, king of Naples (d. 1309)

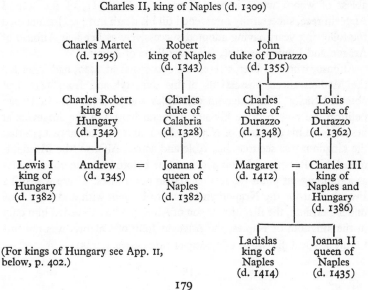

(For kings of Hungary see App. II, below, p. 402.)

Charles Martel (d. 1295)	Robert king of Naples (d. 1343)	John duke of Durazzo (d. 1355)	
Charles Robert king of Hungary (d. 1342)	Charles duke of Calabria (d. 1328)	Charles duke of Durazzo (d. 1348)	Louis duke of Durazzo (d. 1362)
Lewis I king of Hungary (d. 1382) / Andrew (d. 1345)	= Joanna I queen of Naples (d. 1382)	Margaret (d. 1412) =	Charles III king of Naples and Hungary (d. 1386)
		Ladislas king of Naples (d. 1414)	Joanna II queen of Naples (d. 1435)

Provençal, Balkan and Adriatic affairs; his French origin made him the natural ally of the French popes in Rome and in the rest of Italy. All of this led the king to play an ostentatious part in general Italian affairs but there was nothing save further impoverishment to show for it, and he was equally unsuccessful in his repeated campaigns against Sicily. At his death, when his granddaughter Joanna succeeded him, her right was disputed both by the Hungarian Angevins and by the duke of Durazzo. Joanna, feckless and, despite four marriages, childless as well, had a stormy reign. Lewis of Hungary successfully invaded the kingdom in 1347 but his harshness rallied Neapolitan support for Joanna. Two important events marked the last decade of her rule. In 1372 peace was established with Sicily; and in 1380, faced with the pressure of Urban VI (himself a Neapolitan) Joanna sided with the French pope and adopted Louis, duke of Anjou, as her heir. This involved a fresh Angevin dynasty in the fortunes of the peninsula and provoked Charles of Durazzo to seize the throne and murder the queen in 1382. The meteoric career of Ladislas, who followed Charles in 1387 but who did not rid the kingdom of Louis of Anjou until 1399, lay mainly outside Naples, for the conditions of the Schism favoured his successful intervention in Rome and the Papal States. He died, victim of venereal disease, in 1414 at the height of his political influence, but having done nothing for Naples. Under his sister Joanna II the original Angevin dynasty perished miserably. She was forty-five when she came to the throne, distracted by love affairs and at the mercy of favourites, the ablest of whom was Giovanni Caracciolo. Louis II, of the second Angevin race, successfully intervened till his death in 1434. Joanna died the following year, having adopted successively as her heir Alfonso of Aragon and Louis's brother, *le bon roi* René of Anjou.

Alfonso, who had been offered the succession in 1420, had inherited the Mediterranean possessions of his dynasty[1] and from 1416 had obtained Sicily. The kingdom of Naples and a major role in Italian political life now became his aim. General hatred of the Angevins at first assisted his conquest of Naples, although it was not until 1442 that the kingdom was securely his. Able and active, Alfonso 'the Magnanimous', like Robert of Anjou and Ladislas before him, regarded Naples as a jumping-off point for further Italian adventures. There was still a French rival for the Neapolitan barons to bargain with and for a time under Ferrante, the illegitimate son of Alfonso who succeeded him only in the kingdom of Naples, the Angevin John of Calabria was not un-

---

[1] Sicily accepted the change of dynasty of 1412 (above, p. 148).

successful (1458–64). Ferrante, intelligent but weak and cruel, survived the next decades because of the general desire in Italy not to exploit the situation. It was impossible to continue this longer than Ferrante's death in 1494, which precipitated the French invasion—this time led by the king, not by a duke of Anjou. Impoverished by war, divided socially —even the nobility being stratified between Angevin, Aragonese and older Neapolitan strains—the south of Italy was to be the passive prey of the foreign armies of the next decades.

Sicily, thus again divided politically from the mainland at Alfonso V's death, had earlier developed some of the machinery, including Estates (*parlamento*), of the Iberian lands of the Crown of Aragon. A *deputazione del regno* on the Catalan model is found in the late fifteenth century. Under Alfonso and his successors the island was governed by royal vicars or viceroys, appointed for three-year terms of duty, who provided the atmosphere of a court and who governed by decrees approved by a royal council. Other Aragonese policies were less welcome: the introduction of the royal inquisition in 1487 and the expulsion of the Jews, numerous in Palermo and the bigger towns, in 1492. The other Italian island of the Aragonese kings, Sardinia, had been mastered with difficulty in the fourteenth century; Pisa had been induced to renounce her rights in 1326 but Genoa continued to support the rebellious islanders. In the fifteenth century the island came to accept Aragonese rule. There too a *parlamento* of a Catalan type became active, and there too the viceroy made his appearance in the last quarter of the fifteenth century.

Italian ideals and realities

Power in Italy was in practice divided to an extent even greater than that suggested in previous pages, where only a selection of towns and principalities has been briefly discussed. Italian history as such would be almost nonsensical were it not for certain features of public life which bring all or most of the country into focus.

'Italy' was seen by Italians as the framework of their political action. As has been remarked, what thinking Italians wanted—and this remains true even down to the early sixteenth century—was a country so organized that within it the communes and principalities might enjoy their individual liberty. This is strikingly illustrated in many of the works of the greatest of Italian poets, Dante. For the miseries of Italy—the country was compared by him in one stanza of the *Purgatory* to both a

slave and a brothel—Dante invoked the aid of the emperor Henry VII
in his Latin essay *Concerning Monarchy*;[1] and in an even more original
Latin essay Dante analysed the linguistic problem, prescribing an artificial or 'courtly' Italian as a means of reflecting the cultural unities
which he rightly discerned. Over the centuries it was in fact not to be
courtly Italian, but the courtly Tuscan of the *Divine Comedy* which
provided the national language. To this slow dominance of Tuscan the
poetry of Petrarch[2] also contributed. Vehement protagonist of a return
by the popes from Avignon to Rome, bitter critic of the foreigners or
'barbarians' who were ruining the country, Petrarch had no explicit
political remedy for the situation. But even more than Dante he filled
Italy with lyrical consciousness of its shared inheritances, its divisions.
How slenderly held such sentiments were among Petrarch's contemporaries may be seen when Cola called an assembly of all Italian governments, to elaborate a genuinely Italian policy. The response was suspicious and the reaction of the Florentines was typical: they accused
the upstart senator of plotting his own advancement.

Yet Florence herself became the apostle of Italian values soon after
this. At war with the pope from 1376 to 1378 the city claimed that it
stood for Italy against the barbarian mercenaries; and in the next decade,
faced with the growing power of Giangaleazzo Visconti, the republic
again derived strength from its men of letters who painted the Milanese
duke as a monstrous threat to Italian liberty—just as the courtiers of
Giangaleazzo hailed him as the Caesar who had come to abolish division in the peninsula. However important such propaganda might be as
an influence on culture, it remained ineffective. Even in 1494, with the
'barbarians' at the gate, the notion of Italy lacked political roots. There
were indeed political forces making for unity, but they were far from
providing an expression of *italianità*.

As stated earlier, the emperor had all but ceased to be influential in
Italy. Henry VII's expedition had ended in failure and death in 1313.
Lewis of Bavaria sold privileges and intervened in internal politics,
notably on the side of the Visconti in Milan, during his campaign of
1327–30. He was crowned in Rome by an obedient antipope, and coronation in 1355 drew to Italy Charles IV, the son of King John of
Bohemia who had enjoyed the *signoria* of a number of Lombard and
Emilian towns in 1330 and 1331. Wenceslas's main Italian gesture was
the sale to Giangaleazzo of the ducal title for 100,000 florins. Sigismund,

[1] Above, p. 82.
[2] For some consideration of Italian literature as such, see below, p. 345.

with interests in the Adriatic,[1] took his rights more seriously, especially in the north-east. Sigismund came to Italy in 1431 and he was crowned in Rome in 1433; the sale to the Gonzaga of a marquisate marked this visit. Frederick III came in 1452 for coronation and to marry Leonora of Portugal; he made a very poor impression as he haggled with the citizens of Florence and Venice. At this time Borso d'Este bought the title of duke of Modena and Reggio; a flying visit in 1468 was also financed by the sale of titles. All of this activity, which used to bulk so large in histories of Italy, means very little. No later-medieval anticipations can be seen of the sixteenth-century control of the peninsula by the emperor Charles V.

Far more significant for their general effects were the schemes of one or two Italian princes. Of all the lords who secured more than a regional pre-eminence, Giangaleazzo Visconti, Ladislas of Naples and Alfonso V stand out, not least because at the time their contemporaries regarded them as threatening a general overlordship. At Giangaleazzo's death his territories covered Lombardy, included Bologna and the Bolognese, Perugia, Assisi and Spoleto in the Papal States, and embraced enormous areas in Tuscany round Pisa, Livorno, Lucca and Siena. Ladislas and Alfonso from their base in the south seemed at times to be as great a danger. In 1409 and again in the year of his death, 1414, Ladislas seemed about to swallow up the entire Papal States; in 1447 Alfonso claimed the succession to the duchy of Milan. However menacing these gestures seemed at the time they were to prove ephemeral. Giangaleazzo divided his lands between his sons. Ladislas was succeeded by his inept sister; Alfonso, leaving Naples only to Ferrante, while Sicily, Sardinia and Aragon went to his legitimate heir, ensured the ultimate weakness of the Regno. Not even the strong men of Italy seem in the last analysis to have regarded the country as offering the possibility of a united principality, though their court poets and propagandists sometimes wrote as if they did.

In the Italian wars of this period mercenary forces played a prominent part, as they did to a less degree elsewhere. The stipendiary army of the king of England, the 'contract army' of the Hundred Years War, differs sharply from the companies which are found in Italy. France witnessed the existence of organized groups of brutal soldiers under a captain, hired now by the English, now by the French and in times of peace or truce supporting themselves by the blackmail of the countryside. Their military significance in the Anglo-French conflict was limited. In Italy

[1] Below, p. 229.

such professionals became the main source of military power in the course of the fourteenth century.

The beginnings of the 'Free Companies' were to be seen in the troops accompanying the German emperors and the Angevins in the early fourteenth century. The unpaid knights of Lewis of Bavaria were hired by Lucca in 1328; the remnants of John of Bohemia's force terrorized central Italy as self-styled 'Knights of the Dove' in 1334; and in 1339 Lodrisio Visconti grouped some German captains into the Company of St George. The next decades saw other companies led by Germans (such as Guarnieri di Urslingen and Conrad di Lando), by the Provençal known as Fra Moriale, by the Englishman Sir John Hawkwood, product of the Anglo-French wars and the peace of Brétigny, whom the Italians called Giovanni Acuto. Such forces were given a contract (*condotta*) and their generals were termed *condottieri*.

In the mid-fifteenth century these generals were practically all Italians, not foreigners as they had been a century earlier, and the historian Flavio Biondo attributed this development, which he regarded as entirely wholesome, to the Company of St George formed in 1377 by his fellow countryman from Romagna, Alberico da Barbiano. In this company were to serve two famous generals of the next generation, Muzio Attendolo Sforza and Braccio da Montone, both of whom died in 1424. Their main successors were Francesco Sforza, Niccolò Piccinino and Bartolomeo Colleoni. These Italians may (as Biondo claimed) have been less brutal to the Italian population than the 'barbarian' captains of the fourteenth century, but they posed other problems. They were not captains of fifty or a hundred lances, but commanders-in-chief of large armies, and readily developed policies independent of those of their paymasters; and they frequently sought rewards not only in money but also in lordship of land. Braccio, for example, became *signore* of his native Perugia in 1416; of Attendolo Sforza's sons, Alessandro obtained the lordship of Pesaro while Francesco, married at first to a Calabrian heiress, later married Bianca Visconti and made good his title to the duchy of Milan. This trend should, however, not be exaggerated. Few generals carved out principalities, though many a hereditary lord earned his keep by mercenary service (like the Malatesta, the Montefeltro and the Gonzaga) and often a diplomatic alliance, without real military significance, was sealed by the dependent *signore* accepting a *condotta*, as Giovanni Bentivoglio did from Francesco Sforza. It is equally wrong to suppose that professional *condottieri* were usually beyond the control of their masters. The execution of Carmagnola by the Venetians in

1432 is sometimes treated as exceptional: Eugenius IV destroyed his soldier-cardinal Vitelleschi in 1440; Florence had a treacherous general killed in 1441; there are other examples of the murder or imprisonment of *condottieri* and they were always accompanied during campaigns by political commissioners appointed by their suspicious employers.

Nor is it right to accept Machiavelli's erroneous statements concerning the bloodless battles waged by the Italian professionals. It is true that, being *inter alia* business men, they insisted on their pay being secured before they took the field; and captain and hirer accepted the suspension of activity during the winter months. But one can detail the bloody carnage at many battles. At Anghiari on the eastern edge of Tuscany a force serving Milan under Piccinino attempted in 1440 to surprise a Florentine-hired army under Micheletto Attendolo (uncle of Francesco Sforza). Of this action Machiavelli wrote that only one man died and that only because he fell from his horse and was trampled to death. In reality Piccinino lost between forty and sixty heavy cavalrymen dead, 400 wounded and 1,500 prisoners; in fact his whole force was destroyed, though not without ten dead and 400 wounded on the other side.

The wars resulting from Visconti, Angevin and Aragonese ambitions, from the suspicion and greed of Florence and Venice and, more rarely, from the ambitions of the *condottieri*, nevertheless did produce by the mid-fifteenth century a partial peace which united the peninsula in what was, in effect, a precarious balance of power. The disputed succession to Milan had led to the end of the republic there and the acquisition of the duchy by the canny general Francesco Sforza, who now became only too anxious to consolidate his gains. At Florence Cosimo de' Medici, supporter of Sforza after 1451, also wanted peace and helped to make Venice accept the Sforza victory. The Peace of Lodi in 1454 was followed by the Italian League. This went beyond a mere peace treaty: the signatories included all the main Italian powers, including the papacy and (with reservations and not till 1455) Alfonso; the states formed a defensive alliance for twenty-five years and renounced aggression, any aggressor being automatically expelled.

It would be foolish to attribute the existence of the Italian League to any motive but that of a prudence bred of exhaustion although, like earlier treaties, it made use of the notion of Italy. It lead to a great increase in resident ambassadors and the extension of diplomatic machinery. To the fearful eyes of those who were enduring the wars of the next century it seemed to have heralded a period of halcyon peace and prosperity. In reality 'all that was achieved was a policy of tension'.[1] Minor wars continued and there was plenty of evidence that a general conflagration would follow any major change in the main governments such as occurred at the deaths of Lorenzo de' Medici and Ferrante of Naples (1492, 1494). Even before that the play of dynasticism, not least that of the popes, had threatened a general war. The quarrel of the Medici with Sixtus IV over the possession of Imola and other questions led to the murder of Lorenzo's brother Giuliano, in the cathedral of Florence and with papal cognizance of the plot, in 1478; two years later the same pope, in alliance with Venice, attacked Ferrara. Venice was now a great territorial power, her resources greater than those of any of the others. A contemporary estimate of the income of the various governments in the 1470s gave Venice 1,000,000 ducats a year, Milan and Naples 600,000, Florence 300,000, Savoy 100,000, Mantua, Bologna and Siena 60,000 each. The pope, with some 400,000, was only just better off than Florence and had, of course, a much less coherent territory to manage. The situation invited adventurers, inside and outside. There was a fresh wave of Italian intrigue at foreign courts and from France and Spain Louis XI and Ferdinand of Aragon were ready to fish in troubled waters. The threat of invasion, and then invasion itself, did nothing to cancel out ancient regional programmes which, in an attenuated form, were to survive even centuries of foreign domination and to hamper the united kingdom of the nineteenth and twentieth centuries.

Yet the years from 1350 to 1550, when the mercantile and industrial wealth of Italians was smaller than it had been and when the states of Italy were for long periods the victims of self-inflicted war and foreign invasion, were the time in which the literary, moral and artistic attitudes emerged which were to captivate the rest of Europe for three centuries and more. This paradox will be examined in a later chapter.

[1] Mattingly, p. 91; and see his discussion, pp. 83–100, of the 'Concert of Italy'.

VIII

Germany and her Northern Neighbours

If it is hard to write coherently about Italy in this period it is even harder
to treat Germany as a single entity. Italy, or rather the 'Italian idea', did
mean something in the peninsula, as we have noticed, from early in the
fourteenth century. Germany scarcely attained a literary awareness of
cultural let alone political unity until the very end of the fifteenth
century, and then mainly as a negative impulse, in resistance to the
claims of Italians to the intellectual mastery of the west. In Italy the
number of significant political units had diminished during the later
Middle Ages; in Germany it was on the contrary increasing at this time
and it is a temptation to which most historians of the country succumb
to write the later medieval history of Germany in terms mainly of the
emperor. There is nothing to be said for this save its convenience in
offering a theme of sorts, and something to be said against it since it
encourages the illusion that Germany as such was comparable to other

BIBLIOGRAPHY. A survey with full bibliographies in B. Gebhardt, *Handbuch
der deutschen Geschichte*, 8th edn., I (Stuttgart, 1954), ed. H. Grundmann; a
concise narrative in Hermann Heimpel, *Deutschland im späteren Mittelalter*, vol.
I, part 5 of the Brandt-Meyer *Handbuch der deutschen Geschichte*, new edition,
ed. L. Just (Constance, n.d.). Willy Andreas, *Deutschland vor der Reformation*,
6th revised edn. (Stuttgart, 1959), deals mainly with cultural and economic
developments. The best book in English is G. Barraclough, *Origins of Modern
Germany* (Oxford, 1946); a different point of view is found in H. S. Offler,
'Aspects of Government in the Late Medieval Empire' in *Europe in the Late
Middle Ages* (below, p. 399). The older book of J. Janssen, *History of the German
People at the Close of the Middle Ages*, vols. I, II, 2 edn. revised (London, 1905)
is still worth reading. Recent work is reviewed by P. Dollinger and R. Folz in
Rev. historique ccxxxii (1964). In English see: F. L. Carsten, *The Rise of
Prussia* (Oxford, 1954), and the same author's *Princes and Parliaments in
Germany* (Oxford, 1959) which gives useful information on several of the
regions; Henry J. Cohn, *The Government of the Rhine Palatinate* (Oxford,
1965). Scandinavia and the Baltic: an excellent general survey in L. Musset,
Les peuples scandinaves au moyen âge (Paris, 1951).

monarchies. It was not, and this has induced historians, especially Germans, to treat the fourteenth and fifteenth centuries as a kind of no-man's-land between the strong emperors of an earlier day and the princely dynasties who were later to occupy the forefront of the German scene. Much ink has consequently been spilt in regretting the heroic rulers of the eleventh and twelfth centuries and as much again in trying to discern the antecedents of Frederick the Great and Bismarck. Yet if one admits that the nearest German parallel to a fourteenth-century king of England or Aragon is not any emperor but a ruler like the margrave of Brandenburg or the count of Württemberg, or even the emperor as duke of Austria, there is no need to deplore the fact. The result was not necessarily unhappiness nor greater disorder. The German scene is, however, complicated politically. There was an emperor and his subjects recognized him as such, even if their respect and obedience were often minimal. Alongside the emperor there were a multitude of states, lay and ecclesiastical, big and small, including a large number of privileged towns. These units were in many ways politically autonomous.

The kingdom of Germany formed part of the territories of the Holy Roman Emperor, but it was not coincident with them since, as Italians repeatedly pointed out, the Alps formed a political as well as a cultural and to some extent a linguistic frontier. In the later Middle Ages emperors from Henry VII to Frederick III sought papal coronation but there the German connection with Italy more or less stopped.[1] There remained other ambiguities. The western frontier of the Empire followed the valleys of the Rhone and Saône up to Lorraine; there it followed the Meuse to Luxemburg, whence it was formed by the Scheldt. But these rivers were not a clear boundary, for portions of the old kingdom of Arles were still found on the west of the Rhône: the county of Provence had been 'French' from 1246 only in the sense that it belonged to the Angevins; the marquisate of Provence further north crossed the river. A good deal of French intervention had already occurred in this area; Philip IV in 1312 was able to control Lyons and, in prolonged negotiations during 1342–44, Philip VI bought for his eldest son the Dauphiné. Further north the French had already begun effectively to manage the county of Burgundy which lay in the Empire.

The eastern frontiers of the Empire were limited by no obvious natural features. Hungary and Poland were not in the Empire. North of Poland, however, lay the lands of the Teutonic Order, colonized by German knights, burghers and peasants, and the ultimate responsibility

[1] Above, p. 182.

Nidaros
(Trondheim)

N

NORWAY

SWEDEN

FINLAND

Bergen

Oslo

Uppsala

Stockholm

Stavanger

Vadstena

Gulf of Finland

Visby

GOTLAND

North Sea

Kalmar

Baltic Sea

JUTLAND

SCANIA

The Sound

DENMARK

Copenhagen

Lund

BORNHOLM

Falsterbo

TEUTONIC ORDER

SCHLESWIG

RÜGEN

Danzig

Marienburg

Stralsund

HOLSTEIN

Rostock

POMERANIA

Tannenberg

Wismar

Lübeck

Hamburg

MECKLENBURG

Stettin

Bremen

Lüneburg

BRUNSWICK

BRANDENBURG

POLAND

Berlin

Warsaw

Utrecht

Osnabrück

Frankfurt-a-d-Oder

SILESIA

Münster

Paderborn

Magdeburg

CLEVES

WESTPHALIA

SAXONY

Breslau

JULICH

Dortmund

THURINGIA

Leipzig

R. Oder

BERG

HESSE

Erfurt

Meissen

Cologne

WETTIN LANDS

Aachen

Fulda

FRANCONIA

BOHEMIA

Frankfurt-am-Main

Prague

Luxemburg

Trier

Mainz

R. Rhine

PALATINATE

UPPER PALATINATE

Metz

Nuremberg

LORRAINE

WURTTEMBURG

Regensburg

ALSACE

SWABIA

Ingolstadt

R. Danube

Vienna

Stuttgart

Strasbourg

Ulm

Augsburg

Munich

Basel

Ravensburg

Salzburg

AUSTRIA

SWISS CONFEDERATION

TIROL

Innsbruck

Brenner Pass

Brixen

- - - Approximate frontiers

0   100   200 mls

0   100   200   300 km

6. GERMANY AND SCANDINAVIA

189

of pope and emperor. Earlier German colonization also prepared the way for the annexation of Silesia from Poland in 1335 by John of Luxemburg, and thus for its being made part of Bohemia and the Empire.

The Empire: institutions and rulers

The Empire which thus determined the area of the German kingdom had once been the most powerful monarchy in Europe. By the end of the thirteenth century little remained of the grandeur of Ottonian and Hohenstauffen government. The conflict with the papacy culminated in a virtual interregnum (1250–73) after which a series of genuine elections left the country at the mercy of political bargains whenever an emperor died. Something like a dynasty emerged under the Luxemburg rulers (1346–1437) and again under the Habsburgs (from 1438 onwards) but the acceptance of the principle of hereditary succession of itself lent no authority to the rulers concerned.[1] There was, on the contrary, a willingness in these *fainéant* emperors to accept their lack of power that is its own commentary on the realities of politics in Germany. What should be noted, in the following pages, is the way that successive emperors served their private interests and the inability of the electors and the princes to rise above a narrow localism.

Lewis IV was chosen in 1314 largely through the influence of the Luxemburg family, whose own aspirant, the young King John of Bohemia, was not yet of sufficient weight. The Habsburg duke of Austria had, however, some support and was 'elected' by a minority. For eight years there was intermittent warfare until Lewis defeated Duke Frederick at the battle of Mühldorf in 1322, a full reconciliation

[1] *German emperors and kings of the Romans:*
(a) Wittelsbach: Lewis IV, duke of Bavaria, 1314–46 (1347)
(b) Luxemburg: Charles IV, king of Bohemia, 1346–78
　　　　　　　*Wenceslas, king of Bohemia, 1378–1419
　　　　　　　Sigismund, king of Hungary and Bohemia, 1410–37
(c) Habsburg: *Albert II, duke of Austria, king of Hungary, 1438–39
　　　　　　　Frederick III, duke of Austria, 1440–93
　　　　　　　*Maximilian, duke of Austria, 1486–1519
　　For kings of Bohemia and Hungary, see App. II (below, p. 402).
　　Those rulers marked with an asterisk were not crowned by the pope and were technically only kings of the Romans or emperors 'elect'; Lewis IV was crowned by an anti-pope. Disputed elections led to the title being for a time claimed as follows:
　　　　　　　Frederick, duke of Austria, 1314–22
　　　　　　　Rupert, elector palatine, 1400–10
　　　　　　　Jobst, margrave of Moravia and Brandenburg, 1410–11

coming in 1325. The chief factor in Lewis's success was his alliance with John of Bohemia. This did not mean that the emperor restrained his dynasticism as regards the Luxemburgs, for in 1319 Lewis disallowed John's claim to the margraviate of Brandenburg, which was granted to the emperor's son. In 1335 Lewis was able so to play off John of Bohemia and the Habsburgs that the Wittelsbachs were able to get a large share of Carinthia. The astuteness of the emperor nearly led to disaster when John then allied with the duke of Austria; Edward III, in need of continental allies, offered Lewis financial support at this crisis, and the emperor's anti-French policy also restored more general confidence in him in Germany. The pope at Avignon, meanwhile, refused to recognize Lewis's title; Lewis had had himself recognized as emperor in Rome during his fruitless Italian expedition, 1327-30. A gathering at Rhens in 1338 proclaimed that the king of the Romans was created when elected by the electors or a majority of them; to exercise full authority he did not need papal coronation, which merely conferred the right to the *title* emperor. In the bull *Licet juris* Lewis went further and claimed that the emperor could use the full title without papal coronation, a doctrine which did not prevail before the sixteenth century. Two other acts of family aggrandizement ended the reign. In 1342 Lewis on his imperial authority treated as null the marriage of Margaret Maultasch, heiress of the Tyrol, to her Luxemburg husband. Margaret was married to the emperor's son who was granted the Tyrol and Carinthia. And when his brother-in-law William count of Holland died in 1345 Lewis gave the provinces of Holland, Zeeland and Friesland to his own wife, who already had Hainault in her own right. In a quarter of a century Lewis had made the Wittelsbachs one of the greatest houses in Germany.

At this point there was a more general reaction. Charles of Luxemburg, son of King John of Bohemia, negotiated a settlement with the pope in 1346 in which he promised to seek papal confirmation of his election and at Rhens, ironically enough, he was elected by the three archbishops and his father, by now blind and soon to be killed fighting for the French at Crécy. Derisively known as the *Pfaffenkönig* (Parsons' King), but favoured by the death of Lewis IV in 1347, Charles was destined to a long reign which saw imperial power still further reduced. His policy as emperor was, like Lewis's, family aggrandizement: in 1363 he secured rights in Brandenburg with which he endowed his younger sons in 1373; Lusatia was annexed in 1369; and in 1376 his eldest son Wenceslas was elected as future emperor.

The most substantial and far-reaching development of Charles IV's reign was undoubtedly the Golden Bull, devised by the emperor and approved by the electors at Diets at Nuremberg and Metz in 1356. The aim of the document was to avoid disputed imperial elections by defining exactly the rights of the electors; its upshot was the recognition of the wide *de facto* authority of the electors and of all the princes of Germany. The actual rules for an election were relatively unimportant and certainly failed to prevent later strife. Other measures were in the long run to be more influential. In the case of the lay electors, the right to vote was to descend by male primogeniture; electoral principalities were to be indivisible and, if they fell vacant, were to be at the disposal of the emperor, saving the rights of the people of Bohemia to elect their king. The electors were to have regalian rights to mines of metal and salt and to taxes on Jews. They were empowered to mint coins. No subject of an elector could appeal or be appealed to any court outside his territory. And, most indicative of all of the trend reflected in the document, conspiracy against an elector was to be regarded as *lèse-majesté*; the elector was treated as a sovereign and protected by the laws of high treason. As the doctrines adumbrated in the Golden Bull came to be applied to all German principalities the conditions were gradually created within which strong government could emerge at a level below the Empire. The Golden Bull did not itself provoke the 'Germany of the princes' but it allowed it to develop.

Wenceslas (Wenzel) was, by comparison with his immediate predecessors, far less aggressive as a dynast, though he could be twisted to serve the schemes of others, as in supporting his brother Sigismund of Brandenburg's claim to the throne of Hungary from 1380 until it was successful in 1387.[1] The king of the Romans concentration on his own kingdom of Bohemia led, however, to his authority being twice challenged by rivals. In 1400 he was deposed by the electors and Rupert of the Palatinate was chosen as emperor, exercising authority only in the Rhineland, where he excited violent opposition, and weakening his chances of general support by loyalty to the 'Roman' pope Gregory XII who had recognized him; when Rupert died in 1410 the electors, divided by the Great Schism, produced a divided election—Wenceslas's cousin Jobst, margrave of Moravia, and his brother Sigismund, king of Hungary. In 1410 there were thus three emperors as there were also three popes. The political schism in Germany did not last long. After Jobst's death in 1411 Sigismund was able to come to an agreement with Wenceslas

Below, p. 224.

who was to be secure in Bohemia and share the imperial revenues; in 1411 Sigismund was elected as undisputed emperor.

If Wenceslas's reign both before 1411 and after (till his death in 1419. had been centred on Bohemia to the neglect of Germany, Sigismund's significance is also to be found mainly in his non-German activities— his attempts to secure the Bohemian throne, his intervention in the affairs of the Church and especially at the Councils of Constance and Basle, and his massive interests in central Europe. During the reigns of Wenceslas and Sigismund the remaining authority of the emperor was still further diminished, and the only permanent consequences of a century of Luxemburg rulers was the view, which prevailed at Sigismund's death in 1437, that the emperor should come from the eastern part of Germany, clearly threatened now by the advances of the Ottoman Turks.

Albert, duke of Austria, who was unanimously elected in March 1438, was Sigismund's son-in-law and succeeded him as king of Hungary and of Bohemia. He died almost at once from an illness acquired in an eastern campaign against the Turks. His successor, elected in February 1440, was another Habsburg, Frederick of Styria. Not encumbered by the crowns of other kingdoms, Frederick III was in some ways more conscious than his immediate predecessors of the need to preserve the imperial position, but he was less capable than they had been in maintaining authority in his own dynastic lands. His long reign saw determined and on the whole successful efforts to secure at any rate the ecclesiastical integrity of Germany.[1] On the other hand his attempts to assert his authority over all the Habsburg territories, which had been divided since 1379, produced twenty years of conflict. In 1485 Matthias Corvinus drove Frederick from Vienna and the emperor agreed to the election as future emperor of his son Maximilian, who had been married to Mary, heiress of Charles the Bold of Burgundy, in 1477. By the time Frederick died in 1493 Maximilian had gone far to restore Habsburg power in Austria. It was to be his main achievement, for he proved little better than his father at managing the Empire.

By the end of the fifteenth century the 'constitution' of the Empire may be briefly described as follows:

1. The emperor was elected by the three archbishops of Mainz, Trier and Cologne and the four lay electors, the count palatine of the Rhine, the duke of Saxony, the margrave of Brandenburg and the king of Bohemia. Despite the provisions of the Golden Bull, secular electoral

[1] Below, p. 296.

votes were frequently disputed between rival claimants. Possessed of full powers on election as king, the holder of the title needed papal coronation to employ the title emperor.

2. The emperor controlled (apart from the administrative machinery of his own principality, also often used on imperial business as such):.

(*a*) a chancery (*Kanzlei*). The imperial chancellor was an important figure, his office involving much diplomatic activity not only in regard to foreign princes and the pope, but also in negotiations with German princes. The chancery was, however, staffed by a relatively small number of clerks (who from the mid-fifteenth century included a fair number of scholars) in comparison with the chanceries of other countries.

(*b*) A treasury (*Schatz*). Apart from the incidents of a feudal nature, the principal sources of income were taxes on towns and chancery dues, levied for the authentication of a large number of public and private agreements. Imperial revenue in fact hardly existed as such, though contributions were occasionally raised for particular purposes.

3. The imperial Diet (*Reichstag*). This consisted of a number of elements.

(*a*) The princes and nobles. Not all tenants-in-chief of the emperor were summoned or attended, though thirty princes, over 100 prelates and about 150 lords were sometimes involved. Within the larger body the college of six electors (the king of Bohemia not being a member of the Diet) formed a separate group.

(*b*) Representatives of the towns. The larger privileged 'free' cities had by the fifteenth century acquired the right of attendance, but a fluctuating number of other towns were invited to send representatives. Some eighty or ninety towns are represented at late fifteenth-century Diets.

The emperor frequently did not attend the *Reichstag* in person, his place being taken by the chancellor. In the *Reichstag* general ordinances drafted by the imperial chancery were put forward which were frequently opposed by sectional interests and later ignored even when given formal approval at a joint session. The Diet was thus in practice a political forum rather than a legislative body.

4. The Imperial Court of Justice (*Reichskammergericht*). The thirteenth-century imperial court (*Reichshofgericht*) had virtually ceased to operate during the course of the fourteenth century, as a result of the exemption in practice of many princes (recognized in the Golden Bull). But from 1415 the court of the treasury (*Kammergericht*) gradually assumed

significance, at first mainly in matters regarding the fisc, later in a larger sense. Its jurisdiction was enlarged, its personnel exalted, by an ordinance of 1471 and one of the few successful reforms of Maximilian I was the establishment in 1498 of the imperial supreme court on a permanent basis.

The decline in imperial authority from the middle of the thirteenth century was accompanied by increasing lawlessness, and projects for imperial reform are particularly numerous in the fifteenth century, projects which came to grief because none of the powers in Germany was really prepared to allow the emperor to gain strength, and because all reform involved taxation and no one was prepared for sustained contributions to a central government. For example, during the Council of Constance the Emperor Sigismund proposed the creation of machinery to ensure peace in the south and centre of Germany, where the old imperial lands had been thickest and where a petty baronage now made for conditions of intolerable insecurity. The spontaneous development of popular justice in the *Feme*—a series of secret courts especially numerous in Westphalia—showed how urgent the problem was. Yet in essence the proposals of 1415 involved the emperor using towns and town leagues as instruments of government and such an alliance was a bogey which had haunted the German princes since the twelfth century; this led the electors to resist the scheme violently. Sigismund revived a proposal for four circles (*Kreise*) again in 1434 and in his last Diet (1437); and in 1438 Albert also suggested six circles for each of which a senior official (*Hauptmann*) would have been responsible. As for taxation, even the danger of the Bohemian revolution failed to stimulate common efforts to organize effective resistance, though paper armies and illusory contributions were approved in 1420.

The electors constantly resisted imperial pretensions. They had no capacity themselves for sustained, concerted and disinterested organization. Twice—in 1424 and 1455—there seemed a chance that the electors would live up to the important position collectively allocated to them as a body in the Golden Bull. In 1424 the electors solemnly united to defend Germany from Hussite heresy and Bohemian armies; the league barely lasted two years. In 1455 the electors proposed an imperial council (*Reichsregiment*) of the emperor and the electors. This device was, of course, unacceptable to Frederick III though, by recognizing that the Empire was a collection of independent units it continued to attract the attention of reformers, especially among the princes.

Why then was it possible to find princes willing to become emperor? The simple explanation is that the position enabled its holder to advance the interests of his family. The emperor who was lucky could transform his dynastic fortunes: Lewis IV made the Wittelsbachs for a time the greatest house in south and west Germany. All the emperors of the fourteenth and fifteenth centuries were dynasts, save Wenceslas who was childless. Charles IV's zeal in accumulating territory was increased when he had a son in 1361. Even more significant for the future was the treaty of Brünn in 1364. By this arrangement (which also aimed immediately at neutralizing the Habsburgs) Charles IV agreed that if his own heirs or Wenceslas's failed the Luxemburg lands would go to the Habsburgs; if the heirs of Rudolf of Habsburg failed their lands would become the inheritance of the Luxemburg family. In the end of the day this compact was to help the Habsburgs to get Bohemia; it also set a pattern of princely marriage settlements to be followed by dynasts, especially of the Austrian house, in later centuries.

As emperor the ruler of Germany was thus driven to regard the office as an adjunct to his patrimonial power as ruler of inherited or acquired lands. Certain responsibilities were involved—defence of Germany against the Ottoman threat, against the Hussites, and even a lingering sense that the emperor owed the Church as well as Christendom the duty of protection. But in undertaking to be kings of Germany the emperors' main object was no different from that of other German magnates.

Princes, nobles, knights and towns: the Estates in Germany

A detailed map of Germany in the fourteenth and fifteenth centuries will show more clearly than is possible on the sketch map on p. 189 that the emperors of the period came from principalities in the south and east which were larger and relatively more homogeneous than those in the Rhineland and in the north. The difference should not be pressed too far. Bohemia apart, the other provinces providing emperors were less coherent in fact than at first appears. The Habsburg lands were frequently divided between rival members of the family; Bavaria had three Wittelsbach dukes, of Straubing, Landshut and Munich; for a time there was a fourth centred on Ingolstadt. But the territorial complexities of even the bigger units elsewhere in Germany almost defeats cartography as it does brief description.[1]

[1] The second volume of Gebhardt's *Handbuch* (above, p. 187) contains, pp. 437–617, a survey of the German provinces with full bibliographies. The western provinces are dealt with by F. Uhlhorn, the eastern by W. Schlesinger, and the

Disregarding for the time being certain regions which were rapidly losing their German identity, there were five large secular dominions: the county of Württemberg, the Palatinate, the county of Hesse (ruled by landgraves), the Wettin lands associated after 1423 with the electoral principality of Saxony (Meissen and Thuringia) and the margravate and electorate of Brandenburg. Other large areas were ruled by prince-prelates. Of these Salzburg lay between Austria and Bavaria, the others were in the east and north; Mainz, Trier and Cologne were electoral archbishoprics, the archbishops of Magdeburg and Bremen ruled over large areas and so did the bishops of Münster and Würzburg; other prelates enjoyed lands only less extensive—the bishops of Paderborn and Bamberg, for example, and a few religious houses, notably the abbey of Fulda, had enormous liberties.

Just as the Habsburg and Wittelsbach inheritance was rent by feuding princes, so it was with the other large principalities where rival claimants battled for control or wearily partitioned the territory. The large ecclesiastical principalities were less subject to dynastic fission, but even here princely pressures sometimes led to disputed elections and open warfare, especially during the period of the Schism and the councils. Nor were the princely bishops averse to aggressive acquisition of new lands; the archbishops of Trier consolidated their scattered lands by adding scores of adjacent domains in the later Middle Ages. War and acts of brutal aggression were certainly commoner as ways of increasing landed possessions in the Germany of this period than they were in the smaller, tidier monarchies of western Europe. But in Germany, as elsewhere, the quest for political power was pursued at all levels of noble society primarily by purchase and marriage. Treaties between the greater princes securing a reversion in default of heirs, like the Habsburg-Luxemburg agreement at Brünn, are not uncommon. Matrimonial alliances of a simpler kind could also provoke remarkable transformations. The Rhenish counties of Mark and Cleves were thus united in 1368; the duke of Berg became also count of Jülich in 1423; in 1511 the four principalities were united for a century as a result of a marriage treaty drawn up in 1496. Such integration, of course, depended on the luck of heirs and heiresses. All too commonly the ruler

details of the arrangement indicate the intractable nature of the problem: e.g. Dr Uhlhorn has four geographical sections, of which the first, the north German Plain, has six sub-regions. The reader will also find in the 11th edition of the *Encyclopaedia Britannica* many articles, some of which are substantial, on the main German principalities and towns.

was succeeded by two or more sons, each unwilling to give up a share of the patrimony.

The larger lay and ecclesiastical principalities were, however, not only often divided between rival counts or bishops, they were composed of areas which were discontinuous, broken up by independent enclaves belonging to towns, nobles and other princes. Even in Brandenburg a dozen towns gave their loyalty not to the margrave but to the Hanseatic League and two bishops (Brandenburg and Havelberg) had extensive liberties. Elsewhere the situation was much more confused. Hesse and the Palatinate lay each in two disjointed sections, and the Palatinate under four separate rulers; Württemberg both contained imperial cities and was bordered by others. Such a situation at the same time facilitated dynastic division and was an invitation to aggressive war. The superior ecclesiastical rights of bishops and archbishops also offered territorial temptations to ambitious holders of the office in some of the larger ecclesiastical provinces. The sees under the archbishop of Mainz stretched almost from the North Sea to the Alps; the bishoprics of Mainz, Cologne and Trier were very large in comparison with Italian, French or English dioceses and carried with them lordships—the archbishop of Cologne was count of Arnsberg and had claims to the duchy of Westphalia. Magnates only a shade less impressive were established in the north, the rulers of Pomerania, Mecklenburg and Holstein, for example. Smaller nobles abounded everywhere. The most tumultuous and numerous minor nobility was found in the south-west, in the old imperial lands of Swabia and Franconia. Here there were hundreds of independent knights, controlling a castle or two, preying on the traffic of road and river, combining briefly to resist the pressures of the greater magnates and the towns. But the *Ritter* class existed also inside the greater principalities, its members intent on securing for themselves an independence from the authority of count or duke comparable to that which the princes themselves had secured *vis-à-vis* the emperor. Among the knights, as among the princes, dynasticism led to divided domains and private war; and private war readily degenerated into banditry. Descended from the *ministeriales* of an earlier period, some of the *Ritter* were destined to climb into the upper reaches of the nobility.

Granted the uncertainty of public order, the German towns of the period often appeared as islands of relative peace and good government, able to shelter behind their walls from any disorder. Of the government of the towns a little has already been said.[1] Some, privileged by the

[1] Above, p. 122.

emperor, were small sovereign powers, the *Reichstädte* or imperial cities which were mostly found in the south and west. These often controlled a considerable territory, though the jurisdictions under which the country folk lived near such towns were of a bewildering complexity and one must beware of assuming that the greater towns, inventive as they were of administrative machinery, in any sense ironed out the confusions of public life.[1] Many towns also existed within the lay and ecclesiastical principalities, with privileges obtained from bishop or duke.

Territorial lords great and small were in no position in most cases to resist the pressure of their subjects. Weakened by divisions in the ruling houses, the princes both reduced their domain revenues and multiplied the expenses of running their small courts and armies. As a result they were perpetually in debt and compelled to turn for assistance to the clergy, the knights and above all to the towns in their lands. This forms the background to the remarkable development of Estates in Germany in and after the second half of the fourteenth century. In France and England the emergence of representative assemblies can only be understood in terms of the aims of the king; the French *états* and the English parliament are viable in so far as they are instruments of royal government. In Germany the Estates usually evolved in opposition to the prince, somewhat like the *cortes* in the provinces subject to the king of Aragon and especially in Catalonia.[2] When the bishop, count or duke, embarrassed by debts, appealed for help he was forced to accept not only the creation of machinery designed to limit his power, but also the principle that his subjects were entitled to resist him if he infringed the bargain. This legal right to resist (*Widerstandsrecht*) is not to be compared with the *defidatio* or defiance of the feudal vassal in earlier times; it was a corporate sanction placed not on an individual but on an institution.

In the fragmented Bavaria of the fourteenth century nobility, towns and clergy steadily increased their powers. From time to time committees were appointed to supervise the collection and expenditure of appropriated taxes; the duke of Upper Bavaria agreed in 1363 to appoint a council as advised by the Estates; and in the fifteenth century demands emerged for annual meetings of the Diet. In 1392 the Estates of Brunswick-Lüneburg 'forced on the dukes what amounted to a general capitu-

---

[1] See, for example, the remarkable map in Westermann (below, p. 399), no. 81 (1) showing the score of authorities exercising public power in the territory of Nuremberg *c.* 1500.   [2] Above, p. 112.

lation',[1] which left power in the hands of the Estates, a body of knights and townsmen being appointed to see that the contract was observed. In the two parts of Württemberg the counts of the Urach line and of the Stuttgart line both summoned Estates in 1457; in each region promises were extracted that government would be conducted with the advice of the Estates.

Some of these constitutional developments were to have effects which lasted for centuries, as Professor Carsten has demonstrated.[2] Yet the forces which kept the Estates together in most German principalities in the later Middle Ages were negative: the Estates were devices to prevent the exercise of princely power and to advance sectional interest. Paradoxically, in a number of regions the *Landschaft*, the territorial community, promoted the ultimate survival of the prince. One of the perpetual disruptions of public order was occasioned, as has been noted, by divisions in the ruling family. In Bavaria, Württemberg and elsewhere the Estates had sometimes a greater sense of loyalty to the state than the holder of the title, as they had every inducement to reduce the miseries and expenses of fratricidal war and to prevent the prince from denuding himself of resources by extravagant alienations of the domain. The most signal example of the Estates promoting unity in this way was the treaty of Esslingen in 1492 as a result of which Württemberg was reunited under the counts of the Stuttgart line when the Urach line came to an end in 1496.

Not all princes needed prompting by their subjects and there are hints and anticipations of a reconstruction of authority round the ruler in a number of states. This trend, destined in the end to produce the 'princely' Germany of the seventeenth and eighteenth centuries, must not be exaggerated. The margraves of Brandenburg, who offer the most impressive evidence of the process, are often astonishingly casual in their attention to internal government. On the other hand the very situation which had produced the pressure of the Estates was ripe for exploitation by an adroit and persistent count or duke, especially if he was spared the complication of disloyal or rapacious relatives.

The clergy, nobility and townsmen who resisted princely extravagance and disorder were often hostile to each other. It is sometimes difficult to distinguish leagues of self-interested knights and parochial-minded towns from the groups which amalgamated in the Estates. Nobles, hit by economic regression, were jealous of each other, coveted employment by the prince and resented both the immunities of the

[1] Barraclough, p. 328.   [2] *Princes and Parliaments in Germany.*

Church and the wealth of the merchant. The towns of the territory were not only traditionally suspicious of the nobility, they were frequently victims of internal strife, the patricians and the craft guilds struggling for mastery in control of the town council and the assessment of taxation. And, beyond the town walls, outside the gates of the castle, was a peasantry which, in west Germany, had achieved legal independence to find itself at the mercy of extortion and uncertainty. The dark threat of peasant revolts, multiplying as the fifteenth century wore on, could make the prince the only organizer of resistance. The prince in Germany, as elsewhere, could also find allies in the clergy, over whom his rights of patronage had been consolidated as a result of Schism and councils—'the duke is pope in Cleves'—and noblemen could also attain promotion in the church through loyalty to the ruler.

All of this provided opportunities for developments in some German principalities comparable with those which had occurred earlier in France and England: more or less regular taxation, meetings of Estates for this main purpose (i.e. as part of the ruler's administrative machinery), stronger central organs of government, and an acceptance of the identity of the aims of subject and prince. By the second half of the fifteenth century general taxation and more or less regular meetings of the Estates occurred in Austria, Saxony, Jülich, Silesia, Brandenburg, Mecklenburg. 'By the end of the fifteenth century there were few principalities where the *Landtag*, the States-General, created by the princes as an organ for obtaining taxes, had not become a permanent institution for the representation of the land and its inhabitants.'[1] This went with the doctrine that the prince alone controlled the assembly, firmly enunciated by the Margrave Albert Achilles of Brandenburg (1471–86) and by other rulers. It went also with the increased employment of expert councillors, often trained in Roman law, who could produce convenient theories concerning the will of the prince. This 'reception of Roman law', which is often associated with the reconstitution of the *Reichskammergericht* by Maximilian in 1495, in which six of the twelve judges of the court were to be Roman lawyers, did not redound to the exaltation of imperial authority, as it theoretically should have done. It benefited the princes, who treated themselves (like kings of France and England) as possessors of 'imperial' sovereignty. Some such majesty had been attributed to the electors by the Golden Bull in 1356; it now became the ambition of all the German rulers. Another stipulation of 1356, that electoral principalities should descend by male

[1] Barraclough, p. 349.

primogeniture, began to acquire some actuality at this time. The *dispositio Achillea* of 1473 laid down the indivisibility of the mark of Brandenburg and the electoral title that went with it.

The consolidation of territorial states, hinted at in the fifteenth century, lay in the future. The only other possible way that Germany might have attained a modicum of peace and order was through leagues of towns, and these had been proved bankrupt. Through their wealth, the relative maturity of their institutions and their freedom from dynastic complications the imperially privileged German towns had from time to time the appearance of maintaining loyalty both to the emperor and to the notion of general stability. Save for Aachen, Cologne, Lübeck, Dortmund and a few more, the imperial cities were mainly grouped in the south. But that was precisely where disorder was endemic and, in the north, there was a possibility that the Hanseatic League might achieve a position of permanent importance.

During the Interregnum leagues of cities along the Rhine were common and influential. In the fourteenth century they are found in both west Germany and in the east, the cities of Lusatia combining in 1346. It is, however, in the south that the development was carried furthest for there disorder was worse and the ambition of princes more aggressive. In 1349 twenty-five cities were linked by the efforts of Ulm and Augsburg and in 1376 the Swabian league was formed. Fourteen imperial cities, later joined by another score, were associated at the instance of Ulm and in 1381 the Swabian league allied with a reformed Rhenish league which was augmented in 1385 by association with the urban cantons of Switzerland and with Zug. In fact the German towns deserted their Swiss allies who defeated the Austrian army at Sempach (1386).[1] The armies of the Swabian and Rhenish leagues were soon defeated by armies led respectively by the count of Württemberg and the Elector Palatine, and the most notable attempt at urban combination was over by 1389 (Peace of Eger). Like the member towns of the Hanseatic league, the towns of Bavaria, Swabia and the Rhineland were in the last resort jealous of each other, unwilling to collect money to pay soldiers, and averse to the interruptions to commerce involved in sustained campaigning. The parochialism of the ruling cliques made it impossible for the old alliance of emperor and towns to survive the fourteenth century. Town leagues are found later, but they are of local interest, the concomitant of the leagues of knights whose efforts were equally restricted.

[1] Cf. above, p. 124.

A Germany in which the emperors were primarily concerned with their own family fortunes, in which sectional interests could unite only in opposition to each other and to the faint stirrings of a new and auto-cratic concept of princely authority, was naturally unable to preserve what a later age would term 'her territorial integrity'. The German kingdom, which in earlier centuries had steadily expanded, now began to contract.

The shrinking perimeter of Germany in the later Middle Ages

Certain of the regions which effectively left the Empire at this time have already come before us. The Swiss forest cantons, independent of the ultimate control of Austria from the thirteenth century, had been associated with Lucerne and Zürich since the mid-fourteenth century. Augmented still further, the eight 'original cantons' and their dependent territories were more or less recognized as a separate and sovereign unit by Austria by the end of the fifteenth century. This solid development, which was to go far to insulating Germany from Italy, is to be compared with the failure of the town leagues in Germany.

In the western territories of the Empire we have mentioned at the beginning of this chapter the inroads made on the lands of the old 'kingdom of Arles' as a result of which the French controlled Provence and the Dauphiné. Further north the French dukes of Burgundy had made even more serious advances on German territory. Already in control not only of Franche-Comté but of the imperial duchies of Brabant and Luxemburg and of the counties of Zeeland, Holland and Hainault, already effective master of the imperial bishoprics of Liège, Cambrai and Utrecht, Charles the Bold had vaster ambitions—not merely a kingdom, but the reversion of the Empire itself. The duchy of Gelders was the only territory he positively acquired, but he patronized the archbishop of Cologne and secured from Sigismund of Tyrol rights in Lorraine and Alsace in fighting for which he was to meet disgrace, defeat and ultimately death.[1] His death in 1477 showed how flimsy were the pretensions of the Burgundian 'state' but it cannot be argued that Germany gained from its dissolution. Franche-Comté in the end was secured by France; the Low Country provinces passed, not to the Empire as such, but to the patrimony of the Habsburgs, when Charles the Bold's heiress Mary married Maximilian a few months after the battle of Nancy. The subsequent century was to show that the Low Countries had turned their backs on Germany for good.

[1] Above, p. 145.

To the east German influence was also in retreat. In central Europe, where German merchants and soldiers had penetrated in earlier centuries, the self-conscious patriotism of Czechs, Hungarians and Poles took the form of hostility to Germany, as will be seen in the next chapter. The most signal reversal of German fortunes occurred in the north. The Baltic provinces from Danzig to the Gulf of Finland were, by the middle of the fourteenth century, in the hands of the Teutonic Order. Pomerelia, Prussia, and what until 1940 were the states of Lithuania, Latvia and Estonia, formed a principality under the grand master of this crusading Order who was virtually independent of the emperors and the popes (to whom he owed nominal allegiance), and whose authority extended over the bishops of the region. The Order had lost its last connection with the east when Acre fell in 1291 and from 1309 the grand masters had their headquarters at Marienburg. The government of the Order's lands was in the hands of the grand master and a council of senior officials and at a lower level there were twenty commanderies each under a *Komtur*. The peasantry was formed partly of native serfs, partly by free Germans and Swedes; the towns, all German foundations, were active members of the Hanseatic league and were left pretty much undisturbed. In the fourteenth century the Order was imaginatively and aggressively managed by several able grandmasters of whom the most celebrated was Winrich von Kniprode (1357–82). Not only German nobles came to fight the heathen. With Syria lost, the Prussian campaign attracted the chivalry of France, England and other parts of Europe. Nor were the Knights averse to more peaceful advances. Pomerelia had been bought in 1309 and in 1346 Esthonia was purchased from Denmark.

The turning point came with the marriage of the heiress of Poland Hedwig, to the great prince of Lithuania, Jagiello, in 1383. Jagiello ruled Poland as Wladyslaw II[1] and this meant that the Order was now faced with the combined strength of the two countries it had been earlier accustomed to despoil. More than that, the Lithuanians adopted Christianity with their ruler and the crusading Order's very *raison d'être* was gone. In 1410 the Poles defeated the Knights in the battle of Tannenberg and from then on the acquisitions of the Order were gradually eroded, a process to which restive subjects and disobedient Knights actively contributed. The upshot was the occupation by Poland of west Prussia at the second Peace of Toruń (Thorn) in 1466; this left the Knights in possession only of east Prussia and Livonia, cut off from

[1] Below, p. 230.

Germany and theoretically in feudal dependence on Poland. It was this situation, leading the Knights to choose German princes as their grand masters with the aim of maintaining their liberty, which produced the election in 1511 of a Hohenzollern and facilitated the secularization of Prussia in 1525. Livonia became an independent duchy (Courland) in 1561. In the end of the day, when a margrave of Brandenburg succeeded to Prussia in 1618, the province was once again to be fully integrated into German politics, was indeed to form part of the Hohenzollern territories round which territorialized Germany was to be drastically organized in the nineteenth century. This, however, lay far in the future and for centuries the influence of Germany in the Baltic was seriously reduced.

The decline of the Teutonic Order was accompanied by, was partly due to, the fifteenth-century retreat of the Hanseatic League; the slow eclipse of the merchants of north Germany is in some ways the most remarkable of all the evidence of a contraction in German influence. The troubles of the Hansa were not unconnected with the final detachment of territory which must be noticed. The south of Jutland had been erected into a duchy in the thirteenth century. When the Danish king tried to recover it in 1319 Valdemar, the heir of the late duke, was helped by the count of Holstein—who indeed succeeded in making the boy king of Denmark in 1326. The count of Holstein's reward was the grant of the duchy of Schleswig, protected by the promise that the duchy would never be incorporated in the Danish kingdom or be ruled by the Danish king. In the event Duke Valdemar had to hand back the crown to Christopher in 1330 and it was only in 1375, when the royal and ducal lines both ended, that a count of Holstein could seize Schleswig and use the title of duke. In 1460, however, King Christian of Denmark secured his own election to the territories, at the price of swearing to the Estates that they would remain indivisible. In later times, it is true, Holstein was treated as a German principality, and it was of course to enforce this that Prussia was to demonstrate her leadership of Germany in 1864.

It would be wrong to regard these developments—a virtually independent Swiss Confederation, French and Burgundian advances beyond the Rhône and up the Rhine, the defeat of the Teutonic Order and the acquisition of Holstein by the king of Denmark—as German 'losses'. The tradition of German historiography in the nineteenth century undoubtedly exaggerated the unity of earlier times; it would be logical enough in any case to remember that the Danish king who had acquired Holstein in 1460 was in reality a German prince who had been put on the throne by the Holstein dukes of Schleswig; just as it is true that the nobility of Sweden and Denmark as well as the towns of Scandinavia were permanently enriched by German families. Yet down to the fourteenth century German influence had been displayed by the physical advance of German peasants, knights and merchants. In the fifteenth century this came to an end. It would be hard to deny that the regions mentioned detached themselves from Germany because in Germany there was no effective political centre. The ambiguities of East Prussia and Holstein could only have been tolerated in an Empire which had come to mean no more than a loose association of territories, some large, many minute, sharing a common language (divided however into markedly different dialects), and acknowledging in an indistinct way the elected emperor, now hardly ever seen in person in northern Germany. The Swiss were faced now with a situation in which their most powerful neighbour was not the emperor, not even Habsburg Austria, but France. Like the Teutonic Order, the Hansa was confronted in the fifteenth century with a stronger Poland and Lithuania, and the League also had to contend in the North Sea area with kings of England and dukes of Burgundy less easily managed than the princes of previous centuries. It even seemed in the later Middle Ages that in Scandinavia powerful and coherent government might arise to resist the massive advances there of German merchants, and of German language and culture.

The kingdoms of Scandinavia

The first great period of Scandinavian activity had led the Norsemen and Vikings to colonize extensively both west Europe and east. This period ended with the eleventh century, and in the twelfth and thirteenth centuries the more distant territories lost all contact with Scandinavia, save Iceland which was brought under the power of Norway by 1264. Only the Swedes displayed aggressive force, establishing themselves in Finland, where they were long to control the isolated Tatar community whose paganism and non-Teutonic language (Fino-Ugrian) reflected the folk-migrations of a very early date.

The three kingdoms, ultimately associated as they were not only by similarity of language and by royal and noble marriages, had not all reached the same stage of development, politically or socially, by the start of the fourteenth century. Denmark was a plain and easily accessible to men and ideas from Germany; across the Sound, her kings controlled in Scania the flat land to the south of the kingdom of Sweden. Closely involved in the turbulent politics of northern Germany, Danish kings had capitulated before a nobility in which feudalism of a modified form had penetrated—a feudalism which had redounded to the advantage of the vassals who obtained royal lands but who still remained strong in allodial estates. At the same time the free peasantry had declined into servitude and the enormous wealth provided by the herring fisheries off Scania was monopolized by the Hanseatic merchants, putting Danish towns and trade in German hands. In Norway and Sweden politics and economics was dominated by the mountain and the forest. Despite moments of royal power, despite the survival of a free peasantry, the magnates and the prelates were for long periods the real masters.

In the fourteenth and fifteenth centuries these tendencies on the whole continued. Denmark became more Germanized and in Norway and Sweden the magnates were all-powerful. In all these countries nobles emerged in this period who, unlike the great men of earlier days, lived in castles, regarded both king and peasantry as their natural enemies, and enjoyed fiscal immunities. The members of this group controlled senior appointments in the Church and they swayed the royal councils. Conscious of their caste, they sought consorts from other noble families, the Danes frequently in Germany, the Norwegians in Sweden, and the Swedes in Denmark and Norway. This pattern of marriages was also followed in the royal families and was to produce in the late fourteenth century a superficial union of the crowns, though it did not produce any real unification in the government of the Scandinavian territories.

Before the nobility the peasantry slowly retreated. The economic situation of the small independent farmer, the characteristic figure of Scandinavian history up to the thirteenth century, deteriorated and the depopulation and distress of the Black Death did correspondingly more damage. Taxation, customs duties, tolls and levies in kind, hit hardest the rural population, especially in Sweden and Norway. In all these countries the result was the introduction of limitations on peasant liberty, the emergence of personal dependence if not of servitude. First in Denmark, later in Norway and Sweden the relationship of lord and peasant became strained, with concomitant agrarian disturbances: in southern Norway in 1436, in Finland in 1438, in Jutland in 1441. Traditionally the most celebrated of the risings is that associated with Engelbrekt Engelbrektsson in Sweden in 1434. It is, however, by no means clear that peasant discontents alone account for the success of this remarkable demonstration which began among miners who could not export their iron ore because of a blockade. Like many leaders of peasant risings elsewhere, Engelbrekt was a gentleman. The rebellion was backed by many nobles anxious to weaken the king; hostility to foreigners, especially Germans and Danes, was a further motive. Engelbrekt himself, who gained a great domain from the crown as well as the regency of the kingdom, did not live to display any coherent policy; he was murdered in 1436. These peasant protests did not arrest the creation of great estates, especially in Denmark.

Compared with more southerly countries town development also followed a different timetable. Large areas of Norway, Sweden and Finland had virtually no towns at all; nor had Iceland, where the Norwegian governor's residence was a seaside farm. In Denmark by the end of the thirteenth century there were a number of small towns and Copenhagen had emerged as the centre of government; elsewhere towns were rare and very small, the biggest being Bergen with a population of about 6,000 at the start of the fourteenth century. The towns, most of which were not walled (Visby on the island of Gotland was an exception), were governed by a co-opted council in which the richest merchants governed through a burgermaster. But the most remarkable feature of Scandinavian towns at this time was the power attained in them by German merchants, especially those of the Hanseatic League. In Denmark and to some extent in Sweden the Hanseatic trader shared power with local guildsmen in the town council; and in the towns of these countries the Germans often settled permanently. In Norway their depots were quite separate from local urban organization and the Germans were not assimilated to the citizens among whom they dwelt, as at Bergen and Oslo, 'a state within a state'. In Norway German monopoly of trade and manipulation of town government was to continue down to the sixteenth century; in Denmark and Sweden, where German merchants were in any case naturalized, Hanseatic influence steadily declined in the fifteenth century.

Elsewhere in western Europe monarchy at this time had, as we have seen, steadily gained in power and prestige at the expense of the great magnates. The reverse was true in Scandinavia. There the introduction of feudal relations redounded (as in Germany) to the advantage of the vassal rather than the prince, and the kings could not ally with a flourishing bourgeoisie. Royal lands and revenues were alienated. The great officers of the crown tended to be appointed for life and were thus useless as instruments of royal policy; for example the chancellorship in each kingdom was normally attached to a particular see regardless of the quality of the bishop concerned. Above all the council in each of the Scandinavian countries was aristocratic in complexion, being composed of bishops and great landowners, and able to gather under its control the remnants of royal power. Attempts were made to convoke meetings of estates for the whole of each country, but they were never gathered at the instance of the king but rather to demonstrate popular resistance to the exercise of royal authority; and they never concerned themselves with taxation. In Denmark and Sweden from the end of the thirteenth century, and in Norway by the mid-fourteenth, kings were constitutionally obliged to accept the absolute rights of the magnates, not least in the election and recognition of the ruler themselves. Only in Norway was the hereditary principle accepted in the royal house.

It is against this background that the political evolution of Scandinavia must be viewed in this period. Granted the weakness of the monarchy, the independence of the magnates, and the dominant position in trade and urban life of German merchants, it is hardly surprising that even able kings were frustrated in attempts at active government. The fortuitous union of the crowns not merely did not lead to innovation, it provoked bitter and in the end successful resistance.

The dynasties which were formally united in 1397 had, in fact, come together gradually during the previous century, when intermarriage and political accident had already put two countries under one ruler.[1] The ambitious and active Ingebjörg helped her son Magnus Smek to succeed as the ruler of both Norway and Sweden in 1319. Another woman of even greater talent, Margaret the daughter of Valdemar Atterdag of Denmark, who in 1363 married Hakon VI, had a son Olaf who was titular ruler of Denmark and Norway till his death at the age of seventeen in 1387, and then herself obtained the regency in both kingdoms. In 1388 a Swedish faction chose her as regent there and in 1389 she defeated and imprisoned the Swedish king, Albert of Mecklenburg. Already regent in all three kingdoms, Margaret chose as her successor her great-nephew Eric of Pomerania, still a child, who was chosen as king of Norway in 1389 and as king of Sweden and Denmark in 1396. At Kalmar, on the south-east coast of Sweden, a gathering of notables, including the archbishops of Uppsala and Lund, many prelates and a large number of councillors of the three kingdoms, witnessed on 17 June 1397 the coronation of Eric and did homage to him as king of each

[1] The rulers of the Scandinavian kingdoms are shown on page 211 (partly adapted from Musset, p. 295 n.).

country. A few days later a document was drafted which sketched the framework of a permanent union. Eric's successor in each kingdom was to be his heir or, in default of an heir, a single king chosen by the three kingdoms acting in concert; each realm would aid the others in defensive war; the outlaws of any one country would not be received in the other two; negotiations with foreign countries were to be in the hands of the king guided by the councillors of the kingdom he happened to be in at the time; each country should have its own laws and no other country's laws should be introduced. The status of this draft has been disputed and it may never have been regarded as of legal force; a further conference at Kalmar in 1436 laid down that the king should choose his officers from, and divide his time between, his three realms. But this agreement also seems to have had no effect. It certainly did not secure any genuine measure of unification, despite Margaret's promotion of German and Danish clergy to the sees of Norway and Sweden. Eric, ruling after Margaret's death, neglected Norway and Sweden and was by 1442 displaced by his nephew Christopher in all three countries. On the death of Eric's successor Christopher in 1448 the union was in practice finished. The Swedes considered Christian of Oldenburg and his son John as Danish kings and their control of Sweden was episodic or illusory. Karl Knutsson was elected king and later his nephew Sten Sture was regent, preparing the subsequent independence that was to come in 1523. Yet it should be remembered that some Swedes were sympathetic to the union; the wars which brought Karl Knutsson and Sten Sture to power were also civil wars; hostility to German nobles and merchants was a widely diffused sentiment even if it was not enough to make the union of Kalmar effective.

In practice the achievements of Ingebjörg and later of Margaret owed little to the resources of the Crown. They depended on alliances with powerful landed families. Nor was union in any real sense acceptable to the great men as a whole. The magnates insisted on dividing Norway from Sweden in 1344; the Swedes insisted on the separate administration of their country. Elections of child kings like Magnus Smek and Olaf were attractive to the magnates in Scandinavia as elsewhere in Europe because of the opportunities they offered for extracting further concessions. The union was largely acceptable to the Norwegians and the Swedes because it was likely that the superior wealth and population of Denmark would attract all the time and interest of the sovereign. This indeed happened, but in Denmark itself the domination of the counts of Holstein reduced effective royal power.

The table below (see note on page 209) reveals how largely the affairs of Scandinavia attracted the attention of German princely families. Denmark in particular suffered from this, as we have seen also in the complicated connection of the lands of Schleswig and Holstein with the Danish crown. German nobles were firmly entrenched in Denmark by the end of the fifteenth century. In Scandinavia as a whole German influence is particularly to be seen in the towns, also largely Germanized. In all these countries the language of trade and industry was German. The later Middle Ages saw even more radical linguistic changes in Danish as a result of German influence. By the end of the fifteenth century this was, it is true, diminishing, and consequently the Scandinavian peoples had a much greater liberty of action. But there was nothing as yet to indicate that one of these kingdoms, Sweden, was about to emerge as a major force in European politics.

Rulers of Scandinavian kingdoms:

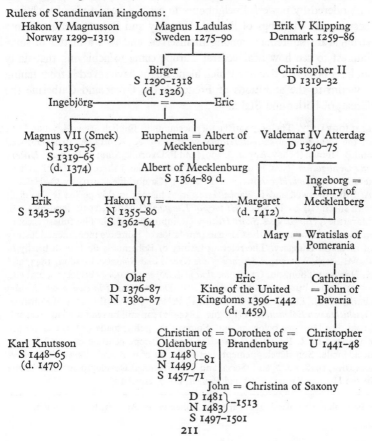

IX

The Central Monarchies

Between Germany and Russia lies a great area of land which was the geographical heart of Europe, and whose inhabitants were mostly Slavs and Magyars. During the latter part of the Middle Ages the Poles, the Hungarians and the Czechs were able to develop as sovereign states unhindered by powerful neighbours to east or west. Free of such preoccupations the kings of Poland, Hungary and Bohemia engaged in a struggle for supremacy among themselves, and it is a matter of some interest to see how near central Europe came to achieving that unity under a powerful dynasty which alone might have saved it from falling a victim to the ambitions of Frederick the Great and Catherine the Great, of Hitler and Stalin.[1]

BIBLIOGRAPHY. The only satisfactory accounts in English are vols. VII and VIII of the *Cambridge Medieval History* written by K. Krofta, A. Bruce Boswell and B. Hóman (below, App. I, p. 399) [and F. Dvornik, *Slavs in European History and Civilization* (New Brunswick, 1962)]. For Poland there are also the chapters in the *Cambridge History of Poland*, I (Cambridge, 1950) by O. Halecki, A. Bruce Boswell and F. Papée. Hungarian history in this period is also dealt with succinctly by D. Sinor, *History of Hungary* (London, 1959) [and by C. A. Macartney, *Hungary, A Short History* (Edinburgh, 1962)]. The fullest account in a western language is the German translation of Hóman's monumental history of medieval Hungary. The relevant history of Bohemia is dealt with briefly in R. M. Seton-Watson, *A History of the Czechs and Slovaks* (London, 1943) and S. Harrison Thomson, *Czechoslovakia in European History* (Princeton, 2nd ed., 1953). Fuller but a bit old fashioned is E. Denis, *Huss et la guerre des Hussites* (Paris, 1878). The German version of F. Palacky's classical history of Bohemia, *Geschichte von Böhmen*, III–V (Prague, 1854–87) can still be read with interest and profit. For Huss see below, p. 299. Some of the points made in this chapter are elaborated in R. R. Betts, 'La société dans l'Europe centrale et dans l'Europe occidentale. Son développement vers la fin du moyen âge', *Revue de l'histoire comparée*, 1948, no. 2, and 'Social and Constitutional Developments in Bohemia in the Hussite Period', *Past and Present*, no. 7, April 1955.

---

[1] For rulers of Poland, Hungary and Bohemia see App. II, below, p. 402.

At the beginning of the fourteenth century it looked as if the achieve-ment of the unification of central Europe would be the work of King Wenceslas II of Bohemia. He was rich and clever, and had gathered round him at his court in Prague a number of very able ministers and expert advisers, some Czechs like himself, but most of them Germans or Italians. He was tempted by the weakness of Poland which had been divided into a dozen or so smallish duchies for the preceding 150 years and which had been cruelly battered by a series of Tatar invasions. The murder of King Przemyslaw of Poland in 1294 was the final disaster which made it possible for the Bohemian king to make himself master of most of Poland, to marry Przemyslaw's daughter and finally to get him-self crowned by the Polish primate in the ancient capital of Gniezno in the year 1300. Many of the prelates and the German merchants who lived in the Polish cities welcomed Wenceslas as the only person who could restore the unity and prosperity of the shattered country. He left Poland to be governed by Czech captains. Their harsh vigour soon aroused the resentment of the Poles who even during Wenceslas's life-time began to look hopefully towards the one man who seemed able and willing to oust the foreigners, the prince Wladyslaw, a member of the ancient dynasty, for the moment a refugee in Hungary.

A year after he became king of Poland Wenceslas of Bohemia was tempted to try for another and equally great prize. In 1301 Andrew III, the last descendant in the male line of the Hungarian ruling house of Árpád, died childless and the united kingdoms of Hungary and Croatia were open to the competition of anyone who could claim descent from a former Hungarian king through females. Three such entered the lists, Charles Robert, grandson of King Charles II of Naples, Otto duke of Bavaria and Wenceslas II of Bohemia. In the year 1301 Charles Robert, who throughout had the zealous support of Pope Boniface VIII, came to Dalmatia and was there tentatively crowned. But Wenceslas proved to be the more skilful in using the situation in Hungary to his advantage. That country, since the destructive Tatar invasion of 1241 and still more since the death of the last Arpadian of any ability, Béla IV, in 1270, had become the victim of the ambitions of a dozen powerful and unprincipled clan chiefs who had partitioned nearly the whole of the country amongst them, destroying the authority of the central govern-ment, and behaving as independent despots each in his own wide domains. These oligarchs, fearing that a resident king might interfere with their liberties, looked for a ruler who would reside in Prague rather than Buda. It was therefore by winning the support of two of the most powerful of these clan chiefs, Matthew Csák and Ivan Köszegi, who between them ruled most of northern and western Hungary, that Wenceslas was able to take an army to Buda in 1301. There, somewhat to the consternation of his allies, Wenceslas had St. Stephen's crown placed on the head not of himself but on that of the young Wenceslas, his son and heir. He left him there with a small army and returned to Bohemia.

The central European empire which Wenceslas had thus created had an even shorter life than that of his father, Přemysl Otaker II, or that of his grandson, Charles IV. Its collapse is a striking example of how dynastic accident has profoundly affected the fortunes of whole nations. But Hungary was virtually lost even before the death of Wenceslas II. The Hungarian prelates, urged on by the papal nuncios, worked hard to seduce the oligarchs from their support of the Czech king and so Wenceslas decided to cut his losses. In 1303 he came again with an army to Buda and escorted his son back to Bohemia, leaving Hungary to be governed by Köszegi as regent. Rudolf of Austria and Wladyslaw the Polish aspirant allied themselves with Charles Robert; the Austrians invaded Bohemia and the Hungarians Moravia, so that when Wenceslas II died in 1305 Hungary was already lost. His son, Wenceslas III (1305–6) at once renounced the Hungarian crown in favour of Otto of Bavaria. He too was crowned in Buda, but by 1307 he faint-heartedly gave up the struggle and went home, leaving the field clear for Charles Robert.

Wenceslas III, an unpleasant and debauched young man, had surrendered Hungary in order to be free to assert his claim to Poland. But the Poles had already shown signs that they were tired of Czech rule. Wenceslas therefore set out from Prague for Poland to get himself crowned in Gniezno. On the way, in Olomouc in Moravia, he was murdered in bed; by whom or why is a mystery. Wenceslas III died childless so that Bohemia too now found itself in the helpless position of being without a male heir to the crown of Wenceslas. Here was the occasion for Hungary and Poland to resume their independent careers, each fortunately under a prince of exceptional abilities.

Wladyslaw the Short

The restorer of the Polish monarchy was Wladyslaw I, called the Short. Returning from exile in 1304 he steadily gained ground and soon after the death of Wenceslas became the master of southern Poland; by 1314 the central and western provinces had recognized him; in 1320, with the approval of Pope John XXII, he was crowned king in Cracow. But the reintegration of the kingdom was never complete. For one thing the new king of Bohemia, John of Luxemburg, would not surrender his claim to Poland, and even though he was unable to prevent Wladyslaw's coronation, John managed to persuade or bully most of the petty dukes of Silesia to accept his suzerainty. Bit by bit Silesia slipped away from Poland, not to be reunited to it until 1945. John of Bohemia, the very pattern of the *roi chevaleresque*, did further great damage to Poland by giving his services to Poland's greediest and most dangerous enemy, the Teutonic Knights. They were now desisting for a time from their crusade against the heathen Lithuanians and seeking to increase their wide lands in Prussia at the expense of their Christian neighbour, Wladyslaw the Short, whose rule had been recognized in eastern Pomerania as early as 1306. The Knights seized Danzig, with the rest of this province in 1308-9 and in the course of a war which lasted off and on from 1326 to 1333 they cruelly ravaged a wide expanse of Polish territory, including Gniezno itself. Despite a victory the Poles won in 1331 at Plowce the Knights remained in occupation of the provinces of Kujawia and Dobrzyn; Poland was completely cut off from the Baltic Sea. Wladyslaw had only been able to save himself from total defeat by allying himself with the young and vigorously expanding Lithuanian state. The preoccupation of Poland and the Teutonic Knights with each other had the important consequence of enabling the Lithuanian princes to subdue the western provinces of Russia without interruption. Prince Gedymin (1315-41) had consolidated his centre of government first at Troki and then at Wilno. His friendly relations with Wladyslaw, whose son Casimir was married to Gedymin's daughter Aldona, allowed him to occupy Brest Litovsk, Minsk and the district around Kiev with little trouble.

All this reads as if Wladyslaw of Poland were an unsuccessful king; but what is important was not the provinces he lost but the fact that he rid his country of Czech rule, preserved in union under the restored crown the all-important provinces of Great and Little Poland and thus made possible the restoration of the greatness and prosperity of the kingdom under his son and successor Casimir III.

Charles I of Hungary

The young Frenchman from Naples, Charles Robert (Carobert) of the house of Anjou, who restored the Hungarian monarchy after twenty-five years of disruption, oligarchy and foreign invasion, was an even abler and more successful ruler than Wladyslaw the Short. After the withdrawal of the Czechs and Bavarians Charles Robert, ably assisted by his French advisers and the papal legates, soon secured the control of the central government such as it was and in 1310 he was crowned in the ancient coronation city of the Árpáds, Székesfehérvár, with St Stephen's crown as King Charles I of Hungary and Croatia. He was then twenty-two years old. His prime task was to destroy the military and territorial power of the oligarchs who ruled most of the country. Of great help was the nuncio of Pope Clement V, the Franciscan cardinal Gentile, who by a judicious combination of diplomatic suavity and ecclesiastical censure persuaded the rich and powerful prelates and some of the magnates to submit to the royal authority. But it needed a great battle at Rozgony in 1319 before the power of the Aba clan in north-eastern Hungary was broken. The now desperate oligarchs sought to save themselves by invoking the aid of their allies, Andrew prince of Galicia and King Stephen Uroš II Miljutin of Serbia. The last to hold out against the king were Matthew Csák, lord of northern Hungary, and Andrew Köszegi in the west; the former died in 1321; the Köszegi sought armed help from the Austrian Habsburgs, but in vain; their last castles fell to Charles's armies in 1327. He was at last master of the whole realm. Austria had to pay the price of having backed the loser by surrendering to Hungary the crucially important city of Pressburg (Bratislava). To insure himself against the ever-threatening danger from the Habsburgs Charles made firm alliance with his Bohemian and Polish neighbours at a famous and ceremonious meeting of the three kings, Charles of Hungary, John of Bohemia and Casimir of Poland at Visegrád in 1335. Charles was already married to Casimir's sister Elizabeth and in 1339 it was agreed that their son and heir Lewis should succeed to the Polish as well as the Hungarian crown if Casimir died without an heir.

The restoration of the unity of Hungary under the undisputed royal authority was the preparatory part of Charles's achievement. He brought to central Europe a monarchy of the type developed by the kings of France and Naples, and, ably assisted by his French adviser, the palatine Philippe Druget, he proceeded to give Hungary an economic and financial organization and a central and local administration which made Angevin Hungary one of the most efficient and powerful states in Europe.

Bohemia under John of Luxemburg

The collapse of Bohemia after the extinction of the male Přemyslids in 1306 seemed likely to undo the work of a century of able government. The ambitious greed of the great lords, the jealous fears of the gentry and the jockeying for some share in political power of the rich German-speaking merchants in the towns rapidly reduced the country to chaos, which was prolonged by the struggle for the vacant throne. Immediately after the murder of Wenceslas III the Habsburg family tried to seize the prize, and the king of the Romans, Albert, was able to get his son Rudolf chosen as king by the Bohemian lords and prelates. But Habsburg rule of Bohemia was to be postponed for two centuries yet, for the young Rudolf, elected in October 1306, died childless in July 1307. The next bid was made by Henry, duke of Carinthia, the husband of Wenceslas's elder sister Anna. But Henry was both obstinate and incompetent and those of the nation's leaders who preferred a more amenable sovereign turned in an entirely different direction. They opened negotiations with the new king of the Romans, Henry VII of the house of Luxemburg; he was relatively poor and was therefore attracted by the possibility of securing the wealth and manpower of Bohemia to support his dynasty. Therefore in 1310 Henry's son John was married to Elizabeth, the younger sister of Wenceslas and sent by his father with a small army which speedily ousted King Henry and put the ten-year old John on the Bohemian throne.

The new king's youth and the promises he had had to make not to allow foreigners to hold offices in Bohemia or Moravia made it inevitable that John could not play the part of a Wladyslaw or a Charles Robert. The great offices of state remained in the hands of the magnates and the lesser administrative and judicial posts were filled by the lesser nobility and the gentry. If only King John had lived permanently in the country he might have restored the authority of the Crown as successfully as Charles was doing in Hungary. But John had no love for Bohemia and not much for his Bohemian wife Elizabeth, who was somewhat older than he. He was a Frenchman by education and inclination, passionately devoted to knightly and military pursuits, restless, inconsequent of purpose, ambitious of fame and glory. He rarely visited Bohemia and then only to raise money for his military enterprises, and the Bohemian people had to pay subsidies of increasing frequency and size to provide for John's expeditions to help his friends, the successive kings of France, and for the banquets and tournaments with which he tried to win the admiration of the chivalry of Christendom. His kingdom was therefore left to the care of Queen Elizabeth, with whom John finally quarrelled in 1319, and to the mercies of the magnate-ministers, especially the clever and power-loving Henry of Lipa, with whom John had to wage unsuccessful civil war during the years 1315 to 1319.

Though King John was an expensive luxury for Bohemia his reign was not entirely without advantage to the state. For one thing, his prolonged absences meant that the magnates and the prelates sometimes met together to deal with public affairs and these meetings were the first stage in the development of a national parliament. Also, in his perpetual anxiety to increase his sources of revenue, John worked hard and successfully to extend the dominions of the Crown of St Wenceslas. By first supporting and later opposing the Bavarian king of the Romans, Lewis IV, he got on lease the strategically situated district of Eger (Cheb) which controlled the route from southern Germany into western Bohemia. In 1320, 1321 and 1346 he secured most of the Slav-speaking provinces of Upper and Lower Lusatia, in the Spree valley north of Bohemia. King John was also responsible for adding most of Silesia to the lands of the Bohemian crown. He considered himself the rightful heir to the Přemyslid claims to Poland and therefore readily accepted the numerous Piast dukes of Silesia as his vassals, for they preferred to be subject to him rather than to the king of Poland. In 1335 Casimir III purchased John's recognition of the validity of his title to the Polish crown by recognizing John's overlordship of all the Silesian duchies except Schweidnitz and Jauer. Another boon John conferred on his realm was in 1333 to make his son and heir, Charles, margrave of Moravia and regent of Bohemia. The young man, twenty-three years old, began at once to reassert the authority of the Crown, to restore order and to restrain the lawlessness of the barons and knights. King John continued his adventurous life free of concern for Bohemia. Though he had lost his sight he conducted two more expeditions to help the Teutonic Knights, in 1337 and 1345. He and Charles went to the assistance of Philip VI when Edward III invaded France and it was entirely in character that John of Bohemia lost his life while leading a forlorn cavalry charge at the battle of Crécy on 26 August 1346.

Casimir the Great of Poland

The middle decades of the fourteenth century in central Europe were occupied by the reigns of the sons of the national restorers. Wladyslaw I was succeeded by his son Casimir III in 1333, Charles I of Hungary by

Lewis the Great in 1342 and John of Bohemia by Charles I in 1346. The position of Charles was complicated by the fact that he became ruler of Germany in the same year, being styled, as king of the Romans and later as emperor, Charles IV.[1] The three central monarchies were now free to develop their potentialities, for neither Germany (except the German offshoot in Prussia) nor Russia was in a condition to oppose their progress. Only the unhindered progress of Lithuania under its princes Jawnuta (1341–45) and Olgierd (1345–77) in expanding its empire over the whole of west and south-west Russia to the Black Sea appeared as a rival to the eastward ambitions of the Polish and Hungarian rulers.

Hitherto Poland and the Lithuanian princes had been allied in opposition to the Teutonic Knights. But in 1343 Casimir made peace with them at Kalisz; he renounced Pomerania to the Knights in return for the restoration of the province of Kujawia. Already there was ground for conflict with Lithuania because another great expanse of Russian territory had become available for annexation. When the Tatars killed Lev and Andrew, the last Russian princes of Volhynia and Galicia, the boyars elected the Polish duke Boleslaw of Mazovia to be their ruler; he turned out to be a tyrant and was assassinated in 1340. At once the Lithuanians occupied the eastern part of the territory, Volhynia, and Casimir the western part, Galicia (Halicz), which, with its orthodox population and its great trading city of Lvov (Lemberg), remained part of the Polish state until the partitions of 1772 and 1795 gave it to Austria. Casimir was able to complete the union of Poland under the authority of the Crown by asserting his authority over the duke of Mazovia in 1351. He also fulfilled in Poland the function that Charles Robert had performed in Hungary, namely that of reorganizing the administration of the state through the institution of royal officers in local government and by making the officers of state of Little Poland the Crown's ministers for the whole country. Casimir established an academy for the teaching of law at Cracow in 1364 and made that city the seat of his court and the centre of his government. Under him the Polish peasants enjoyed the benefits derived from the clearing of new land and from their resettlement under the 'German law' of earlier German colonists; trade and the towns flourished; the customary law was codified. The last of the Piast kings of Poland was with justice called 'the Great'.

[1] Cf. above, p. 191.

The establishment of the Romanian principalities

The principality of Lithuania was not the only new state which established itself in the area to which the ambitions of Poland and Hungary might well be attracted. In the first half of the fourteenth century there also appeared there the two Romanian principalities of Wallachia and Moldavia. The Romanian, or as they were then called, the Vlach people, were in 1300 already settled in considerable numbers in Transylvania as well as in the south-west part of the present-day Romanian Republic, that is, between the southern Carpathians and the lower Danube. Few historical controversies have consumed more paper and ink with less ensuing agreement than that of when and how the Vlachs came to be living in these areas. But whether it be that the Romanian historians are right in saying that these Vlachs of Transylvania and the Carpathians are the descendants of the Roman colonists of the second century A.D., or whether the Hungarians are right in their thesis that these Vlachs were recently immigrated nomadic shepherds from south of the Danube, or whether there is something of the truth in both theories, the fact of the presence on both sides of the eastern frontier of Hungary of these numerous, Romance-speaking Vlach communities made itself very evident during the anarchic period of Hungarian history between 1270 and 1310. As the Hungarian state was fragmented under the oligarchs, so its divisions tended themselves to dissolve. Thus it was that out of the Transylvanian province of László Khan there developed in central and western Wallachia a Romanian principality. Its legendary founder was Radu the Black; in fact the creator of the principality of Wallachia was a chief with the Cuman name of Basaraba (Bassarab). He first appears about 1312 with his seat of government in the foothills of the Carpathians at Arges, on the Danubian tributary of that name. After Charles I of Hungary had reasserted royal authority inside his realm he conducted, in 1330, an expedition to exact fealty and tribute from Basaraba. The Vlachs resisted the royal army and were defeated near Arges, but while the Hungarians were returning home the Vlachs ambushed them on a mountain defile and rained down rocks and arrows on the trapped feudal cavalry, nearly destroying it. The king barely escaped with his life. Basaraba, who lived till about 1342, and his son Alexander were able thereafter to consolidate the principality, free from immediate danger from the kings of Hungary.

A generation later than Wallachia a second Romanian[1] principality

[1] The Vlachs of Moldavia and Walachia did not begin to call themselves Romanians until the seventeenth century.

was established in Moldavia, that is in the area between the eastern Carpathians and the river Seret. This area, with a sparse Slavonic (Ruthenian) population, had since the middle of the thirteenth century been spasmodically visited by tribute-seeking Tatar raiders. To protect his eastern frontier in 1354 Lewis of Hungary settled a colony of Vlachs from the Maramures district of north-eastern Hungary beyond the Carpathians at Cîmpulung and in the valley of the Moldava, a tributary of the Seret. He appointed a Vlach 'prince' named Dragos as its *vojevode*. About the same time another Vlach prince, whom Lewis had dismissed from his office of *vojevode*, took to the same area of Moldavia a band of Vlach settlers; in 1359 Bogdan drove out Sas, the son of Dragos and thenceforward he and his successors ruled the principality of Moldavia, extending its eastern boundaries to the river Dniester.

Lewis the Great of Hungary

Under the second of its Angevin kings, Lewis I, Hungary reached the summit of glory and power. Lewis the Great (1342–82) inherited from his father a united, obedient realm, enriched by Charles's financial reforms and well governed as a result by his introduction of a Franco-Neapolitan type of administration. It is a remarkable witness to the excellence of Charles's work that there was no baronial revolt in Hungary during the forty years of Lewis's reign, even though he only once summoned a parliament. It was not that Lewis was so imprudent as to seek to destroy the liberties and privileges of the nobility. Indeed, at his only parliament of 1351, he extended the principle of hereditary noble privilege to all the nobles, small as well as great, and ensured it by enacting the law of entail (*avaticitas*) which prevented the alienation of noble property. Rather he entered into cooperation with the nobles, condoning their liberties in return for faithful service in the army and the administration of the realm.

Like his contemporaries Charles IV and Edward III, Lewis of Hungary was a great empire builder. He spent an immense amount of energy, time, money and blood in trying in vain, in 1347 and 1350, to acquire the kingdom of Naples from his second cousin Joanna, the much married and dissolute queen of Naples (1343–82).[1] But in almost every other direction he was successful. As the result of a series of wars with Venice Lewis recovered the coast and islands of Dalmatia and won the great trading port of Dubrovnik (Ragusa). When the Serbian empire of Stephen Dušan[2] collapsed after 1355 Lewis sought successfully to

[1] Above, p. 180.　　　　　　　[2] Below, p. 246.

consolidate his southern frontier against the advance of sultan Murad I by asserting his suzerainty over Bosnia, northern Serbia and north-eastern Bulgaria. He forced the *vojevodes* of Wallachia and Moldavia to recognize his overlordship. Lewis's mother Elizabeth was the sister of Casimir III of Poland (who had no male heirs); Casimir had always recognized Lewis as his heir presumptive, so that when Casimir died in 1370 Lewis was crowned as king of Poland, which his mother governed on his behalf. Thus Lewis came to rule the largest political complex of fourteenth-century Europe. His authority extended from the Masurian Lakes to Dubrovnik and from Pressburg to the Dniester.

Charles of Luxemburg in Bohemia

The Bohemian analogue to Casimir of Poland and Lewis of Hungary was Charles I, second ruler of the Luxemburg dynasty.[1] When he succeeded King John in 1346 he was already experienced in the art of government. Unlike John he identified himself with Bohemia, whose position and wealth he saw would provide an advantageous foundation for empire building, one much more reliable than divided and ungovernable Germany. His policy therefore was to confirm the royal power in the Bohemian lands by economic, legal and cultural reforms and to make Bohemia the centre of as large an empire as possible, chiefly by dynastic means for dynastic ends. He spoke Czech.

By repressing bands of brigands he secured the safety of roads and travelling merchants; he introduced the vine into Bohemia; he built a new stone bridge, the famous Charles Bridge which still stands, connecting the two parts of Prague on either side of the Vltava, and he built a new quarter of the city, with its own walls, town hall and town council, which he filled largely with Czechs to counterbalance the powerful German-speaking merchants who had long dominated the Old Town. Charles was no friend of the great landlords who had dominated the country during his father's neglectful absences, and he tried to limit noble privileges by defining them in a codification of the law known as the *Majestas Carolina*. But it is characteristic of the kings of this period that when the nobles took up the position of *nolumus leges terrae mutari* he dropped his plan. However he ignored the infant institution of the Diet, which he regarded as a dangerous product of the days of royal weakness. Charles owed his imperial title to the support of

[1] He was, as Charles IV, king of the Romans and emperor. For his part in the history of Germany, see p. 192.

the papacy; he was also devoutly religious even to the point of superstition and had a genuine concern for the reformation of morals and religion. Already while he was still regent, in 1344, he had secured from his friend and former tutor, Pope Clement VI, the elevation of the bishopric of Prague to archiepiscopal rank, thereby freeing the Church in Bohemia from ecclesiastical dependence on the archbishop of Mainz. He secured the appointment as first archbishop of a zealous reformer of clerical abuses in the person of Arnošt (Ernest) of Pardubice. He also was concerned that his Bohemian and German subjects had no university of their own, but had to make the long journey to Paris or Bologna if they wanted to study. Therefore, again in collaboration with Clement VI, he founded in 1348 the university of Prague, of which archbishop Arnošt was the first chancellor. The university was modelled on Bologna and Paris, and had at first to be manned by German, Silesian and Italian professors, until they had educated a generation of Czechs who competed with them for position and control. Like Lewis of Hungary, Charles drew much of his inspiration from France and, as in Hungary so too in Bohemia, French models influenced everything from the forms of feudal society to architecture and the illumination of manuscripts, as well as the nominalist philosophy of the university scholars. Matthieu of Arras was brought in by Charles to undertake the rebuilding of the Prague metropolitan church of St Vitus.[1] The great castle of Karlštejn which Charles had built on the road from Germany to Prague still looks like a fourteenth-century French château.

Charles's second task, the creation of an empire with which to endow his family was facilitated by his position as German king and by the concentration of the attention of Casimir of Poland on Lithuania and Galicia. He rounded off his father's gains in Silesia by marrying the heiress to Schweidnitz and Jauer, the only remaining independent Silesian duchies, in 1369. His greatest prize was the margraviate of Brandenburg, which by a combination of bullying, craft and main force he wrested in 1373 and 1374 from the sons of Lewis of Bavaria, who had enfeoffed them with it when the Ascanian house died out in 1320. Finally, by securing the betrothal of his second son, Sigismund, to Maria, the infant daughter of Lewis of Hungary, in 1372 he prepared the way for the incorporation of Hungary in the Luxemburg empire.

Within five years of each other the two great political structures of

---

[1] St Vitus was completed, more or less in the form it has today, in Charles's lifetime by an architect and sculptor, Peter Parler, whom Charles imported from Germany.

central Europe were dismembered. Before his death in 1378 Charles IV, ever more careful of the interests of his family than of the unity of his dominions, had secured the imperial election of his eldest son Wenceslas, and had allotted to him the succession in his German lands and in Bohemia and Silesia; Moravia went to Charles's nephew Jobst, Lusatia to his son John of Görlitz and Brandenburg to his son Sigismund. When Sigismund became involved in the business of trying to secure the Hungarian throne he first pawned Brandenburg to Jobst and after Jobst's death he enfeoffed his faithful servant Frederick of Hohenzollern, burgrave of Nuremberg, with Brandenburg (1415), which thereby passed from the brief rule of the Luxemburgs to the dynasty which was to rule it until 1918.

Lewis, king of Hungary and Poland, died in 1382, leaving only two daughters, the eleven-year-old Mary who was betrothed to Sigismund and the nine-year-old Hedwig, betrothed to the young Habsburg prince William. The Poles had no desire to continue to be ruled by a Hungarian sovereign, and therefore, after an unhappy period of civil war, they elected in 1384 Hedwig as their 'king' (under the name of Jadwiga), and to secure the country against disunion and the ever present threat of the Teutonic knights, the Polish lords induced her to renounce William of Habsburg and to accept as her husband Jagiello of Lithuania. Jagiello was an able and experienced man of thirty-six who had been grand prince of Lithuania since 1371. He undertook by the agreement of Krems of 1385 to be baptized with all his heathen subjects if he were married to Hedwig and elected king, and 'to join his lands of Lithuania and Russia to the kingdom of Poland for ever'. This union, so heartbreaking for Hedwig, but so fortunate for Poland, was completed by the election, baptism under the name of Wladyslaw, marriage and coronation of Jagiello in the early months of 1386. Immediately he went on a baptismal tour of his hereditary lands and within a few years the last pagans inside Christendom were converted.

It took even longer to settle the succession in Hungary. The claims of Mary and Sigismund to succeed were disputed by Charles of Durazzo, king of Naples, who brought an army to vindicate his claims. There were five years of bloody strife in which Charles was assassinated and Elizabeth the queen mother was strangled. The death of Charles decided the issue in favour of Mary and Sigismund; they were married in 1385 and in 1387 Sigismund was crowned king of Hungary at Székesfehérvár; in the same year the civil war came to an end and Sigismund was to rule Hungary until his death in 1437.

Bohemia in the early fifteenth century

Neither Sigismund, the new king of Hungary, nor his elder brother Wenceslas (Václav IV of Bohemia; Wenzel, king of the Romans) was of the calibre of their father Charles IV. Wenceslas was an intelligent young man of seventeen, of good natural parts, but without assiduity, persistence or sound judgment. He was inordinately fond of hunting and in later life he drank too much. Like his brother-in-law, Richard II of England (who married Anne of Bohemia in 1382), he surrounded himself with young favourites, men of bourgeois or mean origin, whom he promoted to profitable offices in state and church. Like Richard he was cursed by a number of ambitious relatives, his brothers Sigismund and John of Görlitz, his cousins Jobst and Prokop, who joined forces with the prelates and magnates to oust the favourites, take their offices and revenues for themselves and submit the king to government by a council of great lords. Just as Richard was wasted in his struggle with the Lords Appellant, so Wenceslas was twice, in 1394 and in 1403, defeated by a coalition who on both occasions handed him over to the custody of their ally the duke of Austria. From 1396 to 1403 Bohemia was governed by the aristocratic council. Like Richard, Wenceslas ultimately threw off the yoke and for the last sixteen years of his reign resumed a more or less despotic government, though he was by 1403 so lethargic and besotted that he never was dangerous enough to the aristocracy to incur the risk of deposition from his Bohemian throne.[1]

Throughout his reign Wenceslas was in trouble with the Bohemian Church. Archbishop John of Jenštejn (1379 to his resignation in 1395) proved to be a lesser Thomas Becket. When he was appointed he was a gay, careless young man of twenty; but very soon he suffered a change of heart and became austere, serious and full of a sense of his duty to maintain the administrative, judicial and financial control of his Church against the interference and depredations of the king. Their conflict culminated in 1393 when Wencelas tortured and drowned in the Vltava Jenštejn's vicar general, John of Pomuk.[2] In the latter part of his reign

[1] His neglect of his German kingdom had induced the German electors to depose him from his imperial position and elect Rupert of the Palatinate in his place in 1400. See above, p. 192.

[2] During the Counter-Reformation the Bohemian Jesuits secured the canonization of Pomuk under the name of St John Nepomucene. They regarded him as the martyr of the seal of the confessional, quite erroneously, for there is no truth in the story that he was killed by Wenceslas because he refused to betray the confession of Queen Sophia.

Wenceslas had an even more devastating quarrel with archbishop Zbyněk of Hazuburk. Basically the quarrel was again due to Wenceslas's attempts to control the Bohemian Church and to tap its wealth, but it was embittered by the fact that Zbyněk refused to connive at Wenceslas's withdrawal of obedience from the Roman pope after the Council of Pisa and by Wenceslas's refusal to allow the archbishop a free hand to deal with Huss and Jerome.[1] In 1411 Zbyněk was forced to flee from Prague; he died before he could reach asylum abroad. His successors in the archbishopric were creatures of the king.

The trial and burning of the two leaders of the Czech religious reformation, John Huss and Jerome of Prague, at Constance on 6 June 1415 and 30 May 1416, revealed to Wenceslas and Sigismund, his heir presumptive, that the great majority of the Czech gentry, nobility and masters of the university were strongly behind the reformers. In September 1415 an assembly of nobles and gentry appended their seal to a document which, in the name of the 'regnum Bohemiae et marchionatus Moraviae', declared Huss to have been no heretic and averred its determination to persevere in Huss's principles of the sovereign authority of Scripture and freedom to preach the word of God. King Wenceslas, anxious not to offend Sigismund, feebly tried to stem the rising tide. He imposed a town council of reactionary German merchants on the New Town of Prague. When these magistrates arrested some champions of reform, a ci-devant monk named John of Želiv raised the Prague mob which ended its demonstration by throwing the magistrates of the New Town out of the window of the Town Hall on to the pikes of the mob below. The Hussite revolution had begun. Less than three weeks after the defenestration, on 16 August 1419, the furious and plethoric king died of an apoplectic stroke.

The Hussite revolution was essentially a religious revolt against the corruption, worldliness and superficiality of the Church and churchmen. As such it will be considered as a factor in the religious and ecclesiastical history of Christendom (see chapter XII below). Here it must be treated under its political and social aspects as a part of the history of central Europe in the fifteenth century. Every class of Bohemian society participated in the revolution. The peasants were told by some of the more fanatical Hussite preachers: 'You will no longer pay rent to your lords nor serve under them, but their estates, fish ponds, meadows, woods and all their lordship are to be free to you; everything must be in common and no one must have anything of his own, for who has anything of his

[1] Below, p. 324.

own sins mortally.' Thousands of them left their land and their homes to flock together in 'cities at refuge', to the camps they biblically christened Tabor and Horeb, there to practise for a few months an apostolic community of goods. Even after the prophesied Day of the Lord passed uneventfully and their communistic principles were compromised by the hard necessities of survival, the peasants continued to fight with flail and scythe in a cause which was no longer theirs. The free farmers and gentry were the backbone of the revolution; they fought to rid themselves of the local tyranny of the great secular and ecclesiastical landlords; they fought not only for religious liberty but for social security against encroachments on their property and already diminished rights; in the towns the wage-earning labourers and journeymen, the craftsmen and the poorer masters fought to rid the towns of the rich, usually German, merchant patricians; the nobles, even if not all of them nor for all the time, fought to get the lands of the monasteries and nunneries which were so ruthlessly destroyed, and to secure for themselves the control of government at the expense of the king.

The death of Wenceslas IV removed the last barrier to the flood. His heir, Sigismund, king of the Romans and king of Hungary, came quickly with an army of Hungarians and Austrians to try to secure at once the throne of the country whose resources were so essential to his plans; he came too as the executant of the Council of Constance, to destroy the religious revolt which his own tergiversations had done much to provoke. He did in fact force his way into the castle of Prague in the year 1420, where the archbishop crowned him; but the people of the city, reinforced by the armies of the peasants who poured in from Tabor and Horeb, quickly drove him out; John Žižka, gentleman and professional soldier and most zealous follower of Huss, defeated his effort to enter the Old Town at the battle of Vitkov and again at the Vyšelund, and drove him out of the country, all within the same year. The leaders of the national resistance were determined not to have Sigismund unless he agreed to allow the principles enshrined in the Four Articles of Prague: communion in the wine as well as the bread of the Eucharist for the laity and freedom of preaching of the Word of God, drastic curtailment of the property of the Church, and the punishment by the state of mortal sins. The estates of the realm, lords, gentry and burgesses, therefore assembled at Čáslav in 1421 and there decided to invite a Polish prince to come to be governor of Bohemia; they also set up a committee to carry on the government in his absence. Though eventually Prince Korybut came from Poland and had two spells as a sort of king on approval, he was never crowned king. Bohemia remained kingless from 1420 to 1436, and again from 1439 to 1453; the sovereign body in the land was the Estates, lords and gentry now strongly afforced with burgesses, which not only was sovereign in things temporal but was also *de facto* sovereign in things spiritual, for it appointed and controlled the consistory of priests and masters of the university which governed the Hussite Church right down to 1620.

Sigismund never gave up his endeavours to recover the Bohemian throne. He organized invasion after invasion, from Hungary, from Austria, Saxony, Bavaria; the councils and popes sanctified his expeditions as crusades. But every invasion was defeated, at first by bloody battles, at Žatec in 1421, at Kutná Hora in 1422, and at Ústí in 1425. Žižka and, after his death in 1424, his successor, the Hussite priest Prokop the Shaven, organized the mightiest military instrument hitherto devised, the wagon laager, armed with pikemen, small arms and primitive howitzers, impregnable in defence and overwhelming in attack. Such terror did these armies of the 'warriors of God' strike into the invading crusades that the armies which Cardinal Beaufort led to Táchov in 1427 and, the last of the anti-Hussite crusades, that which the papal legate, Cardinal Giuliano Cesarini led to Domažlice in 1431 fled at the mere sound of the approach of Prokop's host. The Czechs were not content to remain on the defensive. They believed that they had a divine mission to take the word of God to other lands, and their terrible wagon armies rolled destructively through Silesia, Thuringia, Saxony, Bavaria, even in 1433 right through Poland to the mouth of the Vistula.

But yet the Hussite wars were a failure, for they did not succeed in keeping out Sigismund for ever. In the intervals between foreign invasions the Hussites quarrelled amongst themselves, the extremer faction of the peasants and smaller gentry whose centre was Tabor and who wanted no compromise with the Church, against the more moderate party of the lords and the conservative Praguers and masters of the university (the so-called Calixtines), who wanted no social revolution and not to remain for ever as schismatic pariahs in Christendom. In 1434 at the fateful battle of Lipany the Calixtines smashed the Taborites and killed Prokop their leader. They then proceeded to negotiate with the Council of Basle and with King Sigismund. In 1436 a compromise was made at Jihlava, whereby Sigismund returned peacefully to Prague as king in return for promising to maintain the *Compactata*, which embodied the Four Articles of Prague.

Sigismund in Hungary

When at last, in 1436, Sigismund entered peacefully into his Bohemian inheritance it was already too late to rescue his fifty years rule of Hungary from failure. Not even the wealth of the silver mines of Kutná Hora could repair ravages of his luxurious life and costly wars, nor was Bohemia an adequate recompense for the territories that Sigismund had lost. He had indeed been unlucky. In 1403 Ladislas, king of Naples, had renewed the enterprise which had cost Charles of Durazzo his life. He had invaded Croatia and been crowned king of Hungary in Zagreb; he captured Pest and Esztergom and it needed a mighty effort and a great triumph of arms at the battle of Papoc to expel him. Venice too seized the opportunity of Sigismund's preoccupations to renew the struggle for mastery in the Adriatic, and after a series of costly and bloody wars Venice wrested from Hungary the towns and islands of the Dalmatian coast (1411–13; 1418–19). Between 1428 and 1433 western and central Slovakia were repeatedly raided and devastated by incursions of the Hussite armies. Worst of all, the Turks, after they had destroyed the Serbian and Bulgarian empires, ate away at the territories which were subordinated to the Hungarian crown, Wallachia, the banates of Severin and Mačva and Bosnia, so that by the end of Sigismund's reign the sultan ruled right up to the Sava and the Iron Gates.

A ruler as constantly and unsuccessfully at war as was Sigismund had little opportunity to develop or even to preserve the monarchical supremacy established by his Angevin predecessors. He could only keep himself on the throne by allying himself with one or other of the aristocratic factions who used him as a stalking horse for their ambitions and a milch cow to satisfy their greed. He was compelled regularly to consult with the Estates and to enact laws which granted to the nobles, organized in the country courts, wide jurisdictional and administrative powers. So costly a reign could not but be disastrous for the peasants, who ultimately had to pay for it. By the time Sigismund died the Hungarian serfs were paying a tithe to the Church, a ninth of their produce to the lords, one gold florin at least every year to the king and doing increasingly burdensome labour services. Also, in 1435 there was imposed on them the duty of providing one armed knight for every thirty-three *portae*, or servile holdings, to give the state a regular army (*militia portalis*) of 120,000 men.

Poland and Lithuania

More successful than Sigismund was his contemporary and rival Wladyslaw Jagiello, since 1386 king of Poland. It is astonishing how Jagiello, so lately a heathen barbarian, proved himself to be a statesman of the first rank, fully aware of both the opportunities and limitations of his position as the ruler of the largest state in Christendom. His first and greatest achievement was to save Poland and Lithuania from the aggression of the Teutonic knights, who, rightly alarmed at the dynastic union of their two inland neighbours, repeatedly sought to extend their rule into Jagiello's territories. He and his cousin Witold, who was the governor and from 1401 grand prince of Lithuania, waged two hard-fought wars with the Knights (1409–11, 1414–22). The crucial year was 1410 when a great battle was fought and won by the Poles and Lithuanians with their Czech and Tatar auxiliaries at Grunwald (or Tannenberg as the Germans call it) in the Masurian lake district. The grand master was killed with thousands of his army, and though the victors failed to exploit their advantages by destroying the Order, there was never again any possibility of the Teutonic knights recovering their former power. In the course of their later wars with the Knights Jagiello and Witold were able to rescue and retain the province of Samogitia and thus separate the Knights in East Prussia from their affiliated branch, the Knights of the Sword, in Livonia.

Jagiello and Witold were always ready to take advantage of the weakness of their neighbours. While Sigismund was still fighting with the Neapolitans for Hungary, Jagiello brought the Romanian principality of Moldavia under Polish suzerainty. As to Russia, not satisfied with his possession of all its western provinces, Witold imagined that he could take advantage of the infant weakness of Moscow and the decrepitude of the Golden Horde to bring the whole of the country under his rule. Despite a severe check when, in 1399, he was soundly beaten by the Tatars at the battle of the Vorskla, Witold renewed his war with Russia during the minority of the Muscovite prince Vasili II. By the time of Witold's death in 1430 the Polish-Lithuanian state had acquired Smolensk and pushed its frontiers to within a hundred miles of Novgorod and Moscow, while in the south-east it occupied the Black Sea coast between the Dniester and the Dnieper and pushed 200 miles east of Kiev.

Jagiello was far too prudent to offend the Polish lords and the Russian boyars, whose privileges he extended and made uniform. For a time he was friendly with Hussite Bohemia but soon reverted to close collaboration with the Catholic Church, and especially with Zbigniew Oleśnicki, the bishop of Cracow who from 1423 was for over thirty years the leader of the Polish lords and prelates. It was of serious concern to both Jagiello and Witold that the inhabitants of the Russian provinces which they ruled were Orthodox, and a serious attempt was made by the Polish rulers to get the Councils of Constance and Basle to effect some sort of union of the two Churches. Nothing was, however, achieved before the death of Wladyslaw Jagiello in 1434. He was succeeded by his ten-year-old son Wladyslaw III (1434–44) whose youth proved a welcome opportunity for Oleśnicki and the nobility to impose limitations on the royal power and to exact further liberties.

Succession problems in central Europe: Ottoman pressure

The death of Sigismund in 1437, after only a few months enjoyment of his Bohemian acquisition, presented a succession problem to Bohemia, Hungary and Germany, for Sigismund was the last of the house of Luxemburg. He left no son, but his daughter Elizabeth was married to Albert of Habsburg, duke of Austria, who was elected king of the Romans without trouble. The Bohemian Estates also elected Albert, but some of the more zealously Hussite lords were suspicious of so confirmed a supporter of the papacy, and invited in a Polish army which occupied much of Albert's short reign. Hungary too elected Albert as king, and it looked as if a Habsburg era in central Europe had begun. But Albert died of the plague in 1439 and his house had to wait for nearly a century for the Bohemian and Hungarian crowns. Albert had no son, but his wife Elizabeth was pregnant when he died and early the next year bore a son who is known to history as Ladislas Posthumus. Again the three realms had to find a king. The German electors chose Ladislas's second cousin, a young man named Frederick of Habsburg, hitherto ruler of Styria, who became the emperor Frederick III (1440–93). The Bohemian Estates hesitated, and in fact remained kingless for a second period, from 1439 to 1453. The Hungarians were divided between a group of nobles who selfishly welcomed the prospect of a long regency and others, more concerned for the nation's safety in face of the mounting Turkish danger. The first group, the 'legitimists', crowned the baby Ladislas V in May, but two months later the others, those who saw the advantages for themselves in an elective monarchy, induced the Poles to send their young king Wladyslaw III to Hungary where in July he was crowned king of Hungary (1440–44) under the name of Úlászló I.

After a brief civil war his supporters prevailed and the dynastic union of Poland and Hungary was revived.

The supreme purpose of the Polish-Hungarian union was to drive the Turks out of Wallachia, Serbia and Bulgaria and to relieve the eastern empire in its extremity. Pope Eugenius IV sent both Cardinal Cesarini and the energetic and fanatical friar Giovanni Capistrano to urge on the Hungarians to the last crusade which had any chance of damming the Ottoman flood. That chance was the greater because Hungary now had in the person of John Hunyadi a military commander of real distinction. In 1443 King Wladyslaw-Úlászló, accompanied by Cesarini, Hunyadi and the last Serbian prince, George Branković, led a great army acros the Danube. The hosts of the sultan Murad II were beaten back; the crusaders stormed Krusevuć, Nis, Pirot and Sofia, but they failed to force their way through the Balkan mountains. It was already too late in the season to continue to campaign. Therefore the king, well pleased to have rescued northern Serbia, retired and proceeded in July 1444 to negotiate a ten years' truce with Murad, who was away dealing with rebels in Asia minor. Cesarini thought the opportunity for renewal of the crusade too good to be missed. He persuaded the reluctant Wladyslaw that he need keep no faith with the infidel.[1] So only a month after he had sworn not to cross the Danube again the king renewed the war and led a triumphal military parade through Bulgaria as far as the Black Sea. Murad's anger was terrific; with lightning speed he brought his army across the Bosphorus and hurried by forced marches to attack the perjured Christians at Varna. There, on 10 November 1444 was fought the fateful battle. After a hard fight the Christian army was destroyed; King Wladyslaw and Cesarini were killed; Hunyadi barely escaped with his life.

Central Europe after Varna

The tragic death of the king was a domestic disaster for both realms. The Poles for long did not believe he was dead and it was only after three years of confusion that his younger brother Casimir IV was crowned in his place. It was worse for Hungary. There seemed no possible successor except Ladislas Posthumus, and he was a child of four whom his guardian, the Emperor Frederick III, jealously kept in Austria. The best that could be done was to set up in Hungary a regency council of seven, of whom, fortunately, Hunyadi was one. He soon showed himself to have as excellent gifts as a statesman as he had as a soldier. He

[1] Scholarly debate continues on the responsibility for this decision.

based himself on the support of the class into which he was born, that of the lesser nobility, which he championed against the overweening magnates. His task was not easy, particularly because the Slovak parts of northern Hungary were dominated by 'free-companies' of Czech soldiers, who after the end of the Hussite wars had come to batten on Hungary. Their leader, Jiskra, was virtually independent lord of Slovakia from 1440 to 1460. Hunyadi had too to fight against the leaders of the aristocratic faction, the lords of Cilli and Garai. But in 1446 the Diet recognized the still absent Ladislas as king and nominated Hunyadi regent, who was able to force the magnates to accept his authority. Even when Frederick III at last released Ladislas and he came to Hungary to rule in person Hunyadi still remained the effective ruler of the state. Throughout all these years he was almost constantly continuing the war with the Turks and in 1456 he led another national crusade, this time to save Belgrade which the sultan Mohammed II was beleaguering. In a brilliant campaign Hunyadi raised the siege, but within three weeks of his victory he died of the plague, 22 July 1456. The young king Ladislas V died the next year and Hungary for the fourth time in twenty years was without a natural successor to the crown.

The death of Albert II in 1439 had left Bohemia, like Hungary, kingless. The Bohemian Diet, arrogating to itself the right of electing a successor, hawked the once rich crown of St Wenceslas around half Europe; but Frederick III, Albert of Brandenburg and Albert of Bavaria all rejected the opportunity. The royal lands had been so much dissipated or seized by the nobles that no one was willing to assume the financial burden of being king of Bohemia; moreover the catholic princes were hesitant to take on an heretical and schismatical country. Therefore for thirteen years Bohemia was again without a king and that at a time when it needed one most, for only a strong monarch, allied with the gentry and the towns could have arrested the growing power, wealth and independence of the magnates, already enriched by the spoils of the monasteries and the episcopal lands. Since the thirteenth century it had looked as if Bohemia was developing constitutionally on the western pattern and would follow England and France in evolving a strong national monarchy which would defeat the tendency towards feudal oligarchy by relying on the support of the merchants and gentry and by developing a royal council at the expense of an aristocratic parliament. Due to the Hussite revolution and the two long interregna of 1419 to 1436 and 1439 to 1453, Bohemia divagated from the course which the last Přemyslids had set, and drifted into the wake of the politically retárded countries of eastern Europe where it was not the king but the nobility who triumphed. It was not only that the Czech magnates, Hussite and catholic alike, used the opportunity of the interregna to enrich themselves at the expense of the Church, the royal estates and their weaker neighbours, but that through failure of heirs what kings there were were elected and that usually under conditions which limited their power; four of them, Sigismund in 1436, Albert in 1437, Ladislas Posthumus in 1453 and Wladyslaw Jagiello in 1471 were made to purchase the crown by capitulations.

The breakdown of central government after 1439 was rapid and almost complete. The needs of local defence in the religious and civil wars rapidly brought about the parcelling of the country into a dozen virtually autonomous local governments, the so called *landfirdy*, which were governed by councils composed of lords, gentry and burgesses. They were obviously happy hunting grounds for ambitious magnates, one of whom, Hynek of Práček, became the real ruler of eastern Bohemia by uniting under himself as *hejtman* the four Hussite *landfirdy* of Čáslav, Konřim, Chrudím and Hradec Králové. When Práček died in 1444 he was succeeded by *hejtman* of the Boleslav *landfird*, George (Jiří) of Poděbrady, who added his own to the other four. Poděbrady was a young noble of the Kanstát family which had prospered greatly from the opportunities of twenty-five years of lack of governance. In his abilities and career he had much in common with his contemporaries John and Matthias Hunyadi.

George of Poděbrady

In 1443 the Bohemian Estates had recognized Ladislas Posthumus as heir to the throne, but not for ten years were they able to get him out of the clutches of his guardian, Frederick III; thus the Czech lords, with George of Poděbrady at their head, still had a free hand. He strove to establish his own authority and that of the Hussite *landfirdy* over the whole country, but for a time the catholic lords and towns of the southwest, led by the lord of Rožmberk and the city of Pilzeň (Pilsen) leagued together against him. After a brief civil war in 1448 Poděbrady seized Prague; in 1452 the Estates recognized him as governor of the realm. The next year Frederick released Ladislas to become king in fact as well as name of Bohemia and Hungary. But though Ladislas lived in Prague and tried with some success to recover the alienated estates of the Crown and the Church, Poděbrady remained in power in Bohemia, just as Hunyádi did in Hungary. When Ladislas died unexpectedly in

1457 the Bohemian estates elected George of Poděbrady as king, even though there was no drop of royal blood, Přemyslid, Luxemburg or Habsburg, in his veins. It was more a triumph for the aristocratic than the monarchic principle, for George made no attempt to establish a dynasty by securing the succession for his son.

George on the whole served his country well. He brought together the 'external' lands of the Bohemian Crown, Moravia, Silesia and Lusatia, which had almost completely escaped from the authority of Prague during the preceding forty troubled years. He showed great diplomatic skill in building a solid body of support for himself by acting as mediator in the tangled affairs of Germany. He even tried to form a great secular coalition of rulers, led by himself and the king of France, to organize an anti-Turkish crusade quite independently of the pope. Inspired by his French counsellor, Antoine Marini, he seems even to have thought about the possibility of a European confederation of monarchs with some sort of federal European parliament.

King George of Bohemia, representative great landowner though he was, was a good Czech and a good Hussite. It is true that at the beginning of his reign he had secretly promised to work for the reconciliation of his realm with the Roman Church. He even sent an embassy to Pius II. But the pope made it perfectly clear that there could be no reconciliation unless the Czechs surrendered their claim of the Cup for the laity. Indeed Pius solemnly revoked the *Compactata* which had been agreed between the Czechs, the Council of Basle and Sigismund in 1436. His successor, Paul II, in 1466, denounced George as the 'son of perdition', declared him to be deprived of his throne and his possessions, and proclaimed a crusade against him. The pope found it hard to get any ruler to carry out his sentence until in 1468 Matthias Corvinus, king of Hungary, assumed the function, more from territorial greed than from any pure love of orthodoxy. The last years of King George were overshadowed by a bitter war. Matthias made alliance with the league of the catholic lords of Bohemia, invaded Moravia, where he was proclaimed king of Bohemia, and then fought his way into Bohemia. George countered vigorously and in turn invaded Matthias's territories, but when it looked as if he was going to be victorious, he suddenly died, in March 1471. The Bohemian estates tamely gave the crown, not to George's son Viktorin, but to Vladislav (1471–1516), the eldest son of Casimir IV, in the hope that he would secure Polish help against Matthias, not seek to destroy the Hussite Church and be a willing instrument in the hands of the landlords. In the last respect they were well satisfied, for King Vladislav II of Bohemia was the model *roi fainéant* of the later Middle Ages.

Matthias Corvinus

The history of Hungary in the latter half of the fifteenth century runs more or less parallel with that of Bohemia: the brilliant reign of a native king, followed by the enervating rule of a puppet. But Hungary reached a pitch of glory and power under Matthias I Corvinus (1458–90) which surpassed that attained by the pope-harassed George of Bohemia.

When Ladislas V of Hungary died in 1457 there were many candidates for the throne—Polish, Saxon and Habsburg. But the great mass of the gentry and burgesses wanted John Hunyadi's eighteen-year-old son Matthias, whom they elected, on conditions and under the regency of his uncle, Michael Szilágyi. Within a few months Matthias showed that he was going to be the puppet of no faction. He dispensed with his uncle's services and began to govern through a body of ministers, some of them foreigners, of his own choice. His first task was to put an end to a threat from Austria, whence Frederick III was making a bid to incorporate Hungary within the Habsburg complex. Matthias then turned to the opposite frontier and in a series of campaigns recovered some ground from the Turks in Wallachia and northern Serbia. These and other military successes were in large measure due to a thorough reform of the army; for the small and unreliable feudal force of the *banderia* he substituted an army based on the rule that every lord should supply to the king's service one knight for every twenty serfs he owned; lords with fewer than twenty serfs must serve in person, and those with fewer than ten must band together to supply their quota. Matthias also reformed the fiscal system and the gold and silver mines so that he was well equipped to wage the continuous war which occupied his reign and to enrich his court and library without too heavy an oppression of the peasantry.

In 1468 Matthias Corvinus accepted Paul II's invitation to lead a crusade to destroy Hussite Bohemia. The prize was a tempting one, for it might be made the basis of an Hungarian empire which would include not only all the lands of the Bohemian crown, but might well lead to the conquest of the Habsburg lands, even of Germany and the imperial crown. It has been charged against Matthias that he sacrificed to these western ambitions the last chance to put a stop to Turkish expansion in Europe. But in justice to him it must be recorded that he never entirely neglected the Turkish danger. He was fighting them continuously and successfully from 1458 to 1468. During the period of Matthias's campaigns in Bohemia and Austria the Turks renewed their incursions into Croatia, even into Styria. But in 1475, 1476, 1479 and 1481 Matthias turned on them and was able to maintain head against them until his death. He probably believed, and with some justice, that Hungary alone was not strong enough to deal efficiently and finally with the Turkish danger, but needed all the resources in men and money of Bohemia, Austria and Germany to make sure of fulfilling its duty to Christendom. So perhaps he may have justified his great ambitions; that the plan was not impossible of realization is proved by the great measure of success he achieved before his premature death, at the age of fifty, in 1490.

Matthias's attack on Bohemia was of very doubtful success until King George's death in 1471 and the succession of the feeble Vladislav II Jagiello made possible his triumph, which was consummated by the Peace of Olomouc in 1478 whereby Moravia, Silesia and Lusatia were ceded to Matthias, leaving only Bohemia to Vladislav. Both rulers retained the title of king of Bohemia. Next Matthias turned on Austria. In 1477 Matthias's army occupied much of lower Austria; by treaty with the archbishop of Salzburg he gained military control of that vast province; in 1480 he occupied most of Styria and finally in 1485 he besieged and captured Vienna. When he died in that city in 1490 he was lord of an Hungarian empire that occupied and dominated the whole of south-central Europe. None of his contemporary sovereigns could equal him in power and glory. It seemed as if the future of Europe lay with the Hungarian king.

Casimir IV

When King Wladyslaw III disappeared on the disastrous battlefield of Varna his Polish subjects refused to believe he was dead and it was not until two years afterwards that they elected his younger brother, Casimir IV (1447–92) to succeed him. Though Casimir was only seventeen he had already gained some experience in government as grand prince of Lithuania. His long reign, which overlapped both George of Poděbrady and Matthias Corvinus, was of great importance in the history of Poland and Lithuania.

First, he dealt finally with the Teutonic Knights. Since their defeat at Grunwald in 1410 they had ceased to be a danger to Poland and Lithuania; indeed their anomalous position as a religious Order ruling the now Christian and Germanized Prussian lands made them rather a temptation. Many of the subjects of the Teutonic Knights, especially the German landowners and the German inhabitants of the Prussian towns, disliked the monopoly of power of the arrogant Knights. They formed the so-called 'Prussian Union' and began to look to Poland to set them free. Casimir rushed at the opportunity. In 1454 he began the Thirteen Years' War by invading Prussia, having purchased the support of the Polish *szlachta* by granting them, by the charter of Nieszawa, the right to be consulted in their local Dietines (*sejmiki*) the right to give or withhold their consent to any new legislation or general armed levy. The first Polish attack on the Knights was badly defeated at Chojnice (1454), but Casimir persisted, greatly helped by the Danzigers and by the navy of his Danish ally, Eric VI. The decisive victory was won by the Polish general Peter Dunin at Puck in 1462. In 1464 Bishop Langendorf of Warmia (Ermland), the most important prelate in Prussia, deserted to the Poles. In 1466 Casimir's armies finished off the war by capturing Stargard and Chojnice. The Teutonic Knights made peace at Toruń. The grand master became a vassal of the king of Poland; the eastern half of his territory, that is the whole of the lower Vistula area, together with Danzig, Elbing, Toruń, Marienburg and Warmia, was incorporated in the kingdom of Poland as 'Royal Prussia'. Poland again had a coast on the Baltic and what was left of the lands of the Order, 'Ducal Prussia', lingered on as a fief of the Polish crown. The remaining twenty-six years of Casimir's reign were relatively uneventful. He was much concerned at the extension of the Turkish empire round the western end of the Black Sea. Bayezid II took Kilia on the Romanian coast and Akerman south of the mouth of the Dniester in 1484, and Poland was cut off from the Black Sea coast.

When Casimir died in 1492 he was not succeeded by his eldest son, Vladislav king of Bohemia and Hungary. The Polish senate deliberately preferred to make an election, for they distrusted the principle of hereditary right. They chose Casimir's second son, John Albert (Jan Olbracht) as king of Poland; his younger brother Alexander became grand prince of Lithuania.

Weakness of central European monarchy

In appearance central Europe at the end of the fifteenth century seemed to constitute a Jagiellonian empire. One brother, Vladislav-Ujászló, was ruler of the three kingdoms of Bohemia, Hungary and Croatia, together with Moravia, Silesia and Lusatia; another, John Albert, was king of Poland, together with Galicia and royal Prussia; the third, Alexander, was grand prince of Lithuania and lord of the Russian provinces of

Podolia, White Russia and the Ukraine. The rival dynasties of Luxemburg, Poděbrady and Hunyadi were extinct. The Habsburgs, under Maximilian I, seemed to be only interested in the Netherlands and Burgundy. But there was no Jagiellonian empire, no confederation amongst the brothers. In 1500 Poland seemed to be in the happiest position, for John Albert was a cultivated and able ruler who was developing a monarchy of the new type under Renaissance influences. Nevertheless the situation in Poland was precarious. Even so competent and energetic a monarch as he was handicapped by the elective character of his office; he had no allies within the state, for the towns were not well developed or nationally conscious, most of the burgesses being Germans. John Albert had repeatedly to make concessions to the *szlachta* who only gave him support for his wars in return for the grant of concessions at the expense of the peasants[1] and the towns. In 1496 when he was preparing for a great struggle with the Turks he had to grant, at the Diet of Piotrków, the right of the lords to bind their serfs to the soil, to forbid townsmen to own agricultural land and to allow the lower house of the Diet a full share in legislation and the granting of taxes. If ever the Jagiellonian line in Poland should entirely fail (as it did in 1572) the supremacy of the *szlachta*, political and economic, would be assured.

The fate of Bohemia and Hungary had already been decided when George of Poděbrady died in 1471 and Matthias Corvinus in 1490. The lords of both countries definitively and permanently established their sovereignty by electing the negligible Vladislav Jagiello as their king. He is known to history as 'king very well' because of his ready acquiescence in everything proposed to him. During his long reign in Bohemia of forty-five years the magnates steadily accumulated power, property and privileges; they dominated the Diet, of which the upper house was composed of the great lords and the lower house of representatives of the knights and gentry. In Bohemia too the peasants were made *adscripticii* by statutes enacted in 1497 and 1500. So entrenched was the nobility in control of the state that not even Ferdinand I in the following century was able completely to assert autocratic principles there.

In Hungary after Matthias Corvinus there was no great king. During the reigns of Vladislav (Úlászló) Jagiello (1490–1516) and his juvenile son and successor Lewis II (1516–26), the magnates and the prelates, who were members of the great noble families, were in absolute control. Through the Diet they made laws to their own advantage; the towns and

[1] For the peasants in central and eastern Europe see above, pp. 40-2.

the peasants were steadily and progressively repressed. Both Hungary and Bohemia were inevitably cursed with faction fights between the great noble families, and at the moment when the Ottomans were preparing to break through the frontiers which had been held against them for a century none of the three countries which might be expected to oppose them first was either united or efficiently enough governed to avert catastrophe.

0   100   200   300   400 miles
0   200   400   600 km

Novgorod

R. Volga   Kazan

Pskov
Tver
Riga   Vladimir
LIVONIA (Teutonic Order)
R. Dwina   Moscow
Memel   Kasimov
                              Riazan
SAMOGITIA   WHITE
Koenigsberg   Smolensk   Kulikovo Pole
Baltic   Sea
PRUSSIA   Vilno   RUSSIA
Danzig   WARMIA   Troki
POMERANIA   Elbing   Minsk
Stargard   Tannenberg   Marienburg
Berlin   Torun   Dobrzyn   R. Niemen
BRANDENBURG   Gniezno
Pinsk   LITHUANIA
LUSATIA   POLAND   Kalisz
MAZOVIA   Brest-Litovsk   R. Pripet
Gorlitz   SILESIA   Piotrkow   Lublin   Kiev   R. Dnieper   R. Vorskla
Jouer   Schweidnitz   Cracow   VOLHYNIA   UKRAINE
BOHEMIA   Prague   Kutna Hora   GALICIA   Lvov
R. Eger   Pilzen   Chrudim   Olomouc   CARPATHIAN   PODOLIA
R. Malau   Caslav   MORAVIA   Lisov   MTS.   R. Dniester   R. Bug
BAVARIA   Krems   Vienna   SLOVAKIA
AUSTRIA   Pressburg   Rozgony   Seret R.   Sea of Azov
STYRIA   Buda   Pest   R. Tisza
CARINTHIA   Papa   Szekesfehervar   MOLDAVIA   CRIMEA   Kaffa
Zagreb   TRANSYLVANIA   Galati
Venice   CROATIA   HUNGARY   Cimpulung   Kilia
DALMATIA   Ruma   Belgrade   Iron Gates   WALLACHIA
BOSNIA   Nicopolis   Danube R.   Black   Sea
SERBIA   BULGARIA   Varna
Krusevac   Nis   Pirot   Sofia   Trebizond
Dubrovnik   Kossovo   OTTOMAN   TURKS
(Ragusa, V)   Adrianople   Constantinople   Bosphorus
ALBANIA   MACEDONIA   THRACE   Pera   Nicomedia
Otranto   Thessalonika   Gallipoli   Sea of Marmara   Nicaea   BITHYNIA
Athos (G)   Brusa   Ankara
EPIRUS   Lemnos (G)
Corfu   THESSALY   Lesbos (G)   ANATOLIA
(V)   Negroponte (G)   Phocaea
GREECE   Corinth   Chios (G)   Smyrna   Konya
Athens   (G)
PELOPONNESE   Samos (G)   Ephesus   Adalia
(MOREA)   Nauplia (V)   RHODES   CYPRUS
Modon   Mistra   Duchy of Naxos   Nicosia
(V)   Kithira   (V)   (V)
(V)   Candia   Beirut
CRETE (V)

Adriatic   Sea

N

7. CENTRAL AND EAST EUROPE

X

Eastern Europe

It is logical enough to discuss the eastern Mediterranean area and the nascent Russian state in the same chapter. The latter had owed its distant origin to Scandinavian settlements on the overland route to Byzantium and at the end of the day Russia, with a Greek Orthodox Church and a language which employed the Greek alphabet, was to inherit some of the ambitions of the vanished empire of Constantine. Yet for much of the Middle Ages the two areas had little contact and in what follows pride of place will be given to the Greek Empire and its fall, for this at the time directly involved the fortunes of other European communities.

BIBLIOGRAPHY. The subjects dealt with in this chapter are discussed in volume IV of *Cambridge Medieval History* which has appeared in a revised two-volume form, ed. by Professor Joan Hussey (1966–7). The best account of the Byzantine Empire is G. Ostrogorsky, *History of the Byzantine Empire*, trans. Hussey (Oxford, 1956); W. Miller, *Latins in the Levant* (London, 1908) is still useful; a recent work is by F. Thiriet, *La Romanie Vénitienne* (Paris, 1959). The final catastrophe is the subject of modern treatment by Steven Runciman, *The Fall of Constantinople: 1453* (Cambridge, 1965). On Byzantine civilization see: S. Vyronis, *Byzantium and Europe* (London, 1966) and F. Masai, *Pléthon et le Platonisme de Mistra* (Paris, 1956). The canonical history of the Ottoman Turks is J. von Hammer-Purgstall, *Geschichte des osmanischen Reiches*, 10 vols. (Pest, 1827–35). A recent and valuable account of Ottoman beginnings is by P. Wittek, *The Rise of the Ottoman Empire*, Royal Asiatic Society Monographs (London, repr. 1958); see too F. Babinger, *Mahomet II le conquérant et son temps* (Paris, 1954) and D. M. Vaughan, *Europe and the Turk* (Liverpool, 1954). The crusade and crusading literature is the subject of A. S. Atiya, *The Crusade in the Later Middle Ages* (London, 1938). For Russia see: V. O. Klutchevsky, *History of Russia*, trans. C. J. Hogarth, I (London, 1931) and the fuller account by Vernadsky in G. Vernadsky and M. Karpovich, *History of Russia*, III, IV (Princeton, 1953–59); J. L. I. Fennell, *Ivan the Great of Moscow* (London, 1961) deals mainly with foreign relations. A. T. Luttrell discusses the fourteenth-century crusade, and D. Obolensky Byzantium and Russia in *Europe in the Late Middle Ages* (App. II, below, p. 399). Cf. Dvornik, above, p. 212.

Byzantium in the later Middle Ages

The Eastern Empire never forgot its august origins nor the world dominion claimed by Constantine and his successors. The city had remained enormously wealthy at a time when barbarian invasions reduced the towns of the western Empire to shadows. A paid civil service and army, a church obedient to the emperor, a tradition of Greek learning, all combined to make Byzantium for long the most imposing centre of civilization in the Christian world. From the twelfth century, however, there was a change. Massive threats to the Greek Empire appeared and its survival was achieved at the cost of loss of territory to Seljuk Turks and crusaders, who fought over Asia Minor, and to Slavonic peoples slowly pressing into the Balkans from the north. At the same time cultural and religious antipathies exacerbated political tensions between the West and the East. The final stages in this were reached in the thirteenth century. In 1204 the Fourth Crusade captured Constantinople and a Latin Empire was established, greatly to the advantage of Venetian traders in the east Mediterranean. The conquest of Greek lands was, however, not complete; there were Greek rulers in Epirus, at Trebizond and at Nicaea. From Nicaea the Palaeologi were established on the imperial throne, with Genoese help, in 1261. For the remaining two centuries of its existence the Greek Empire suffered the consequences of these events. There were Frankish rulers in Achaia, the Venetians were in control of Crete and many of the Aegean Islands, and the Genoese were established in Pera (Galata), the port adjoining Constantinople; the mountainous Balkan provinces were now the home of indigenous Serbian and Bulgarian princelings; in Asia Minor the area ruled from Nicaea was the object of attack by warlike Turkish tribes, one of which was to take its name from its leader Osman, who inherited power in 1281. To the east the advent of the Tatars had disrupted trade across the steppes (though this was to recover) and sealed off Russia.

The history of the area was thus in practice deprived of the unity which had been earlier provided by aggressive emperors; one is compelled to compare the resulting disintegration with the falling apart of Germany after 1250. Just as the history of Germany must be conceived in regional terms, so with the fragments of the Eastern Empire. Indeed this is even truer of the Eastern than of the German Empire of the Middle Ages, for in Germany a common language and a common (if often tenuous) loyalty to the emperors survived, which in the nineteenth century were to inspire the reunification of the country. In the nineteenth century in the Balkans, on the contrary, linguistic (equated with ethnic) differences joined with national sentiment to encourage the development, not of a revived Greek Empire, but of a coherent Greek kingdom and separate states in Albania, Serbia, Bulgaria and Romania.

Properly to illustrate the regional history of the Balkans and the east Mediterranean is impossible in the present context. It would mean chronicling the disturbances which were endemic in the Balkan countries; describing the Angevin principalities on the coast facing Italy and their relationship with Naples and Provence; dealing with the successive Frankish, Catalan and Florentine dukes of Athens, as well as with the Venetian families who ruled in the duchy of the Archipelago (the Cyclades), the Genoese in Chios, the Hospitallers in Rhodes. Some idea of the intricate politics of the area may be gained from the ma (p. 241) and from the main developments in the slow decline of the Empire to its final collapse.

The first of the restored Palaeologi[1] tried, with some success, to re-establish a meaningful authority, but on the death of Michael VIII the problems of government defeated his successor Andronicus II. This was not (as used to be said) because Andronicus was inept, but because the problems he faced were beyond his resources. Feudal relationships

[1] Palaeologi emperors:

Michael VIII
(d. 1282)
|
Andronicus II
(1282–1328, d. 1332)
|
Michael IX
(d. 1320)

Andronicus III John VI Cantacuzenus
(1328–41)   (1341–54, d. 1383)
| |
John V = Helena
(1341–91)

Andronicus IV   Manuel II
(1376–79, d. 1385) (1391–1425)
|
John VII
(1390, d. 1408)

John VIII Constantine XI Thomas
(1425–48) (1449–53)
|
Ivan III of Moscow = Zoe (Sophia)

steadily increased to the advantage of the great landowners and the detriment of the Crown, for the nobles evaded taxes and tended to accumulate tax-paying lands of lesser landowners and peasants, while they failed to render the appropriate military service. There was thus even more need for a mercenary army and even less money with which to pay it. The gold currency of Byzantium, once the greatest in the Mediterranean area, crumbled. The emperor had trouble with the Greek province of Epirus, virtually independent under its own despot, as well as with the Venetians who attacked the Empire because of favour shown to the Genoese; the Italian republics gained from the war but the Empire lost. At the same time the Asiatic provinces of the Empire fell to the Ottomans. In an effort to secure help, Andronicus hired a Catalan mercenary company under its leader Roger de Flor. The Catalans won a victory over the Turks but then ravaged Thrace before moving to Thessaly where they overthrew the Franks and established a Catalan duchy based on Athens and Thebes which lasted until 1379. As for his northern neighbours Serbia and Bulgaria, Andronicus perforce tried to pacify them with bribes and royal marriages. Thus was set the scene for the disasters of the fourteenth century.

It was a time of civil war. For this there are a number of reasons. The Empire really consisted of separate regions and this almost inevitably led to devolution of the central authority of the emperor. In any case the Latin Empire of the thirteenth century had encouraged provincialism and in the latter-day acceptance of feudalism there was a sympathy for the appanage which cut across the whole autocratic tradition of an earlier day. It was now customary for an emperor's heir to be crowned co-emperor; this gave a ready-made focal point round which opponents of the ruler could gather. Finally, in the desperate straits to which the economy had been reduced, social groups came into open conflict, the rich being attacked by the poor, especially in the cities. In such circumstances an adventurous politician could make a dramatic career for himself. But likewise the situation offered endless opportunities for the hungry peoples, Slavonic and Turkish, on the flanks of Byzantium and for the parasitic activities of Genoa and Venice. There were, however, certain alleviations in the grim picture: the Bulgars and Serbs suffered from primitive social and political organization and were potentially even more divided than Byzantium; the Ottomans had enemies in the other Anatolian emirates; Venice and Genoa were deadly rivals. A strong government in Constantinople might have been able to divide and rule its enemies. But strong government did not emerge.

Andronicus II, whose sober policy of retrenchment was unpopular, was challenged in 1321 by a conspiracy led by a rich noble, John Cantacuzenus, and a self-made soldier, Alexius Apocaucus, who succeeded in getting for Andronicus III (crowned co-emperor in 1325) the province of Thrace, while the old emperor retained the capital and the other small fragments of the Empire. In 1328 Andronicus II was deposed and forced to enter a monastery. Cantacuzenus, whose title was Grand Domestic (commander of the armies), was now the real power. He succeeded in recovering for Andronicus III some authority in Epirus, and planned to extend control also to the Morea when he assumed the regency for the nine-year-old John V in 1341. In the event Cantacuzenus was faced by a further civil war, provoked by the jealousy of Apocaucus. Cantacuzenus had himself proclaimed emperor. At the same time a severe social upheaval occurred, an anti-noble movement which was particularly violent in Adrianople and Thessalonica. Encouraged by Apocaucus radicals took over the government of Thessalonica in 1342 and held power for the next eight years. But Apocaucus died in 1345; Cantacuzenus entered the capital and married his daughter Helena to John V. Devolution went on. Cantacuzenus made part of the Morea into a despotate ('despot' was the highest title the emperor could confer) for one son and created an appanage in western Thrace for another. In 1353 he had his son Matthew proclaimed emperor as a result of John V's reaction. But in 1354 Cantacuzenus was deposed.

The real gains in this period went to the Ottomans (with whom Cantacuzenus was regularly in alliance and whose fortunes are dealt with later in this chapter), and to the Serbs and the Genoese, who profited from the civil and class war in Thrace, Macedonia and Thessalonica. The predatory advances of the Serbian boyars against Greek territory were galvanized and unified during the meteoric reign of Stephen Dušan, who had been made king in 1331 and who controlled Bulgaria as a result of his marriage to the sister of its ruler. In the next few years all of Macedonia was occupied, the Serbian patriarchate was detached from obedience to Constantinople and in 1345 Dušan assumed the title 'emperor of the Serbs and Greeks'. Albania and Epirus were overrun. Dušan's 'realm now stretched from the Danube to the Gulf of Corinth and from the Adriatic to the Aegean coast'.[1] When he died at the age of forty-six in 1355 his power was at its greatest extent. But conquered territory had been granted out to the Serb and Albanian nobles;

[1] Ostrogorsky, p. 467.

despite Dušan's reputation as a lawgiver and his evident ambition to rule as a Caesar, there was no political structure to support a weaker king. Under his successor Uroš (1355–71) the Serbo-Greek empire broke up, to fall victim in its turn to Turkish occupation. As for the Genoese, Cantacuzenus boldly tried to divert merchant shipping from Pera to Constantinople itself and also with difficulty raised funds to build much-needed shipping. The Genoese, who monopolized trade to the extent of collecting 87 per cent of the customs dues of the Bosphorus, went to war and destroyed the Byzantine ships in 1349. A few years later Cantacuzenus joined the Venetians in a further attack on the Genoese. He was, however, compelled to treat with Genoa and the upshot was Venetian support for John V in the struggle with Cantacuzenus which now opened, though it was with the help of a Genoese adventurer, Francesco Gattilusio, that John V obtained undisputed power and was able to get rid of his rival. Gattilusio was given John's sister as a wife and the island of Lesbos as her dowry.

John V and his successors felt obliged to turn to the west for help, recognizing that the price to be paid was a union of the two Churches. John V wrote in 1355 to Pope Innocent VI promising obedience in return for an army and a fleet, which did not materialize. In 1366 the emperor went to Hungary to beg help from King Lewis; he got nothing for his pains. In 1369 John went to Rome, where he personally accepted the Roman faith. His successor Manuel spent two fruitless years in the west (1400–1), where his pathetic state aroused much pity but led to no results, and John VIII also visited the west in search of help in 1423. Finally, in 1437 John VIII left for Italy with a large company and, in 1439 at Florence, accepted the union of the two Churches at the papal council.[1] These gestures were without effect not least because in the last century of its existence the mantle of imperial pride was carried by the Orthodox clergy, rather than by the emperors. To the ancient suspicion of Rome was added a growing consciousness of the uniqueness of Greek Christianity and of the scholarly background on which it rested.[2] During the period 1394–97 the Patriarch Antony issued a stern rebuke to the grand duke of Moscow for daring to maintain the Orthodox Church without a corresponding loyalty to the emperor. 'It was not the State which stood behind the Church', writes Professor Ostrogorsky, comparing this situation with that of an earlier day, 'but the Church which supported the State.'[3] Even Manuel is quoted by a contemporary Greek source as saying 'we should make use of the project

[1] Below, p. 290.   [2] Below, p. 250.   [3] Ostrogorsky, p. 492.

of reunion to conciliate the Latins when we need their support: we should never try to make reunion effective'.[1] On the eve of the fall of the city an imperial official expressed a view which may well have been general: 'I would rather see the Muslim turban in the midst of the city than the Latin mitre.'[2]

Under John V the emperor became a client of the Ottomans. This further decline in power directly led to further palace revolutions. In 1373 Andronicus revolted against his father unsuccessfully. In 1376 he rebelled with more success, aided by the Genoese in Pera anxious to prevent John V handing over the island of Tenedos to the Venetians. Tenedos, commanding the entrance to the Dardanelles, was finally neutralized (1381) after a bitter war fought in the western as well as the eastern Mediterranean. John V and his son and heir Manuel were restored with Turkish help in 1379. The only compensation for the declining power in Constantinople itself (and by the end of the fourteenth century only the capital city remained of the Macedonian and Thracian provinces) was the success of the Greek despots in the Morea. Cantacuzenus's son Manuel had started a process, carried on by the Emperor Manuel's sons, which by 1430 had put practically the whole of the Peloponnese under their control. The despotate of the Morea was to survive the fall of Constantinople, succumbing to the Turks after 1460.

Why did Constantinople not collapse before 1453? The brief answer to this question is that the Turks were defeated by the Mongol Timur in 1402, an event which disrupted Ottoman power for a decade. The defences of the city were also extremely strong on the land side, defeating a siege in 1422, and at sea the Turks were as yet inexpert and weak. Nevertheless when the Turks really exerted themselves the result was a foregone conclusion. The siege lasted from 7 April 1453 to 29 May when the walls, battered by excellent Turkish artillery, were carried, the defenders overcome and the city sacked. Constantine XI was killed in action. And so was Giovanni Giustiniani, captain of a small Genoese company which had reached the city just before the siege began.

Before turning to the Ottomans who thus became undisputed masters of great tracts of Europe and Asia, a further matter deserves consideration: the character of Greek civilization in these last centuries of the Empire. This has direct political relevance for it helps to explain why the 'Hellenes' (as the Byzantine governing class began to regard them-

[1] The historian Sphrantzes, quoted Masai, p. 323n.
[2] Ostrogorsky, p. 505.

selves at this time) were so unwilling to accept union with the Latin west, which might have secured for them more effective help in their resistance to Ottoman invasion.

Byzantine civilization

One of history's frequent paradoxes is found in this period. While the Empire of the Palaeologi was crumbling the cultural activity of the Greeks was entering a fresh and lively phase. Indeed it is not entirely inappropriate to talk of a Byzantine Renaissance in the fourteenth and fifteenth centuries. This renewed artistic and intellectual activity was moreover far from being monopolized by the capital city. Like all the big Greek towns, Constantinople had suffered seriously from the Black Death; many districts were deserted and in ruins. The city which had once been enormously wealthy was now threadbare. We read that the emperors of the mid-fourteenth century banqueted with earthenware vessels rather than the gold or even the silver of an earlier day. The Palaeologi did their best to maintain the splendid walls of Constantinople in good condition. But that was almost the limit of construction there, though some artists were still at work at the start of the fourteenth century. The fourteenth and fifteenth centuries are chiefly interesting because of the decentralization of art, the spread of Byzantine painting and mosaics in the Balkans and in the Aegean.

In one field in which the Greek Empire had been pre-eminent there was no recovery. The legal system codified by Justinian, which was immensely influential in the west during the Middle Ages and which at this time was rapidly developing further in many parts of the continent, meant little in its disorganized homeland. Legal reforms were undertaken from time to time, but the courts and the judges were corrupt and the whole notion of an emperor-focused jurisprudence was meaningless in a state which existed only in scattered and isolated portions. Andronicus II and Andronicus III appointed 'supreme justices of the Romans' but the effort to curb regional judicial autonomy failed. The clergy took a much larger part in judicial administration than in earlier centuries.

The Byzantine Church had often in the past experienced the influence of oriental mysticism; the image-breaking movement (iconoclasm) of the eighth and ninth centuries was such a moment and it left an indelible mark in the austere and hieratic art of the Greeks. In the fourteenth century occurred another intense spiritual development, known as hesychasm (the cult of devout silence). Mystical and ascetic practices were not unknown among Greek monks. The teaching of

Gregory of Sinai revived them in the early fourteenth century, especially among the well-endowed monks of Mount Athos in the south of Macedonia. There was, however, dispute about the theology of the divine light, a vision of which these spiritual exercises were designed to provide. The Greek-speaking Calabrian monk Barlaam (who failed to teach Petrarch the language of Homer) when at Constantinople attacked the hesychast monks, claiming that the divine light which they experienced must be God Himself, a contradiction since God was not visible to men. The defender of the movement was St Gregory Palamas (d. 1357–58), who argued that the light was not God but a manifestation of God. Gradually hesychasm won adherents in the Greek hierarchy and its final victory was assured when it gained the patronage of John Cantacuzenus and his aristocratic party. The doctrine was officially approved at a council in 1351 and remained the active ingredient in Orthodoxy in the Empire till its collapse. It was, in fact, a return to an older pattern and it intensified the difference between the rationalist Roman church and its schismatic rival. During and after the negotiations which culminated in the Act of Union in 1439 it was adherents of hesychast principles who constituted the most stubborn opponents of accommodation with Rome: the most notable of these was Mark Eugenicus, metropolitan of Ephesus, whose disciple George Gennadius Scholarius became the first patriarch of Constantinople under the Turks.

Another and more ancient stream in Greek culture surfaced in the fifteenth century, but one utterly opposed both to the transcendentalism of the hesychasts and the Aristotelian logical position of western Latin thought, which had had adherents in Byzantium from the twelfth century onwards. This time the centre was even further removed from the capital, at Mistra in the Morea, though the extraordinary man behind it, George Gemistus, who gave himself the surname 'Plethon', was born about 1360 of an important clerical family at Constantinople. After the usual education of a well-to-do Byzantine, he acquired (probably from a Jew) a profound knowledge of Aristotelian, neo-Platonic and Jewish Cabbalistic thought while residing at the court of the Ottoman sultan Murad I. He then returned to the capital where his teaching displeased the orthodox clergy, and he was given an official magistracy in the Morea sometime after 1405. He remained there until his death in 1452, interrupting his residence by only one major absence when he went with the emperor to the council of union in 1438–39.

It is easy to exaggerate the significance of Plethon, for he was the only thoroughgoing Platonist of his generation, or indeed of the whole of the later Middle Ages. His teaching, moreover, has tempted historians to associate him with the syncretism slowly growing up in the Florence of Marsilio Ficino and Giovanni Pico.[1] In reality it was utterly opposed to any accommodation between Platonic teaching and either Aristotle or Aquinas. More important, Plethon was not a Christian; in that lies his lonely distinction. Nor was he an atheist in any strict sense of the term (and it must be remembered that the word was applied abusively in the late fifteenth and sixteenth centuries to many men who deviated from the orthodoxies of Catholicism or, later, of Protestantism). Plethon is rather, and accurately, to be described as a pagan. Below the Supreme Being he ranged the Ideas, identified with the Gods of Olympus, and there seems no doubt that a few intimates at Mistra were initiated into rituals which had as their aim the encouragement of the morality which Plethon drew from his inspiration in Plato. It was above all in his ethical and political doctrines that Plethon envisaged a revived Hellenism which he tried to instil into the despot of the Morea and into the emperor: he

> thus advanced . . . an absolutely revolutionary political ideal: instead of summoning the emperor and his compatriots to the defence or the re-establishment of the old Byzantine empire, he invited them to change their political aim, to abandon their interest in the Asiatic and European provinces . . . now lost to Hellenism, in order to concentrate on the defence and unification of the Greek fatherland properly so called. This was defined as 'the Peloponnese and the adjacent part of Europe with the neighbouring isles', because 'this was the country which the Hellenes have always occupied'.[2]

The practical recipe for this was a national and not a mercenary army: one part of the population would fight for the community, the other (analogous to the helots of old, but free and with strictly determined financial dues) would work; individuals would choose which role they would fulfil; the land would be held in common. In its turn this attempt to steer the future course of his people and to digest its past history stemmed from a conviction that human affairs were divinely governed, that Plato had established the principles for understanding man and his place in the scheme of things, that there was an 'eternal wisdom'.

Plethon's Hellenism represented a tradition consciously inimical to Christianity and one which had incurred political and ecclesiastical censure whenever it had manifested itself earlier in Byzantine thought.

[1] Below, p. 343.   [2] Masai, p. 88.

Plethon himself was bitterly attacked (notably by the theologian George Gennadius Scholarius) but was protected by his absence from the capital. The fall of the Empire denied a future in Greece for Plethon's teaching. The lectures given at Florence, however, by the 'prince of the Platonic sect' in 1439, when he was attending the council, inspired Ficino and undoubtedly encouraged Italians to a livelier interest in Plato. It may well be questioned how many of them really appreciated that Plethon was genuinely a disciple of Plato, that he accepted the Ideas in a way which made nonsense of western 'idealism', that he believed in polytheism. It does seem established that the devout Bessarion, who stayed on in Italy and became a cardinal, both knew of his former master's real beliefs and yet continued to regard him as a profound thinker. Ironically Plethon found an Italian resting place. When Sigismondo Malatesta acted as Venetian general in a campaign in the Morea in 1464 he captured Mistra and brought Plethon's body back to be placed in one of the sarcophagi set in the niches round the 'temple' into which he had turned the church at Rimini.[1]

Plethon was the most unusual thinker and writer of the period, but there were many more. The old connection between the emperor and literature was maintained both by John Cantacuzenus, who wrote his lengthy memoirs after his deposition, and by Manuel II, a highly cultivated man who wrote on theology and rhetoric. An outstanding literary figure of the early fourteenth century, Nicephorus Gregoras (d. 1360), wrote a large *Roman History*, which contains a particularly elaborate account of the Empire from 1320 to 1359. Three other notable historians were at work in the period immediately after the fall of the city in 1453. Plethon's pupil Laonicus Chalcocondyles (1424–1511) described in a manner deliberately based on ancient models the rise of Ottoman power down to 1463; Ducas (dates unknown), who was sympathetic to union and to the Genoese, wrote in detail of the period 1389 to 1462; the history by George Sphrantzes (1401–78) goes down to 1477. The lively and continuous religious and philosophical controversies over hesychasm and over the Union of the Churches, produced a vast literature. The most impressive of these writers was Demetrius Cydones (c. 1334–c. 1400), neo-Platonist, companion of John V and supporter of union with the Latin Church and critic of hesychasm who, among many other works, translated into Greek the *Summa Theologiae* of Aquinas. Both Cydones and Sphrantzes held high office in the Empire.

Finally the artists of latterday Byzantium deserve respect. Their

[1] Below, p. 352.

mosaic pictures and fresco paintings break fresh ground. 'There is a new lightness, a new delicacy, the approach is more human and, although none of the old ethereal quality of the art has been lost, it has at the same time gained a new intimacy.'[1] The main centres seem to have been in the Morea and the art of the churches at Mistra has been most fully examined. After the fall of Constantinople and the Turkish conquest of the Morea the monks of Mount Athos took up the new style and it is also found in Crete, the homeland of Domenicos Theotocopoulos, 'El Greco', the Greek.

The culture of the Empire which disappeared under Ottoman conquest was thus more than merely respectable. It had, however, little or no future in its own area, and its influence must be traced elsewhere. In the arts Byzantine painting had influenced Italian painters like Cimabue, Duccio and Giotto, though the long-term result was to be a school of painting which rejected (in Vasari's words) the 'clumsy Byzantine manner'; in the sixteenth century El Greco was to bring his genius, and a peculiarly Byzantine spirit, to Venice and then to Spain. The future of the Greek style was also assured in parts of the Balkans and above all in Russia. Likewise with philosophy and literature, it was in the west that its Greek roots were to be cherished, thus constituting the 'Byzantine Background to the Italian Renaissance'.[2] At the time this direct Greek influence was confined to a handful of scholars and it should not be conceived as constituting a major element in the Italian or European Renaissance.

The advance of the Ottoman Turks

The Ottomans owed their name to an early leader. They owed their fortune to two circumstances, one arising from the character of the Turkish peoples of Asia Minor and the other from the situation in the Empire. The Seljuk sultanate of Rum, based on Konya (Iconium), had harboured militant Muslim warrior bands known as Ghazis for border defence against the Byzantine Empire; these groups of soldiers had a knightly ethos and, whenever successful, they attracted swarms of recruits (including some of the *akritai*, Byzantine frontier troops). When the Seljuk power at Konya declined in the thirteenth century the Turkish Ghazi bands set up a number of independent emirates of which one was situated near the Byzantine towns of Brusa and Nicaea,

[1] D. Talbot Rice, *Byzantine Art* (London 1954), p. 102.
[2] The title of the study by Kenneth M. Setton in *Proc. Amer. Phil. Soc.*, 100 (1956), pp. 1–76.

in the area south of the Sea of Marmora. Hostilities for this body of Ghazis meant attacking major fortified positions, but they also meant that major rewards and rich booty were the prizes of adventure. On the side of the Empire, the thirteenth century saw the destruction of the old Empire by the Latins. The Palaeologi, who from Nicaea recovered power in 1261, inherited both a diminished and weak Empire and familiarity with the marcher forces of the Turks, now established in areas till recently part of the Greek dominions. In generations of fighting both Greeks and Turks came to know each other and each other's territories. The Turks in particular were tolerant of their Christian neighbours' civilization while at the same time never abandoning their role as conquerors for Islam. In 1281 Osman inherited power from his father. The Ottoman (or Osmanli) emirate had acquired the ruler whose name it was later to bear.[1] Under Osman the advance was mainly at the expense of other Turkish emirates but at the very end of his life his son Orchan captured Brusa.

The Byzantine rulers of the past had often allied with Turkish rulers, had often recruited auxiliary forces from the Turks. The Palaeologi, dis-

[1] The following is a simplified genealogical table of Ottoman rulers:

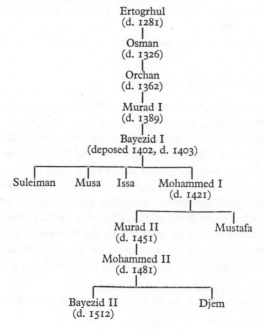

254

tracted as they were by civil wars, intensified the need and multiplied the occasions when Turkish troops were employed by Greek rulers. In 1345 (by which time the Ottomans had captured Nicaea and Nicomedia from Byzantium as well as extending their control over further parts of Turkish Anatolia) John Cantacuzenus was helped against John V by large bodies of Ottoman troops who served in Thrace. The upshot was that Cantacuzenus accepted Orchan's rule in the former imperial province of Bithynia, and the Turks came back from service with Cantacuzenus with a clear notion of where their future expansion should lie —not only in Asia Minor, but in Thrace and Macedonia in Europe. Cantacuzenus gave his daughter to Orchan in marriage and he has been blamed for admitting the Ottomans into the European Empire when he granted them a fortress near Gallipoli on the northern shore of the Dardanelles in 1352. But the opposite faction had also tried to secure an Ottoman alliance and in fact Seljuk mercenaries, hired to fight Cantacuzenus in 1346, invaded and ravaged Bulgaria. The Ottomans captured Gallipoli itself in 1354 and were now poised for further advance.

Under Murad the Ottoman centre of gravity moved to Europe. Thrace was conquered and in 1365 the Turkish capital was moved to Adrianople. Ottoman policy was now deliberately organized to further expansion, not 'by independent Ghazi hosts', but as 'deliberate and well-organized state enterprises'.[1] There was an efficient army and a growing executive fortified by the Moslem clergy, trained in theological schools established in the main towns. As the Turks moved into long established Greek areas they also recruited experienced Greek soldiers and administrators. By Murad's death not only was Thrace occupied but a systematic occupation had begun of Macedonia and attacks were launched on Bulgaria. An army of Serbs and Bulgars was defeated in 1371 and the Serbs were again beaten at Kossovo in 1389, although Murad fell in the battle. The Balkans were virtually at the mercy of the Ottomans. Murad did not neglect expansion in Anatolia, which was accomplished largely with the help of imperial contingents. John V was in practice a Turkish vassal: he himself fought with Murad in Anatolia in 1373 and he and his successors were compelled to pay tribute in men and money. Under Bayezid I the process continued at an accelerated pace and by the end of his reign nearly the whole of the Empire and much of the Balkans had come under the Ottoman government. Constantinople still remained behind its great walls but the emperors were helpless puppets whose only hope of relief now lay in western

[1] Wittek, p. 45.

help; by defeating the one major crusade at Nicopolis in 1396 Bayezid had shown how little he had to fear from that quarter.

Momentary relief came when Bayezid was destroyed by the last great Mongol conqueror Timur who, having established himself in central Asia, completed a vast marauding expedition through India, Persia, and Syria by defeating the Turkish army at Ankara in 1402. Timur had no desire to occupy Anatolia and died in 1405 on his way to China. For a time the Ottoman government was totally disrupted. Bayezid's four sons fought over the inheritance, Suleiman from Europe and the others in Asia Minor. Musa defeated Suleiman and Mohammed defeated Musa, with the help of the emperor Manuel, in 1413. The Ottoman lands were once more under one ruler but Mohammed I's reign was devoted to healing the wounds of civil war and he remained on good terms with his ally, the Emperor Manuel.

When the phil-Hellene Mohammed was succeeded by Murad II, Ottoman aggression revived. Murad at once laid siege to Constantinople, which was saved not only by its landward defences and the lack of Turkish seapower, but also, by the existence of a Turkish pretender, Murad's younger brother Mustafa. The siege of 1422 was lifted but Turkish pressure on Thessaly and in the Balkans continued, though there the penetration was now slower as the Ottoman armies encountered more serious resistance, and even an occasional defeat, as in the Albanian mountains where George Castriota (Skanderbeg) organized a brilliant resistance from 1443 to 1468. This meant that it was dangerous to tolerate longer the independence of Constantinople. Murad II's successor besieged and took the city in 1453. Remaining Greek territory fell piecemeal: the despotate of the Morea was conquered in and after 1460; Trebizond, on the south-east shore of the Black Sea, fell in 1461; Genoese possessions in the Crimea were overrun in 1475. There remained under Christian control in the eastern Mediterranean only Rhodes, the island base of the Hospitallers, and Cyprus which passed in 1489 from the ancient dynasty of Lusignan to Venice. Venetian and Genoese colonies and protectorates also came under attack in the later fifteenth century. Genoa had made its first treaty with the Ottomans in 1387, and Venice soon followed suit. In fact no accommodation was possible for long. The Ottomans were unwilling to go on tolerating Venetian colonies in the Morea or in the islands, and Venice, despite prolonged and exhausting campaigns in the 1460s and 1470s, was unable adequately to protect her territories from an enemy increasingly important as a sea power. Negropont (Euboea) fell in 1470 and at the peace signed in 1479 the Venetians were forced to buy at a heavy price the right to trade in Turkish lands. Rhodes, besieged by the Mamluks in 1440–44, was attacked by the Ottomans in 1480 (though it did not fall till over forty years later) and in the same year Rome was thrown into a panic by the temporary occupation of Otranto by a Turkish band. Under Bayezid II attacks on the west were halted. The Sultan was immobilized by the presence of his younger brother Djem in Christian hands. Latterly the pope received an annual payment from Bayezid for keeping Djem under guard and this went on till he died in 1495 when Charles VIII of France (who had taken Djem from the pope as part of his crusading plans) returned his body to the Sultan.

In 1453 Mohammed the Conqueror acquired not only Constantinople but an imperial view of his dominions, which already covered large areas of two continents. In all their European possessions the Turks came as a conquering minority. Governors of provinces were appointed, and below them fiefs (timarets) were granted in return for military service, but the bulk of the population was not dispossessed. That the Turks were able to spread so fast and so securely depended on several factors. Their enemies were divided not only politically and militarily, but on religious grounds as well. This last was important not only in frustrating the union of the Churches, but also during the Ottoman advance in the Balkans, where Orthodox tributaries were not unwilling to fight for them against the hated Latin Christians of Hungary and central Europe. In any case the structure of Orthodoxy survived. The Christian communities under the Ottomans had their bishops and clergy. There was still a patriarch. They paid heavy taxes for a religious freedom which reduced them to political servitude, but at least they were not ravaged by the mercenary armies, civil wars and Turkish raids of earlier times. In any case the religion of Islam was monotheistic. The sultan was an autocrat in religion and in politics, as the Greek emperors had once been, and much of the administration was Greek as were many of the administrators. The machinery of government and many of the elaborate procedures of the Ottoman court were adapted from Byzantium—many such borrowings going back far behind 1453.

Some of the most effective institutions were original enough. Mohammed II laid down as a law that the son who succeeded to the Ottoman empire must destroy his surviving brothers, and he himself on his accession had procured the murder of his youngest half-brother. The fratricide which thus entered Ottoman practice was perhaps an unavoidable consequence of the harem; the eunuchs who also went with the harem had already figured for long at the Byzantine court. Much more important was the army. This consisted partly of the cavalry force of Spahis, the territorial force supported by the timaret system, partly of lightly armed auxiliaries, thrown into battle first to take the first shock of the assault, and the janissaries or New Army. The janissaries, and for that matter many of the highest officials of the Ottoman administration, were recruited from the subject Christian population by the process known as *devshirme*. This, which was found under Murad II but may have been older, was the forcible recruitment, region by region and every five years, of boys between the ages of ten and fifteen. The number taken varied between 2,000 and 12,000. They were removed from their homes and educated in the sultan's palace at Constantinople or in the homes of Turkish families in the capital. After learning the religion and the language of the Ottomans they then entered the ranks of the officials at court or reinforced the janissaries. At the end of Mohammed II's reign this force numbered about 10,000 men, who were fanatical in the service of Islam and bound to each other by a religious and puritanical code. Finally Mohammed II greatly increased and improved artillery, as well as creating a powerful navy.

These were some of the characteristics acquired by the Turkish tribe which, from the mid-fourteenth century, gradually turned itself into a state. The sense of mission, the military efficiency of the Turks and the flimsiness of the immediate obstacles to their advance frightened the Latin west from time to time. Why therefore was there relatively little concerted resistance?

The west and the crusade

There were many reasons why western Europe could not react in the later Middle Ages as it had in the eleventh and twelfth centuries. Crusading had become debased by being used by popes for purely political purposes: in this period, for example, John XXII declared a crusade against Lewis of Bavaria, Bishop Despenser in 1383 led a so-called crusade for Urban II against 'Clementist' Flanders and John XXIII proclaimed a crusade against Ladislas of Naples in 1411. The crusade had originally been essentially a Frankish activity; now the Mediterranean contained complicated political and economic power groups—Angevin, Catalan, Genoese and Venetian—which were far more interested in pushing their own interests than turning the Levant upside down in pursuit of an ideal.[1] The thirteenth century had shown how easily the

[1] For commercial activity see below, chap. xiv.

Byzantine Empire could be exploited and this was not forgotten by those best placed to help. Moreover the armies of the later Middle Ages were paid forces and there was no hope of raising a force on a voluntary or speculative basis, as was done in the first crusade. The crusade of Nicopolis, for example, involved the payment of very large sums to the knights and the men-at-arms enlisted. In any event what was needed was not a few great gestures, but a persistent military and naval counter-attack. Europe at large, engaged in massive internal wars, was in no position to mount this, and the resources of the military Orders were (as far as the Levant was concerned) now reduced to those of the Hospit-allers who did keep up a steady resistance to the Anatolian emirs near Rhodes and joined in other crusades. The popes at Avignon, though they supported crusading proposals, were further away from the scene than they had been at the time of Urban II or Innocent III. The papacy was later divided and ineffectual during the Schism and thereafter enmeshed in Italian politics.

Despite these difficulties—perhaps because of them—the propaganda for the crusade increased in the Latin west in the fourteenth century. Pierre Dubois (d. *c.* 1321) in his *De recuperatione terre sancte* made the recovery of the Holy Land part of a vast scheme of world peace. The Mallorcan Ramon Llull (1235–1315), a man of remarkable scholarship, spent a lifetime trying to organize a united crusade on the one hand and a programme of conversion on the other. The Dominican Burcard addressed a *Directorium* (1332) to the king of France, in which he analysed the crusading problem from a firsthand experience of the Near East. Another writer who knew the terrain was the Venetian Marino Sanudo (d. 1343), who based his plan on sea power and economic war-fare. Philippe de Mézières (d. 1407) indefatigably urged the creation of a new order of crusading chivalry. These are a few of the figures in a remarkable stream of polemicists, some of whom had been pilgrims or had actually crusaded in person, like Philippe de Mézières. In the fifteenth century, it seems, there was a decline in propaganda for a crusade and more stress was laid on conversion. This is seen even in Pius II who, while trying at the congress of Mantua to convoke an army to go to the relief of eastern Christians, also wrote the curiously equivocal 'letter to Mohammed' in which he urged the sultan to adopt Christianity not only because that was a proper thing to do but because it would enable Mohammed to be another Constantine.

The results of the literary activity are hard to measure. Although the crusade was preached by popes from time to time, most of the active 'crusading' was the result of pretty mixed motives. The Hospitallers took Rhodes from the Greek Empire between 1306 and 1310 but thereafter were perhaps less selfish than the other parties to crusades. The Venetians and Genoese were in general concerned to protect their sea routes and damage each other's trade rather than recover Jerusalem or attack the Turks. A papally-sponsored crusade on the Anatolian coast commanded the support of the Venetians and Genoese because the ports there were important centres of Turkish shipping: Smyrna was taken in 1344 but defence was then left to the Knights, and the merchants of Italy lost interest; the town fell to Timur in 1402. Humbert of Dauphiné conducted an expedition to the Levant in 1345–47; the Genoese, jealous that the Venetians might gain advantages from helping the dauphin, were provoked into attacking and occupying the Greek island of Chios in 1346. Pierre I de Lusignan, king of Cyprus and titular king of Jerusalem, was a man of high purposes and had every practical inducement to support crusades which might relieve his island from Muslim pressure. His aim was to secure a strong land base in enemy territory. He took Adalia on the Anatolian mainland in 1361 and held it for a few years. In the major crusade of 1365, which followed on a tour of European countries in which Peter sought help, the king commanded a large expedition which sailed to Alexandria, the richest infidel city of the Middle East. It was sacked, but the crusaders refused to follow Peter's advice to hold the city and made off in galleys, laden with plunder. This destruction at Alexandria was at the expense not only of Muslims but of helpless Coptic Christians and of western merchants with establishments in the city. Afterwards the Venetians and Genoese were insistent that peace should be established between Cyprus and Egypt so that normal trade could be resumed.

It was at this stage not clear to western statesmen that the advent of the Ottoman Turks was changing the situation. Fourteenth-century crusading literature was still directed at the old aims of retaking Jerusalem or of damaging Egypt. The earliest major expedition to come into contact with the rising power had been led by Amedeo count of Savoy, who in 1366 went to the aid of the Empire and retook Gallipoli from the Ottomans. He also helped to redeem the emperor John V, who was his cousin and who had been captured by the Christian ruler of Bulgaria. But the intention of Amedeo and his contingent had been to join Peter of Lusignan's campaign and there is nothing to show that an attack on the Turks formed part of the count of Savoy's original aims. It was, in fact, only when the Ottomans occupied Bulgaria and directly menaced

Hungary that a more elaborate effort resulted. Under the patronage of the duke of Burgundy and under the leadership of Sigismund, king of Hungary (and later emperor) a great army marched to the Danube where it was routed, after a violent battle at Nicopolis, by Bayezid (1396). The folly of the French and Burgundian contingent and the uncertain loyalty of the Transylvanian and Wallachian elements (who were suspicious of Sigismund and the Hungarians) led to divided policies and chaotic tactics; the Christian allies of Bayezid fought loyally. Sigismund escaped down the Danube and back to Hungary by way of the Dardanelles and Ragusa; a handful of great men were held to high ransom; a few younger crusaders were sent to slavery; and the rest of Bayezid's captives were butchered.

Although a few western soldiers continued to serve in Constantinople to the end, the crusading effort really ended with the disastrous campaign of Nicopolis. In the Balkans fighting naturally went on, for the Hungarians had to defend themselves. It was in this long war that John Hunyadi emerged as a national hero.[1] He was far from universally successful and in particular suffered a serious defeat at Varna in 1444; but his victory at the siege of Belgrade in 1456 held up the Ottoman advance for two generations. In these efforts Christendom mildly participated. Cesarini as papal legate in Hungary was largely responsible for the provocation of Murad II which led to the battle of Varna; in the retreat from this the cardinal was killed. The Observant Franciscan Giovanni Capistrano preached the crusade in Austria and Hungary, encouraged the defenders of Belgrade in 1456 and died in Hungary of plague.[2] Pope Calixtus III appointed Skanderbeg captain-general for the Turkish war in 1457 and the next year summoned a conference at Rome to concert action against the Ottomans—an assembly as ineffective as that called to Mantua by Pius II in 1459. The Venetians did, as has been pointed out, conduct a long war against the Ottomans, but it was a war fought to protect their commercial interests and not to protect Christendom, a fact frequently complained of by Italian contemporaries who themselves did nothing to compensate for Venetian lack of zeal.

It was not the case that the crusade was entirely dead as an idea. It was to linger on for centuries, to justify wars between European powers, to stimulate maritime exploration, to bedevil the policies of a sovereign like Charles V who took his responsibilities seriously. But in practice the Italian states, including the papacy, had come by the end of the fifteenth

[1] Cf. above, p. 233.   [2] Cf. below, p. 318.

century to accept the Ottoman as an uncomfortable but unavoidable neighbour. The rest of Europe soon followed suit.

The inheritor of Byzantium: Russia

In no part of Europe did the Mongol invasions of the thirteenth century have profounder consequences than in the principalities of north-eastern Europe. The rule of the khans of the Golden Horde, based on Saray on the lower Volga, was indirect by the fourteenth century, the dukes being required to secure confirmation of their authority from the khan and to collect from their subjects tribute to be paid to the Tatars. This arrangement lasted throughout the fourteenth century, though there were serious dynastic rivalries in the khanate in the second half of the century. The khan of the Golden Horde clashed with Timur[1] from 1387 till 1396, and, after a brief resumption of united direction during the first twenty years of the fifteenth century, the Golden Horde then broke up into three sections. In the north a khanate was established at Kazan (1445), in the south another emerged based on the Crimea (1449) which was soon to be the object of sustained Ottoman attack. The remainder of the Golden Horde survived on the lower Volga. By this time the Tatar hosts had abandoned notions of conquest and permanent control. They conducted raids on each other, on Lithuania and the states of Russia, solely for the purpose of capturing booty and slaves, who found their way into the Mediterranean market.

It was Lithuania which first expanded as the result of the decline in Tatar power and this was at first mainly at the expense of Russian territory. Gedymin (1316–41) occupied the area of the middle Dnieper. Olgierd who succeeded him (1341–77) also pursued this policy, several times raiding as far as Moscow; but he also turned south and in 1363 pushed Lithuanian power to the shores of the Black Sea. Lithuania indeed for a long period looked like being the unifier of the divided Russian states. The personal union of Poland and Lithuania which followed the marriage of Jagiello (1377–1434) to Hedwig of Poland in 1386,[2] while it introduced Roman Christianity among the formerly pagan Lithuanians and thus made for conflicts in the principality with the Orthodox Christians of the Russian areas, did not in fact lead to Polish domination. Jagiello, as king of Poland, had to accept his cousin Witold as prince of Lithuania, and Witold during a long reign (1398–1430) was much more powerful than any of his Great Russian neighbours. Both Witold and Casimir (1447–92), who again united Poland

[1] Above, p. 256. [2] Cf. also chapter IX.

and Lithuania) successfully leagued with the Tatar khans to embarrass the grand dukes of Moscow, but at the same time they were weakened by tensions between Lithuania and Poland and by the continued need to protect themselves from the Teutonic Order. By the second half of the fifteenth century there was a dynamic and aggressive power in Moscow. In 1494 a peace and marriage treaty was signed between Russia and Lithuania; this not only precluded further Tatar attacks on Moscow, which had occurred intermittently from 1460 to 1481, but also gave Russia control of some of the territory taken by Gedymin over a century before.

In the treaty of 1494 the Lithuanian prince Alexander accepted Ivan III's description of himself as sovereign 'of All Russia'. There was little in the position of the duke of Moscow and Vladimir at the beginning of the fourteenth century to suggest that two hundred years later his successor would have acquired such a primacy. Of the several more or less separate and independent units which, under the khans, existed in Greater Russia, Moscow had, it is true, certain advantages over the duchies of Riazan and Tver and the city states of Novgorod and Pskov. It was the centre of a river system which made communication easy. It was becoming the effective centre of the ecclesiastical hierarchy and the normal residence of the metropolitan of Kiev (ruined by the Tatar invasion in 1240, Kiev never recovered its ancient importance and was by the mid-fourteenth century under Lithuanian control). Moscow could normally depend on an alliance with Novgorod. It was well fortified, had on the whole a loyal population and enjoyed the government of a series of princes who were both tenacious of their rights and willing to take risks when occasion offered. Such occasions multiplied with the schisms in the Golden Horde. In 1380 Duke Dmitri Donskoy defeated a Mongol army at Kulikovo Pole. This was a temporary gesture in that a Mongol army penetrated the walls of Moscow by a ruse in 1382 and put the town to sack, but it was none the less a sign of new times that a Russian army could defeat a Mongol host.

The further troubles of the Tatars and their break up unto three khanates enabled more rapid advance to occur under Vasili II (1425–62), who recruited Tatars into his service on a considerable scale. His reign had its inauspicious moments: in 1445 he was defeated and captured by a Tatar force which was in process of establishing itself as the independent khanate of Kazan; on his release he was deposed and blinded by his cousin Dmitri Shemiaka, the conspiracy being successful because the duke's Tatar vassals were unpopular. By 1447 Vasili had recovered power and the next years saw a series of significant increases in Muscovite power. The duke of Riazan accepted the suzerainty of the grand duke of Moscow in 1447. In 1448 a synod of Russian bishops elected—in defiance of the pope and the patriarch of Constantinople, technically now united by the Council of Florence—a metropolitan of Kiev.[1] In 1452 Vasili's Tatar chiefs and their men were resettled in a client khanate round Gorodets (renamed Kasimov in 1471 in honour of its first khan), thus establishing a buffer against the Tatars to the southeast. And in 1456 a first step was taken to limit the independence of Novgorod.

Under the cautious and able rule of Ivan III (1462–1505), the first grand duke who had no patent from a Tatar khan confirming his authority, Vasili's goal of increased authority and wider dominions was steadily and effectively pursued. Of the two more or less independent duchies Riazan was immobilized by a marriage treaty in 1464 and Tver was forcibly incorporated in the Muscovite state in 1485. The subjugation of Novgorod proved more difficult. The town, which had an enormous hinterland, was a Hansa port, looked to Baltic trade and readily allied with Lithuania. Faced with just such a Lithuanian alliance Ivan in 1471 attacked Novgorod and compelled the town both to accept that it was part of his domains and to promise never to ally with Lithuania again. After a further rebellion in 1478 the town was governed by lieutenants appointed by Ivan, lost its enormous eastward provinces and saw the bell used to summon the popular assembly taken away to hang in a Moscow church. The fall of Novgorod also entailed a diminished independence for Pskov, though the city did not entirely lose its liberties until 1510.

The steady increase in the authority of the grand duke of Moscow was accompanied by social changes. The nobility ('service-princes' or titled descendants of formerly independent dukes) and boyars greatly extended their possessions in these centuries and power gradually deserted the Russian towns for the countryside. This was accompanied by a sharp decline in the independence of the civic popular assembly (*veche*) not only in major commercial centres like Novgorod and Pskov where it represented traditions of independence, but also in other towns of Greater Russia, including Moscow. The dominant social group by the end of the fifteenth century were the boyars, who had gained much land by the redistribution of the great territories formerly belonging to Novgorod, and who had absolute rights to their estates. Their assembly

[1] See below, p. 301, for the mission of Isidore to Russia.

(the *duma*) was consulted by the grand duke on all important matters, and there was only one occasion under Ivan III when the lesser gentry were convoked. The latter were, however, a potential counterweight to the boyars and under Ivan a great many were granted fiefs on state land in return for military service. The army consisted under Ivan of his own retinue and those of the princes, Tatar auxiliaries, boyars and the gentry with military tenures; when infantry was needed it was conscripted from the towns. These changes all conduced to the autocracy of the grand duke, though he had to exercise his powers temperately in dealing with the great boyars. This growing absolutism should be compared with the constitutional limitations imposed by the boyar class in Lithuania on their prince; as in Poland, the nobles and gentry of Lithuania were gradually entrenching their powers in constitutional practice. In both Muscovy and Little Russia the status of the free peasantry was dropping, but the progress of advancing serfdom was more rapid in Lithuania.

Russia had emerged by 1500 as a distinct state. Isolated during earlier centuries by Lithuania to the west, by the Cumans and then by the Golden Horde to the southeast, the country had now to face less serious danger from the steppes. Her enemies and her ambitions in future were to lie rather in the opposite direction. Further, the decline of the Tatar hordes had been followed by the rise of the Ottoman Empire, and Constantinople, whence had come the Orthodox faith, the art and the alphabet of the Russians, was now an Islamic town. It would be false to see under Ivan III a conscious attempt to don the mantle of Byzantium, though he did (after a characteristically lengthy period of reflection and negotiation) accept Pope Paul II's suggestion that he should take as his second wife Zoë, niece of the last Greek emperor. The marriage took place in Moscow in November 1472, when the princess adopted the name Sophia. For a time this seems to have encouraged Italian influences at Ivan's court—there were Italian architects at work in the Kremlin from 1473 to 1491. In the last years of Ivan's reign, when he had to choose as his heir between Dmitri, the grandson of his first wife, and Sophia's son Vasili it was the latter who was in the end preferred. Traditionally this has been attributed to Sophia, along with other ideas and practices that Ivan and his intimates were borrowing from the Greek past. There is, in fact, not a scrap of evidence to suggest that Sophia played any part in this. Nor should the Byzantine elements be exaggerated: the double eagle of the eastern Empire was adopted as a ducal state emblem in the 1490s; the rituals used in the crowning of Dmitri as co-ruler in 1498 (who was later set aside in favour of Vasili) had a strong Byzantine flavour and in them is used the word 'tsardom' for the first time (tsar = Caesar). It would have been strange if this kind of development had not taken place, for, whatever conscious attempts Ivan III may have made to emulate the practices of his second wife's ancestors, he could not help being, like them, the guardian of Orthodoxy. In 1510 Abbot Filofei of Pskov was to write a letter in which he told Vasili that he was the sole protector of the Greek Church. It was in this connection that he sketched a picture of the three Romes in which Christianity had been centred, Rome itself, then Constantinople, and now Moscow—'the only sanctuary of Orthodox Christianity'.[1]

In any case Ivan needed no adventitious proofs for his concept of power. When an emissary of the Emperor Frederick III offered him a king's crown in 1489 the grand duke replied in forthright fashion:

By God's grace we have been sovereigns in our own land since the beginning, since our earliest ancestors: our appointment comes from God, as did that of our ancestors, and we beg God to grant us and our children to abide for ever in the same state, namely as sovereigns in our own land; and as beforehand we did not desire to be appointed [sovereign] by any one, so now too do we not desire it.[2]

[1] Vernadsky, *Dawn*, p. 169.   [2] Quoted Fennell, p. 121.

XI

The Papal Monarchy:
The Church as a State

'The pope' wrote St Thomas Aquinas, 'has a plenitude of power like a king in a kingdom.' This remark (with its tacit implications for secular paramountcy) was given its fullest development by the able legists who occupied the see of Peter during the two generations during which the popes were at Avignon. If kings of France or England disposed of much greater material resources than the vicar of Christ it is to be doubted whether even by the end of the fifteenth century they had as sophisticated an administration. In the fourteenth century it remained a unique object lesson in bureaucracy.

BIBLIOGRAPHY. For the period down to 1378 the classic manual of G. Mollat, *Les papes d'Avignon* (9th rev. edn., Paris, 1949) gives a balanced account and full bibliographies of sources and secondary works. The English translation (Edinburgh, 1963) omits the bibliographies. The sources of church history after 1378 will be found in bibliographies to *Cambridge Medieval History*, VIII, esp. for chaps. 1, 2 and 5. The Schism and the councils are covered by N. Valois, *La France et le grand schisme*, 4 vols. (Paris, 1896–1902) and *Le pape et le concile*, 2 vols. (Paris, 1909). The councils are also dealt with in C.-J. Hefele, trans. and ed. H. Leclercq, *Histoire des conciles*, vol. VII, pts. 1, 2 (Paris, 1916); J. Gill, *The Council of Florence* (Cambridge, 1959); and in the early chapters of H. Jedin, *A History of the Council of Trent*, 1 (London and Edinburgh, 1957). The legal aspects of the origins of the Schism are discussed in W. Ullmann, *Origins of the Great Schism* (London, 1948). The theory and practice of papal collation is the subject of G. Barraclough, *Papal Provisions* (Oxford, 1935). For papal finances see W. E. Lunt, *Papal Revenues in the Middle Ages*, 2 vols. (New York, 1934—a collection of illustrative documents in translation with a long and useful introduction), and A. Gottlob, *Aus der Camera Apostolica des 15. Jahrhunderts* (Innsbruck, 1889). Among general histories first place goes to L. Pastor, trans. Antrobus, *History of the Popes*, vols. I–V (London, 1891–98), the work of a conscientious Ultramontane; A. C. Flick, *The Decline of the Medieval Church*, 2 vols. (London, 1930) contains useful material but must be used with caution; M. Creighton, *A History of the Papacy from the Great Schism to the Sack of Rome*,

The popes at Avignon have been criticized on many counts and by writers of many persuasions. To many Roman Catholics (other than Frenchmen) they have seemed the occasion for the Schism and thus responsible for the conciliar movement, national churches and the Reformation. Protestants have shared in this only the antipathy for a Church made, as they assert, the tool of the French monarchy. And there is a general criticism of their fiscal policy and of what one writer has called the 'mechanization' of papal administration.[1] It is hard to sustain such views. The French popes[2] were on the whole able and disinterested men, only the first of them being guilty of supporting French policy as such. Avignon, where the curia settled in 1309 and where the great palace began to rise in 1336, was a fief of the Neapolitan Angevins, not bought by the popes until 1348, and was separated from France by the wide Rhône: it was nearer to the English in Bordeaux than to the centre of royal power in the Île de France.

Individually John XXII and Benedict XII stand out from the others. John, elected after a protracted and difficult conclave, was about seventy-two when he came to the papal throne, but he threw himself into controversy with reckless energy. At odds with Lewis of Bavaria in Italy, he supplied him with allies by attacking the current Franciscan doctrine of poverty and affronted theologians and common men by his views on the Beatific Vision; he held the doctrine, to be formally repudiated by his successor, that the souls of the blessed must wait until the Last Judgment, before they enjoyed the sight of God. Benedict XII, who had been an active bishop, devoted himself to reforming the religious orders in

---

6 vols. (London, 1897) is still suggestive, though its quotations and references are sometimes inaccurate; in the *Histoire de l'église*, ed. by A. Fliche and V. Martin, relevant volumes are XIV, E. Delaruelle, E.-R. Labande and P. Ourliac, *L'église au temps du Grand Schisme et de la crise conciliaire* (Paris, 1962–4), XV, R. Aubenas, *L'église et la Renaissance 1449–1517* (Paris, 1951), with good bibliographies and useful chapters on Spain by R. Ricard; see also works by Gregorovius and Partner in bibliography to chap. VII, above, p. 163. The main regional studies of the church are: A. Hauck, *Kirchengeschichte Deutschlands*, vol. V, 2nd edn. in 2 pts. (Leipzig, 1911–20); E. de Moreau, *Histoire de l'église en Belgique*, III, IV (Brussels, 1946–49); A. Hamilton Thompson, *The English Clergy and their Organization in the later Middle Ages* (Oxford, 1947). For the clergy, see above, p. 45.

[1] Knowles, *Religious Orders*, II, p. 170.
[2] Popes at Avignon: Clement V, 1305–14; John XXII, 1316–34; Benedict XII, 1334–42; Clement VI, 1342–52; Innocent VI, 1352–62; Urban V, 1362–70; Gregory XI, 1370–78.

systematic fashion, only the Dominicans managing successfully to resist. It is, however, as a singularly coherent group that the Avignon popes are remarkable. All were university-trained men, save Clement VI, the *bon viveur* who succeeded the austere Benedict, and they brought ever-increasing system into papal business. And, although they did not deliberately follow a pro-French policy, they went far to making French the senior *cadres* of the clergy. The officials of the curia were mainly recruited from the south of France, and, more striking still, of the 134 cardinals promoted by the Avignon popes 113 were Frenchmen.[1]

The clergy and the pope

Wherever kings were strong they continued to appoint the prelates of their choice, as they had always done, but no one challenged the papal right to provide incumbents for the greater offices of the regional church. A bishop or archbishop was thus normally elected by the chapter and provided by the pope; the king's part was to permit the chapter to elect (*congé d'élire*) and tell them who had to be chosen, just as he asked the pope to provide the same man. The system worked well enough, for it gave princes the ultimate control but allowed the pope the theoretical powers and financial advantages[2] of nomination.

All over Roman Christendom the bishop was the key figure in the administration of the Church. There were some 700 sees, spread unevenly across Europe,[3] of which some were enormous in extent, some minute. The small ones, especially some of the 138 in the kingdom of Naples, were incredibly poor, not rating (in papal taxation) as much as a two-hundredth part of the income from Winchester, Rouen or the vast German bishoprics. It was the duty of the bishop to train, examine and ordain clergy, to supervise the spiritual life of the clergy and laity in his diocese and the material conditions of the churches. He was also a judge, and to his court came all clerical offenders (if they were not irregularly dealt with by laymen impatient of the lenience of ecclesiastical tribunals) and many cases involving the laity: oaths, matrimonial questions, wills and heresy. Finally, the bishop was always regarded as a secular magnate and frequently his feudal lands made him a very influential public figure.

In discharging his wide duties the bishop, who was in any case often

---

[1] There were thirteen Italians, five Spaniards, two English and one from Geneva. The absence of Germans was an old story.
[2] Below, p. 275.
[3] See totals in note to table on p. 272, below.

an absentee attending to the public business of his prince or the pope, depended on a number of officials to whom he formally deputed authority to deal with his administrative commitments. Those of a specifically spiritual nature, and notably the ordination of priests, needed a bishop and many threadbare prelates with sees *in partibus infidelium* or in remote and inhospitable lands like Ireland earned a precarious living supplying such services to their wealthier and busier brethren. Diocesan administration, which turned on regular visitation, was neglected and perhaps especially so on the continent, where the archdeacon was losing the importance he maintained in England. Nor were episcopal synods held regularly in the later Middle Ages, despite their obligatory nature. Supervision of the bishops lay normally in the hands of an archbishop;[1] here too traditional machinery was weaker than it had been and in particular provincial synods were less frequent, save when they were summoned in response to the demands of royal policies and royal desire for taxes from the clergy.

Papal supervision of the provinces of the Church had of old been undertaken in three ways. Bishops and especially metropolitans had been encouraged to visit the curia on appointment; the affairs of the Church as a whole had been debated in general councils which by the thirteenth century were entirely amenable to papal control; and the pope had sent legates to the faithful. In the fourteenth century it is only the last which continued to operate. Papally appointed legates were of two kinds. The *legatus a* or *de latere* was a curial official of great seniority, dispatched by the pope with wide powers for a specific period and area. The *legatus natus* was a local prelate exalted by a title and by powers which raised him above his fellow bishops.

In practice, as already noted, princes usually controlled the appointment of prelates, just as (subject to episcopal approval and induction) patrons of livings appointed priests. Yet the papacy in the fourteenth century exercised much influence and derived a large income from the practices of general reservation and provision. These dated from an earlier period but were completed and fully exploited by the popes at Avignon. Their basis lay in the pope being the universal 'ordinary' or bishop, and in the plenitude of his powers.

The first such general reservation was promulgated in 1265 when Clement IV gave himself and his successors the right to nominate to all benefices vacated by persons who died at the papal court. Boniface VIII

---

[1] Certain bishops had no archbishop and, in theory, depended directly on the pope; the first archbishopric in Scotland was St Andrews, erected in 1472.

extended this to cover clergy dying within two days' journey of the court. Under Clement V and John XXII the Avignon popes built greatly on these foundations. They reserved all benefices vacated by the deposition of the incumbent, or surrendered by him to the pope; all benefices vacant due to papal provision or translation of a clerk; and all benefices held at their deaths by cardinals and officials of the papal curia. Gregory XI reserved all patriarchal, archiepiscopal and episcopal sees and all convents of men. The popes did not threaten the rights of lay patrons, but all prelacies and practically every other benefice in the gift of the clergy were in theory at their disposal. 'Never, perhaps, in any period of history had the pope so largely exercised his powers of jurisdiction.'[1]

Historians have long argued the merits of this development. It has seemed defensible on two grounds, both advanced at the time by the papacy: it secured the appointment of men better trained and less liable to be merely socially acceptable than those who were often given nominations by electing bodies or ecclesiastical patrons; and it did a lot to curb the appalling quarrels in electing bodies, who often produced two or more 'elect' with resulting vacancies or even armed conflicts. On the first point there is no doubt, as we shall see, that university men were in general well served by the arrangement. On the second one can produce terrible evidence that the old machinery was faulty. Of the six moments between 1306 and 1356 when the bishopric of Constance fell vacant the noble canons four times elected two rivals; and similar instances could be produced wherever there was a weak secular authority and a consequent survival of genuine elections. Yet papal action in providing to reserved benefices or even to benefices not yet vacant (expectatives) tended all too easily to have regard only to the legal issues, and the care of souls was forgotten in the litigation which often resulted. To contemporaries two other criticisms seemed even more important. Reservation and provision were frequently the handmaid of papal politics and what seemed to matter to the popes was the financial consequences of their rights of collation. In the fourteenth century, when they were Frenchmen residing on the border of France, this exacerbated among Germans, Englishmen, Italians and Spaniards the ancient hatred of the popes as financiers and statesmen.

It is not easy to control exactly the chauvinistic criticism of contemporaries. We can count papal provisions and expectatives, but it is a laborious and sometimes an impossible task to determine how many were effective and to discriminate between provisions asked for by

[1] I paraphrase Monsignor Mollat here and quote his conclusion, p. 528.

princes and other patrons and those cases when the pope was pleasing himself or rewarding a servant. Certain calculations have been made for the eight years' pontificate of Benedict XII:[1]

PAPAL PROVISIONS AND EXPECTATIVES 1334-42

	Major benefices	Capitular benefices	Priories	Lesser benefices	Expecta-tives	Total	Total of foreigners
France	93	435	140	327	1411	2406	111
England	6	20	0	9	69	104	12
Empire	15	50	0	12	184	261	22
Spain	22	120	1	32	144	319	42
Italy	142	163	23	31	191	550	15

It seems certain that Benedict was more moderate than his predecessor or successors. The scale of intervention in the normal machinery of election and collation is impressive, especially for France, even if the curia and the pope apparently took pains not to intrude foreigners save exceptionally, and perhaps nearly always at the request of the local civil or ecclesiastical authority.

Two further groups came under papal control: the regular clergy and the universities. The monks and friars who followed a rule were the subject of a good deal of reforming attention from the Avignon popes. There was much to reform. The Benedictine monks were slack in their observances and their supervision was difficult. Some monasteries were directly under the pope. Others, not so exempt, were visited by the local ordinary. The papal remedy, reiterated and systematized by Benedict XII in 1336, was to impose on these monasteries a discipline applied by provincial chapters, thus making them roughly correspond to the arrangements of the Cistercians and the friars, who met in provincial assemblies, as well as having the general chapters characteristic of Cluny. This and other papal directives stressed the direct dependence of the

---

[1] B. Guillemain, *La politique bénéficiale du pape Benoit XII* (Paris, 1952) p. 129. The sees as enumerated in C. Eubel's *Hierarchia catholica* i (1913):

Italy and islands (incl. the pope and 6 cardinal bishops)	302
France	131
Iberian countries	56
British Isles (England and Wales 21, Scotland 11, Ireland 35)	67
Scandinavian countries	25
Germany	48
Central Europe (Prussia and Livonia 8, Poland 18, Hungary 19)	45
TOTAL	674

Of the sees in the Balkans and S.E. Europe only a few were in practice filled, usually by Italians.

religious on the pope. This dependence should not be exaggerated. The upheavals in the Franciscan order were beyond papal remedy and the Dominicans thwarted Benedict's attempt at reorganization. The increasing practice of granting monasteries *in commendam* is a further example of the ambiguous nature of papal power. Forbidden in theory, the popes made frequent exceptions, and in this way encouraged an increase in pluralism, confused the secular clergy with the religious, and weakened monastic organization and finance.

As teaching institutions the universities will be dealt with later. Papal concern with them, as sources of trained clerks, theologians, preachers and heretics, was of long standing and by the opening of the fourteenth century it was accepted that only the pope could make a true *studium generale*; even those established by an imperial privilege sought papal confirmation later. Certain of the older universities, notably Paris, were as yet imperfectly responsive to regulation by the pope, but the extension of papal provisions enabled the curia to offer positive advantages to university men. John XXII favoured Paris graduates in provisions and by the time of Clement VI the university regularly sent rolls of graduates and others to the curia for provision of benefices. Oxford started at about the same time and soon every university prepared an annual *rotulus beneficiandorum,* arranged in order of faculties and within faculties by seniority. Occasionally at Paris and always at universities where the students formed the corporation, the roll included the names of undergraduates. The earlier rolls did not specify the benefices, but later the diocese and the income hoped for were indicated. A deputation of masters carried the roll to the curia and stayed for a considerable period arranging the detailed provisions. The resulting provisions were, of course, not always effective. They normally conferred only a title to a future vacancy in a chapter. But the graduate clerk rapidly came to feel that he had more likelihood of support from papal patronage than he could expect from the local bishop. In the event this was to mean that a large and vocal element in the clergy was vehemently in favour of papal provisions when this question, as part of general reform, came to be debated at Constance.

The curia at Avignon

Any description of the administration inherited from the past by the popes at Avignon and perfected by them, must begin with the financial departments, for in all ways the *camera apostolica* came first in both influence and status. The office was under the *camerarius*, who was always a bishop or archbishop and who normally became a cardinal. He had complete authority over all deputies and servants and as a result became very important in general papal policy; from Benedict XII onwards he was also the head of a confidential secretariat. The immediate deputy of the *camerarius* was the treasurer and below him came three or four 'cameral clerks', men of great executive importance. These, with the *camerarius* and the treasurer formed the cameral college, which dealt regularly with the accounts and had judicial functions (normally exercised by an 'auditor'), concerning both civil and criminal action arising out of the actions of cameral agents.

The chancery was less important, for it had no independent authority but, under the *vice-cancellarius*, worked entirely to papal mandates. Seven main offices functioned under the vice-chancellor, the bulk of their activity arising from the requests put to the pope by petitioners (impetrants). The impetrant in quest of papal action had first to submit his request in due form to the pope by the intermediary of a cardinal or some official in daily personal contact with the pontiff. The resulting document was characterized as being in common form (*litterae communae*) or exceptional, in which case it had to be read to the pope again before it was finally issued (*litterae legendae*). The petition, marked with the pope's approval, went first to the office of requests, then (in all cases where preferment was in question) to the office of examinations where the qualifications of the impetrant were scrutinized. In the 'minuting office' an abstract or draft (*minuta*) of the final document was prepared and it then went to the engrossing office (*grossa*) to be drawn up in full. The office of correction then scrutinized it and at this stage the *litterae legendae* were given final papal approval. In the sealing office the letter was given its lead *bulla* and, lastly, if the petitioner wished he could have the document recorded in the register.

Judicial administration was also important, for the high quality of papal justice and the frequent litigation provoked by papal action, especially in matters of benefices, brought a great deal of legal business to the curia. The pope, sitting with the cardinals in consistory, was a supreme court of appeal; it was commoner, however, for appeals to the pope as judge to be delegated by him to a cardinal who normally heard the case through an auditor. But the bulk of business flowed through the *audientia sacri palatii*, known after 1330 as the Rota. Here papal *auditores* heard cases and, after consulting their colleagues, gave decisions. The Rota heard all cases remitted to it by the pope or the vice-chancellor and had a special competence in cases pertaining to benefices.

The auditors were distinguished canonists and could normally expect high preferment at the end of their careers.

The primacy of the *camera apostolica* turned on the efficacy with which it dealt with the bewilderingly complicated revenues of the see of Rome. These were of many kinds and of differing antiquity and can only be described briefly here. Administratively a distinction can be made between those rendered direct to the curia and those collected provincially.[1] Of the former the most important were 'common services', which consisted of a third of the annual value of benefices worth more than 100 cameral florins per annum, and they were paid by all clergy given such preferment by the pope or whenever such preferment was confirmed by him; the bull of preferment or confirmation was not issued until the individual had pledged himself and his benefice to meet the debt. Other taxes were related to common services. Lesser services were levied for the benefit of certain servants of the pope and cardinals; the *sacra*, one twentieth of common services, was shared between the *camerarius*, the cameral clerks and other officers; the *subdiaconum*, a third of the *sacra*, went to the pope's subdeacons. Chancery taxes were levied by the offices in the chancery for the issue of the relevant documents. Next in order of importance came 'compositions', the sums collected for compounding of penances. These were mainly received through the apostolic penitentiary, a cardinal with a considerable staff of *penitenciarii minores*, who (in the pope's name and usually after consultation with him) issued absolutions or remitted penalties in cases, mainly of excommunication, reserved to the pope. Lesser in importance, and more variable as sources of income, were visitations *ad limina apostolorum*: all prelates were required to make regular journeys to Rome, the frequency depending on distance, but they normally made only a 'verbal visitation', paying a tax in lieu. Of oblations laid on the altars of Roman churches the pope got a share; this was valuable in years of jubilee. The profits of curial law courts were also considerable. But the ancient *census* or tribute from vassal kingdoms[2] was virtually never paid in this period, and the sale of offices, begun by Boniface IX, was not yet a significant source of revenue.

Taxes were levied provincially mainly by the collectors, officials of the camera, stationed in the provinces of the Church where they were accorded diplomatic status; in the Papal States and other territories

---

[1] Here, as elsewhere in this section, I follow Mollat. Lunt, *op. cit.*, enumerates (with equal logic) by the order of origin of the various taxes.

[2] Poland, England, Sicily, Castile, Aragon, Portugal.

directly administered by the pope a treasurer was attached to the governor *(rector)*. The oldest of the provincially paid revenues were not now of much account: feudal dues from the papal lands, Peter's Pence (from England, Sweden and half a dozen other kingdoms), and the tribute of 'exempt' monasteries, i.e. those which had placed themselves directly under the pope. Papal tithes, on the other hand, were not negligible, though their collection involved the connivance (to be paid for) of the local ruler. Far more significant were 'annates' or first fruits, the income of a benefice for the first year of an incumbency collated by the pope. This was paid by all benefices valued at less than 100 florins (that is, those which were not liable to common services) which fell vacant at the curia or were covered by general or particular reservations. From the extension of provisions came the right to the income of vacant benefices reserved to the pope, the *fructus medii temporis*. 'Procurations' were levied on clergy by prelates making visitations and, as a source of money for the curia, consisted of a proportion of the sum in question, the prelate being authorized to exact the money without making the visitation in person. Other sources of cash were of less significance: charitable subsidies (voluntary gifts now enforced, when they were granted, by ecclesiastical censure) and the *jus spolii* (which gave the pope the right to the goods of deceased clergy in reserved benefices). Indulgences were as yet a minor source of money, although, in the form of the jubilee, they began to bulk larger. There were jubilees in 1350 and 1390. Merit could be earned without making the pilgrimage to Rome, by compounding for the cost of the journey and purchasing the indulgence locally. The large sums collected provincially were remitted to Avignon or wherever the pope had need of the money, by specially nominated Italian banking firms, whose depots and agents now covered virtually the whole of Christendom. Such transfers were normally effected by credit operations and they did much to encourage further sophistication in commercial technique.[1]

It is tempting to try to estimate the total revenues of the popes in the fourteenth century, but the exercise has not much significance. Popes, like kings, derived power not only because they collected money, but because they could exempt from payments due. Moreover from John XXII onwards there was a privy purse, and ever larger sums were attributed to it, so that the income recorded in cameral accounts is no longer an adequate indication of total resources. What can be said with certainty is that papal expenses were normally very high. John XXII

[1] Below, p. 376.

accumulated considerable treasure and Benedict XII was also economical. Thereafter, mainly because armies in Italy were so expensive and
so constantly used, the camera was in difficulties and these were not
lessened by the very size of the papal curia and household, of whom
there were usually some 400 members to be provided for. 'My predecessors did not know how to be popes', said Clement VI. It was an
attitude which, with its attendant luxury, legalism and fiscal exactions,
made contemporaries savagely critical of what Petrarch christened the
'Babylonish captivity' and St Bridget called 'a field full of pride, avarice,
self-indulgence and corruption'.[1]

The college of cardinals

Petrarch in particular stigmatized the cardinals, rich, insolent, rapacious.
This was not how they saw themselves and, in view of the crisis of 1378,
it is necessary to consider the position of the score of men who held the
title at any time in the fourteenth century. The cardinals existed corporately as a college. Sitting with the pope in council they formed consistory. At his death they met in conclave to elect his successor. The
three aspects are worth examination.

In consistory the cardinals formed the pope's council and this recognized their important place in curial administration. We have noted that
important judicial work was often committed to a cardinal. Likewise for
important diplomatic work the pope frequently appointed legates *de
latere* from the college, and certain of the most senior posts, such as
those of the *camerarius* and the penitentiary, were often held by cardinals. Since they frequently saw the pope, they were the channel by
which many petitions were presented to him. Kingdoms and important
towns often retained one or two cardinals to represent their interests.

The college as such was mainly of financial significance. From 1289
the cardinals were given as a body a share in common services, visitations, and half the feudal income from the patrimony. The cardinal
camerarius ensured that this income was properly received; he normally signed demands and acquittances jointly with the papal *camerarius*.
This income was shared among those cardinals present in curia only;
but a cardinal on active duty in the provinces got very handsome procurations. The income of a cardinal could be augmented in two other
main ways. He was, as noted, sometimes retained as spokesman of a
government. And, being exempt from all restrictions on pluralism and

[1] A masterly account of the papal establishment in B. Guillemain, *La cour
pontificale d'Avignon* (Paris, 1962).

in a good position to petition for benefices, he often accumulated a large income at the expense of the Church at large; one cardinal at Avignon held six archdeaconries.

To the prestige and wealth enjoyed by cardinals was added the power of electing a new pope, and in the transactions of the cardinals during the conclaves (made much more comfortable by a constitution of Clement VI in 1351) of the second half of the fourteenth century we have overwhelming evidence of their dissatisfaction with their position. However wealthy some of them might become, whatever panoply surrounded them, they were in practice creatures of the pope and, since they were in his entourage, might suffer from his plenitude of power more than clergy who were remote from the curia and protected by a strong prince. What remedy had the cardinals? How might they protect their corporate interests against a pope who might neglect their advice, squander their revenues, multiply their number so that they were individually poorer? Their answer was to try to bind a future pope to pursue policies compatible with their interests, and to do this during the conclave. From 1352 we find a series of 'election capitulations'; each cardinal in conclave swore that, if chosen as pope, he would respect them.

The capitulation of 1352 may be summarized thus.[1] Not more than twenty cardinals were to exist at any one time and there would be no further creations till the number had dropped to sixteen. Every such creation was to have the consent of all or at least a two-thirds majority of the cardinals. The pope would not depose or imprison a cardinal without the unanimous consent of the college; he would not excommunicate or censure him, deprive him of his right to vote, of his right to wear the hat and attend consistory, or take away his benefices or income, without a two-thirds majority of the college. The pope would not confiscate the goods of a cardinal, alive or dead. The pope must not alienate church lands without good cause and a two-thirds majority. The college was to have half the income of church lands in accordance with the decree of Nicholas IV. High secular officers of the papacy were not to be appointed or dismissed without a two-thirds majority. The marshal of the papal court and rectors of church lands were never to be relatives of the pope. No tithes or subsidies were to be given by the pope to a lay prince without a two-thirds majority. When cardinals were asked for their opinions, the pope should allow each to speak freely. All the cardinals present

[1] G. Mollat, *Revue d'histoire ecclésiastique*, 46 (1951), p. 100, part of an excellent article (pp. 22–112, 566–94) on the college in the Avignon period.

swore to observe these stipulations in their entirety if elected, and to ratify them as soon as elected; if in doubt the elect would be guided by a two-thirds majority.

This remarkable document offers a clue to the interpretation of the history of the Church in the next two generations. Its immediate fate is no less significant. The new pope, Innocent VI, had disclaimed it within six months of his election. However tightly the cardinals in conclave might bind the old pope's successor, the irregularity of such proceedings was a permanent impediment to their acceptance and in any case the cardinals could scarcely limit the powers of one who was admitted to possess the power of St Peter to bind and loose.

The Great Schism

A return to Rome became more urgent in the 1360s. It was urged on the pope by many earnest Christians, and the ravaging of the Rhône valley by soldiery released from formal war by the treaty of Brétigny made Avignon uncomfortable as a residence. The partial pacification of the papal states had been accomplished and the presence of the pope in Italy was necessary to prevent further trouble there. Urban V took the curia to Rome in 1367 but encountered attacks from all his Italian enemies; he returned to Avignon in 1370. Gregory XI almost at once announced his intention of returning but was held up by lack of cash and by involvement in Anglo-French war and negotiation; in Italy in 1375 Florence encouraged a rising in the Romagna and thus provoked the 'War of the Eight Saints', as the Florentine war council was called. None the less Gregory XI entered Rome on 17 January 1377. During the next twelve months the Papal States had more or less been brought to obedience, especially after a terrible massacre at Cesena directed by the papal legate Robert of Geneva, and a peace conference assembled at Sarzana in March. Gregory died in Rome on 27 March 1378. His successor hurriedly accepted a settlement with Florence.

Passionate feelings have always been roused by the events of 1378 which produced two lines of popes, and later three.[1] From the Schism,

[1] Popes of the Great Schism:

Rome	Avignon	Conciliar (Pisa)
Urban VI (1378–89)	Clement VII (1378–94)	Alexander V (1409–10)
Boniface IX (1389–1404)	Benedict XIII (1394–	John XXIII (1410–dep.
Innocent VII (1404–6)	dep. 1417, d. 1423)	1415, d. 1419)
Gregory XII (1406–res.	Clement VIII (1423–29)	
1415, d. 1417)	'Benedict XIV' (1425–	
	c. 1430)	

[continued next page

as from the residence at Avignon, it has seemed possible to trace the main future development of organized Christianity; and to these matters national sentiment has added vehemence, not to say venom. The facts may be summarized shortly. At Gregory's death sixteen of the twenty-three cardinals were in Rome—eleven French (of whom seven were from the one French province of Limoges), four Italians and one Spaniard. The Limousins could not agree with the rest of the French majority during the conclave, which took place in a city seething with discontent at the likelihood of a French pope. A compromise candidate was hastily, but canonically, elected who was not a cardinal; Bartolommeo Prignano, archbishop of Bari, known as a tried servant of the Avignon popes. The angry mob invaded the conclave during the last stages of the election and the cardinals made a rapid withdrawal, leaving behind the old cardinal Tebaldeschi, at first taken by the people to be the successful candidate. When it was found that an Italian, if not a Roman, had been elected the city took the news quietly. Cardinals who had fled from Rome made their way back and Urban VI, elected on 8 April 1378, was duly crowned on 18 April. On 20 September 1378, however, thirteen cardinals met at Fondi and there elected as pope Robert of Geneva, the 'victor' of Cesena. He took the title of Clement VII and the Schism had begun.

Why had this occurred? The cardinals who had caused the Schism gave as their reason that they had acted at the conclave under fear and claimed therefore that the election of Urban VI was invalid. This cannot be accepted save as a rationalization and defence of their later action. The plain case seems to be that Urban VI, chosen by a flustered conclave, proved to be wholly intolerable to the cardinals who elected him, whether or not he was unsuitable as pope. Neurotic and violent in his behaviour, the particular object of his bile was the status, privileges and wealth of the cardinals, whom he accused of simony and luxury, and whom he neglected or insulted in curial business. If Urban VI's behaviour is placed in the context of the election capitulation of 1352 the election of Clement VII is readily understood. Before they acted the cardinals had to ensure some political support and among others they consulted Charles V of France. He naturally preferred a French pope and had no means of determining the legal position save through the

---

The title John XXIII was chosen by the pope elected in 1958. He thus stigmatized the earlier pope of this name as an anti-pope. By inference approval has also been given to the 'Roman' line of popes.

tendentious reports of Urban's enemies. In August the French cardinals, whose number had risen to twelve, and one Spaniard withdrew from the curia and circulated to princes their disavowal of Urban's election; this they expected to bring about his resignation. In fact, on 18 September Urban took what was the unforgivable step of creating no fewer than twenty-five new cardinals—an entire college—thus at a stroke destroying the wealth of the members of the existing college and nullifying the effects of their defiance. At the same time they were fortified by a letter from Charles V promising support for a new pope. When the French cardinals elected Robert of Geneva, the three Italian cardinals (Tebaldeschi had died) took no part but signified that they approved of the step. Alberico da Barbiano, Urban's general, succeeded in maintaining his master in Rome and Clement VII retreated to Avignon.

For the next fifty years we cannot talk of papal policy, for the only programme common to all the popes was to secure the obedience of as many provinces of the Church as possible, and at almost any price, and to harm their rivals. Christendom meanwhile bore the brunt of two papal administrations and, in areas of weak civil government, of competing provisions, irregular vacancies and disintegrating discipline.

The 'Roman' popes were insignificant as men and leaders. Urban found the cardinals of his own promotions no easier to get on with than those who had deserted him in 1378; his brutal temper brought five of them to their death. His successors struggled ineffectively with King Ladislas and the Roman mob, and the last of them, Gregory XII, led a wretched life under the protection of Carlo Malatesta at Rimini. At Avignon Clement VII was under pressure from the French crown and sought to embarrass his Roman opponents by interesting French princes in the spoils of Italy; he turned practically all the Papal States into the 'kingdom of Adria' as a bait for the house of Anjou. He was succeeded by Pedro de Luna, an Aragonese, as Benedict XIII, far and away the most influential of all the popes of the Schism. Forced to leave Avignon, he withdrew to Perpignan in 1408 and then to Peñíscola, a coastal fastness in Valencia where he died in 1423. As a last act of intransigence he made the four cardinals at his death-bed elect a successor in the person of 'Clement VIII', a Spanish canon who made his submission to the reunited Church in 1429. One of Benedict XIII's cardinals who was absent from the 'conclave' of 1423 in 1425 secretly elected a French pope who took the title of 'Benedict XIV' and whose misty person disappears from view when the count of Armagnac came to terms with Martin V in 1430.

These last grotesque developments came after all Christendom had accepted Martin V, the pope elected at Constance. The early days of the Schism saw each region of Europe following one or other pope. France, Aragon, Castile, Navarre, Scotland and, at times, Naples supported the pope at Avignon; most of Italy and the Empire, with England and Portugal, obeyed (the word is too strong) the pope at Rome. There were some curious borderlands, as in the duchy of Burgundy where the French territories looked to Avignon and the German lands (including Flanders) to Rome. France as a whole was the first country to find the Schism not only morally shocking but also, not least because of heavy papal taxation, materially embarrassing. Her doctors and publicists were the earliest and most successful expositors of doctrines designed to end the Schism,[1] and her kings were among the leaders of princely attempts to end the division in the Church. France joined with England and Castile in a mission sent in 1397 to each curia. In 1398 France tried the bold step of withdrawing obedience from Benedict, which produced chaos in the French church; in 1408 she declared her neutrality.

The popes protested their desire to reunite Christendom, but it was hard to bring them to effective action. Once more the cardinals in each obedience resorted to election capitulations. At Avignon in 1394, when the conclave ignored the French king's request not to elect, the capitulation involved the elect in promoting unity and resigning if called upon by his cardinals to do so. Similar oaths were sworn in the Roman conclaves of 1404 and 1406. Why (one must ask) did not the cardinals simply refrain from electing? The answer for both obediences was that they sought a protector to secure their own interests and, besides, were often convinced of the legitimacy of their case. Indeed as time wore on Benedict XIII could fairly claim that, as the only pre-schismatic cardinal, he alone could straighten out the muddle. There remained the possibility of direct negotiation. This produced abortive negotiations for a meeting at Savona in 1407–8. The popes did not meet but their cardinals made contact. The upshot was the decision taken by thirteen Gregorian cardinals and nine Benedictine cardinals (later joined by a further cardinal from each obedience) to settle the matter at a council which they summoned to Pisa.

The cardinals at Pisa acted in good faith and, if the council was not widely attended when it opened in March 1409, the deposition of Gregory XII and Benedict XIII which it pronounced in June were generally acceptable to the faithful. All the cardinals present joined in

[1] Above, p. 87.

the election of a new pope, Alexander V, and, this done, the council dispersed. It had demonstrated implicitly that in an emergency a council was superior to a pope; it had explicitly called for a council to be held in three years' time to reform the Church. Neither of the deposed popes accepted their sentence: Gregory had some support in Italy, Benedict could still depend on Aragon, Navarre, Castile, Scotland and the count of Armagnac. But France, England, Germany and most of Italy regarded Alexander V as true pope. Alexander V deputed to his powerful supporter Cardinal Baldassare Cossa the task of recovering power in Rome and the Papal States. And when the pope died at Bologna in 1410 it was Cossa who succeeded him, taking the title of John XXIII. The new vicar of Christ was neither lovable nor respected. He was also singularly unsuccessful in making headway against Ladislas's all-victorious progress. It was as a refugee in Florence, where he made friends of the Medici family who later commemorated him in the lovely tomb in the Baptistry, that he agreed unwillingly to the summoning of a general council in the imperial Free City of Constance. This was the price of the protection of the Emperor Sigismund.

The consequences of the Schism may sometimes have been over-stressed, but by any account they are important. The exhibition by the rival servants of the servants of God of ruthless intrigue and intransigence on a continental scale had profoundly stirred the Christian conscience. The unity of Catholic Christendom under the pope, striven for by generations of clerks for a millennium, had been shattered, not by the political pressure of kings and emperors, who had in earlier centuries found it profitable to promote occasional anti-popes, but by weaknesses in the very headquarters of the Church itself. Princes were, however, the beneficiaries, for they enjoyed the rare chance of choosing their own popes and then admonishing them. These popes were in no position to resist royal demands for graces and privileges, however outrageous. Lorenzo de' Medici in 1477 was surely expressing the general view of civil governments when he wrote that 'the division of power is advantageous and, if it were possible without scandal, three or four Popes would be better than a single one'.[1] Not least important was the emergence of a realization in all countries of the viability of national churches, for the chief ecclesiastical victims of the Schism were the international orders of monks—Cluniac, Cistercian and Carthusian—whose headquarters in the Avignonese obedience led to new provincial arrangements being made in areas looking to Rome. This chimed in with a

[1] Pastor, IV, p. 300.

widespread trend to locally organized religious groups, in marked distinction to the days of St Bernard and St Francis.[1] Above all, the Schism led directly on to the Councils of Constance and Basle, and the attempt to create a papacy with limited and prescribed powers.

The Councils of Constance, Basle, and Ferrara-Florence-Rome

At Pisa a future council had been given the task of reforming the Church. John XXIII summoned the Council of Constance because of his political embarrassment in Italy. The fathers who assembled at Constance in 1414 were confronted with the two main tasks of reforming the Church and of ending the Schism. In the event they ended the Schism but failed to accomplish reform.

John had hoped for a council which, in conformity with recent practice, would obey a papal president and he felt he could secure this through the large number of Italian prelates who attended. But both pope and Italians were suspect; with some Pisan precedents to go on the vote was given to doctors and princes (or their proxies) as well as prelates, and organization rapidly evolved along 'national' lines. The 'nations' at Constance, like the nations at many medieval universities, were based to a large degree on geographical considerations rather than on the national factors (largely linguistic) which prevail today. At Constance there were at the beginning four nations: Italy, France, Germany and England. Matters were first debated within a nation. The business was then presented by delegates of the nations to a congregation of all nations. If agreement was thus reached resolutions were tabled at a *plena sessio*. The place of the pope in this arrangement was solved by John XXIII's flight on 20 March 1415—a move designed to draw from Constance the curia and the cardinals, and so to deprive the council of both validity and prestige. It failed, not least because the cardinals stood firm. It nevertheless put the college in a curious position. As senior clergy the cardinals claimed primacy. For a moment the kind of oligarchy sketched in the election capitulation of 1352 seemed within their grasp; and they could reasonably argue that they were a weightier group than some of those to which the Council had given authority (there were sixteen cardinals as against the three prelates and twenty members of the English nation). But the Fathers likewise refused to budge. The cardinals were told firmly in May 1415 that they must vote with their respective nations. This was, in the upshot, of some significance. While attached to their own nations, the cardinals still continued to meet as a

[1] Below, pp. 314-17.

group and to put forward collective proposals. Since most were French and Italian, they acted at a critical moment in bringing together these two nations.

John's flight also facilitated, if not reunion, at any rate the deposition of his rivals. Deserted by his Austrian protector soon after his flight, he lacked powerful lay adherents and this was also more or less the case with Gregory XII who went through the form of himself summoning the council to which he resigned in July 1415. Benedict XIII was better supported and of a less pliant disposition. Not till the emperor Sigismund had directly negotiated with the Spanish sovereigns was the stubborn old man rendered practically powerless. In October 1416 Spanish representatives arrived at Constance and eight months later, on 26 July 1417, Benedict XIII was deposed. The Schism was over, the way open to the election of a new pope. At this point arose the greatest crisis at the Council. Which was to come first—reform or a new pope?

Reform at Constance had been the theme of scores of sermons and pamphlets: the old European libraries have volume after volume of this material, and we shall see later how deep the disquiet was, how long it had existed and what violent forms it occasionally took.[1] In July 1415 the Council had both handed Huss over to execution and appointed a reform commission consisting of eight members from each of the nations together with three cardinals. But there are plenty of reasons why little was then done, even apart from a failure to agree on the exact steps which should be taken. Sigismund, who encouraged active policies, was absent from July 1415 until the end of 1416, engaged on negotiation with the Spanish kings and an attempt to mediate between England and France which aggravated the situation by ending in an Anglo-Imperial alliance. The Council was also heavily engaged in routine administration, for there was no pope and curial business had to be carried on. With the deposition of Benedict XIII reform had, however, to come to the centre of the picture. All reform turned on the way the pope controlled the Church, on papal taxation, reservation and provisions, and on the place of the cardinals. The view of the German, French and English nations was that reform should precede an election, so that the new pope would not be able to revert to the old bad ways.

By this time, the spring of 1417, delegates from Castile had arrived and they urged the opposite, as did the cardinals who were prepared to allow an election in which delegates of the nations would, for this time only, take part. A compromise was reached in July 1417 which laid down

[1] Below, pp. 317-28.

that a partial reform should precede the choice of a new pope. Yet even partial reform proved unattainable. Some of the Fathers, including a few cardinals, were radical in their views, others were reactionary. The cardinals saw themselves as a corporate check on the pope; for most delegates it was axiomatic that the wealth and power of the cardinals should be reduced. In general the prelates present were hostile to papal provisions; but the university men wanted them, though they would have happily destroyed common services and annates. To these tensions within each nation were added others between the nations. England and France were engaged in bloody war and the hostility was not absent from the Council. These national animosities were excited by the prolonged debates concerning the status of the new Spanish nation. The stalemate led the French, Italians and Spaniards to side with the cardinals in urging an early election and the English began to waver in September 1417. In October it was decided to promulgate a decree affirming that reform would be seriously undertaken after an election, to enact forthwith such reforms as were agreed, and to arrange for the election. At the thirty-ninth session, on 9 October 1417, this was done. The agreed reform consisted of the decree calling for regular councils[1] and making detailed arrangements to deal with any future schism; a newly elected pope would be required to swear faithfully to defend the Catholic faith according to the apostolic tradition, the oecumenical councils and the Fathers; prelates were not to be translated against their will without good cause to be communicated to them; and papal abuse of procurations and *spolia* were condemned. Enactment of these reforms was followed by a fierce wrangle on the way the pope should be elected. In order to avoid a pope who had not the suffrages of a majority of his cardinals a French suggestion was accepted that the elect must secure a two-thirds majority both among the twenty-three cardinals and in each national delegation of six men. The conclave was thus to number fifty-three, the cardinals and thirty other prelates. On 30 October 1417 it was laid down that the pope to be elected would, before he dissolved the Council, reform the Church in head and curia in respect of eighteen named problems. The conclave opened on 8 November and on 11 November 1417 the Italian Cardinal Oddo Colonna was elected as Martin V.

The factors militating against agreement on fundamental reform remained, and were not helped by Martin's immediate renewal of the rules of the papal chancery on reservations and taxes—the most con-

[1] Below, pp. 287-8.

tentious of the problems needing attention—and his liberal exercise or papal grace reminded delegates of the advantages of the old order. In the event a few minor reforms were promulgated in March 1418. These, together with specially negotiated concordats between pope and nations, were accepted as fulfilling the reform stipulations of the session on 30 October. Delegates, many of whom had been at Constance for several years, were weary for home and the provinces of the Church were tired of the endless bickering.

The most elaborate of the concordats was the German one. Its main provisions were as follows. Cardinals to a total of twenty-three were to be chosen proportionately from different provinces of the Church. Papal reservations were to be drastically reduced; in collation graduates were to be preferred to non-graduates and one-sixth of cathedral canonries were to be reserved for them. Only bishops and abbots were to pay common services, and the scale of annates was to be revised. Appeals to the pope were to be reduced. Large monasteries were no longer to be given *in commendam*, lesser ones only to cardinals who would otherwise be poor. Dispensations and indulgences were to be granted sparingly. The other concordats were similar—the French mainly differed in two respects: only half annates were to be paid for five years because of the devastation of war; and no agreement was found possible on providing for graduates. The English (who had had what amounted to a concordat ever since Provisors and Praemunire in the mid-fourteenth century had made it an offence for an Englishman to accept papal provision or carry an appeal to the Rota) were content with a much shorter document, which, if it had been effective, would have strengthened the power of bishops. If, indeed, any of the main reforms of Constance and the concordats had been effective the whole pattern of the future might have been different. This is, of course, especially the case with the definition made of the relations between pope and council.

Conciliar supremacy over a pope was implied by the cardinals' proceedings at Pisa. At Constance it was stated in as many words, in the exciting days after John XXIII's flight. There was much anxious and indeed stormy debate, but in the fifth session, on 6 April 1415, five decrees dealing with the crisis were duly passed, of which the first, *Sacrosancta*, ran: 'The Council of Constance, an oecumenical council, derives its power direct from God and all men, including the pope, are bound to obey it in matters of faith, of ending the Schism and of reforming the Church in head and members.' This was completed at the thirty-ninth session in October 1417 by the decree *Frequens* which laid down that general councils were to be held more often, the next in five years, then another seven years later, and thereafter every ten years. The pope and cardinals together could shorten these intervals, but not lengthen them. Prior to the dissolution of a council the venue of the next was to be determined. Machinery was also laid down in the event of the cardinals being faced with another crisis like that of 1378: this too would be settled by the council. In this way the Fathers at Constance reversed the thousand-year-old process which had turned the pope into an absolute monarch. The Church was given a written constitution.[1]

The failure of *Sacrosancta* and *Frequens* was not immediately apparent. Though it seems clear that Martin V did not accept the limitation on papal supremacy he had necessarily to accept the Council and its actions in general, for it had elected him. The next council met at Pavia, five years after Constance, though the pope empowered his legates to transfer it elsewhere, which was certainly not in keeping with *Frequens*; they transferred it to Siena. Divided into nations, hostile to the pope, but poorly attended, the Council did little but name Basle as the place where its successor would meet; the legates hastily dissolved it on 7 March 1424. Pavia-Siena was a failure in part because no great prince supported it. Hussite problems led the emperor to press for the meeting called for Basle and in the end Martin capitulated, naming as his legate Cardinal Cesarini, already chosen as leader of the crusade against the heretic Bohemians.

Eugenius IV inherited this situation when he became pope in 1431. His Italian troubles, but above all the disastrous failure of Cesarini's crusade, made him vulnerable to Sigismund. At Christmas 1431 he dissolved Basle, but in the next two years he gradually climbed down until on 14 December 1433 he accepted the Council fully. By that time some 500 clerks had been incorporated into the Council, it had the support of the emperor and many German magnates, and Cesarini was convinced that it offered the only hope for a settlement in Bohemia. Among the bulls which the pope had to revoke was *Deus novit* of September 1433, in which he had declared the doctrine of conciliar supremacy to be heretical.

The constitutional arrangements of the Council of Basle were very different from Constance. Broadly speaking, all clergy had the vote. Business was transacted in four committees or 'deputations'—of faith, of peace, of reform and for general matters (*deputatio communis*); within each deputation there were equal numbers for each of the four

[1] Above, p. 87.

nations of Italy, France, Spain and Germany. The deputations met thrice weekly and the united deputations each month elected a small group to determine to which of them matters should be referred. The transactions of each deputation were communicated to the others and when two or more were in agreement on a question it was put before the general congregation. If three deputations were then in agreement a resolution went to a plenary session.

The relations of pope and council remained uneasy, but the final breach did not come till 1436. The Compacts of Prague were signed in July 1436.[1] This left as the next great task a union with the Greeks, who had been driven by Turkish advances to negotiate their submission to Rome. Both Council and pope were in touch with the Greek emperor and both were anxious for the privilege and the prestige which would attach to the ending of a schism which had lasted since 1054. Faced with a divided Roman Church the Greeks opted for the pope, who had offered them a council at Ferrara.

It was not merely hostility to conciliar doctrine that prompted Eugenius to break with Basle, but also the reform measures taken by the Council. From the twelfth session (13 July 1433) to the twenty-first (9 June 1435) the Council proceeded steadily to strip the pope of his resources. Reservations and provisions were abolished; chancery fees, common services and annates were suppressed. In August 1435 the Council, where a rudimentary curia was growing up, ordered all payments to the *camera apostolica* to be sent to Basle; and in March 1436 the papal curia was reformed in detail. Eugenius acted. On 18 September 1437 the bull *Doctoris gentium* condemned the inactivity and truculence of the fathers and transferred the Council from Basle to Ferrara. Many senior prelates now left, including Cesarini himself. When the Greeks accepted the papal Council, Basle lost its *raison d'être*.

The clergy left at Basle still, however, had influential support. Aragon and Milan were the enemies of Eugenius, France was neutral and, although Sigismund died at the end of 1437, so also were the German princes. Extreme measures were now taken. In May 1439 conciliar supremacy was declared to be an article of faith; in June Eugenius was condemned as an obstinate heretic and was deposed; and in November he was replaced as pope by Amedeo of Savoy[2] who took the title Felix V. The last years of the Council were devoid of constructive action. The rump quarrelled with their pope, and though there was still some German support for the Council, Christendom at large was strongly in

[1] Above, p. 228; below, pp. 327-8.   [2] Above, p. 170.

favour of Eugenius. Felix V left Basle in 1442 but it was not until 1449 that a face-saving formula was evolved. In April of that year Felix resigned and the Fathers elected the Roman pope, Nicholas V.

The failure of Basle was in great measure due to the success of the Council of Ferrara—summoned and controlled by the pope in traditional fashion. It opened on 8 January 1438 under the presidency of Cardinal Albergati and did its business in three groups determined by status: the cardinals, archbishops and bishops, abbots and other prelates, and the doctors; a successful motion needed a two-thirds majority in each estate. The Greeks, led by the emperor, the patriarch of Constantinople and twenty-two bishops, arrived in March 1438. The debates on the doctrinal points were long and sometimes bitter and were continued in Florence when the Council was transferred there in January 1439. The main issues were the procession of the Holy Ghost, the use of unleavened bread, the doctrine of purgatory and the primacy of Rome. Only the first and last of these proved difficult. Very unwillingly the Greeks accepted the Latin position by which *filioque* had been added to the Creed.[1] The primacy issue was smoothed over: the Greeks recognized Rome but saved the rights and privileges of the Eastern patriarchs. The decree of union, in Latin and Greek, was signed on 5 July 1439. The practical effect on Greek Orthodoxy and on the political situation in the eastern Mediterranean was negligible.[2]

The union, published by Eugenius in a triumphant bull to all provinces of the Church, greatly increased his public stature. Other unions followed, with the Jacobites (monophysites in the Middle East) and, after the transfer of the Council to Rome in 1443, with the Mesopotamian, Chaldean and Maronite Churches; even the Manichaeans of Bosnia made formal submission. More important still, the Council made no reference to its successor; indeed so completely obedient was it to the pope that we do not know exactly when it ended, save that it predeceased Eugenius himself, who died in February 1447.

Conciliarism, as we can now see, was over, the final blow being the bull *Execrabilis* of 1460 in which Pius II declared it to be anathema to appeal from the Roman pope to a future council. Yet to contemporaries this was less clear. Many such appeals continued to be made both on religious grounds and as a way of embarrassing the pope by his political opponents, especially in Italy. And even in the early sixteenth century many an earnest and orthodox Catholic wondered why councils had not

[1] '. . . I believe in the Holy Ghost . . . who proceedeth from the Father *and the son* . . .'   [2] Above, pp. 247–8.

assembled in conformity with the terms of *Frequens*, which had not been explicitly repudiated by the papacy. Perhaps the most important long term consequence of Constance and Basle was the fear it bred in later popes of all such meetings, a fear which, in the crisis provoked by Luther, prevented the summoning of a council till it was too late.

The re-established papacy

The Councils had other and more immediate effects on the line of popes stemming from Constance and Martin V.[1] Martin himself and Eugenius IV were severely handicapped in all spheres by the existence or the imminence of councils, which legitimized the political activities of their enemies in Italy and their unruly subjects in the Papal States. Martin did much to secure some of the lost authority in his territories and, after a long residence at Florence, finally entered Rome in September 1420. His Venetian successor Eugenius, austere and autocratic, undid much of this by an attack on the Colonna and the ensuing troubles culminated in the pope's undignified escape from the City in 1434. For nearly ten years Eugenius IV was also in Florence. The Romans themselves were soon brought to heel by the pope's ruthless and able agent Vitelleschi, soldier, bishop, patriarch and cardinal, who then turned his attention to the area round Rome until he was murdered, perhaps with Eugenius's tacit connivance, in 1440. Cardinal Scarampo, with a not dissimilar background of medicine and war, succeeded him. These tough men, together with an understanding between the pope and Alfonso of Naples in 1442, enabled Eugenius to return to Rome the following year.

Nicholas V, who came to the papal throne in 1447, was a man of humble origins, who had risen by his scholarship and who was the first pope to patronize and encourage the new artists and men of letters.[2] The

---

[1] The popes after Constance:

Title	Family	Region of origin	Reign
Martin V	Colonna	Rome	1417–31
Eugenius IV	Condulmaro	Venice	1431–47
Nicholas V	Parentucelli	Sarzana	1447–55
Calixtus III	Borja	Valencia	1455–58
Pius II	Piccolomini	Siena	1458–64
Paul II	Barbo	Venice	1464–71
Sixtus IV	della Rovere	Savona	1471–84
Innocent VIII	Cibò	Genoa	1484–92

[2] Below, p. 350.

importance of these activities for the papacy lay in the future. More significant at the time was the re-emergence of a fresh school of papal propagandists and the demonstration of general pleasure in a united Church through the enormously successful jubilee of 1450, which helped to reinforce papal finances. An old man succeeded Nicholas in 1455—the Valencian Cardinal Borja who had been given the hat as part of the papal-Aragonese settlement of 1442. Calixtus III urged the crusade, somewhat ineffectively; he also promoted the careers of many Catalans and advanced to the dignity of cardinal his nephew Rodrigo Borgia, who was to achieve notoriety as Alexander VI.

Aeneas Sylvius Piccolomini was the surprising successor of Calixtus III, surprising because, though of gentle birth, he lacked influence and also because in his earlier days he had been a warm supporter of conciliarism and Basle. All of this, which he put aside on reconciliation with Eugenius in 1445, we know about from his own voluminous writings, which include the *Commentaries*.[1] Despite his unregenerate youth and his facile pen he proved a meritorious enough pope. His condemnation of the Council in *Execrabilis* expressed the new and more confident attitude of the curia. A draft bull of reform was prepared in 1460. And the pope took even more earnestly than Calixtus the threat of Ottoman advance. The call to a crusade by Christian princes at the poorly attended Congress of Mantua in 1459 did not deter him and he died in 1464 at Ancona, vainly awaiting the forces to assemble which he had summoned to defend Christendom.

Paul II, though by no means unsympathetic to the new culture of Italy, took the step of purging the papal administration of men who had entered it as a means of literary advancement, and suffered from the bitter portrait which one of them drew. Platina, in his *Lives of the Popes*, obtained a lasting revenge. Paul's short pontificate was hampered by divisions among the cardinals.

The last two popes to be considered here mark a decisive turn in Church history. The Franciscan Sixtus IV embarked on a policy of nepotism not new in papal history, but on a scale not known earlier. This led to the disastrous struggle with the Medici, and to fighting in the Papal States. The Genoese Innocent VIII was also devoted to his family; his son married Lorenzo de' Medici's daughter. In 1489 Giovanni de' Medici was promoted cardinal at the age of fourteen, though this was not published till 1492. Innocent's pontificate was the heyday of Cardinal Rodrigo Borgia, who was to follow Innocent in 1492

[1] Above, p. 11.

and whose son Cesare was to be the most striking example of papal favouritism.

The popes of the second half of the fifteenth century gradually begin to play the role, not of the pontiff of a universal Church, but of an Italian prince. This change has sometimes been justified on the ground that otherwise they would have become the victims of kings of Naples or dukes of Milan. The promotion of their relatives, especially to high office in the Church itself, has also been explained by arguing that the reigning pope needed about him cardinals whom he could trust; and certainly in the 'cardinal nephew' we can discern the future cardinal secretary of state. Yet the pope could never be a prince like his dynastic contemporaries. On his death he was invariably followed by a pope from another family, intent to dissipate his predecessor's gains. The result was that the pope and his relatives had to work quickly and could not gradually accumulate lands and power. The quarrel between Lorenzo de' Medici and Sixtus IV was directly due to the speed with which the pope and his family pressed on with their ambitious plans.

In this situation the college of Cardinals rapidly became the focal point of diplomatic intrigue, each great family trying to be directly represented. As a group the cardinals had not yet entirely abandoned hope of limiting the exercise of papal powers in their interests. Election capitulations continued, their tenor much the same as earlier: to bind the pope to secure the assent of the college in all matters of policy and to safeguard the cardinals' income. Cardinals in the conclave of 1458, which elected Pius II, swore if elected to prosecute the war against the Turks, to reform the curia, to consult the college on all appointments in the curia and to bishoprics, to observe the Constance decrees on the appointment of cardinals (especially that they should be made in consistory), to safeguard the rights of cardinals to benefices and *commendams*, to make concessions to princes only with the consent of the college, to ensure that all vassals and governors in the Papal States were responsible to the college as well as the pope, and to make up the stipend of each cardinal to a minimum of 4,000 gold florins per annum. Though Eugenius IV did embody the capitulation of 1431 in a bull, these attempts to tie up the future pope were quite unsuccessful. Popes accepted them with the saving clause: 'consistently with the honour and integrity of the apostolic see'. If the pope tried to be a prince, the cardinals had little alternative but to become courtiers and succumb to the attractions of high life, ostentation and political intrigue. This was what most of them did.

The administrative machine perfected before the Schism continued with remarkably few changes, although the work it had to perform altered in certain respects. On the financial side the main innovation was the decline in the non-Italian revenues of the camera. Enormous sums were still paid as common services, and much cash came from the annual influx of pilgrims to Rome and the greater numbers attracted by the jubilees of 1450 and 1475.[1] But Italian income—from indirect taxes in Rome and the Papal States, from the alum mines discovered at Tolfa, and from the sale of offices at the curia—bulked larger and further encouraged popes to behave like Italian princes; a symptom of this was that the transaction of business inside the curia after 1480 was not in Latin but in Italian. The sale of offices went with a rapid increase in bureaucracy and with the growth of a bureaucratic attitude among the large number of clerks placed in the 'colleges' of abbreviators, sealers and secretaries. Another growing source of income was the sale of indulgences.[2] The upshot was that the income from the 'spiritual' side of the curia was slightly greater than that from the temporal lordship of the pope. A typical year of Sixtus IV produced income as follows:[3]

		ducats
1. Curial functions:		
annates and common services		60,000
sealing and registry		36,000
compositions		12,000
sale of offices		15,000
indulgences		10,000
	Total	133,000
2. Temporal lordship:		
Papal States		83,000
Rome		40,000
	Total	123,000

Together with irregular income from gifts and jubilees the popes in the later fifteenth century probably had about 400,000 ducats a year, which made them (as far as material resources went) a medium Italian power.[4] Their largest commitment was the army. Even in peace time garrisons and troops ran away with about 100,000 ducats annually, and in general a chronic shortage of money limited papal action. This was intensified by certain aspects of papal policy. The bribes to Frederick III, the cost of transporting and supporting the huge Greek delegation for the union,

[1] Below, p. 306. [2] Below, p. 307.
[3] Gottlob, *op. cit.*, pp. 253–5. [4] Above, p. 186.

and the lavish building programme at Rome all severely strained resources and led to further unsavoury searching for cash.

Christendom after the Councils

The great power which a prince exercised over the Church in his lands
before the Schism was increased by the events of 1378 and in the system
of concordats recognition was given to the existence of provincially
organized and distinct Churches. This process was carried furthest and
with least trouble in England and, on the continent, in the Spain of
Ferdinand and Isabella. In France and Germany, however, there were
prolonged tensions between the papacy and secular and religious authorities after Constance.

The fifteenth century is the period when the 'liberties of the Gallican
church' were self-consciously canvassed by king and clergy. Bedevilled
by hostility between the hierarchy and the universities (especially Paris),
and by the civil war, the only thread of constancy is the general desire
to reduce to a minimum papal taxation in France. Paris University was
anxious to reestablish papal provisions for graduates after 1418: *parlement* was vehemently opposed to this, and from this point onwards the
lawyers in *parlement* were at the heart of Gallican sentiment. Hard
pressed by England, Charles VII could not always afford to flout the
pope. The concordat of Genazzano (1426) went far to nullifying Gallican
liberties and gave French bishops the disposal of only a third of nominations to benefices. *Parlement* registered this under protest. After 1435
Charles was stronger and ready to adopt a more popular policy. A
council of French clergy at Bourges in June 1438 advised acceptance of
the reform legislation of the Council of Basle and this was embodied by
the king in a solemn ordinance known as a Pragmatic Sanction. This not
only enacted the moral reformation of Basle (regularity of services,
condemnation of concubinage and so forth) but also conciliar supremacy
over the pope. Canonical election was laid down and, though a few concessions were made to Eugenius IV for his lifetime, reservations and
annates were abolished.

The Pragmatic Sanction of Bourges became the basis of future
Gallicanism, but it remained at the mercy of the political situation.
There was much to be gained by the use of papal prerogative at the
behest of a king. Louis as dauphin had opposed the ecclesiastical policy
of his father and as king he revoked the Pragmatic Sanction. When
Pius II failed to support royal nominations and did not aid French
policy in Naples the Pragmatic Sanction (with other anti-papal measures)

was brought back in 1463–64. Similar gambits were tried with Paul II in 1467 and with Sixtus IV. In practice, whatever his momentary relations with Rome, Louis was master of the French clergy, as were his successors.

The German story lacks the simplicity to be found in centrally-governed France. Dislike of papal politics was engrained in Germany. The support for Constance and Basle came from emperor, princes and prelates. From 1378 to 1437 there had been in practice freedom from papal interference in the German church, and when the emperor began to see advantages, temporary or permanent, in an arrangement with the pope, he was resisted by the electors and many bishops. At Sigismund's death in 1437 the electors declared their neutrality between pope and council. This was also the policy of the Emperor Albert II. The *Acceptatio* of Mainz, in March 1439, went further and received into German lands the main legislation of Basle—as the Pragmatic Sanction had received it in France. Frederick, who followed Albert in 1440, was faced with a pope whose fortunes were rising and with electors who supported Felix V as an anti-imperial gesture. In the ensuing negotiations of 1445–46 a large part was played by Aeneas Sylvius Piccclomini, who had moved from service of the Council of Basle into the imperial chancery. In February 1446 the bargain was struck. Frederick recognized Eugenius IV in return for rights of presentation in six German sees for his life and the huge sum of 221,000 ducats, 121,000 from Eugenius and the balance from later popes. The archbishops of Trier and Cologne, leaders of the anti-papal forces, were deposed, but this only closed the German ranks. Long and piecemeal intrigue now followed, pope and emperor detaching the magnates lay and clerical from their intransigent position. The pope's concessions, made on his deathbed and therefore devoid of much significance, promised a council and recognized the validity of appointments made during the period of neutrality; the rebellious archbishops would be forgiven and a legate would settle outstanding differences. On these terms neutrality was at last abandoned, culminating under Nicholas V in settlements at Aschaffenburg in 1447 and at Vienna in 1448, which were in the end to be more or less accepted throughout Germany. The emperor gained extensive patronage and princes continued to treat the Church in their lands as they wished. Stormy episodes still occurred in papal relations with Germany, such as the conflict between Nicholas of Cusa and Sigismund of the Tyrol,[1] or the rivalry for the archbishopric of Mainz;

[1] Below, p. 319.

both troubled the Church in Germany from 1460 to 1464. But there was a real gain for the pope: the abandonment—at any rate officially—of the doctrine of conciliar supremacy. It proved a temporary pacification. Luther was born in 1483.

The affairs of the post-conciliar Church have been briefly illustrated from France and Germany. The dominant position of the secular ruler could equally well have been demonstrated with other regions: from Scotland, for example, where in 1487 Innocent VIII agreed to delay for eight months all provisions so that royal wishes could be known; and where in 1493 an act of parliament decreed outlawry for clerks petitioning Rome for benefices without the king's consent. Or from Burgundy, where the duke in 1437 forced an unwelcome papal nominee to Cambrai to withdraw and where, to the large ecclesiastical patronage of Philip, the popes frequently added block reservations to be filled at the ducal pleasure: ten abbeys were put at his disposal in 1442 and in 1448 no fewer than 108 benefices in the diocese of Tournai. Not the least abundant evidence of lay control of Church appointments comes from Italy itself. Milan, Venice, Florence, Naples and the smaller principalities all demanded the obedient collaboration of the pope and reacted violently if their nominees were passed over. When in 1459 Pius II made the Venetian Cardinal Barbo (later to be Paul II) bishop of Padua, this conflicted with Venetian wishes. The cardinal's family were attacked viciously by the signory and Pius II had to give way, though the agreed candidate had to pay Barbo a substantial compensation from the income of the see. In Spain the Inquisition[1] was also a step in the direction of royal control of the Church, and episcopal nominations were strictly controlled by Ferdinand and Isabella. Ferdinand successfully obtained the mastership of the influential military Orders of Calatrava, Alcántara and Santiago.

The regionalism promoted in these ways was reflected also in the organization of the religious Orders. Those with headquarters in the obedience of Avignon were compelled during the Schism to develop fresh provincial arrangements in areas looking to Rome. These divisions were on the whole not reversed after the reunification of the papacy, and indeed, quite apart from the Schism, provincial autonomy increased among the friars. The Dominicans had 'congregations' or groups of houses in Lombardy, Holland, Spain and France, each with a vicar general whose relations with the master general were often tenuous. The distracted Franciscans were even more split up. Two great groups were

[1] Below, p. 331.

officially recognized, the Conventuals and the Franciscans of the Strict Observance, or Observants. In 1415 the French Observants obtained a vicar general who was merely confirmed by the minister general; and this also happened in Spain in 1434. In 1446 Eugenius IV divided the Observants into two great groups, Cismontane and Ultramontane, each with a vicar general. We will see, when we come in chapter XII to discuss religion as distinct from the Church, that movements for reform and movements of outright rebellion are both provincial in this period. Such a development was perhaps not surprising in a world where national sentiment was playing a larger part, where princes were stronger, and which had endured two generations of schism followed by popes for whom Christendom was less important than Italian politics.

XII

The Bonds of Religion

By 1300 the Cross had been planted in all but two small areas of Europe, Lithuania and Granada, though the Crescent of Islam was soon to penetrate territories in the southeast of the continent. The advance of Christianity was slower now than it had been, and in the hands of politicians rather than evangelists. The conversion of the last pagan people of the Baltic region occurred not as a result of the desultory

BIBLIOGRAPHY. Relevant books will be found in connection with chapters IV and XI. Volumes 14 and 15 in the Fliche and Martin *Histoire de l'église* respectively by Delaruelle and others and by Aubenas and Ricard, contain useful material (the latter being particularly valuable for Spain), and so do the relevant volumes of Pastor's *Popes*. Monsignor Mollat's contribution to the Lot and Fawtier *Histoire des institutions de France au moyen âge* and his *Papes d'Avignon* range widely beyond the constitutional. G. G. Coulton, *Five Centuries of Religion*, IV (Cambridge, 1950) is a confusing and badly put-together book but contains a mass of information and is based on wide reading of the sources; see also E. Delaruelle, 'La pietà popolare alla fine del Medioevo' (in French), *X Congresso Internazionale di Scienze Storiche, Relazioni*, III (Florence, 1955), pp. 309–32. For England: W. Capes, *A History of the English Church in the Fourteenth and Fifteenth Centuries* (London, 1900); W. A. Pantin, *The English Church in the Fourteenth Century* (Cambridge, 1955). For a significant part of the Low Countries: Moreau, *Histoire de l'église Belgique* (above, p. 268). For Germany: A. Hauck, *Kirchengeschichte Deutschlands* (above, *ibid.*). Mysticism: Evelyn Underhill in *Cambridge Medieval History*, VII, chap. 26; A. Hyma, *The Christian Renaissance* (Grand Rapids, 1924); E. F. Jacob, 'Brethren of the Common Life' in *Essays in the Conciliar Epoch* (rev. edn. Manchester, 1953). Wycliffe: the most recent account is K. B. McFarlane, *John Wycliffe and the Beginnings of English Nonconformity* (London, 1952); the fullest account of his religious teaching is H. B. Workman, *John Wyclif*, 2 vols. (Oxford, 1926). A recent sober and valuable work on Huss is by a Benedictine monk, P. de Vooght, *L'hérésie de Jean Huss* (Louvain, 1960). For radical heresies see N. Cohn, *The Pursuit of the Millennium* (London, 1957); G. Leff, *Heresy in the Later Middle Ages* (Manchester, 1967), and H. C. Lea, *A History of the Inquisition of the Middle Ages*, 3 vols. (London, 1888), the fullest treatment of its subject. A useful discussion of the Jews by Cecil Roth is in *Cambridge Medieval History*, VII, chap. 22.

crusading of the Teutonic Knights and visiting cavaliers, who found in Prussia the most economical centre for the display of religious bellicosity, but through the marriage of the Great Prince Jagiello to the Angevin princess, Hedwig (Jadwiga) 'king' of Poland. This took place in 1386 and in the decades that followed a large area was won for the Latin rite which might otherwise have ultimately come under the sway of Greek Orthodoxy. Bishoprics were established at Wilno (1387) and Miedniki (1417) under the metropolitan of Gniezno. A century later, following the marriage-union of Aragon and Castile, the Moorish kingdom of Granada finally fell. Granada had been the last remnant of Islamic Spain; its 'bishop' had held his see *in partibus infidelium*, as had the bishops of Almeria and Guadix; on 10 December 1492 Granada was raised to metropolitan rank as a sign that a whole province had been recovered for Christianity. Such advances were, of course, followed by difficulties. There were Orthodox Russians and pagan Samogitians in Lithuania who took ill to the new arrangements. In Granada the forcible conversion of the Moors was (so Spaniards later thought) superficial.

In Poland and Lithuania the Greek and Roman Churches confronted each other, and a similar situation was found in the Balkans, especially in the mountainous territory in Bosnia. Elsewhere the boundary between Greek and Roman obedience was clearly drawn, for even in the islands controlled by the Latins, like Crete and Rhodes (where there were Latin bishops) the population was Orthodox Greek. In the course of the fourteenth century the Ottoman Turk absorbed Greek Asia Minor and began to penetrate deeply into the European provinces of the eastern emperor. By the end of the fifteenth century the Turks controlled all the Balkans up to the Save. This did not mean the extinction of Orthodox Christianity in these areas; the Turk tolerated religious diversity at the price of taxation and other penalties. But it deprived the eastern Christians of leadership from Byzantium.

The fear of engulfment by the Turk gave urgency to the old problem of ecclesiastical relations between Rome and Constantinople. These had been strained to breaking point since the eleventh century, and the breach had been worsened by the Latin conquest of the Eastern Empire in the thirteenth century. It was a measure of Greek desperation that at the Council of Florence in 1439 the emperor and a large Greek delegation finally agreed to end the Schism.[1] The agreement not only did not lead to western aid of any significance for the beleaguered Greeks: it did

[1] For Ottoman-Greek relations see above chapter x; for the Council of Ferrara-Florence see above, p. 290.

not command popular, or even perhaps official, support in Constantinople, where the city was divided into unionist and anti-unionist camps; the latter gained the upper hand in both court and hierarchy. The fall of the city in 1453 solved this situation and made the union nugatory. By this time, however, a new centre for a Greek rite independent of Rome was emerging. Isidore, metropolitan of Kiev, who led the Russian delegation at Ferrara and Florence where he was a warm advocate of union, was made a cardinal by Eugenius and apostolic delegate for Russia. When he finally got to Moscow in 1441 Prince Vasili imprisoned him for a while and totally rejected the Act of Union. A few years later, just before Constantinople fell, Jonas was elected metropolitan of Kiev and All Russia without the agreement of pope, emperor or patriarch. Russia was to be the citadel of Orthodoxy in centuries to come.

However momentous for the future was to be the transference of Greek Christianity to the patronage of tsars, however immediately important the Act of Union was in reinforcing Eugenius IV's prestige and weakening the Council of Basle, these developments did little to affect the character of religion in Christendom.

The quality of Latin Christianity

Evidence that all was not well with the Church comes from every century of the Middle Ages. A sound and aggressive religious spirit is as likely to urge reform as is one beset by doubts. The fourteenth and fifteenth centuries certainly afford plenty of examples of men and women who were dissatisfied with the role of religion in their lives and with the structure of the organized Church. Such questioning and criticism came now not only from zealous priests and regular clergy but from an ever more literate laity. It ranged from attacks on papal and episcopal rapacity (simony, trafficking in church preferment, made a man a heretic) and luxury among prelates (St Catherine of Siena compared the papal court unfavourably to a brothel), to condemnation of ignorant and boorish priests, and of monks and nuns who led scandalous lives.

At the end of the fourteenth century in England we have the sad and savage testimony of William Langland (1332–1400) in *Piers Plowman*:

> Friars? All the four orders,   I found them there,
> Preaching to the people,   and glosing the gospel
> For their own profit . . .
> Look there, a Pardoner   preaching like a priest.

A papal bull he brought,   sealed by the bishop
He can assoil them all,   of fasting, falsehood and of
            broken vows . . .
If the bishop were holy   and worth both his ears,
He would not send his seal   to deceive the people.
But against the bishop   your Pardoner preacheth not.
For the parson and the Pardoner share the sermon-silver,
Which the parish poor would get if the Pardoner were away . . .
Bishops and deacons,   masters and doctors,
With cures under Christ   and tonsured to show it,
Who ought to shrive their people and pray and feed their flocks,
They lie in London,   in Lent, ay, all the year.[1]

To balance Langland's 'Field full of folk' we have the pilgrims in Chaucer's *Canterbury Tales*, where the spiritual members of the party are (save for the poor parson) the gayest. Was Lady Eglentyne's nunnery the smart house Langland wrote about?

I have an aunt, a Nun,   another an Abbess.
They would sooner faint or die than suffer any penance.
I was cook in their kitchen,   I served the convent
Many months with them,   and many with the monks.
Broth for the prioress I made and for other poor ladies,
Broth and soup I made out of
   chatter.   Thus it went:
'Sister Joan was a bastard
Sister Clarice a knight's daughter her father a cuckold;
Sister Pernell a priest's wench not fit to be prioress;
She bore a child in cherry-time all the chapter knew it,
They challenged her with it   at her election day.'[2]

Amor (as Chaucer's Prioress had it in the 'A' of her equivocal golden broach) *vincit omnia*.

The literary evidence from England is paralleled by a mass of similar material from other countries. The clergy in Boccaccio's *Decameron* in the mid-fourteenth century are like those in the even fiercer tales of Masuccio of Salerno in the late fifteenth, and the intervening Italian novelists are no different. In France it is the same with the *Cent nouvelles nouvelles* and the poems of François Villon. These writings

[1] *Piers Plowman* (Everyman's Library), pp. 5–6.
[2] *Piers Plowman* (Everyman's Library), pp. 78–9.

certainly stem from an old tradition and notably from the *fabliaux*. But there is no doubt that the audience for light literature in the later Middle Ages took for granted a norm of priest, monk, friar and nun which cast them readily for parts involving lechery, trickery and sloth.

Nor is this picture contradicted, though it is toned down, by such impartial evidence as is supplied by visitation records and the canons of provincial councils. The visitations carried out in the archdeaconry of Josas, in the diocese of Paris, have survived for the years 1458–70. They provide a melancholy picture of ruin and carelessness, where priests were absent or ignorant, churchwardens not much better and hatred so uniformly found between parson and people that the Visitor, Jean Mouchard, recorded not the strife but the few occasions where there was peace in a parish.[1] This was a part of the world where the French civil war and the English occupation had wreaked havoc down to 1435, and where Louis XI's troubles led to further fighting; and it was near enough to Paris for many of the clergy to seek the solace of the capital. Yet allowing for this and allowing for the melancholy fact that the malefactor is more newsworthy than his law-abiding contemporary, the state of Church affairs here was deplorable. It is borne out also in other records, which are fuller for conventual than for parochial establishments. Decayed monasteries with one or two brothers are found not only in ravaged France, but in Italy where Ambrogio Traversari attempted in and after 1431 the reform of the Order of Camaldoli of which he was general; passages from the journal of his tour, the *Hodoeporicon*, are the basis of chapters 28 to 33 in volume IV of G. G. Coulton's *Four Centuries*. The sober conclusions of Dom David Knowles on the visitation material for England from 1350 to 1450 gives a fair picture of one of the best regulated of the provinces of Christendom:

> The religious houses . . . were undoubtedly several degrees more distant from fervour than they had been in 1300. At almost all the barrier which was their physical separation from secular life had fallen. In some cases complete decadence was manifest; at others only a general want of zeal.[2]

For an indication of the overall situation we can conclude with some of the canons of one of the relatively infrequent provincial councils held

[1] *Visites archidiaconales de Josas*, ed. J. M. Alliot (1902); a convenient and full analysis by Ch. Petit-Dutaillis in *Revue historique*, 48 (1905), pp. 296–316.
[2] *Religious Orders in England*, II, p. 218.

in the later Middle Ages. In 1429 a provincial synod at Paris enacted forty-one canons.[1] The following need no commentary:

2. Clergy are forbidden to gossip or laugh in church, or to play foolish and unbecoming games on holidays, at any rate during divine service.

4. Canons and prebendaries will only share in alms if they have been present at matins, mass and vespers.

5. Town clergy, with prebends in several churches, run in their ecclesiastical habits from one church to another: this abuse will be repressed.

6. No canon or prebendary of a cathedral will leave it on a feast day for another church where he has a prebend on the grounds that the latter is more valuable.

7. The sacred vessels and appointments will be kept clean; dancing, profane songs, games and markets will not be held in sacred precincts.

8. Bishops will not ordain any clerk not of good life, who does not know the Epistles and Gospels, who cannot read and sufficiently understand the rest of the service. Some who wish to have the sub-diaconate are unaware that this involves continence: they must be told in advance. No one shall be inducted into a cure of souls without previous examination, with particular reference to the administration of the sacraments and his own morals.

9. When prelates ride abroad they will wear their proper hats; in church they shall wear below their vestments (which shall never be ornamented with velvet or silk) a linen rochet, neither too long nor too short.

11. The officers of episcopal courts extort money and perpetrate every kind of irregularity; bishops will reform their courts . . .

14. Abbots and monks will not dwell outside their monasteries. They will follow exactly the old rules for costume. In particular they are forbidden to wear short tunics, long cloaks, silver belts etc.

15. Entrance fees will not be charged by monasteries from those who wish to enter an Order, though gifts may be accepted.

20. Bishops and rectors will ensure the complete compliance with the legislation concerning the life and conduct of clergy and especially in regard to the prohibition of clerics frequenting inns, in-

---

[1] Hefele-Leclercq, *Histoire des Conciles*, VII, i, p. 650.

volving themselves in temporal matters, trade, dealings in wine and cereals, playing ball in public . . .

22. Blasphemy and perjury among the clergy should be punished twice as severely as among laymen.
23. Concubinage is so common among the clergy that it has given rise to the view that simple fornication is not a mortal sin. No bishop will tolerate any clerk living in concubinage, still less will he allow his connivance to be purchased.

There are some hair-raising stories of clerical ignorance and immorality in these centuries, but the overall picture is probably rather of sluggishness and lack of conviction. Councils and bishops reiterate demands for the regulations to be observed with such monotonous frequency that one can only suppose admonitions had little effect. Does this mean that the inspiration of the altar and the scriptures had lost their significance? Here one meets the problem of what men and women believe in and how far their beliefs influence their actions. It is an impenetrable question in our own day and no easier in earlier centuries. One is left with the external evidence only.

There are a good many indications of changes in the currents of popular devotion. The respect for the Virgin Mary, which had gathered strength in earlier centuries, grew ever stronger. The doctrine of the Immaculate Conception still attracted the *furor theologicus* in the fourteenth century, Dominican scholars opposing it and Franciscans supporting it. By the end of the century it had gained much support at the university of Paris, the stronghold of Catholic theology; in 1439 at the Council of Basle the Fathers declared it to be an article of faith. With this should perhaps be associated the use of the rosary, which (with Dominican encouragement) became widespread in the fifteenth century. Another example of popular pressure on doctrine was provided by the promulgation as a dogma of the Beatific Vision.[1] Older forms of piety were not neglected. The latterday pilgrims thronged the routes to the great centres—Compostella, Rome and Jerusalem—as well as to Canterbury, Aachen, Mont-Saint-Michel and hundreds of less celebrated shrines. The way was now less fraught with heroism and, though the poor went too, pilgrimage was now no longer identified with poverty as such; a holiday element was perhaps more noticeable. The Venetians provided regular ships to carry pilgrims to the east; some 600 or more were carried annually in the fourteenth century though the numbers had

[1] Above, p. 268.

dropped by 1500. Handbooks were provided for visitors to Rome, listing not only the churches but the monuments. The transport and accommodation of pilgrims was an important mercantile activity as well as an object of continuing charity. We read that between 40,000 and 50,000 pilgrims came annually to Rome and that the German hospice alone dealt with between 3,000 and 5,000 a year. It has been argued[1] that with the jubilee of 1450 the popes deliberately tried to make Rome the centre of popular devotion, the 'capital of prayer'.

A new and less wholesome form of piety was displayed by the flagellants. In groups numbering hundreds and sometimes thousands they wandered over Germany and France in the first half of the fourteenth century. The height of the mania seems to have been reached in the aftermath of the Black Death. Prayer and fasting accompanied the regular whipping; but so did anti-Jewish demonstrations and anticlerical vandalism. In 1349 Pope Clement VI solemnly condemned the flagellants and called on all bishops and civil rulers to disperse and imprison them; there were, however, later outbreaks. These waves of hysteria were of course prompted by the conviction that the body was physically vile, and they had respectable antecedents in the austerities of individual monks and saints. But they should also perhaps be linked with the later medieval cult of the Passion. Christ as the Man of Sorrows, Mary as the *mater dolorosa* entered the canon of religious painting. The Instruments of the Passion were frequently employed as symbols; the cult developed of the Stations of the Cross. The blood shed by Christ was one of the most cherished relics and its merits provoked yet another fierce debate between Franciscans and Dominicans, the latter asserting that the blood had been 'reassumed' by Christ at the Resurrection. The argument became so violent that Pope Pius II was forced in 1462 to prohibit discussion of the question.

The reality of religion in more concrete forms was also doubtless encouraged by both art and drama. The Italian primitives and later the Flemish primitives conveyed with an immediacy which must at the time have been startling the lives of Christ, of the Virgin and saints. Placed in familiar settings, the streets and churches of a known town, the humanity and sufferings of Jesus, the meekness and charity of his mother, had come down from the remote and hieratic distance that formerly separated them from the devout. When a worshipper looked at Masaccio's *Crucifixion* he must have felt he was himself a witness, that the Agony of the Man was above him on the wall. The painters also

[1] By Delaruelle, *art. cit.*

depicted religious events with familiarity since they had before them the acted story in the Miracle Plays, the *Sacre rappresentazioni* of Italy and their equivalents everywhere. Religious drama had long left the church for the market place; craft guilds and confraternities of citizens undertook the production of the plays, often under municipal control. The great day was, significantly, the feast of Corpus Christi (instituted in 1311), when the elements were carried in grand procession through the streets and the earthly story of Christ was enacted scene by scene. Although rural miracle and mystery plays are not unknown, the countryman who wished to marvel at the religious art and drama of the period normally had to visit a town of some size.

Even small rural parish churches, however, often had a wall covered with the Last Judgment. Here again a new note of realism and pity are to be found together with an insistence on the omnipresence of death and the likelihood of damnation. The skeletons of the *Danse macabre* are depicted in wood, stone and paint all over northern Europe in the century after they first appear in sculptured form in the Church of the Innocents at Paris in 1408. In Italy the equivalent late medieval theme is the Triumph of Death. The north of Johann Huizinga's *Waning of the Middle Ages* had no monopoly of the charnel house and the worm as goads to virtue. 'The awareness of death and the love of life'[1] jostle each other in the whole of Europe in the fifteenth century; by 1500 the skull and bones have already entered the iconography of sepulchral monuments.

An obsession with the need to die well, for which dozens of writers and artists catered, also lies behind the fresh urgency acquired by indulgences at this time. The notion that the pope could shorten the penalties of sin on earth and in purgatory by drawing on the Treasury of Merit, the abundant satisfaction of Christ augmented by the 'superfluous' merits of the Virgin and saints, was not a new doctrine, for indulgences had been given by popes in earlier centuries, especially in connection with the crusades. But the first official declaration on the doctrine comes with a bull of Clement VI in 1350. At first regarded as exceptional, perpetual and plenary indulgences multiplied and could be obtained for cash down. The theologians never wavered in demanding contrition before indulgences were effective, but for ordinary men and women the purchase of an indulgence or the visit to a privileged church became a simple act from which grace flowed automatically. The

[1] A translation of the title of an important book by Alberto Tenenti, *Il senso della morte e l'amore della vita nel Rinascimento* (Turin, 1957).

censorious pre-Reformation critic blamed the hierarchy for the rapid development of indulgences, for their sale involved evident profits for the pope or his nominees; Protestants and (since the Council of Trent) Catholics have echoed such censure. But it is well to remember the consumer demand for the spiritual comfort of the indulgence: the pardoner, who flogged these dubious documents to the public, was execrated by reformers in the later Middle Ages, but he never lacked patrons; the multiplication of indulgences was one of the first tasks of the early printers; pilgrims flocked to Rome now for the grace afforded by the pope rather than the relics in the churches.

The terror of purgatory also partly accounts for the elaboration of masses for the dead. These, either in perpetuity or for a period of years, the rich provided for in their wills and the less well-to-do secured by membership of a religious confraternity. From this practice sprang the large numbers of chantries and chantry priests, particularly in towns. The aisles of the bigger churches were flanked by little chapels and even in country districts confraternities as well as local magnates founded private chapels. This development doubtless offered easy jobs for lazy priests, as contemporaries regularly pointed out. But it is one of the channels through which endowments flowed to the Church in the later Middle Ages and it had certain indirect benefits for the community. The chantry priests often kept small schools. The confraternities were often patrons of the arts, particularly in some of the bigger towns. Venice offers some striking examples of works of art commissioned by pious guilds.

When one descends from these generalities to the actualities of parochial life in the fourteenth and fifteenth centuries it is clear that there was still a chasm between the rules and the practices of the Church. For reasons which will come before us below the supervision of the clergy was defective. Absenteeism meant that parishes often lacked the services not only of the rector or vicar but of the curate who was supposed to act for him; for months or for years no mass might be said in a remote rural church, which became ruinous or was maintained as a barn or stable. The level of education of the average parish clergyman was low, his manners boorish, his stipend so meagre that he insisted on his petty privileges in cash or kind—for burying, for marrying, for baptizing, even for giving Easter communion—in mean ways which often angered and alienated his flock. The condition of religious life depicted in the visitation of the archdeaconry of Josas was undoubtedly due in part to war and the clerks revealed in this record may not be as repulsive as

those revealed by the thirteenth-century records of the diocese of Rouen
—one of the few areas of France for which earlier visitation records
survive. But the squalor of the parishes in this part of the Île de France
in the second half of the fifteenth century is a grim reminder of how far
the Church could sometimes be from serving the people. Baptism
(which could be given in an emergency by the laity) and burial were the
more or less unavoidable moments when a priest was needed. For the
rest he was less essential. Marriage was basically a contract before
witnesses: the priest, if available and if his services could be afforded,
merely blessed the union; the ceremony (in which by canon law the
spouses are the ministers) had in any case as yet got no nearer to the
altar than the porch of the church. Of episcopal confirmation of the
laity as an actual practice we hear very little anywhere in Christendom.[1]

It must be stressed that this stark picture has many exceptions,
particularly in towns. Yet it is not only in the savager parts of Europe
that we hear, more insistently as time goes on, of the deeper and more
primitive rituals of witchcraft and sorcery. Controversy has been fierce
over the question and it is likely that we are confronted not only by
increasing credence in popular magic but also a new resolution on the
part of the Church authorities to eradicate it; the greater documentation
is thus not necessarily due to greater superstition. One must also distinguish from popular mysteries the scientific use of astrology, patronized by practically all princes and great men under the conviction that
the stars influenced terrestrial events.

With all due reserve it seems likely that witchcraft or black magic was
more widely accepted as part of the fabric of society in the fourteenth
century and later than it had been in the preceding period. Much of it
was innocent enough, as we can see from the *Inquisitor's Manual* (*c.* 1322)
of Bernard Gui.[2] He lists questions concerning charms for infertility
and for promoting (and destroying) conjugal love; he refers to incanta-
tions which cure the sick, and others which spy out the future. But he
also enquires into the profanation of the consecrated elements, the
baptism of figurines in wax and lead. When priests were often not available or when they shared in the pagan assumptions of their parishioners,
when qualified medical attention was confined to town hospitals and
rich men's households, it must have been useful to know 'how to gather

---

[1] It was not registered by bishops, though the child was often given a sacred
memento of the occasion, as Platter was (see above, p. 55n.).
[2] Edited by G. Mollat, 2 vols. (Paris, 1926–27).

herbs on one's knees, facing the East, saying the Lord's Prayer'. In any case belief in demons was orthodox. Princes and prelates did not hesitate to practice sorcery against their enemies. The bishops of Cahors, Toulouse and Ganos tried to kill John XXII by magic in 1317 and Matteo Visconti tried again in 1320. Many of these shadowy activities are, of course, as old as man; and some of them have survived the Enlightenment into the twentieth century, and not only among the ill-educated. What is not in doubt is the new vehemence of the attempted suppression. It may indeed, as the historian of the Inquisition H. C. Lea thought, have advertised the very observances it sought to quell.

Reform and the clergy

Some of the influences which weakened the Church were also impediments to the reform which, as we will see, was insistently demanded.

First must be considered the pope, the cardinals and the curia. The popes of the Avignon period were not unable men, though they were hampered outside France by a widespread suspicion of their political integrity. From 1378 to 1417 there was a Schism with two and then three popes, and then till the mid-1440s a doubtful period of conciliar activity. When this was over the popes are no longer figures of real significance beyond Italy. In general it is fair to say that there is no serious or sustained papal encouragement of reform in the fourteenth and fifteenth centuries. As for the cardinals, predominantly French at Avignon and overwhelmingly Italian by the second half of the fifteenth century, they contained some illustrious and devoted men; we have noticed the important role played by some of them in ending the Schism in 1417; we will encounter others among the reformers. But by and large the college in the later Middle Ages was devoted corporately to protecting its own powers against papal encroachment and had even provoked the disastrous events of 1378 in the pursuit of such an aim. Defeated in their ambition to control the pope, most cardinals consoled themselves with large incomes and high living. No attempt was made to respect the reiterated demand of councils and concordats to secure a college representing fairly the different provinces of the Church. The monopoly of the French first and later the Italians in the offices of the curia was another standing grievance to which small attention was paid. But, more important than that, the large establishment of curial clergy, which got even bigger in the decades after 1447, depended financially on the rigorous collection of administrative taxes. Since offices were increasingly sold, this problem grew more intractable as time went on. Rome was associated above all with money and hardly at all with moral leadership.

Though the fiscal activity of the popes and the curia was universally disliked and was generally blamed for the luxury and worldliness of the headquarters of the Church, clerical opinion was far from being sure of the remedy. If one had a pope and a curia this had to be paid for somehow, and each group of clergy looked only to its own interests. Above all there was a cleavage between the university men and the rest. Popes were accepted as more reliable patrons of graduates than local bishops. Universities sponsored the annual roll of members seeking the grant of livings, and papal reservations and provisions, which carried with them papal taxation and were disliked by bishops and most other clerks, were popular with masters and doctors.

Overall it may be assumed that the revenues of most livings were smaller than they had been, for landed income had declined in the fourteenth-century slump. This led to larger churches 'appropriating' income from parishes of which they had the patronage, a process (however necessary it may have been) which still further reduced the value of livings served by ill-paid vicars or curates. This in turn encouraged absenteeism. The non-resident parson was no new problem. In the later Middle Ages he was encountered more often and it is hard to be censorious of men who abandoned the misery of rural parishes; those who stuck by their flocks were often pretty unwholesome.

Absenteeism was not found only among the parish priests. It was found among the archdeacons and bishops whose job it was to survey and discipline the clergy of a diocese. Episcopal visitations are rare. When they occur it is all too plain that bishops were often either long-suffering or complaisant and hesitated to take the drastic steps which would have removed scandal and abuse. Moreover money was involved here too. The visitor claimed substantial fees (procurations); his tour was thus made even more unpleasant for his clergy. Or sometimes the visitor sought and obtained from the pope the right to these payments without undertaking the visitations, in return for the papal camera receiving a half of the procurations. Visitation thus often led merely to another tax.

The failure of the bishops properly to fulfil their functions was perhaps the most serious single impediment to reform. Dependent as they now were on princes and popes for their promotion, bishops tended to be men of the world. Their diocesan duties were delegated to deputies; their spiritual functions were performed by suffragans. At the councils of Pisa and Constance they were subordinated to the nations, at Basle to the structure of 'deputations' and at the papal council of Ferrara-Florence they were merely one—if the most senior—of three estates. In the machinery of Church government the bishop was still a key figure. In practice he had abdicated or been deposed. For eleventh-century reformers the main aim had been to secure a righteous, independent and effective episcopate; to achieve this Gregory VII set all Christendom by the ears. In the fourteenth and fifteenth centuries no pope and few reformers saw the bishop as the means of effecting reforms. Reform had to come either from above—from the prince, or from below—from the people.

It was, perhaps, the slow emergence of this antithesis which discouraged popes from embarking on general measures. Particular and limited problems were grappled with, especially in the fourteenth century. John XXII in 1322 tried to solve the dilemma of property in the Franciscan Order: he declared that the Holy See no longer held Franciscan property; in 1323, in *Cum inter nonnullos*, he defined as heretical the Franciscan doctrine of the absolute poverty of Christ and the apostles. Benedict XII was even more active than John, turning his attention to all the religious orders and in particular issuing the 'Benedictine bull' *Summi magistri* in 1336. This attempted to deal with the question of discipline by grouping Benedictine houses into thirty-five provinces, and at the same time laid down rules for monastic education. Yet this measure was ameliorated by the laxer Clement VI; and the Franciscans succeeded in 1430 in having the ownership of their property once again vested in the papacy. The one major review of clerical discipline was due to Pope Pius II. A weighty commission was appointed in 1458. Two outstanding men supplied detailed suggestions for reform. Cardinal Cusa based reform on three Visitors who would have been responsible for the whole Church, abolishing pluralism, appropriations, fraudulent indulgences and miracles, and ensuring that the curia itself should conform to the rules of the Church. Domenico de' Domenichi, a Venetian and a senior member of the curia, argued that reformation should begin with the pope and radiate out from him; his proposals concentrated on purity in the papal court. Pius embodied these and other notions in a draft bull (1460). This legislated first for the pope: he was to be the supreme example of devotion, uprightness and good management. Cardinals were to be pure and their say in government enhanced: those created before Pius II were not to have more than sixty servants and forty teams of horses; those created by Pius II were to have no more than twenty servants and four teams of horses; they were not to possess any benefice worth more than 4,000 florins, they were not to hunt or have banquets (save for diplomatic occasions). Other rules affected the administration of the penitentiaries, the chancery and cameral officials. Members of the curia were to get rid of frivolous members of their households, to expel concubines and loose women: any curial official found having commerce with a prostitute was to be fined heavily. Pluralism was to be drastically reduced: a convent with more than eight inmates was not to be given in commendam and no cardinal was to have more than three convents in commendam. There were other minor regulations.[1] But all of this remained a project. Like other such attempts—the so-called reforms at Constance, at Basle, in the concordats—this provides interesting evidence of the corruption of the clergy, of the awareness of that corruption among men of authority and good will, and of the feeble ineffectiveness of positive action. Cusa and Domenichi were bishops and it should not be forgotten that in every province of the Church there were men of their rank who took their episcopal duties with high seriousness. An example of such activity will be given later.

There can be no doubt that the main impetus to reform in this period came not from the clergy themselves but from the laity. In this the later Middle Ages offer again a contrast to earlier ages, when popes, monks and friars were the advocates of rigour and renewal. The laity in the fourteenth century, and even more in the fifteenth, were more insistent on their spiritual needs and better able to express them. Lay aspirations took mystical forms.

Mysticism and the laity

A yearning for direct contact with God, a conviction that such contact had been established, a desire to communicate the ecstasy to others, all of this is almost as old as Christianity. In the earlier Middle Ages, however, mysticism is found predominantly among the clergy and particularly among members of religious orders. The books they wrote and the exercises they devised were intended for other religious. In the later Middle Ages, though many mystical writers were still clergy, their public was predominantly lay. The impulse behind this remarkable diffusion of lay devotion is probably to be traced back to the popular religious movements of the early thirteenth century, both those which were more or less unorganized (like the Beghards and Béguins) and the friars who

[1] The bull is summarized in appendix no. 42 in Pastor, *Popes*, III, pp. 397–403.

tried to enlist the laity in austerity and purity through their Third Orders. From this came not only orthodox mysticism but also heresy.

Individual mystics were found everywhere in the later Middle Ages. In northern France and in the Rhineland there developed a corporate mysticism. This seems to have been largely due to the influence of both Dominican theology and the Dominican preachers Eckhart (1260–1327) and, in the next generation, Suso (1295–1315) and Tauler (1290–1361). Their centre was at Cologne and their vernacular teaching and writing spread in the convents of neighbouring cities, in the *béguinages* where a more radical spirituality was often displaced by Dominican influence. The aim was a reinvigoration of the Christian symbols and of the eucharist, and it was fundamentally orthodox and obedient to authority. In this atmosphere grew up the Friends of God and the Brethren of the Common Life. The Friends of God were groups of dedicated men and women in the cities of the Rhineland, especially in Cologne, Strasbourg and Basle, under spiritual direction of Dominicans and striving to be an élite in a corrupt world.

The Brethren of the Common Life owed most to the initiative of Ruysbroeck (1293–1381) and Gerard Groote (1340–84). Ruysbroeck was a secular priest who was drawn to mysticism partly by the combat against heresy in Brussels, and who became an Augustinian in 1343. His influence was exerted mainly through his writings and his chief disciple, Gerard Groote. Groote had in 1379 sponsored a community of women living a corporate life of devotion but without vows, very similar to the *béguinages* of an earlier day. The Brethren had an organization no more elaborate. The young copyists who made their living in the book trade and who lived in the house of a Deventer vicar and admirer of Groote, Florence Radewijns (1350–1400) adopted a similar pooling of resources. From this modest beginning the Brethren spread. Soon there were houses not only at Deventer and Zwolle, but at Amersfoort and Delft. In the fifteenth century, besides other houses in Flanders, the movement established itself in Dutch and German towns, and it began to acquire an educational programme, a natural enough consequence of an interest in books. As the houses multiplied and attracted endowment, organization became more elaborate, but with remarkable persistence the Brethren continued till the Reformation to embody the '*nova devotio*', the ideal of a devout lay society.

Another offshoot of Groote's inspiration was the foundation in 1386 of a house of canons regular of St Augustine at Windesheim of which for a time Radewijns was also prior. This house—a good example of the perfectly conventional framework within which Groote and Radewijns moved—became the nucleus of a group of reformed Augustinian convents, one of the 'congregations' to which reference will shortly be made. The congregation is important in the history of mysticism not only because it inherited the Flemish traditions represented by Groote, but because it included St Agnietenburg (near Zwolle), the house of Thomas à Kempis (1379–1471), the author of the *Imitation of Christ*. This collection of separate treatises, which the author revised over a long life, was to become the most celebrated mystical work ever written. Its simple and concrete terminology, its quiet piety and common sense, exactly reflect the spirit of Flemish mysticism.

Elsewhere in Europe, outside Flanders, the Low Countries and western Germany, we find not corporate mysticism but isolated though sometimes extremely influential figures. In England, Margery Kempe (d. about 1440), an illiterate Norfolk woman who dictated her experiences to sympathetic priests, and Juliana, a 'dame' of Norwich (d. about 1413), who wrote the *Revelations of Divine Love* were, like their predecessor Richard Rolle of Hampole (d. 1349), not working from the philosophical basis of Eckhart and his successors; they were not concerned to organize group devotion, like Groote; they were sometimes directly and often by implication critical of the clergy around them, but they scarcely qualify as reformers. Above all these English mystics attracted little attention at the time compared to some of their continental contemporaries.

The devout women of the period naturally gravitated to this form of religious experience. For them works of Latin piety were translated into vernacular languages and the tenderness and lyrical quality of certain kinds of mystical writing had a peculiar appeal. Female recluses and devout nunneries attracted great contemporary respect, but it is the emergence of powerful personalities from such milieux which is most striking. St Bridget of Sweden (1303–73) and St Catherine of Siena (1347–80) are the two most notable. Bridget, daughter of a nobleman and wife of another, had undertaken the pilgrimage to Compostella before she became a widow; she died in Rome after a pilgrimage to Jerusalem. In 1349 she set off to France and Italy consumed with her mission to purify the Church and to persuade the pope to return to Rome. Her revelations, written in Swedish, were soon translated into other vernaculars and Latin and after her canonization in 1391 the religious foundation she established at Vadstena (to which her remains were carried) became the centre of a new order; the Bridgetines were organized in twin convents of monks and nuns under the control of an abbess. The scathing attacks on abuses by St Bridget were continued by St Catherine of Siena, whose humble urban background was very different but who was also, in Miss Underhill's phrase, a 'militant mystic'. Her influence in securing Gregory XI's return to Rome has doubtless been exaggerated, but it was exaggerated at the time, an indication of her reputation with contemporaries.

The saints of the later Middle Ages are evidence that holiness was both practised and revered. During the fourteenth and fifteenth centuries some 200 individuals lived who were accorded beatification or sanctification either during this period or later.[1] Of these a considerable majority were Italian and a significant number were female: of the seventy-seven fifteenth-century Italian saints listed in Pastor's *History of the Popes* twenty-four are women. Yet these devout men and women are for the most part not well known. Those whose fame is more than local do not number more than about eight. Apart from St Bridget and St Catherine of Siena, already mentioned, there was another woman whose life in many ways resembled theirs, St Colette (d. 1447); she devoted herself to the reform of the Franciscan nuns, or Poor Clares, in Flanders and northern France. St Roch (d. 1327) was a citizen of Montpellier and gained his reputation in the tireless administration of succour to plague victims; the onset of the Black Death and its repeated returns ensured a wide diffusion for his cult. In the first half of the fifteenth century three men lived whose names transcend one region. Two were Observant Franciscans and will come before us later: Bernardino of Siena and Giovanni Capistrano. The third, St Vincent Ferrer, conducted campaigns of evangelization in Spain and France; born in Valencia in 1350 he died in Brittany in 1419. It will be noted that none of these holy figures reaches the height of universal reverence attained of old by a Bernard or a Francis. The lesser names are often obscure. Few Englishmen will know the only one of their compatriots from these centuries who was canonized, St John, prior of Bridlington, who died in 1379 and was canonized in 1403.

The preceding paragraphs do far less than justice to mysticism in its later medieval forms. It invaded practically every aspect of life. It spilled out in art and literature. It coloured education, especially in northern Europe. It affected not only individuals intent on the attainment of

[1] I have counted 211 listed in Mas Latrie's *Trésor de chronologie* for this period, in conjunction with the much fuller list of fifteenth-century Italian saints in Pastor, v, pp. 86–8; 138 were Italians, 19 French, 11 Spaniards.

divine illumination but on men of affairs like Jean Gerson (who used by some to be considered the author of the *Imitatio Christi*). It lay behind some of the political speculation of Cardinals d'Ailly and Cusa. From time to time it touched the multitude when a great concourse was listening to Vincent Ferrer or Bernardino of Siena. It could divagate into radical movements and be stigmatized as heresy. But it could and did provoke sober and methodical attempts at righting wrong.

Orthodox reform

Reference has been made above to the bull of 1336 in which Benedict XII tried to reorganize and discipline the Benedictine order. In broad terms the pope mitigated early rigour and sought to make the provinces of the monks the units for visitation and regular chapters. The general effect of the bull was not great. But it pointed to what was to become a feature of monastic rehabilitation, the grouping of monasteries in regional 'congregations'. Eight Reformed Augustinian houses in Flanders and the Rhineland had clustered round Windesheim by 1402; by 1419 there were twenty and towards the end of the fifteenth century there were over eighty in eighteen dioceses. The Benedictine house of Bursfelde in Brunswick became in 1446 the centre of a congregation which numbered ninety abbeys by 1490; similar Benedictine congregations were based on the abbeys of Melk on the Danube and Santa Giustina at Padua. The principle behind groups of associated houses was the pooling of moral resources and the aim a restoration of the rule. Such monastic developments did not usually affect the laity save by eradicating scandal and mismanagement.

The reform of the mendicant orders did, however, have larger consequences, especially in the case of the Franciscans, for it unleashed a further wave of evangelical activity. It may fairly be said that St Francis had founded an order which automatically generated reform. The persecuted Fraticelli of the thirteenth century were, after all, a minority who could claim their master's inspiration, at all events before they succumbed to millenarian dreams, and a few Spirituals avoided heresy, like Olivi and Angelo Clareno (1247–1337) who established his Poor Hermits in 1294, with the help of that pope, Celestine V, whom Dante denounced for his resignation of the papacy. From Clareno stems a thin stream of Franciscan reformers who secured limited approval from sympathetic generals of the Order. This process culminated in 1368 with Paulluccio dei Trinci who was allowed to establish a hermitage at Brugliano near Foligno. In 1380 he was put in charge of twelve reformed convents in

Umbria. The Strict Observance had begun. In 1517 it succeeded in becoming in a sense *the* Franciscan Order, for in that year Leo X directed that the Observants should be governed by a minister general and that all reformed Franciscan communities were to be united in the Observant family. There were by then several such reforms: the reform began more or less spontaneously in France in 1388, in Aragon in 1389, and a little later in Portugal and Castile; later it was deliberately carried into Hungary, Germany, Poland, Scotland and (by the late fifteenth century) into England. At every stage the Conventuals resisted this advance (often made by taking over their convents) and the competition between the two branches was often anything but edifying.

It would be wrong to assume that the Observants were able to secure their pre-eminence solely on merit. They were helped by the Schism, which led to the Conventuals being divided: just as there were two and later three popes, so there were two and later three ministers general; popes in the Schism were proud to privilege a reforming order as it offered a chance to embarrass their rivals and demonstrate their keenness for religion; the first independence of the Conventuals was given to the Observants by the Council of Constance in 1415. Likewise reforming princes and town councils sometimes gained financially by supporting the Observants against the better-endowed Conventuals. Nor did the Observants really observe the rule *ad literam*, as was their aim. Their discipline was harsher than that of the slacker Conventuals but it soon tolerated an attenuated form of conventual life, educational standards were raised and, because of the popularity of the reformed friars, endowments were steadily offered to them and accepted. Above all the Observants released a further wave of practical evangelism, especially in Italy where three saints played a full part in the reforms in public life in Italy. Bernardino of Siena (d. 1444) was the greatest preacher of his day and a fortunate chance has preserved the texts of some of his racy vernacular sermons, preached at Siena in the great *piazza* before the Palazzo Pubblico on which is still painted the Holy Name, surrounded by radiant beams of light, which was his symbol. Here at dawn the citizens gathered to be castigated, cajoled and entertained by this remarkable man who could for a time rid a city of its vendettas and raise its moral standards. James of the March (d. 1476) was only less celebrated than Bernardino, and Capistrano (d. 1456) carried his fervour into Austria, Germany and Poland; he died of plague in Hungary where his eloquence had been put to the service of Hunyadi and the crusade.[1]

[1] Above, p. 261.

With the Obervant reform should be linked the Minims, a new Order (1474), consciously based by its founder St Francis of Paola on the apostolic poverty of St Francis of Assisi.[1]

The Dominican Order also developed an Observant branch, stimulated by the reforming activities of Raymond of Capua, minister general from 1380 to 1400. Just as the Dominicans had successfully resisted the attempt of Benedict XII to rationalize their status as mendicants in 1337, so the internal reform attempted by Raymond of Capua led on to unseemly wrangles between the two branches, similar to those found among fifteenth-century Franciscans, but with less redeeming fire.

Not all bishops were absentee or slothful even if few were models of activity or sources of inspiration. One outstanding bishop was Nicholas Krebs of Cues (Cusa), former conciliarist, cardinal (1448) and one of the intellectual giants of his day.[2] Nominated legate for Germany in 1450 Cusa undertook a wide visitation, attempting not only to win over a country especially sympathetic to the Council of Basle, but to inspire and to reform by means of his personal example, provincial synods, and the appointment of Visitors with powers delegated from himself to regulate the main religious Orders. The difficulties encountered by Nicholas of Cusa in his work form a considerable part of the material used in G. G. Coulton's book[3] and they may be illustrated from his own experience in the diocese of Brixen, to which he was provided by Nicholas V in 1450. The chapter at Brixen, supported by Sigismund count of Tyrol, for long disputed this nomination. Sigismund championed the dissolute Benedictine nuns of Sonnenburg; they had been directed to observe claustration by Nicholas of Cusa in 1451 but the wrangle went on until in 1458 the nuns were finally evicted from their convent by force; the Franciscan nuns (Poor Clares) of Brixen were almost as troublesome. The bishop of Brixen had to hire mercenary troops to defend himself. Sigismund ignored an interdict, evaded the attempts of Pius II to effect a compromise, and finally captured Cusa in 1460. At this point the dispute widened and involved the whole question of the obedience of the electors and the German Church.[4] It should be noted that it was not only from a handful of undisciplined women and a recalcitrant magnate that resistance came. The clergy of the diocese as a whole resented Nicholas of Cusa as a Rhenish stranger, foisted on them

---

[1] The Jesuates constituted (1367) another Order of *pauperes Christi* under the inspiration of Giovanni Colombini, a citizen of Siena.
[2] Below, p. 342.
[3] Above, p. 299.   [4] Above, p. 296.

by a Roman pope, and as an interfering purist. They were content to be left unreformed.

The mantle of reformer was sometimes donned by the secular power. Duke Albert of Austria, who became emperor in 1438, lent his personal influence to the rehabilitation of the monasteries in Austria. The duke of Brunswick, Frederick the Pious (1445–78), not only supported reformers but from 1459 to 1471 withdrew from the world to the Franciscan convent he had established. Great princes, however, seldom demonstrated their religious convictions by such positive action, though many of them were still assiduous collectors of relics: Alfonso V of Aragon in 1423 carried off from Marseilles the relics of St Louis of Anjou. No king of France of the later Middle Ages can be described as a Church reformer, and in England Henry VI was advanced as a candidate for beatification by Henry VII on the grounds of personal holiness and not because he was a doughty champion of a reinvigorated clergy. Only in Aragon and Castile after the union of the Crowns was there major royal support for Church reform. The reasons why the Catholic sovereigns extended their control over senior Church appointments was no doubt largely fiscal and administrative. But one result was the promotion to episcopal office, especially in Castile, of men devouter and less aristocratic than the bellicose nobles of the fourteenth and early fifteenth centuries. Above all the pope in 1491 empowered Ferdinand and Isabella to reform the monastic orders and their instrument for this was the rigorous Franciscan Observant, Jiménez de Cisneros (Ximenes), who destroyed the Conventuals in Spain and whose reforms spread slowly into other orders. With these developments must be linked the Spanish Inquisition, mentioned later in this chapter.

A common feature of all orthodox reform was the sermon, the importance of which is seen in the multiplying manuals for preachers and in the elaboration of the contemporary pulpit. Popular preaching had, of course, been an activity greatly extended in an earlier day by the friars, especially the Franciscans and Dominicans. The Franciscan Observants of fifteenth-century Italy continued this traditional function of their Order. But it is equally evident in the work of Nicholas of Cusa, who preached in the vernacular all over Germany and is said to have delivered eighty sermons in Brixen alone. One of the rare monk bishops of the later Middle Ages, Thomas Brinton (or Brunton), bishop of Rochester (1373–89), preached indefatigably in his own cathedral, in London and elsewhere. The taste for the fiery sermon was unquenchable and it even transcended the understanding of what was said. St

Vincent Ferrer preached in the north of France to English soldiers, who cannot have comprehended his words, but who were gripped by the gestures, the symbolism, the magic of the occasion. Capistrano preached through an interpreter in Austria and Hungary, but his message got through. Very large audiences attended the sermons of a celebrated revivalist. A Carmelite preacher, Thomas Couette of Rennes, who reformed several houses of his Order in the south of France from 1424 to 1428, on one occasion preached in the cathedral of Arras suspended by ropes from the roof in order to be seen by the vast concourse.[1] Preaching was, moreover, sometimes regarded as of almost sacramental significance. Here is an extract from a vernacular sermon of St Bernardino, preached at Siena during Lent in 1427:

> What would become of the world, I mean, the Christian faith, if there were no preaching? In a short time our Faith would die away. And so the church has ordered that there shall be preaching every Sunday; there may be little or much; but some there must be. And she has ordered you to go and hear Mass. And if of these two things you can only do one—either hear the Mass or hear the sermon—you should let the Mass go rather than the sermon . . . There is less peril for your soul in not hearing Mass than in not hearing the sermon. . . . All you have and know comes from God's word; and, as a general rule, what we hold concerning the faith of Jesus comes through preaching alone; nor will the faith ever fail, so long as it shall be preached.[2]

This faith in the efficacy of the sermon was shared by the heretics of the period.

Heresy

The line between an orthodox evangelist like St Bernardino and a heretic like John Huss is a fine one, depending (we may suspect) on times and places as much as on doctrinal variations. By the start of the fourteenth century the Church was, of course, familiar with esoteric opinions, not only among the learned, where they had always tended to grow up, but also among the people at large. In the later Middle Ages it had to deal with a new situation: the academic heresy which gained popular support.

Popular heresy of an earlier day still lingered on. The Waldensians survived as a persecuted minority in the western foothills of the Alps and so did the Fraticelli in Italy. The laity who gravitated to the teaching of Beghards were often led to doctrines which invited persecution

[1] Vallet de Viriville, *Bibliothèque de l'école des chartes*, 33 (1872), pp. 96–9.
[2] A. G. Ferrers Howell, *S. Bernardino of Siena* (London, 1913), pp. 218–19.

and suppression. An undercurrent of apocalyptic resentment can be detected in many areas, linking with anti-clerical sentiments which could easily be deflected into heretical forms. Nor must it be forgotten that the clergy were still the fiercest critics of their own condition. The diatribes of saints like Bridget or Catherine of Siena are echoed in the denunciations of clerical corruption which we find in the sermons of the Observants or Thomas Brinton. The friar seldom resisted the temptation to illustrate the vices he was reproving from the persons of the local parson or bishop. Out of this situation, and in the peculiar circumstances of the Great Schism (1378–1417), were to come two very different heresiarchs, Wycliffe and Huss.

Unlike Italy, the Low Countries and western Germany, medieval England had been virtually free of heresy until the advent of John Wycliffe (c. 1320–84). A brilliant academic teacher at Oxford, Wycliffe espoused a variety of realism,[1] but it was not until the later years of his life, after he had been employed by the Crown as a diplomatic agent, that he began to develop doctrines at variance with Church teaching. Gregory XI censured a number of propositions of Wycliffe which suggested that the secular power could deprive an unworthy clergyman of his endowments, that a bad pope was not pope and that the pope was not necessarily the head of the Church. John of Gaunt and other magnates found some of these opinions congenial and saved Wycliffe from the full effects of the condemnation. But in the next years two developments occurred which changed the whole situation: Wycliffe began to argue against transubstantiation, and the Peasants' Revolt broke out. The nature of the consecrated elements had troubled theologians long before Wycliffe. He, however, made his view widely public: in essence this was that the bread did not become the Body of Christ; from this it logically followed that the Mass and the priesthood had a diminished significance. The Peasants' Revolt of 1381 made it impossible this time for Wycliffe to remain undisturbed. He was not responsible for the anti-clericalism of the rebels, but their views coincided with some of his and his aristocratic patrons withdrew their protection. In 1382 he was condemned by a synod in London and forced to remain in his living at Lutterworth where he died in 1384.

Wycliffe's Bible fundamentalism and his attack on clerical possessions were to be more important in securing a following for him than the philosophy or the theology which lay behind such attitudes. Two vernacular versions of the Scriptures were due to his inspiration. The first

[1] See below, p. 339.

was a rigidly literal translation. The second, probably made by Wycliffe's disciple and secretary John Purvey, was much more idiomatic and soon became very popular. Despite ecclesiastical censure it survives in nearly 200 manuscripts and it was possessed by a host of entirely orthodox readers; only if an owner of the translation was suspected of heresy on other grounds did the English Bible aggravate the offence. Through this work, more than through the relatively small number of 'field-preachers', Wycliffe influenced fifteenth-century English folk, though the later post-Reformation Protestant tradition has probably tended to exaggerate this influence. In the decades immediately following Wycliffe's death there was a more substantial response to his advocacy of a Church stripped of its landed endowment. This came from a number of gentry, the 'lollard knights', and culminated in the rebellion of Sir John Oldcastle in 1414. This was never a really serious challenge to authority; Oldcastle was a fugitive when he was captured and executed in 1417. There were to be a few English lollards throughout the rest of the century, but they lacked academic support or the attention of the magnates and gentry. The contemporary European estimate of Wycliffe depended, however, on the outbreak of a much more serious challenge to the established Church in Bohemia. John Huss was widely regarded as a Wycliffite.

The Czech movement had in fact origins much deeper than mere contact between the dons of Oxford and Prague. Charles IV had done much to encourage both popular piety and a sense of provincial loyalty in his kingdom. Similar if more erratic encouragement came from his successor Wenceslas. As a result, a number of evangelical preachers were to be found at work, especially in the Bohemian capital, from about 1360. Their message, delivered in German and later in Czech, urged private devotion and purity, and (like all preachers) the reformers bitterly attacked the sloth and corruption of the clergy. The people of Prague in particular revered the saintly John Milič, whose vernacular sermons, mystical and intense, were complemented by the practical organization of a community where former prostitutes were rehabilitated, and by an insistence on frequent communion. Milič was involved in constant quarrels with the clergy and made several visits to the curia to justify himself. It says much for his integrity (and the wisdom of the popes) that even his conviction that Antichrist had come was not ultimately held against him; he died in Avignon in 1374. A number of substantial laymen aided reform: Thomas Štitny (d. 1402) compiled mystical writings in Czech; Wenceslas Křižand and John of Mühlheim founded in 1391 the Bethlehem Chapel in Prague, where vernacular preaching was to take place twice every Sunday and feast day. In 1402 Huss was appointed to the post of priest of the Bethlehem Chapel, where he continued the tradition of Milič.

Huss (b. 1369) was a university-trained theologian, brought up in the new Caroline university, where there was a large German element which provoked corresponding anti-German feeling among the Czechs. Many of the Czech masters were attracted by Wycliffe's philosophical doctrines, for his realism contrasted with the fashionable nominalism of the Germans who controlled three of the four 'nations' at the university. Sympathy for realism was allied often with sympathy for Wycliffe's attack on the papacy; the Schism of 1378 had made papal claims and papal ambitions both more scandalous and less effective than they had been earlier. Some Czechs were attracted further towards Wycliffe's denial of transubstantiation, but this offended much that was fundamental in the Milič-Huss position. Far from denying the Eucharist, both men exalted it, and in his careful scholastic works in Latin as in his lively vernacular sermons and pamphlets Huss never budged from the orthodox view of the sacrament.

Tensions in the university culminated in the expulsion (furthered by Wenceslas) of the Germans in 1409. Thereafter the situation developed rapidly. Huss, with considerable popular backing, challenged the authority of the 'Pisan' pope John XXIII, especially over the indulgence preached to raise funds for the pope's campaign against Ladislas of Naples. There were disturbances in Prague; many Czech masters at the university now went over to the conservative side. Wenceslas hesitated between supporting reform and alienating the pope; the Empire had slipped from his grasp in 1400. A papal excommunication of Huss in 1410 forced him to leave Prague and apprehension of Wycliffite tendencies mounted, not only in Bohemia; basically unjust though this was, it influenced many sane and moderate men (Jean Gerson and the theologians at Paris, for example) to demand that the matter should be determined at the Council of Constance, when that body was convoked in 1414. Wenceslas by now was openly siding with Huss and his supporters. Sigismund, Wenceslas's brother, was emperor and his heir; he urgently wished to end the tension in his future kingdom and offered Huss protection to the Council and a fair hearing from the Fathers.

At Constance, where he arrived in November 1414, Huss was interrogated exhaustively on his views, particularly with regard to condemned points in Wycliffe's teaching. As time went on he was treated as a prisoner and it was as potentially guilty that he appeared before the whole Council early in June 1415. He then stoutly refused to condemn all the points from Wycliffe, though he rejected many of them, and he refused to renounce *en bloc* errors allegedly to be found in his own writings; likewise he adhered to the principle of communion in both kinds by the laity (who normally were not offered the consecrated wine, which was drunk by the priest only), a practice which was rapidly gaining adherents both in Bohemia and among Czechs at the Council. Efforts were made to induce Huss to recant. He agreed to change his views only if he was convinced of their error on scriptural authority. On 6 July he was condemned as a heretic and handed over to the lay power, the Emperor Sigismund. He was immediately executed by burning. In May 1416 his friend Jerome of Prague was similarly condemned and executed. In these proceedings Wycliffe's heresy was authoritatively condemned and, a pathetic sequel to the tragic pyres of Constance, the Englishman's bones were disinterred in 1428, burned and flung into the river Swift at Lutterworth.

There is no doubt that Wycliffe by disputing the doctrine of transubstantiation was in conflict with the teaching of the Church. Huss consistently in his writing and preaching disowned this side of Wycliffe's doctrine and his whole practice was to exalt communion and emphasize its effects. Was Huss a heretic? The Benedictine scholar Dom Paul De Vooght has recently tried to answer that question in his warm and generous book. There is no doubt that Huss erred in his denial of papal supremacy, yet, as Dom De Vooght points out, the Council that condemned him had itself declared popes subject to councils. For the rest Huss's doctrine of the Church and the priesthood was basically orthodox, though often expressed in confusing and even dangerous ways. In his desire to 'snatch men from sin' he wildly exaggerated the importance of the Church of the Saved as against the Church Visible here below; he argued that no bishop or priest in a state of mortal sin was really worthy of his office, but not that his acts were invalid; he stressed the authority of the Bible, but he did not deny the teaching of the Church. On such points

> ... the *doctrine* of Huss is irreproachable. All the applications of it were not, nor the indiscreet fashion with which he proclaimed such applications. The danger to the established order derived from this, but even the most aggressive of Huss's points would have been utterly inoffensive save for the existence of corruption everywhere.[1]

[1] De Vooght, p. 470n.

This calm appraisal was not possible in the early fifteenth century and especially in Bohemia. There many Czechs had gone further than Huss. He cannot be described as a Wycliffite, though some of his contemporaries and many Hussites later can be so described. Apart from their totally opposed views on the Eucharist, there remained profound differences between the teaching of the two men. Some Hussites were prepared for revolution, for a kingdom of God on earth, while Wycliffe had argued for passive obedience—'God must obey the devil'. Wycliffe had seen reform coming from above, from the king; for Huss and for his direct disciples it must come from below, from a purified people. But the chief distinction between Wycliffe and Huss is to be seen in the history of England and Bohemia. The condemnation of Huss unleashed a national movement and encouraged millenarian religious excitement, while the condemnation of Wycliffe had little or no consequences for English society or English Church history. The extraordinary reactions to Huss's death in Bohemia were due in part to the way he had been betrayed by Sigismund (for this was how the emperor's action was regarded, perhaps unfairly). Huss, so it seemed to very many Czechs, had scourged the sins, the sloth and the luxury of the senior clergy and the men he had exposed sat in judgment on him. Bohemia itself had been condemned as a nest of heretics. Whatever had been the position before Huss's martyrdom, heresy was soon accurately to describe the position held by many Czechs.

The political consequences for Bohemia have been touched on earlier.[1] The religious consequences were at first dramatic and some of them proved in the long run to be permanent. The nobles of Bohemia and Moravia had indicated their support for Huss during his trial. When news of his execution reached Bohemia, 500 gentlemen set their seals to a document repudiating the council's condemnation of Huss and of their country. They pledged themselves to resist the council, to obey a future pope only if he did not offend God's teaching, to allow free preaching and to submit doctrinal problems not to the hierarchy but to the university of Prague. In 1417 the university authorized communion in both kinds and in 1420 the Four Articles of Prague were formulated. They represented, broadly speaking, the traditional position of Milič and Huss: there was to be unimpeded preaching; communion for the laity was to be in both kinds; clerical possessions were to be largely abolished; sin was to be punished, and especially simony. This remained the programme of the Utraquists (*sub utraque specie*, under both kinds) or

[1] Above, chap. IX and p. 226.

Calixtines (*calix*, a chalice); it appealed to the nobility and gentry of Bohemia on grounds both of religion, patriotism and self-interest (they obtained much confiscated church property). But the situation was extremely fluid. After all the cup for the laity had hardly been an issue when Huss left Bohemia but became one while he was at Constance. Disturbances of a popular kind were becoming common in Prague, and from the start it is possible to discern a radical wing to the Hussite movement. For a time this was concealed by the overwhelming danger of attack. Wenceslas died in the summer of 1419. His successor Sigismund battled through to Prague a year later at the head of a crusading army but was driven out and defeated a second time in November 1420. For the next fifteen years, with no king and no central government, Hussitism developed into less defensible forms. The new town of Tabor, in south Bohemia, became the centre of extremist peasants, who believed in a Second Coming, preceded by a Time of Troubles. The leader was a knight called John Žižka, who had considerable military experience and was an inventive and resourceful general, though even he could not stomach the wilder varieties of chiliasm. Radicalism had little appeal to the burgesses of Prague or the Utraquist gentry and Žižka came into conflict with the moderates. When Žižka died in 1424 Taborite leadership came under the control of an equally gifted man, the priest Prokop.

The divergent tendencies of the two wings of revolt were forgotten from time to time in the urgent need to repulse foreign armies or to undertake expeditions into neighbouring countries or into Catholic areas of the lands belonging to the Bohemian Crown in Silesia and Lusatia. But extreme views were multiplying. Žižka had to destroy an Adamite sect which tried to practice rationalist communism, but he failed to prevent the spread of Wycliffe's views on the sacraments: with transubstantiation were jettisoned purgatory, saints and relics, and the whole distinction between priests and laymen; the Taborite bishop existed but had virtually no function. Social protest by the lower orders made the Utraquist burgesses and nobles anxious for a settlement; the military threat of the Hussites convinced Sigismund that he must make concessions. The Council of Constance had precipitated the Czech revolt; at the Council of Basle steps were taken to arrange a reconciliation. Indeed it was the rout of yet another 'crusade' at Domažlice on 15 August 1431 which convinced Cardinal Cesarini that the council was the only way by which the situation could be saved.[1] Negotiations by a Czech delegation at Basle and then by a conciliar delegation at Prague

[1] Above, p. 288.

resulted in November 1433 in the 'Compacts' of Prague. This was a victory for the conservatives. Calixtines and Catholic nobles enforced it at Lipany in May 1434, at which battle Prokop was killed. The moderate John Rokykana was elected archbishop of Prague a year later and in August 1436 Sigismund entered the city as king of Bohemia.

The Compacts of Prague, though based on the Four Articles, really conceded only the right to communion in both kinds. This was soon opposed as erroneous by the Council of Basle itself and it was subsequently totally repudiated by the popes, who refused to confirm Rokykana's appointment. In desperation the Hussites turned to the eastern Church and, until the fall of Constantinople in 1453, there was a serious possibility that Bohemia would accept Greek Orthodoxy; an even more remarkable by-product of the situation was the project of King George Poděbrady in 1462–64 for a congress of European powers to be in permanent session with the aim of securing peace and resistance to the Turks. In the event the Utraquists survived and the Compacts remained the official basis of the religious settlement until the seventeenth century. More important, in the long run, was the re-emergence of an extreme religious movement, also destined to survive. The Unity of the Brotherhood followed the teachings of Peter Chelčický (d. 1460) and took the place of Tabor, finally subjugated in 1452. The members of the Unity of the Brotherhood accepted a break with both Utraquist and Catholic. They deliberately established their own organization and abandoned not merely the established Church but attempts to reform it or to establish a variant within it. Persecuted and harried the puritanical sect survived to become the quietist Moravian Brethren of the eighteenth century.

Anti-German sentiment, social tension, dynastic uncertainties inside Bohemia and the weakness of the Church during the Schism and Councils, had all led to the permanency of religious innovations in Bohemia. Outside the kingdom heresy remained endemic in Christendom, but it was not significant. The violent and millenarian sentiments which had for a time found expression in Bohemia were to lead a subterranean life until they surfaced again in the Anabaptist movement released by the Lutheran revolt. Luther himself was to find inspiration in Huss and the Hussites. But the one serious challenge to the Church in the later Middle Ages was at the time contained. The very hostility to Germany which had in large measure provoked the Czech movement prevented it from spreading in neighbouring lands.

Repression of heresy: The Inquisition

One of the functions of a bishop was the moral welfare of his diocese. Defence against heresy therefore depended on the vigilance of the bishop. From the start of the thirteenth century the papacy had created a further bulwark in the Inquisition, which was regularly established in 1233 and which had a systematic provincial structure by the end of the thirteenth century. The inquisitors were normally Dominicans, the region that of a Dominican province, and the inquisitor and his subordinates were appointed by the provincial. At the time of the inception and early growth of the Inquisition it was naturally developed most fully in areas of heresy, in the south of France (Cathari), in the foothills of the Alps (Waldensians) and in Italy (Fraticelli), and these territories continued to be the main arena of inquisitorial activity, which hardly existed in Germany, Scandinavia or England. In the pontificate of Clement V inquisitors were ordered to act in conjunction with bishops but in practice the latter tended to delegate their powers and the inquisitor, backed by the lay power which was responsible for carrying out the more serious sentences, was often all-powerful.

Procedure was secret and, as men's thoughts were the subject of investigation, the only satisfactory evidence was confession. From this flowed consequences which made the Inquisition frightening at the time and repugnant to later ages: torture was employed, statements were accepted from discreditable persons, and one sign of conversion which was invariably demanded as an indication of sincerity was the naming of the heretic's former companions in error. Repentance and conversion could save a heretic only once; for the relapsed heretic there was no hope. The technique must strike a twentieth-century reader as familiar enough from current totalitarian practice in purges and brain-washings. The penalties, inflicted in ceremonies to which maximum publicity was given, ranged from penances of a mild kind, to pilgrimage and imprisonment. For the most serious offences the penalty was death at the stake. This death sentence was, of course, not pronounced in as many words by the public tribunal which at the end of the process produced its verdict, for clergy were not allowed to kill even in the process of law. But the secular authority which did not carry it out would have itself incurred ecclesiastical penalties, would have been aiding heresy. The weapon of the Inquisition was never used in the later Middle Ages to effect the appalling holocausts of the thirteenth century, and often it was used with humanity. When Bishop Jacques Fournier of Pamiers (1317–

1326), later pope as Benedict XII, was actively assisting the inquisitor of Carcassonne, he is said to have rid his diocese of heresy while only executing four Waldensians and one Cathar. But it was sometimes responsible for fierce and sustained persecution, as by Bernard Gui, whose manual (*De modo, arte et ingenio inquirendi et examinandi hereticos*)[1] represents his practice as an inquisitor from 1307 to 1324 in the area of Toulouse. In April 1310, for instance, he secured the condemnation of twenty persons 'to wear crosses and perform pilgrimages, sixty-five were consigned to perpetual imprisonment, three of them in chains, and eighteen were delivered to the secular justice and were duly burned'.[2] Gui was a well-educated and conscientious zealot. Some inquisitors were only zealots. Conditions in the prisons of the Inquisition were occasionally terrible, and inquisitors were often surrounded by braggart 'familiars' who caused disturbances under cover of their masters' privileges. Moreover the confiscation of the heretic's property gave an unwholesome motive for the bishop and the papal Camera who in Italy shared them with the local secular authority and the Inquisition, and for the Crown which largely participated in the spoils in Naples and France.

It is curious that these efforts, while in the end they effectively stamped out Catharism, did not eradicate the Waldensians or the Fraticelli. It is equally important that local opposition in the north of Europe frustrated any significant inquisitorial activity in those parts of Christendom where popular heresy was rapidly multiplying in the later Middle Ages. In Germany papal inquisitors are found, but episodically: Huss carried with him to Constance a certificate of approval from the inquisitor in Prague. In England papal inquisitors had operated (very ineffectively) during the prosecution of the Templars from 1309 to 1311, but the supporters of Wycliffe caught the hierarchy quite unprepared and hasty legislation was necessary, culminating in the statute *de haeretico comburendo* of 1401, to strengthen the authority of bishops and to compel the execution of sentences by lay authorities. The most celebrated heresy trial involving the English was that which led to the burning of Joan of Arc at Rouen in 1431. Her technical error was sorcery but she was destroyed because she was politically dangerous; in these proceedings the papal Inquisition was involved but only marginally so. Suppression of witchcraft was, of course, a major preoccupation of the hierarchy in the fifteenth century. The bull *Summis desiderantes* (1484) of Innocent VIII focused attention on the problem in Germany.

[1] Above, p. 309, n 2.
[2] Lea, *History of the Inquisition*, I, p. 393.

The bull was addressed to the inquisitors Jacob Sprenger and Henry Institoris, whose book the *Malleus Maleficarum* (Hammer of the Witches) collected and digested material for the prosecution of witch-craft.

During the fourteenth and early fifteenth centuries the Inquisition was not active in the Spanish peninsula, save intermittently in Aragon. Yet it was in Spain that there arose a peculiar off-shoot of the Holy Office which, under state control, was to become in effect a completely separate institution. In 1478 Sixtus IV authorized Ferdinand and Isabella to nominate inquisitors for Castile, persuaded that there was a real threat from the instability of the converted Jews or *conversos*. The pope, who had thus deprived the Dominican provincial of his traditional responsibility, regretted his action, repeatedly tried to moderate the savagery he had unleashed, and tried to limit both the scope and independence of the new tribunal. In this he failed. The Catholic sovereigns insisted on extending their Inquisition to the whole of their dominions; appeals to Rome were denied. An inquisitor general was appointed in 1483 (the Dominican Thomas de Torquemada) and in the same year was established a royal council for the Inquisition, the '*Suprema*' (*Consejo de la Suprema y General Inquisición*), which was responsible to the Crown for the operations of regional inquisitors and the administration of confiscated property which went to the royal treasury. At a later stage the Spanish Inquisition was to deal severely with Protestants and Moriscos, and to act as the custodian of *limpieza de sangre* or purity of blood, as that dubious quality gradually became an important factor in Spanish society. In the fifteenth century its task was primarily the problem of the converted Jew and it is likely that zealous *conversos* were themselves responsible for its initiation and early severity. *Conversos* and Jews had been prominent in Spanish commerce and administration. Now the former lived in terror of denunciation as relapsed heretics. It was to remove the temptation of the *converso* to revert secretly to the practices of his orthodox brethren that all Jews were expelled from Spain in 1492. Many *conversos* left at the same time.

The Jews of medieval Europe had, in fact, never constituted a real problem, although from time to time they had suffered cruel persecution. In Canon Law a Jew was tolerated. He only became liable to prosecution as a heretic if he accepted Christianity and later abjured it. But the Jew could not normally hold landed property or become a full citizen, he had to wear distinctive clothing and he usually lived in an urban ghetto. As a result Jews tended to concentrate on money-lending and commerce, aided in this by the Church's prohibition of usury among Christians. Under royal protection Jews were taxed heavily, to the point where there was no further revenue to be got from them. The Italian banker was now available to lend money, and on a greater scale than Jews could provide it. In 1290 Jews were expelled from England, in 1306 from France. Pogroms were fierce in the fourteenth century, especially in the cities of the Rhineland and after the Black Death; it was at this stage that sizeable Jewish communities began to establish themselves in Poland and generally in eastern Europe. In Spain the first wave of persecution came, after centuries of relative tranquillity, in 1391; the end of the story has already been mentioned. Two small exceptions were to be seen to western Europe's rejection of the Jews in the later Middle Ages. Some found a minutely regulated existence in the cities of north Italy. And in the Comtat Venaissin the papal legates continued to tolerate Jewish communities at Carpentras and other towns, as the popes themselves had done during the Avignon residence.

Religious regionalism

In the earlier discussion of the organized Church (chapter XI above) it was evident that the provinces, especially those provinces which coincided with kingdoms, were in practice becoming more important. There was by the early fifteenth century a Gallican Church, a Church 'of England', and it was in the sphere of Church government that Ferdinand and Isabella first really unified the kingdoms of Aragon and Castile. The religious story is in broad agreement with this trend. Reform was limited to 'congregations'. Heresy was only serious when based on patriotic antipathy, as in Bohemia.

To that extent the title of this chapter, 'The bonds of religion' may seem a misnomer. Yet it should be remembered that, save for the incipient Unity of the Brethren in Bohemia, there was virtually no attempt to create new churches distinct from that which looked to Rome. At the end of our period, as at the beginning, practically everyone in Christendom accepted the pope; the clergy performed the traditional services; the laity complained of abuses and urged rehabilitation, but men did not aim to destroy the old order of religious life. There were, however, indications that the ancient priorities were in the end to be challenged, and in Italy during these centuries a new scheme of morality was slowly being evolved. That will be one of the topics discussed in the next chapter.

XIII

The Bonds of Education, Literature and Art

The eminent place in world literature of three Italian writers (Dante, Petrarch and Boccaccio) in the fourteenth-century and the fifteenth-century development in art, literature and ethical thought in Italy, summarized in the word 'Renaissance', make it tempting to discuss the subjects of this chapter in two halves—the Italian and the non-Italian world. Yet to do this would falsify the picture. Some differences, and important ones, there were between the Italian peninsula and the rest of Europe. And in the sixteenth and seventeenth centuries Italian values were to penetrate the whole area. Yet they would scarcely have done this if there had not already been many features of the cultural scene common to most parts of the continent. It is with these common elements that

BIBLIOGRAPHY. There is no satisfactory book dealing with schools in this period, but see G. R. Potter's chapter in *Cambridge Medieval History*, VIII and its bibliography, and P. S. Allen, *The Age of Erasmus* (1914), chaps. 1–4. For universities the basic book is H. Rashdall, *The Universities of Europe in the Middle Ages*, new edn. by F. M. Powicke and A. B. Emden, 3 vols. (Oxford, 1936). For later medieval thought: Maurice de Wulf, *Histoire de la philosophie médiévale*, III, 6th edn. (Louvain, 1947); A. Combes, *Jean Gerson* (Paris, 1940); E. Cassirer, *The Individual and the Cosmos in Renaissance Philosophy*, trans. Domandi (Oxford, 1963) for Cusa and Pico. On medieval science see A. C. Crombie, *Augustine to Galileo*, 2nd edn. (London, 1959), and Herbert Butterfield, *Origins of Modern Science* (London, 1949). For vernacular literature see the national literary histories, e.g. *Storia letteraria d'Italia*, vols. by N. Sapegno (fourteenth century) and V. Rossi (fifteenth); J. Bedier and P. Hazard, *Histoire de la littérature française illustrée*, I (Paris, 1926); vols. in *Oxford History of English Literature* by H. S. Bennett and E. K. Chambers; there are useful surveys of particular *genres*, such as the brilliant book by C. S. Lewis, *The Allegory of Love* (Oxford, 1936). For the culture of northern Europe, J. Huizinga, *Waning of the Middle Ages* (trans. 1924), is essential; H. Baron's chapter in *New Cambridge Modern History*, I (below, p. 399) should be consulted, as should Franco Simone, *Il rinascimento francese* (Turin, 1961, Eng. trans. 1970). For the Renaissance: J. Burckhardt, *Civilisation of the Renaissance in Italy*, trans. Middlemore (many edns.); J. A. Symonds, *Renaissance in Italy*, 7 vols. (many edns.); D. Hay, *Italian Renaissance in its Historical Background* (Cambridge, this chapter begins. They may be indicated briefly as systematic education and the rise of vernacular literature.

Education during the later Middle Ages

Not very much need to be said about what is now called primary education. A child in a literate family could pick up the faculty of reading and writing with the aid of a mother or a domestic priest. That more and more children did this is evident from the number of townsfolk and country gentry who could read and write, especially by the fifteenth century. Opportunities for the very humble were more casual, but many a priest had to train a boy sufficiently to say the responses during services, and others who could read sometimes made an honest penny instructing children in dame schools or in association with chantries. Facilities like these were obviously precarious; they were to be found most regularly in towns of some size; but overall they must have been fairly extensive.

'Secondary education' was provided more systematically. Grammar schools were often maintained by cathedrals and by town councils, and in a big city there would be several. The grammar taught was Latin. Manuals (Donatus, Priscian and the very popular twelfth-century verse compilation of Alexander de Ville-Dieu) had to be learned by heart in order to acquire the disciplines of the *trivium*—grammar, rhetoric and dialectic. Rhetoric (the art of expression, both spoken and written) and dialectic (logic) were mainly tested by oral exercises. Scholars at such a school progressed through the various forms, promotion depending less on age than ability. They were normally assumed to have reading and elementary Latin grammar before they arrived; the vernacular was

1961); Wallace K. Ferguson provides a guide to the vast literature in his *Renaissance in Historical Thought* (Boston, 1948), and there are several pertinent papers in *Italian Renassaince Studies*, ed. E. F. Jacob (London, 1960). Indispensable for the Florentine Renaissance are the following works by Hans Baron: 'Cicero and the Roman Civic Spirit ...', *Bulletin of J. Rylands Library*, 20 (1938); 'Franciscan poverty and civic wealth', *Speculum*, 13 (1938); *The Crisis of the Early Italian Renaissance*, 2 vols. (Princeton, 1955 and new ed. 1966). Relevant chapters in E. H. Gombrich's *Story of Art* (London, 1956) make an excellent introduction; a helpful recent survey is P. and L. Murray, *The Art of the Renaissance* (London, 1963). For music, E. E. Lowinsky, 'Music in the culture of the Renaissance', *Journ. Hist. Ideas*, 15 (1954). Printing: the British Museum has issued an admirable booklet by V. Scholderer, *Johann Gutenberg* (1963); a useful general introduction is the Penguin volume by S. H. Steinberg, *Five Hundred Years of Printing* (3rd ed. Harmondsworth, 1966).

usually the medium for teaching in the lower forms, though it was not itself expressly taught. Classical Latin authors were read a good deal, but not often in their entirety or for their own sakes, but rather to illustrate grammar and style—much (alas) as is often the case today in grammar schools in western Europe. Grammar schools varied in quality, but all had what would now be regarded as a poor 'staff-student ratio'. William of Wykeham, who founded Winchester College in 1382, envisaged a schoolmaster with an usher to assist him to look after seventy scholars and ten commoners in seven forms; soon the number of commoners was greatly increased. In the time of Hegius (Alexander of Heck, 1433–98) the famous school at Deventer, where the influence of the Brethren of the Common Life was much in evidence, enrolled over 2,000 boys in eight forms. This last should remind us that too much emphasis has perhaps been laid on the 'reform' of education by the Brethren. Their schools contained some splendid moral figures, but the curriculum was basically the old curriculum and at Deventer (for example) only a handful of senior pupils actually made contact with Hegius himself. Erasmus, a pupil at this time, described the school as 'barbarous'. The fifteenth-century grammar school was still geared to a programme of studies which aimed at producing clergy, either for the universities to train further, or for parish work. Nevertheless there were plenty of boys at the grammar schools who had no intention of becoming clergy. Even at Winchester College, established in order to increase the supply of clergy, most of the boys who attended were not aiming at a religious career. The three authorized schools in London (increased to six by the mid-fifteenth century) were supplemented by private schools, some of high quality, and Miss Sylvia Thrupp suggested that in these centuries about 40 per cent of London merchants could 'read a little Latin';[1] *a fortiori* a larger number could read and write in English. Giovanni Villani in his *Chronicle* (XI, 94) estimated that each year there were between 550 and 600 boys at four grammar schools in Florence in the 1340s, there to learn *grammatica e loica*.

Villani further estimated that 1,000–1,200 boys went also to what may be termed 'commercial' schools, where they were taught *l'abbaco e algorismo*; there were six such schools, providing instruction in arithmetic. Clearly this was as necessary for the budding businessmen as Latin and, being free from the supervision of the Church, such schools could easily be established; many were set up by town governments in the later Middle Ages—as at Lübeck, Brunswick and Hamburg. A

[1] *op. cit.* (above, p. 45), pp. 156–7.

business training, however, like training in other crafts, was essentially accomplished by apprenticeship. For the vast majority of European men and women that apprenticeship was to farming, and education largely passed the peasant by. He had no use for it.

If every sizeable centre had one or more grammar schools and an even larger if fluctuating provision of elementary schools (Villani talks of 8,000–10,000 Florentine children of both sexes learning to write) it was slowly becoming the case that every country had one or more universities. The multiplication of universities can be demonstrated much more clearly than that of schools, for in general they have had a continuous or at any rate a long existence. Yet the increasing provision of facilities for higher education depended, it must be stressed, on the existence of large numbers of schools of a more modest kind. The position in the fourteenth and fifteenth centuries is tabulated[1] as follows:

Universities	Italy	France	Eng-land	Scot-land	Spanish peninsula	Germany etc.	Other
Founded prior to 1300	11	5	2	—	5	—	—
Founded 1300–1400	7	4	—	—	3	5	3
„ 1400–1500	2	9	—	3	6	11	3
Total	20	18	2	3	14	16	6

There were, however, not as many more effective universities at the end of our period as these figures suggest. Nor did more universities necessarily mean more students. Many new foundations took students who would have swelled numbers at an older *studium generale*: the proliferation of French universities (especially in the fifteenth century) was, in this sense, at the expense of Paris and it reflected divisions of a political kind (Caen 1432, Bordeaux 1441, were in 'English' parts of France); the Scots who went to St Andrews (1413), Glasgow (1451) or Aberdeen (1494) might have otherwise gone to Paris or, more likely, to Oxford. When Prague expelled its German masters they set up shop at Leipzig (1409). And the motives of founders were often mixed: Louvain (1425) was established by city fathers who hoped thereby to increase the prosperity of a declining community. Nor were all the universities equally successful. Some maintained a precarious existence, with grumbling and underpaid (or not paid) masters and few students; some died out; many (especially in Italy) experienced 'a mere succession of extinctions and revivals'.[2]

There were two main types of *studium generale*. At Paris and Oxford,

---

[1] Adapted from Rashdall I, p. xxiv.   [2] Rashdall, II, p. 68.

and some other universities which derived from them, the *universitas* or corporate body consisted of the teaching or regent masters, who were responsible for discipline and academic standards; the senior officer was the vice-chancellor. The other type, associated with Bologna, was based on the student body and it was, at any rate in theory, the students who were responsible for the choice of professors just as they elected the rector. On balance it was the second type of institution which developed in Spain, in Scotland and in Germany, as well as in Italy. But in practice there was considerable amalgamation of features from both systems, as in the French foundations of the fifteenth century. Common to all universities were the faculties, though only the greatest universities had faculties of civil and canon law, theology and medicine as well as the big basic faculty of arts, which was divided (for administrative purposes) into 'nations'. In some universities there was a high degree of specialization: Paris remained the main university for theology throughout this period; Bologna retained its pre-eminence in law, though one or two of the new universities both in Italy and France were primarily intended to teach law. Some other peculiarities are not without significance. There were no significant theological faculties in Italian universities. At Oxford and Cambridge canon and civil law had not the practical relevance they had on the continent, and the common law of England was taught in the Inns of Court at London.

The curriculum changed little. Except at Bologna and other law universities, where undergraduates tended to be older, the student began in his mid-teens (or younger) a course in arts which led, in four or five years, to a first degree (bachelor) and then in a further three years to the M.A. Thereafter two years of teaching or regency were required before admission to one of the higher faculties, where a doctorate might be gained in a further seven or eight years. At Paris from 1366 the minimum period for the M.A. was reduced to four and a half years. Throughout, training consisted of hearing lectures which took the form of commentaries on set texts; the examination was always oral. The subjects studied in arts consisted of the *trivium* and the *quadrivium* (arithmetic, geometry, astronomy, music). The *trivium* was much the more important and in essence the arts curriculum consisted of rhetoric, logic and metaphysics, moral philosophy and natural philosophy (physics). The frequent debates or disputations of the logic course, the illustrative contemporary cases which the civil lawyer studied, could and often did produce sharp minds, useful to the community. But the course was hardly inclined to interest the general run of young men and one may suspect that boredom or lack of funds explains the small proportion of those starting who actually proceded to even a first degree. What is of interest in this connection is the rising number of youths who attended for a year or two and who clearly had no intention of completing a formal degree. On balance it cannot be argued that they were keeping out the 'poor scholar': a feature common to all non-Italian universities of the later Middle Ages was the multiplication of colleges and bursaries for the poor—at Oxford, Cambridge and Paris, indeed, the colleges were already practically dominating the university by 1500. It was thus possible to get a university education if one tried hard. The adventures of Thomas Platter and Johann Butzbach in the later fifteenth century display two humble boys who, at the price of great personal sacrifice and misery, finally became scholars.[1]

The universities of the later Middle Ages were in general better endowed but less independent and less international than they had been in the thirteenth century. Founders of new institutions tried to compel their subjects to attend: the count of Provence fined Provençals who attended universities other than Aix when he founded it in 1409. Kings of France and England found it intolerable to have Church–State relations discussed at Oxford or by the doctors of the Sorbonne; though the latter played a significant part during the Schism (when the French monarchy was divided and weak) their liberty of action dwindled in the later fifteenth century; Oxford was brought to heel over Wycliffe by the English government and had no further public role of any significance.

Traditional scholarship

Just as the universities continued the traditions they had established in the thirteenth century, so the patterns of learning associated with them at that time continued to dominate the European world of learning. No better tribute to the firm foundation of the arts subjects and law, theology and medicine (which had been laid in the first two centuries of the universities' existence) can be found than the persistence into this period of the same intellectual preoccupations and even the same texts. Provision was now increasingly made for university libraries, but they contained for the most part the old books; specialist 'professors' were also appearing, but their chairs were more or less tied to the received curriculum.

At school (as we have noted) and at the university the basic gram-

[1] For Platter see above, p. 55; for Butzbach, see Allen, *Erasmus*.

matical manuals were Priscian and Donatus; other works presented
were the twelfth-century *Graecismus* of Everhard of Béthune and the
slightly later *Doctrinale* of Alexander de Ville-Dieu. No fresh dictionary
of Latin was constructed in our period, and the fortunate treasured their
copies of Papias's vocabulary (mid-eleventh century), the *Liber deriva-
tionum* of Huguitio, bishop of Ferrara (d. 1210), and the epoch-making
work on alphabetical principles, the *Catholicon* of the Genoese Dominican, Giovanni Balbi, which he completed in 1286; the *Catholicon* was
not to be superseded until R. Étienne produced his Latin dictionary in
1532. The basic courses in logic, metaphysics and physics were based on
the works of Boethius and, above all, Aristotle, as they had been since
the second half of the thirteenth century; in medicine the writings of
Averroës and Avicenna were by now basic; in civil law the *Digest* and the
Institutes; in canon law Gratian's *Decretum*; and in theology the Bible
and the *Sentences* of Peter Lombard (d. 1160), in which patristic sources
were collected.

From these ingredients the thirteenth century had constructed a vast
philosophical and theological edifice, which reached its most notable
development in the work of the Dominican Thomas Aquinas (d. 1274),
who was canonized in 1323. One of the main controversies which
Aquinas had been involved in is traditionally known as the debate between 'realists' and 'nominalists' and Aquinas was a subtle but uncom-
promising realist. That is, he argued for the real existence of abstractions and denied that they were mere intellectual counters useful for
speculation. In the fourteenth century this position lost ground in both
Paris and Oxford, and in general terms it can be said that nominalism
was the dominant intellectual position of the philosophers and logicians
of the later Middle Ages. Yet Thomism was far from being uninfluential.
It was, for example, actively developed at the Dominican house at
Cologne, associated with Eckhart and his disciples; the municipality
founded a university here in 1388 which gained authority from the
teaching of Denis (1402-71), prior of the Charterhouse of Roermund
and a prolific mystical writer. It is important to recall that both Wycliffe
and Huss would have regarded themselves as realists. In the early
fifteenth century a canonical defence of Aquinas was issued by Jean
Capreole (1380-1444); Pico della Mirandola was as much a Thomist
as anything else. In the sixteenth century the doctrines of Aquinas were
once again to acquire a commanding position among what must then be
described as Roman Catholics, and they were also held in high esteem
by the English Protestant divine Hooker.

Thomism, then, was far from moribund in the fourteenth and fifteenth centuries. But there is no doubt that the bulk of active philosophical work at this time was hostile to Aquinas. Nominalism owed its wide acceptance largely to the work of the English Franciscan William Ockham (*c.* 1290–1349). We have encountered Ockham already as a critic of the papacy and as supplier of arguments which justified conciliarist action.[1] His persecution by the hierarchy, his linking up with Lewis IV and the emperor's other intellectual supporter, Marsilio of Padua, may have encouraged Ockham to astringency of thought. It is, however, clear that in the early years of the fourteenth century many thinkers were groping towards a position which would release speculation from the ordered legalism of the thirteenth-century scholastics, which would admit the perception of 'individuals' rather than accept only an awareness of abstract form or essence wrapped up in 'accidents' of texture, colour, shape and the like. Many men were feeling their way towards a direct intuitive knowledge of the physical world; Ockham established such a view as a respectable intellectual position although (perhaps because) it carried with it the awareness of God by the same intuition. Ockham and his nominalist or terminalist adherents were recognized as offering the *via moderna*, and they set the pace in faculties of arts for the rest of the Middle Ages. For them logic was the main occupation of the philosopher, not the argued steps from created to Creator. The abstractions of the realists were bundled away as merely being names or terms coined to facilitate speculation.

One historian of medieval thought has compared Ockham to Lenin, as a solvent of the accepted contemporary categories.[2] Time will tell if this is a fair comparison. Ockham's metaphysical scepticism, which was further developed by some of his successors, often led to logic for logic's sake. Their debates centred on intricate problems of expression which to many seemed utterly void of moral content. Such seemingly verbal exercises earned them the contempt of the humanists of the late fifteenth and early sixteenth centuries, but it is significant that modern logicians have stimulated a new interest in nominalism. It is also the case that the 'Dunces' stigmatized by Erasmus and his confrères derived their name not from a nominalist but from a Franciscan from the Scottish lowlands, Duns Scotus (1266–1308), who was on the whole a follower of Aquinas. By the time the Renaissance came, one may infer, scholasticism would have been attacked by the humanists whatever the philosophical position adopted by its exponents.

[1] Above, p. 86.   [2] David Knowles, *Evolution of Medieval Thought*, p. 320

For Ockham and for many of his followers there was no question of doubting the truths of religion; all that was argued was that they could not be proved. In fact nominalism was partly responsible for some of the fresh spirituality of the period, by releasing thought from too narrow theological trammels. It could also, of course, lead to a wider scepticism, but this was found less among nominalists than among a handful of thinkers, in Italy and in Paris, who were captivated by the teaching of the Arab philosopher Averroës. Averroës's writings came in during the twelfth and thirteenth centuries as part of the Aristotelian *corpus*; Averroës however interpreted Aristotle in ways incompatible with Christian doctrine, and notably denied the immortality of the individual soul. Averroists are much talked about in the later Middle Ages, for their audacious speculations could only be accommodated to the Faith by denying that they were *believed* in by their adherents: they were truths in philosophy only, not in faith. One of the most celebrated Averroists of the period was the Frenchman Jean de Jandun (d. 1328), wrongly accused by John XXII as part-author of Marsilio's *Defensor Pacis*.[1] Apart from the fear that it engendered among the orthodox, the most significant effects of Averroism are perhaps to be seen in the release it gave to reflections on the physical universe, to 'science' in the modern narrow sense of the term. This was also the effect of nominalism.

So important is physical science today that it is easy to exaggerate the place it occupied in centuries earlier than the seventeenth. Much work has been done on the scholars who concerned themselves with science in the Middle Ages and there is no doubt that slowly and hesitatingly, and with an almost complete lack of interest in experimental method, advances were made on which scholars in later centuries were to build. In the fourteenth and fifteenth centuries, with the greater freedom of speculation induced by nominalism and Averroism, the pace of scientific enquiry became a little quicker. At Paris a number of secular masters who were Ockhamists developed original notions. Jean Buridan (d. 1358) showed how irrational was Aristotle's explanation of motion and substituted for it a doctrine of *impetus* which he tried to establish by observation. Nicholas Oresme (d. 1382) was a considerable geometrician and the German Albert of Saxony (d. 1390) carried further Buridan's investigation into motion. To some extent at Montpellier and Paris, but chiefly at Padua, the teaching of medicine was improved by more frequent (but still not common) dissections of the human body. Yet at Padua what the professors were really interested in were questions of logical induction,

[1] Above, p. 86.

and there is much to be said for the view that medieval logic was more influential than medieval 'science' in the development of physics and anatomy in the sixteenth and seventeenth centuries. Astrology was universally accepted as worthy of serious attention, and the influence of the stars was also accepted in the mysterious operations of the alchemist. There was plenty of practical and inventive horse-sense about—in collecting simples for remedies, in constructing lofty arches and great domes, in plotting the coasts for the mariner's portolan, or using compass and astrolabe. But very few of the intellectuals of this age were interested in analysing their universe empirically or in constructing a coherent system of causal relationships on the material plane. The one solid achievement, Alberti's understanding of perspective, hardly makes him a scientist.

It may appear from the foregoing that, apart from adventures in logical analysis, the later Middle Ages produced little that was novel in its universities. This is not so and three men may be advanced who were original thinkers while being in the full sense academic.

Jean Gerson (1364–1429) has come before us as an advocate of conciliar supremacy, as a bitter enemy of Huss, and as a mystic. He was in the fullest sense a Paris man, getting his doctorate in theology in 1392 and being elected chancellor of the university in 1395. He was (as the episode of Huss shows) fanatically orthodox, yet he gave his own sister the Huss-like advice not to enter a nunnery if she wished to lead a life of piety. His alert intelligence was not only devoted to the conventional exegesis of philosophical texts, but also to the whole question of the quality of university teaching of philosophy. The nominalists claimed him as one of their luminaries, and in general he agreed with much of Ockham. But he deplored the division of universities into rigid sects of opposing philosophical colour, and he disliked the mandarin self-satisfaction which went with much speculation: 'they [the theologians] freely invent for themselves technical terms incomprehensible to other doctors and masters'.[1] Beyond that he was a frequent preacher and was sympathetic to literature, interested in the Latin classics. He cannot be neatly categorized.

Nor can Nicholas Krebs of Cues (1401–64), whose activities as a model bishop and legate are referred to elsewhere.[2] Like Gerson he was a great mystic, but he was even more like him in being a great university man. At school at Deventer, where he was touched by the spirit of the Brethren of the Common Life, he subsequently attended the universities of

[1] Wulf, III, p. 152.   [2] Above, p. 319.

Heidelberg, Padua and Cologne, which gave him successively an understanding of nominalism, Averroism and Thomism, so that his education
incorporated each of the main strands in later medieval thought. Of the
several works composed by the cardinal, sandwiched into a hectic public
life, two are of considerable originality, the *De concordantia Catholica*
(1433) and the *De docta ignorantia* (1440). The first has a self-explanatory
title: it was written for a Christendom divided by Huss, divided by the
ancient hostility between Rome and Constantinople and by the traditional enmity of popes and emperors; and it proposes mathematical
measures to reassert unity. The *Catholic Concordance* is a large work,
which examines the relations of Church and Empire, with many inci-
dental comments on earlier ages which display Cusa as a shrewd historian: among other points he demonstrated the falsity of the Donation
of Constantine—or at any rate showed that it had left no trace in contemporary records.[1] The essential basis of the work is a conviction that
popular consent is at the basis of law, that election is the foundation of
government. For the Church this means that the pope, as its monarch,
should be elected by cardinals representative of the whole of Christendom, and that a council derived its powers directly from Christ. The
Learned Ignorance is a smaller, more difficult and profounder book. In it
Nicholas took issue against formal metaphysics, whether Thomist or
nominalist. He argued for the ultimate impossibility of rational explanation, and for the possibility of intellectual or intuitional knowledge,
illustrating his points by reference to geometry. He advanced the
paradox that logical contradiction is no impediment to spiritual truth.
It is possible to say what God is not, rather than what God is. The
sources of his thought have occasioned much debate: he knew (mainly
by way of Latin versions) a wide range of Plato's works; he was much
influenced by neo-Platonic writers, especially Proclus; and he was
heavily indebted to the mystical tradition of the Rhineland, notably
to Suso.

The third academic is usually discussed as a 'humanist' but in fact the
rich Italian noble Giovanni Pico, count of Mirandola (1463–94), is far
better looked at as a product of the universities of Bologna, Padua, Pavia
and Paris, rather than as a member of the Florentine 'academy' (which
will be mentioned shortly). His contact with Ficino was important, but
neo-Platonic notions were widely diffused among medieval scholars and
what Pico owed most to Florence was a knowledge of Hebrew and of the
Jewish Cabbala. Not only was Pico's basic training academic in the

[1] Below, p. 353.

traditional sense: his Latin was anything but humanist; and his initial reputation was occasioned by his publication in 1486 of nine hundred theses which he offered to defend at Rome in public disputation— another conventional feature of the university, though on a vaster scale than was usual. The theses display his syncretism, his amalgamation of truths from diverse sources, and they can best be read as summarized in the 'Oration on the dignity of Man' written as an introduction to the disputation.[1] This debate did not take place. Innocent VIII condemned thirteen of the theses as heretical and Pico took refuge in France. He came to Florence again in 1488 and completed there his major work, the *Heptaplus*, in which he interpreted Christian doctrine through the Cabbala. This further irritated Innocent VIII, and it was only in 1493 that Alexander VI was persuaded by Lorenzo de' Medici to absolve Pico from the charge of heresy. The last years of Pico saw him increasingly attracted to a Savonarolan renunciation of the world, though he embarked on a work designed to reconcile the teaching of Plato and Aristotle and he completed a vigorous and solid attack on judicial astrology and the charlatans who foretold the future from the stars.

We are told that the main criticism of the later medieval university is that it was doctrinaire:

> The thirteenth century had been the era of great personalities. In the fourteenth began the reign of schools of thought. As such schools established themselves, men of mark became rarer. From 1330 to 1450 the majority of philosophers depend on the thought of others.[2]

The term 'Thomists' begins to be used from 1341; 'Scotists' and 'Occamists' follow. The *via antiqua* was opposed to the *via moderna*, and the opposition was sometimes violent. Yet it is all but impossible to classify Gerson, Cusa, or Pico under any sectional label, and it is worth insisting that their training in universities allegedly dominated by arid scholasticism failed to quench a profound and mystical Christianity.

The rise of vernacular literature

The linguistic situation in medieval Europe was complicated by Latin being the only language formally taught. Among the many results of this, two are particularly important. First, the vernacular remained for long without any norm of grammar and orthography, and many local variations existed within the broad regional areas—there was no one

[1] Translated by Elizabeth L. Forbes in *Renaissance Philosophy of Man*, ed. E. Cassirer, P. O. Kristeller and J. H. Randall (Chicago, 1948).
[2] Wulf, p. 214.

French, Italian or German. Second, serious work was written in Latin and only ephemeral matter was usually composed in the vernacular. The period covered by this volume saw changes in each of these fields. Slowly there emerged a conscious artistic cultivation of vernacular language, and with it there came a tendency for one variety of each language to acquire primacy. At the same time (though here the steps were taken more hesitatingly) there were attempts to make the vernacular languages do work which had earlier been left to Latin. In this second process the revived Latin of the Italian humanist was, in the event, to provide an example of one all-sufficient language; it was an example which was to be observed and emulated by writers in English, French and other tongues in the sixteenth century, when most modern European languages really attained their majority.

The whole development[1] is seen in action earliest in Italy and one might fairly claim that, in so far as Italy has ever developed one national language, this had pretty well happened by the end of the fourteenth century. If there was relatively little Italian literature prior to Dante (by comparison for example with the riches of the French epic and *fabliaux*) Italians were nearer to the disciplines of Latin than other peoples and Dante's vernacular works, *Vita nuova*, *Convivio* and *Divine Comedy* are of astonishing linguistic maturity. Dante Alighieri died in 1321; his poetry still directly communicates with a modern Italian; one may hear unlettered Florentines quoting him in a café, which is not the sort of place in England where one would hear Chaucer. Dante was a layman, though his great poem is theological in structure. Francesco Petrarca (1304–74) was technically a clerk, drawing an income from church endowments. His love poetry *Le Rime* was inspired by Laura; he also wrote the *Triumphs* in honour of his mistress. The contemporary and friend of Petrarch, Giovanni Boccaccio (1313–75), who also wrote much vernacular verse, is above all known as the author of the *Decameron*, which was set in the plague year 1348 and was written soon after that. Dante, Petrarch and Boccaccio were all Tuscans, and their poetry and Boccaccio's prose *Decameron* were to ensure over the centuries that Tuscan became the main literary language of Italy. It should, however, be noted that each was a scholar and wrote much serious work in Latin.[2] No

---

[1] No attempt is made in what follows to summarize the content of the works referred to, which are mostly accessible in modernized versions and in English translations.

[2] For references to some of their Latin writings see above, pp. 82, 182, and below, p. 348.

writer in the vernacular of anything like the same greatness was to emerge in the fifteenth century, but the entire competence of the language was assured.

In France the literary tradition of the *langue d'oil*, the northern language which in these centuries reduced the *langue d'oc* more or less to a patois, had a long tradition behind it: courtly epic and lyric, fabliaux (mostly comic and in verse), the romances in poetry and prose. In the fourteenth century this literature (in broad terms) moved from verse to prose; the laity were reading for themselves rather than listening to professional reciters. At the same time a new and consciously 'rhetorical' style crept into artistic (professional) prose and verse. This reached its apogee in the writers attached to the Burgundian court, and not least in the historian who succeeded Froissart as chronicler of chivalry, Georges Chastellain (1404?–75).[1] Amidst all this preciosity later ages look with an admiration which would have puzzled his contemporaries at the verse of François Villon (born and died no one knows where or when), an M.A. of Paris in 1452 and still in trouble with the authorities ten years later. Racy and pathetic by turns, and almost entirely obscure to the modern reader without a learned commentary, Villon reminds one of the goliardic poets of the twelfth century. In his own age he was a freak.

Among the literatures of the Spanish peninsula, Catalan slowly declined and Portuguese was relatively unimportant in the later Middle Ages. It was in Castilian that real advances took place, perhaps because of the richness of the linguistic and literary inheritance—Hebrew and Arabic as well as Castilian itself. The strength of the literature lay in lyrical poetry, much of it oral and only written down later, but there was also a more sophisticated and rhetorical school in the fifteenth century, borrowing from both Italian and French models. Both tendencies are seen in the work of Iñigo López de Mendoza, marquis of Santillana (d. 1458).

Among the literatures of Teutonic peoples only English developed significantly at this time, to produce in John Gower (*c.* 1330–1408) an important poet, and in Geoffrey Chaucer (*c.* 1340–1400) a great one. Thereafter the literary scene darkens for a century and a half, apart from the so-called Scottish 'Chaucerians' at the end of the fifteenth century— Robert Henryson (*fl.* 1470–80) and William Dunbar (*c.* 1460–1515). The advance was, however, limited mainly to verse. How inadequate the language was for serious prose can be seen in Chaucer's version of

[1] Cf. above, p. 4.

346

Boethius, or in the laborious English works of the unfortunate Reginald Pecock (d. *c.* 1460), bishop of Chichester, who got into trouble with the hierarchy for the imprudence of his arguments against the lollards.

It may well be felt that the emergent vernaculars should hardly figure in a chapter devoted to the 'bonds of literature' for they went far to cancelling out the earlier unity conveyed by Latin or the more limited regional associations provided by Anglo-Norman and French, by Provençal in the south of France and Italy, or in the Catalan culture which ignored the boundaries of France and Aragon. There is much truth in this; a world increasingly dependent on the vernacular was obviously liable to erect new cultural barriers. Certain lively forms of popular literature were clearly not capable of crossing linguistic frontiers. The later Middle Ages is the greatest period in the ballad—in the Anglo-Scottish borders, in Denmark, in Castile. Yet by turning the Bible into the vernacular (and this happened everywhere at this time) one of the great common influences of European literature and ideas was spread to even larger sections of the population, a process which was also encouraged by the miracle and mystery plays which are a feature of all countries at this time.[1] Beyond that, there was an astonishing degree of interdependence of theme and inspiration. Chaucer was the translator of the *Roman de la Rose*, and borrowed material from Boccaccio. French romance spread into Germany in its prose forms, as it had earlier in verse, while in England Thomas Malory (d. 1471) produced his *Morte d'Arthur*. In Italy the long popular interest in the old French epics arrived at court in the *Orlando Innamorato* of Matteo Boiardo (1441–94), a gentleman who served the Este court at Ferrara. The cultural world of the fifteenth century had certainly not entirely abandoned older shared literary manners. And in Italy a new set of cultural values was emerging at this time which was in the end further to bind together the nations of Europe.

The Italian Renaissance

Properly to understand the novelty of the Italian Renaissance one must abandon the view, held by Burckhardt and Symonds, and by many subsequent writers, that the 'rebirth' was basically the rediscovery of the values of ancient civilization. A new excitement in the literature, the ethical teaching and the scholarship of the Roman and Greek worlds was indeed experienced, together with a new reverence and sympathy for the monuments and the art of antiquity. But the impulse behind these

[1] Cf. above, p. 307.

evolving attitudes was the desire of a steadily multiplying number of men to define afresh their moral, intellectual and aesthetic purposes, and to acquire the skills by which these purposes might be adequately expressed. Likewise the older opinion, that the Renaissance constitutes the beginning of the 'modern' world, cannot now be sustained, if by modern we mean the world of our own day. It can be reasonably argued that it inaugurated a period of European civilization which lasted till the eighteenth century, with consequences lasting on in an attenuated form to our own day. That in itself is a remarkable achievement deserving of investigation. But it cannot properly be investigated unless another assumption of Burckhardt is seriously modified: that the Renaissance, overall and from the start, was a general Italian phenomenon. It was not. The Renaissance began in Florence and spread fairly quickly into the smaller courts of Italy, much more slowly into the only two great principates, Naples and Milan.

Between about 1380 and 1440 the cultural world of Florence was largely transformed. A growing group of patricians began to patronize scholars bent on 'recovering' the ancient world and artists who, from Masaccio (1401–c. 1428) and Brunelleschi (d. 1446) onwards, painted and built in a new realistic and 'classical' style. There had been earlier indications than this of an interest in antiquity, both artistic and literary. Nicola Pisano and his son Giovanni (*fl.* 1260–1314) had based much of their sculpture at Pisa and Siena on classical sarcophagi; Giotto (1266–1337) painted with a new solidity and care for reality. There were many lawyers in Italian cities who were interested professionally in the world which had produced the Roman law which they studied at the university and applied in the courts; Florence had a reputation for producing good notaries. Petrarch had fallen in love with Latin and demonstrated its enormous capabilities in his letters, in his introspective *Secretum*, in his poem *Africa* and in many other works. Boccaccio, like Petrarch, was passionately interested in Latin literature and compiled a big manual of ancient mythology called the *Genealogy of the Gods*. But there was no permanent home or support for such studies until they seemed relevant to a wider public. As good a date as any for that acceptance is the appointment of Coluccio Salutati (1331–1406) as chancellor, the only senior executive officer of the government, at Florence in 1375. Salutati, a lawyer by training, was what a later age would call a humanist: his interest in the literature and life of classical antiquity had a passion like Petrarch's; but Salutati put his talents to the service not of letters for their own sake, but of the Republic of which he was the servant. He was the centre of a group of younger scholars. Other groups formed round Luigi Marsili and Niccolò de' Niccoli.

Coteries such as this were not new. Scholars and *littérateurs* had gathered in such ways from time to time—not least in those moments called the 'Carolingian Renaissance', the 'Renaissance of the twelfth century', and in Florence and other Italian towns in the fourteenth century. In the decades round 1400 at Florence, however, something else happened: the ruling oligarchs (who had appointed Salutati, and whose powers rapidly increased after 1381, when the popular revolution[1] was over) took an interest in the new learning which was both lively and, more important, sustained. An even more impressive scholar was appointed to succeed Salutati, Leonardo Bruni of Arezzo (1374?–1444), and two other outstanding humanists followed Bruni: Carlo Marsuppini (1398–1453) and Poggio Bracciolini (1380–1459). These men gave the new letters a permanent establishment in Florence, and one is driven to ask why the hard-headed business men who formed the *signoria* considered it worth their while, individually and collectively, to patronize learning in this way; not all the patricians were cultivated like the Alberti, whose gardens formed one of the gathering points for the new generation of intellectuals.

The answer which seems most convincing is that in these years Florence was enduring a prolonged political threat of encirclement, perhaps of extinction. Her scholars and men of letters fortified the Florentine will to resist Giangaleazzo Visconti, Ladislas of Naples, Filippo Maria Visconti. They explained the essence of the Florentine ethos and advocated republican liberty against the Caesarian peace professed by Visconti propagandists.[2] In letters, pamphlets and larger works (like Bruni's *History of Florence*) the glories of the past were related to the freedom of the city. Even more important, the humanist scholars went on to show that it was virtuous to lead a life of action in the world, that the possession of wealth was not of itself a bad thing. Petrarch had condemned Cicero for spoiling himself as a philosopher by meddling in politics and had affected to despise Dante's involvement in marriage and public life. Bruni and his contemporaries considered that Cicero and Dante were great men precisely *because* they had been both poets and active citizens. The ancient teaching of the Church had stressed the moral primacy of the monk and the recluse. Now the integrity of the citizen was proclaimed. To serve one's family and one's community was

[1] Above, pp. 174–5.
[2] For what follows see the works of H. Baron (above, p. 334).

to obey God's law; to be rich enabled one not only to avoid the furtive meanness, the liability to corruption and the practical certainty of moral ugliness, of poverty—it enabled one to glorify the Creator and make life more gracious and comfortable for one's fellow men.

These staggering claims were not all made at once, and poverty in particular proved a hard nut to crack: St Francis was still a potent influence in 1400. Nor did the humanists of this early Florentine Renaissance ever claim that the active life was the only road to Heaven, that wealth necessarily made a man virtuous. They merely put involvement in the world on a par with renunciation, but that was enough to start an intellectual change which was gradually to affect the whole of Europe. For the dilemma between activity and renunciation was not just a Florentine problem, or even an Italian or an urban problem. It was universal and, when the envelope of aggressive republicanism had been removed from the new doctrine, it could and did move freely into the courts of the peninsula and thence into the courts of Europe at large. So it was also with the artistic innovations.

The coincidence of the new art with the new morality is striking and suggests that the burgesses of Florence found the same kind of satisfaction in Ghiberti, Luca della Robbia and Donatello as they did in the ethical and political doctrines of the humanists. Brunelleschi's Pazzi Chapel, in the cloister at Sta Croce, was completed by 1446—the first entirely Renaissance building in a city which was to be transformed in the course of the next two generations. The Florentine art of this period is generally familiar and need not be insisted on here. Yet it should be stressed that the works produced in the first forty years of the fifteenth century represented a break with the past as remarkable as that achieved in the field of moral values at the same time.

From Florence the new art and the new notion that literature and learning were guides to proper public life gradually spread. They were curiously neglected for some time in the other republics, presumably because there was no love, only jealousy and political apprehension, of all things Florentine even at Genoa and Venice, let alone at nearby Lucca and Siena. Nor could 'tyrants' like the Visconti, or kings like Alfonso of Aragon in Naples, be expected to welcome attitudes which at first were redolent of communal liberty. But the lesser dynasts accepted the morality, the literature and the art and quietly forgot about the republicanism. At Mantua the Gonzaga patronized humanist letters and art; so did the Este family at Ferrara and the Montefeltro family at Urbino. Pope Nicholas V, himself the product of a literary career which had taken him to the top of the ecclesiastical tree, encouraged scholars and artists to frequent the papal court and employed them in the curia; from that time onwards the papacy, consciously and unconsciously, increasingly adopted Renaissance values and sought to bolster the declining spiritual authority of Rome by making the City the centre of art and scholarship. Finally, by the end of the fifteenth century we find Renaissance art and humanist ideals establishing themselves in Milan and Naples, under the patronage of the Sforza dukes and King Ferrante, though in neither city was the reception particularly noteworthy in its immediate manifestations.

In the second stage of development, when Florentine discoveries were being accepted outside Tuscany, steps were taken to put them on a permanent footing. This was largely the work of two inspired teachers, both working under princely auspices: at Ferrara Guarino da Verona (1374–1460) and at Mantua Vittorino da Feltre (1378?–1446) taught the children of their patrons and others, both rich and poor, in an entirely new manner. Their aim was not the production of clergy, or even scholars as such, nor (in any traditional sense) of a devout laity. Their ambition was to train young men in the humanities—grammar, poetry, rhetoric, history, moral philosophy, as exemplified in the classics, especially the Latin classics—in order to bring out their full potentialities for life and public service. Vittorino expressed his view thus:

> Not everyone is called to be a lawyer, a physician, a philosopher, to live in the public eye, nor has everyone outstanding gifts of natural capacity, but all of us are created for the life of social duty, all of us are responsible for the personal influence which goes out from us.

And it can be fairly said that both men applied Bruni's programme of education which was based on two assumptions: learning should be broad and based on the humanities; learning must be fruitful, capable of use.

> That high standard of education . . . is only to be reached by one who has seen many things and read much. Poet, orator, historian and the rest, all must be studied, each must constitute a share. One's learning thus becomes full, ready, varied and elegant, available for action or for discourse. . . . But to enable us to make effectual use of what we know we must add to our knowledge the power of expression . . . Where . . . this double capacity exists—breadth of learning and grace of style—we allow the highest title to distinction and to abiding fame.[1]

[1] Vittorino in W. H. Woodward, *Studies in Education during the Age of the*

The men taught by Guarino and Vittorino became the rulers of the next generation, their secretaries, ambassadors and councillors; others of them became schoolmasters and, as the new humanities were slowly accepted by universities, professors in faculties of arts—teaching *literae humaniores* (as classical studies are still called at Oxford). The reception of the humanist curriculum by Italian universities was relatively easy; there were no entrenched divinity schools to resist, and the dominant lawyers were in general sympathetic. It was to be less easy in the universities of northern Europe, though there the new grammar school, lycée or gymnasium was to be even more impressively developed in the sixteenth century than it had been in Italy.

In this courtly phase many of the features of earlier or (as it is now often termed) 'civic' humanism were changed which, like republicanism, did not commend themselves to dukes or popes. Instead of designing town houses of magnificence for patricians and oligarchs, which the architect was called on to do in Florence, the princely patron wanted him to build a castle-cum-palace, such as the splendid building erected at Urbino on a hill-top; or old buildings had to be furbished up in the new manner, like the Palazzo Schifanoia in Ferrara or the Gonzaga stronghold in Mantua. By the second half of the fifteenth century the men commissioned to build or decorate such buildings were either Florentines or men bred in Florentine artistic manners. Two final examples may be given of this activity. In 1459 and the next years Pope Pius II turned the tiny hill town of Corsignano whence he came into a miniature jewel of Renaissance art: he himself reconstructed the church (and elevated it to the status of a cathedral) and built a sober and serene palace, complete with a 'classical' garden. Other buildings were erected by complaisant cardinals in this hamlet in the Tuscan hills and its name was changed by the pope to Pienza. In 1446 Sigismondo Malatesta, lord of Rimini and Pius's arch enemy (the pope accused him of every sin from atheism downwards) had Alberti cloak the walls of the church of San Francesco at Rimini with a Renaissance mantle, while inside artists and sculptors turned the Gothic building into a 'temple'.[1] As one moves round Italy today it is the Renaissance churches which strike one; hardly a building which stood in 1400 was not to be draped, if not rebuilt, in the new manner in the course of the coming two centuries.

For, whatever else the new mood did, it did not make Italians either

_____

Renaissance (Cambridge, 1906), pp. 12–13; Bruni in the same writer's *Vittorino da Feltre and other Humanist Educators* (Cambridge, 1897), pp. 132–3.
[1] Cf. above, p. 252.

more or less religious than they had been before. A growing number of pictures were painted of mythological scenes, but they remained a tiny minority compared with the madonnas and the saints. The religious subjects were treated in a new way. In sculpture and paintings there was an air of realism mingling with the heroic which was very different from the Byzantine austerities and angularities of earlier Italian art, as it was from the Gothic art of the thirteenth century in France or England. But one has no right to assume (as tended to be done in the nineteenth century in northern Europe) that prayer and praise can only ascend efficaciously from dreaming spires. Nor did the new scholarship produce atheism. Some few there were who toyed on the one hand with philosophical scepticism or on the other with Epicureanism; the great philologist Lorenzo Valla (1407–57) was one of these. Yet he remained a conventional enough Christian. The damage he did to the Church was of a practical kind and came less from his philosophy than from his demonstration of the falsity of the Donation of Constantine; in this action he had independent and contemporary companions.[1] There were undoubtedly men who were both learned and dissolute in the service of the papacy: and some of the popes, like the Franciscan Sixtus IV and the Borgia pope Alexander VI are, in different ways, scandalous figures. But their dynasticism (and Alexander VI's debauchery) cannot be attributed to the culture of the day. The scholars who might be tempted towards intellectual error were more likely to be old-fashioned Averroists than humanists.

At the end of the fifteenth century there was indeed a positively religious or at any rate mystical aura about some of the new humanists. This was particularly the case in Florence where the forms of a republican polity were still largely maintained, but where the outside world accepted that a principate had in fact emerged with Lorenzo de' Medici. Contrary to the legend, 'il Magnifico' was not as significant a patron as his grandfather Cosimo had been, but among the scholars in the ambience of Lorenzo's court there stands out Marsilio Ficino (1433–99) who had been encouraged by Cosimo to translate Plato into Latin. This was the origin of the group of men who regarded themselves as an academy, the first of many such learned societies in Italy and Europe at large. In the sixteenth and later centuries such academies were to acquire premises, constitutions and publications, and become the most important *foci* of advanced scholarship and research, first in the humanities and later in the sciences. This lay in the future. There was no system

[1] Cusa (above, p. 343) and the Englishman Reginald Pecock (cf. above, pp. 346–7).

in the discussions of the friends who met at Ficino's villa at Careggi, where most of the participants were not professional scholars like Ficino but men of affairs and men of art and letters, who were sympathetic to his general attitude. Ficino was convinced that Platonic doctrine was not only compatible with Christianity, but that it enabled men to rise to a transcendental awareness of God. Such an approach, carried even further by bringing in the mysticism of the Hebrew Cabbala, characterized Ficino's most famous disciple, Giovanni Pico of Mirandola (1463–94).[1] It is obvious that teaching like this could and did marry well with the *nova devotio* of the North, much of which stemmed also from Platonic and neo-Platonic inspiration.

North–south cultural contacts in the later Middle Ages

In any account of literary, artistic and spiritual links between the new movements of Italy and the new movements in northern Europe, stress is normally and rightly placed on the reception north of the Alps and in Spain of the values and practices invented in Florence and adopted elsewhere in Italy. The Italian Renaissance became the European Renaissance in the course of the sixteenth and seventeenth centuries. It is nevertheless important to recall that in traditional literature and scholarship the continent was still bound together by the cultural activities sketched at the start of this chapter, and it is equally important to note that traffic in intellectual and artistic influences was far from being exclusively from south to north. Indeed a strong case can be made that the prevailing wind was in the contrary direction during much of the fourteenth and fifteenth centuries.

The most remarkable aspect of this is to be seen in the fine arts. In the course of the fourteenth century the painters and sculptors of the north evolved a light but dramatic style which enmeshed realistic and decorative detail in a framework of fantasy. At the same time Gothic architecture moved into a highly complicated and swirling 'decorated' style, to be followed by even loftier and more attenuated walls of windows and columns which reached their furthest development in English 'perpendicular'. At the end of the fourteenth century and at the beginning of the fifteenth there is an astonishing homogeneity in European art which has been called the 'international Gothic'. The terms art historians use to describe it—lyrical, elegant, delicate and so on—suggest aristocratic patrons and it is in fact a courtly and highly cultivated manner. It may be the case that Giotto had something to do with

[1] Above, pp. 343–4.

its origins and that Avignon in the time of the papal residence acted as a radiating point for the Florentine art of the early fourteenth century. There is, however, no doubt that the international style in the later fourteenth century penetrated into Italy—again, perhaps, from papal Avignon. At Siena Simone Martini (d. 1344) and at Florence Lorenzo Monaco (d. 1425?) are its influential representatives, and echoes of this international style are found in Italy right through the fifteenth century down to Fra Angelico and Botticelli. Nor should we forget that northern sculpture had early attained extraordinary solidity and realism which may have helped the innovators of Florence. Again, though in Italy Gothic architecture had never been strong and was destined soon to be overwhelmed by the glories of Renaissance style, the most ambitious church of the peninsula in the later Middle Ages, the cathedral at Milan, begun in 1386, was a kind of apotheosis, almost a caricature, of the Gothic. And the portrait, regarded with some reason as the hallmark of patrons and artists interested in the depiction of an actual world, comes first not in Italy but in France, Bohemia and England in the period 1360–80.

Nor did the admiration for northern art die out in Italy with a generation gradually coming to prefer Masaccio, Donatello and their successors. The Low Countries in the fifteenth century witness a transformation of international Gothic in the direction of further and more compelling attention to realistic detail. Painting the world as it was became the painter's main aim, though the traditional decorative patterns died hard. The man who transformed the old style was Jan van Eyck (c. 1390–1441) who worked at Lille and Bruges under the patronage of the duke of Burgundy. His reputation was high, and not only in Burgundian territory. He greatly affected the remarkable painters who overlapped and succeeded him in the Netherlands, Roger van der Weyden and Hugo van der Goes; he was also influential in France, and especially in the Avignon school, and in Italy. Bruges was the most important commercial centre of northern Europe in the later Middle Ages. Italian business men there patronized Flemish artists and at home Italians ordered Flemish paintings, for they were regarded as being both deeply religious and beautifully executed. Above all in technique Italian artists looked up to Jan van Eyck as the inventor of oil painting (as opposed to egg tempera, the normal medium with which colours had been mixed). This is probably an exaggeration but it is one which indicates the sense of indebtedness with which Renaissance painters in Italy regarded the masters of the north.

A somewhat parallel development exists in the case of music, though it needs an expert properly to describe and illustrate it. The precious *ars nova* style, deriving its name from the title of a work (*c.* 1320) by Philippe de Vitry, was in fact found generally in Europe in the fourteenth century, corresponding in some degree with the International Gothic in painting. The major innovations thereafter are Netherlandish, the patronage of the dukes of Burgundy once more being a significant factor. Partly perhaps because of the influence of the English composer John Dunstable (*c.* 1390-1453), court musician to the duke of Bedford when he was Regent in France, a fresh and invigorating direction was given to Flemish music by Guillaume Dufay (*c.* 1400-74) who has been compared in musical history to Jan van Eyck in painting. For the greater part of the fifteenth century and the first quarter of the sixteenth the Low Countries dominated European music; they produced great composers and executants whom they exported everywhere in Europe; and they contrived to innovate in both choral polyphony and instrumental music. This leadership was due partly to much bigger professional (and lay) choirs in certain large centres, like Antwerp, and partly to a succession of brilliant musicians of whom the greatest was Josquin des Prez (*c.* 1450-1521), who was in Italy for many years—at Milan, at Rome and with the Este family at Ferrara—and then at the French court. In the sixteenth century the great centres of musical development were to be found in Italy, at Rome and Venice. But the roots of this development are to be found in fifteenth-century Flanders.

If the painters of the Low Countries exercised considerable influence in Italy in the later Middle Ages, if the advance in music was almost entirely to be concentrated in the same area, the most impressive of all northern innovations was to emerge in the adjacent area of the Rhineland. In the mid- and late 1430s Johann Gutenberg (1394/99-1468) of Mainz began the experiments which culminated by about 1453 in the production of the first book printed with movable metal type, the massive '42-line' Bible. Printing had been known in China for centuries, and the Chinese invention of paper had already reached the west. The printing of Chinese ideographs had, however, little relevance for Gutenberg, even if he knew how it was done (and there is no evidence that he did). The western alphabet involved the juxtaposition of twenty-six characters in a multitude of combinations arranged in parallel lines, and Gutenberg, who had a traditional family connection with goldsmiths, solved the problem with movable metal type, made by pouring lead into matrices cut to resemble the characters of the current 'book-hand' of the best scriveners. The details of the earliest pieces of printing in the 1440s and 1450s are still the subject of learned debate, but Gutenberg's primacy is not now disputed. From the point of view of the general historian the invention and rapid adoption of printing have multiple significance. It seems impossible to doubt that pressure on the resources of manuscript copyists was such that they could not meet the demand, and this is further evidence for the literacy of the laity in the Rhineland, where we have encountered so much lay mysticism. That printing met not just a local problem in south Germany is seen by the extraordinarily rapid spread of the technique in ensuing decades. Two Germans established the first press in Italy at Subiaco in 1464 and then moved to Rome in 1467; by 1471 printers were also established at Venice, Milan, Naples and Florence. The production of books spread early in Germany and Switzerland; it began in Paris in 1470 and Lyons in 1473, at Valencia and Bruges in 1474, at Westminster in 1476 and in London in 1480. Soon every large town and university centre had its printers. (The first printed music is found at Esslingen in 1473.) Equally revealing of the public reaction is the kind of book produced by the printers of the fifteenth century, the 'incunable' or cradle period of the art.[1] On the whole the printer-publisher issued relatively small editions (200 to 1,000) of books he knew he could sell. Ninety-four Vulgate Bibles had appeared by 1500 and thirty editions of translations of the Scriptures into vernacular language. Thomas à Kempis's *Imitatio Christi* came out ninety-nine times in the same period. Service books, grammars (like *Donatus*) and school books of all kinds were steadily reprinted. The bulk of incunables are in Latin as far as numbers of printings are concerned though there is evidence that the size of editions of vernacular works tended to become larger, while editions of Latin books tended to become smaller. It is in any case clear that the new invention made the old books more readily available. In the absence of copyright the printing press hardly affected the career of authorship. Of itself it did nothing to promote new ideas, but it undoubtedly hastened the circulation of existing ideas, just as it further encouraged the growing literacy which had initially provoked the whole development. By the end of the fifteenth century the most important centre of printing was at Venice, partly because of the number of presses (about 150 by 1500) and partly because of the establishment there in 1490 of the first great scholar-printer, Aldus Manutius (*c.* 1450–1515). The

---

[1] Down to 1500. For this period there are relatively complete lists, covering the whole of Europe, of all books published.

prestige of the classical texts issued by Aldus was enormous and, among other things, it ensured the rapid conquest of the north by the 'roman' type (to be followed early in the sixteenth century by the italic) —a victory for Italian values which is a fair symbol of the spread of the Italian Renaissance into the northern Gothic world.

At this point, in the last decades of the fifteenth century, Europe as a whole was on the brink of the Renaissance: Dürer's visit to Venice in 1494 typifies the beginning of a period when Italian cultural values were to root themselves generally outside the peninsula. It is remarkable how suddenly and how thoroughly this was to happen in the sixteenth century, how unfruitful Italian influence had been prior to this point. Petrarch had lived much of his life in France and had many friends there, but the Petrarch admired there was not the man of introspection and humane letters, not the Latinist whose excitement for the language and literature of antiquity gave his writing a new vigour and homogeneity: it was the old-fashioned in Petrarch which was admired—his criticism of the world, his dislike of matrimony; much the same is true of Chaucer's borrowing from Boccaccio, as we have already noted. In the fifteenth century a few English aristocrats, of whom Humphrey duke of Gloucester and William Gray, bishop of Ely, are the most significant, patronized humanists and collected Italian books, though their preferences were for what was most traditional in humanist scholarship. A rather more vigorous and sustained interest in Italian culture may be seen in Spain (especially Castile) and above all in the towns of south Germany. At Augsburg and Nuremberg and in the Rhineland generally there were burgher aristocracies which were sympathetic (as the patricians of Florence had been) to the new learning. In such a milieu it was possible for Rudolph Agricola (1442–85) to flourish. This Dutch-born scholar had spent over ten years in Italy before going to Germany, where he spent his last years at Heidelberg. He and Conrad Celtis (1459–1508), who was the first German poet to be laureated in the Petrarchan manner (1487), had a more thorough understanding of Italian values than their contemporaries in England or France.

It was, however, to be nobles like Duke Humphrey who were to be the real patrons of the Renaissance in the north after kings had secured its success. Princes soon found it essential to have 'Latin secretaries', humanist-trained diplomats, literary apologists of an up-to-date kind. The Renaissance came to the courts of the north from the courts of Italy, and from the prince it radiated out to the nobles, and to the gentry and the burgesses who aped their ways.

XIV

The Bonds of Trade

It is useful to distinguish three kinds of trade in this period. There were local markets in most towns where the products of the immediate region were bought and sold. Certain larger centres had markets where such business was transacted but which also handled commodities which had originated in more distant parts of Europe. Finally there was a limited traffic in exotic products from the east. This last might be termed intercontinental trade, in contrast to the continental trade of the second category and the provincial traffic of the first. These are, of course, not

BIBLIOGRAPHY. There are several recent works with good bibliographies. Vol. II of the *Cambridge Economic History* (1952) has two stimulating chapters, one on the trade of the north (by M. M. Postan) and one on the south (by R. S. Lopez), as well as useful accounts of the woollen industry, mining and building. Vol. III (1963) is devoted to 'Economic organization and policies'. M. Mollat and others contribute a review of recent literature in vol. VI (Florence, 1955) of the *Relazioni* of the Tenth International Congress of Historical Studies. A brief but valuable account is provided by Heers, above p. 26. Some important studies of particular questions: E. Power and M. M. Postan (eds.), *Studies in English Trade in the Fifteenth Century* (London, 1933); Y. Renouard, *Les relations des papes d'Avignon et des compagnies commerciales et bancaires* (Paris, 1942); R. de Roover, *Money, Banking and Credit in Medieval Bruges* (Cambridge, Mass., 1948) and *The Rise and Fall of the Medici Bank* (Cambridge, Mass., 1964); J. Le Goff, *Marchands et banquiers du moyen âge* (Paris, 1966). A brief and lucid account of Venetian shipping is provided by F. C. Lane, *Venetian Ships and Shipbuilders during the Renaissance* (Baltimore, 1934) and there is a useful study by A. R. Bridbury, *England and the Salt Trade in the Later Middle Ages* (Oxford, 1955). For a general study of Italian commercial activity see: Y. Renouard, *Les hommes d'affaires italiens au moyen âge* (Paris, 1950) and A. Sapori, *Le marchand italien au moyen âge* (Paris, 1952); there is a popular but rewarding study of Datini by Iris Origo, *The Merchant of Prato* (London, 1957). For the Baltic see Dollinger, above p. 79 and J. Gade, *The Hanseatic control of Norwegian commerce during the Late Middle Age* (Leiden, 1951). For the Mediterranean, R. S. Lopez and I. W. Raymond, *Medieval Trade in the Mediterranean World* (New York, 1955). Cf. economic histories noted above, p. 26, and now H. A. Miskimin, *Economy of Early Renaissance Europe* (Englewood Cliffs, N.J., 1969).

water-tight compartments; wine could be bought in a small market in Gascony which could form a staple of continental commerce; eastern spices were retailed in small places even if the wholesale trade was channelled through a handful of routes.

It is the continental trade of Europe which formed at this time a genuine link between different regions and which helped to give a sense of economic coherence to politically divided and sometimes warring areas. The continent was bounded by three seas—the Mediterranean, the Atlantic Ocean and North Sea, and the Baltic. To the east lay a series of rivers running from north to south which also formed a means of communication and transport, though by the fourteenth century interruptions of a serious kind were experienced here. If the overland and river routes of the eastern edge of Europe were now less significant than in earlier ages, the other three sides of the continent were even more important than they had been, for large-scale commerce was leaving the land routes and taking to ships. What made trade effective in coalescing different parts of the continent was the complementary nature of the natural products to be found in north and south and the emergence in particular places of industrial and commercial techniques which could themselves be exported.

Communications and trade

Land transport was limited by bad roads. Apart from a few places in Lombardy, there was no network of metalled roads made as we know today, so that the haulage of carts was severely restricted even in good weather, and often became impossible in winter rains. It is true that Roman roads were regularly used and that they were less decrepit than they were to become later;[1] but it is also true that, outside Italy, they seldom went to the main centres of medieval trade. Charity and self-interest led individuals and corporations to repair and maintain bridges and stretches of highway, but state supervision was seldom present to ensure that the main routes were passable to more than a man on foot or on horse. Much was, however, transported by cart, not only to local fairs but also to relatively distant markets, and much continental commerce was carried on pack animals or, where the routes were steep, as in the Alpine passes, on the backs of porters; the St Gothard was opened to pack animals in 1237, and in 1338 a road was made across the

[1] See the interesting discussion of transport by Postan, *Cambridge Economic History*, II, pp. 143–8; he argues that roads were better than is suggested above; the account I give rather follows Lopez in *Past and Present*, no. 9 (1956).

Septimer Pass for small carts. Even in the thirteenth century and earlier, when the existence of the Champagne fair towns as the main entrepôt is an indication of the importance of land transport, merchants preferred to send bulky goods by inland waterways. Rivers were navigated wherever possible, and in favourable areas like Flanders and the valley of the Po canals were dug; in Lombardy irrigation often preceded transport as an impulse to canal construction as it did in the Naviglio Grande between Milan and Pavia. Nevertheless the disadvantages of rivers were in some ways even greater than roads, for they attracted the predatory lord who imposed tolls on the traffic passing through his territory. Convoys of carts and pack animals could and did avoid plague and fiscality as well as the obstacles of landslide and flood and the hazards of private banditry and official war, by simply altering routes; but a bargeload of cloth, wine or salt was an easy victim. Riverine tolls increased in the later Middle Ages, perhaps because territorial lords were harder up than they had been. There were tolls on the Seine and the Garonne every six or seven miles. Other continental rivers were sometimes even more heavily oppressed; at the start of the fourteenth century there were thirty-five tolls on the Rhine and this had nearly doubled by 1500. Where monarchy was strong (as in England) this never became an impediment; where a prince controlled territory effectively (as the dukes of Milan did) a long stretch of inland waterway could be operated with economy; but in general by the fourteenth century the inland transport of anything but small and precious commodities, or of local goods going relatively short distances, tended to be expensive.

In the general economic decline of the later Middle Ages the incentive to improve roads and waterways was thus continuously present: the smaller the profits the more important it became to reduce transport costs. Princes were more powerful and more concerned to encourage commerce for the revenue it brought them and to facilitate the passage of large armies and heavy artillery; town councils and urban republics were anxious for their supplies of necessities, guildsmen for their raw materials. As a result roads begin to be improved, canals widened and the gradients of mountain paths modified: acts of piety, acts of prudence and acts of state. Among the most impressive works may be mentioned the canal joining the Haff and the Niemen which linked Danzig and Kovno in the early fifteenth century, and the canal (1398) which linked tributaries of the Trave and the Elbe to assure barge traffic between Lübeck and Hamburg, and thus between the Baltic and the North Sea; the traditional systems of waterways at Venice, in the Po

Valley, in Flanders and Holland were maintained and extended. It will however be noted that these activities are nearly all in maritime areas. The extension of canals near the Adriatic, the North Sea and the Baltic indicates what was the main transport change of the late thirteenth and early fourteenth centuries: long-distance commerce had taken to the sea.

There is no doubt that the difficulties of land routes referred to above were mainly responsible for this. At the same time there were new and better equipped ships available. Much shipping still hugged the coasts, was small and confined to local transport. But merchants in the Mediterranean and the Baltic disposed of much bigger vessels. Galleys, swift if expensive, grew progressively bigger. The great merchant galley of Venice was normally powered by sail and used oars only when entering or leaving harbour or in battle. By the end of the thirteenth century Genoese and Catalan vessels were sailing to the North Sea,[1] where they met the tough Baltic cog and its fifteenth-century successor, the hulk. In the Mediterranean the 'round ship' became more important and the amount of freight carried rose from 100 tons to 500 tons and even higher (700 or 800 tons) in some Italian ships. By the end of the fifteenth century, in both north and south, faster and roomier caravels and carracks were making their appearance. In general the ships of the North Sea and Baltic tended to be slower and bigger than contemporary boats built in Italy or Spain. The cargoes they carried for long distances were bulkier and inherently less valuable.

Along with the bigger and faster ships went improved navigational equipment. The compass was in general use by the thirteenth century, and with the compass, the astrolabe and the lead (particularly valuable in northern waters), the sea captain could now steer a course from port to port rather than from headland to headland. He also disposed of sophisticated marine charts. The elaborate 'portolan-chart', which had been devised under Catalan inspiration (and probably at Majorca) by the third quarter of the thirteenth century, plotted the coastline of the Mediterranean and Black Sea with extraordinary fidelity and the 'wind-roses' on it enabled the mariner to follow the compass-bearing best suited to his course. The *portolani* were gradually extended to cover the Atlantic Coast as this came to be a regular route for Mediterranean shipping.

On all routes freight costs were lower on long journeys by sea. It has been calculated that transport added between 15 and 20 per cent

[1] The first Venetian convoy to the North Sea was in 1314.

to overland costs compared with 2 per cent (or perhaps 6 per cent allowing for insurance) for costs by sea in the case of silk sent from Venice to Flanders. In the north, freight charges were very much higher on average, for the goods transported were bulky: the cost of carrying a cargo of corn from Danzig to Bruges in the early fifteenth century was about 48 per cent of the value of the cargo; Portuguese salt taken to Bruges involved a charge of 85 per cent, for the route was long and dangerous. But the cost of long-distance land transport of timber, grain, fish or salt would have been prohibitive—indeed such distances could not have been traversed with heavy loads of relatively cheap commodities.[1]

By the use of sea routes the merchant avoided being exploited by the tolls levied on land transport. Ships might also be organized in convoys and could carry a high degree of armed protection against pirates and attacks by enemy shipping. But the convoy, whether organized by groups of independent merchants or (as at Venice) under the minute supervision of the state, made for slowness. And at sea storms and contrary winds could paralyse movements for months at a time. Even in the Mediterranean it was not until the fourteenth century that Venetian convoys operated virtually all the year round.

How slow was commercial traffic? On land an unencumbered man on a tolerable horse, following a regular road without obstacles on it, could average something like fifteen miles in an hour and, with regular changes of horses, some remarkable performances were achieved: the 400-odd miles between Paris and Avignon were covered in four days in 1394 by a courier sent by Charles VI to anticipate the conclave; other feats were the two days and two hours taken from Barcelona to Valencia (220 miles) or the even more impressive achievement of Rome to Venice in a day and a half (360 miles)—an average speed of over eleven miles an hour. Edward IV in 1482 arranged relays of riders to cover the 200 miles between Newcastle and London in two days. But these were emergency journeys. The usual messenger did not ride by night; papal couriers in the fourteenth century covered in a day about sixty miles in good terrain and only half that in mountain areas. Merchants' letters were normally slower still. And all schedules were liable to be put out by illness, lack of horses, or the suspicion of the authorities through whose territories the messenger passed. Consequently even for urgent despatches the margin between prompt delivery and late delivery was

[1] For these figures see G. Luzzatto, *Storia economica d'Italia* (Rome, 1949), I, p. 311; Dollinger, *Hanse*, p. 195.

enormous. Late fifteenth-century Venetian information gives some of these margins:

	Maximum (days)	Minimum (days)
Venice to Augsburg	21	5
„ „ Florence	13	1
„ „ Genoa	15	2
„ „ Paris	34	7
„ „ Vienna	32	8

And the moment sea routes were also involved the uncertainty was even greater: Venice–London could take only nine days, or it could take over fifty.[1]

If this was the speed of news, and financial and other documents, the slowness of commodities in land transport can readily be imagined. A convoy with horses and mules might cover between fifteen and twenty miles a day. Packhorses took seventeen days to carry loads of wool from La Rochelle to Nîmes (375 miles); and even on a favourable network of canals and rivers the speed was no better. Goods came down the Rhône valley at about twenty-one or twenty-two miles a day. It was reckoned normal for barges to take about eighteen days to cover the distance between Milan and Venice, a journey which a fast boat could do in three days. At sea, while ships could make seventy-five to eighty miles in a day, they were usually able to steer straight for their destination only for very short periods and consequently even a fast boat seldom averaged as much. The voyage from Venice to Candia (Crete), which could be done in eighteen days in favourable conditions, normally took between twenty-three and thirty in summer, between forty-five and sixty in winter. From Lübeck to Bergen might take between nine days and twenty. Long voyages, such as those undertaken by Venetian fleets to Southampton and Bruges, or by the Hansa to Bourgneuf at the mouth of the Loire (for salt) were in any case always undertaken in convoy for security reasons and this, as we have noticed above, usually made for slow progress. A record voyage (1509) from Southampton to Otranto brought the Venetian Flemish galleys over the 2,500 miles in thirty-one days.[2]

[1] Y. Renouard in *L'histoire et ses méthodes*, ed. Samaran (Paris, 1961) pp. 112–14; P. Sardella quoted by F. Braudel, *La Méditerranée et le monde méditerranéen à l'époque de Philippe II* (Paris, 1949), p. 318; C. A. J. Armstrong, 'Distribution and speed of news at the time of the Wars of the Roses', *Studies in Medieval History Presented to F. M. Powicke* (Oxford, 1948), pp. 129–54.
[2] Lane, p. 16.

Local trade and local fairs

Economic historians have naturally concentrated their attention on the
great centres of trade and on the capitalist economy engendered by
long-distance commerce. One may guess that the greatest volume of
trafficking was to be found in the sum of exchanges in small and even in
tiny centres. The little towns which are sprinkled still over the Pennines,
the Massif Central, the Apennines were, for the most part, already there
in the later Middle Ages, in some cases not much smaller than they are
today. They and the only slightly larger settlements of the plains, were
the scene of local markets in which regional products were bought, sold
and bartered. Such places had no resident wholesalers and might not
even have a regular shop. Their needs were met by stalls put up once a
week, or less frequently, in the main street or the market place, to which
farmers of the region brought their surpluses; less frequently a fair for
sheep, cattle, horses would be held. That is not to say that commodities
of more distant origin never found their way to small towns. They did,
but in small quantities, and the trade resembled more that of the pedlar
than the merchant. Likewise buyers from bigger centres came to acquire
the specialities of the region at the seasonal fairs. The bulk of the business was, however, local products being exchanged by local people:
animals, locally-woven cheap cloth, the goods and services of small
craftsmen, smiths and carpenters above all. 'Throughout Italy towns
and their districts were commercially interdependent.'[1] Cloth and cattle
were the principal complementary services of town and country everywhere in Europe.

Sologne [an area south of Orleans on the Beuvron] does not export
cloth far afield: the wool there is too poor in quality and the cloth
not much regarded. Yet even there the peasants are carders and
weavers; many fulling mills are found along the streams. To this
activity should be added leather: tanning mills which pound the bark
of the oaks, tanneries, bootmakers and skinners in each village. The
covered market at Courmesnin, where only peasant customers came,
in 1455 held twenty-four stalls for drapers, sixteen for mercers and
ten for tanners. The fairs in Sologne, purely rural occasions where
local products only were disposed of, were held regularly three or
four times a year in the bigger villages, sometimes merely at cross-
roads: at Salbris, Brinon, La Ferté-Nabert, La Ferté-Hubert, La
Ferté-Avrain, Chapelle-d'Anguillon.[2]

[1] Lopez, p. 327.   [2] Heers, p. 125, from J. Guérin, La vie rurale, p. 99.

The picture was no different in other rural areas. Such modest enterprise was, of course, a source of excitement as well as a means of replenishing stores or selling stock for the dwellers in outlying hamlets and isolated farms. A visit to the small town might be an occasion not only of buying and selling but perhaps of going to church, certainly of meeting friends and relatives. And it furnished the broad basis of the total purchasing population. Professor Russell's figures suggest that the bulk of the population in England in the late fourteenth century lived in centres numbering between fifty and 200 souls.[1]

At any borderland where markedly different economic regions met more significant though still essentially local activity was found. This is particularly evident where moorland or mountain met the *plat pays*. The villagers in Wales or, to an even greater extent, in the Alps and the Pyrenees could not grow enough grain and bartered their cattle, dairy produce, timber and quarried stone with the villagers of the adjacent open country: from such activity was to spring the prosperity of Swiss towns like Basle, Zurich and Geneva, of Pamplona and Perpignan on the borders between France and Iberia, and dozens of smaller centres. Occasionally an isolated town, depending on local or seasonal commerce, could acquire great significance. Thus the shepherd fairs at Medina del Campo, on the route of the Mesta,[2] developed under Castilian royal patronage into the financial centre of the kingdom.

As soon as a town itself reached a certain size it had, of course, its own demands. The townsmen depended on the countrymen for food. The bigger the centre the more important became the importation of cereals, vegetables and wine, the more regular had to be the services provided for the consumer. University towns, cathedral cities, centres of government had relatively large populations. Wholesalers and retailers, craftsmen, lawyers, clergy, with servants, workmen, porters swelled the community. Such a market was permanent though its trade remained predominantly local. Indeed one effect of the multiplying tolls of the later Middle Ages, which have been referred to above, was to encourage the greatest possible dependence on the resources of the immediate region. Only towns on or near the sea could afford to import raw materials or manufactured goods from any distance. That such maritime centres did depend on the sea and comparatively distant sources of supply is vouched for by the very lively coastwise trade of small boats, not only in the Baltic and Mediterranean, but on the Atlantic seaboard. The small ports of Normandy, Brittany and the Basque country were

[1] *op. cit.*, pp. 308–9.　　　　　[2] Above, p. 39.

only on the margin of long-distance trade and derived their vitality from local demand.

The scattered and individually unimportant centres of commerce, however rudimentary in themselves, constituted a total volume of production and consumption which was undoubtedly influential in metropolitan trade. Much wine reached big towns from distant and unimportant vineyards, rather than through the organized trade from Bordeaux, La Rochelle, or the valleys of the Rhine and Rhône. Likewise local cloth from towns in Catalonia was exported to Italy, not in competition with the fine woollens of Flanders and Florence, but for a humbler market. The main sources for salt production were concentrated in a few areas, as we shall see, but salt made in many small places found its way into the main entrepôts. Likewise the consumption in villages and small towns of the articles of international commerce was minute in each particular centre. But in aggregate the demand for pepper, fine cloth, wine, was enormous and was satisfied by the dispersion of these goods through a multitude of small merchants.

Finally a few towns must be mentioned which had grown to a size which made them of the very greatest commercial importance although they were themselves not the scene of indigenous industry or of mercantile inventiveness. Paris and London were very big towns, augmented regularly by visitors drawn to the centre of administration and justice in a big kingdom. Rome, though it was for much of the fourteenth and fifteenth centuries in a sorry state, was an attraction for thousands of pilgrims, and, when the pope was in residence and especially at a time of jubilee, contained an enormous floating population. The pacemakers in commerce, the merchants and bankers serving the long distance trade (to which we must now turn), never neglected the possibilities, hazardous though they often proved, of these and similar centres.

Metropolitan and intercontinental trade

The 'grand commerce' of later medieval Europe was concerned with practically every available raw material and manufacture. In certain large regions, however, a few commodities were more actively exchanged; and some of these formed the staples of a truly continental system.

Within the Mediterranean the basic traffic as far as bulk was concerned was in grain. The large cities of north and central Italy were never able to sustain themselves with the cereals produced in the rural areas they controlled and had to import from the south of Italy, from Sicily, from

North Africa, from the Black Sea. Other basic materials of the region were olive oil, salt, wool and cloth, not only the fine cloth of Florence, but cheaper materials from Catalonia and Lombardy, the sweet wines of Cyprus and the Aegean, wax and hides from the Muslim states of Tlemcen and Tunis. Far surpassing these commodities in value were the goods imported by Italian and Catalan ships from the eastern Mediterranean, Asia Minor, North Africa and beyond: gold, spices, drugs, silk, small in bulk but high in price, and the bulkier loads of alum for the cloth industry. In return Italians exported cloth to Asia Minor and the Black Sea and (this in particular was a Venetian speciality) timber to North Africa and the Middle East.

· The Atlantic–North Sea area saw exchanges of wine from Bordeaux against grain from England. Wool from England was exported to Flanders; later English cloth penetrated the whole of the north. Salt from Portugal and above all from the Bay of Bourgneuf was shipped to all the main centres in the west. There was also very considerable trade in skins and in dairy produce in the North Sea region.

In the Baltic, where again there were towns which needed to import cereals, grain came increasingly from Prussia. Beer was exported from north Germany to Scandinavian countries in large quantities; from Sweden came iron and dairy produce. Above all the fishing grounds off the Scanian coast were the richest in herring, and the tall timber of Norway and Sweden furnished the shipyards of Lübeck and Danzig.

These are the maritime regions. Other parts of Europe, distant from the sea, produced major markets in the necessities and near necessities of life. In northern France and in southern Germany flax played the part of wool elsewhere, and linen cloth was widely worn. Saffron, used like pepper, was grown extensively in south-central France, in the valleys of the upper Rhine and Danube. Above all in Westphalia, in Saxony, and in Bohemia iron was found; copper and silver and a little gold came also from the mountains of the Balkans and the Tyrol.

Attention has always been given by economic historians to those products which moved in substantial quantities not only within these regions, but between them: wool from Spain and above all from England, which fed the looms of Flanders and Florence, and the resulting high-grade cloth, which was sold to the rich in every part of Europe; the wines of Gascony and Cyprus, which were traded everywhere; alum, which moved from the Near East to all centres producing cloth of quality, and the dyestuffs (pastel, madder, cochineal, woad) which were fixed by the alum; timber, hemp and tar, exported by Baltic countries to the Atlantic ports where ships were made; salt from the Bay and Lüneburg and the salted fish from Scania; metals from Spain, Scandinavia and central Europe; and the exotic produce of the Orient. Such materials were certainly responsible for the most striking advances of business technique, for they compelled adventurous men to new methods of financing economic activity.

No trade had been more stimulating in earlier centuries than that between Europe and the East. Compared with the exchanges of necessities touched on above the quantities involved were relatively small but their economic significance was as high as their intrinsic value. At the start of the fourteenth century commerce with Asia Minor, with the East Indies and with the Far East was channelled almost exclusively through Venice and Genoa, entrenched in the main entrepôts of the Middle East: Caffa in the Crimea and Tana on the sea of Azov tapped the resources of the south of Russia and formed one outlet for the overland routes to India and China; Trebizond, on the southern shore of the Black Sea, was a terminus for the caravans arriving from Persia; Alexandria was the Mediterranean port for the traffic from the East over the Indian Ocean and up the Red Sea. Genoa was more powerful in the Black Sea area and at Constantinople, and in the Aegean had the island of Chios as a base. Venice's predominance was above all in Alexandria, the Syrian ports and in the islands of Cyprus and Crete. Originally, and still in the early fourteenth century, this oriental trade was mainly significant for the importation of precious commodities: pepper, ginger, spices of all kinds, sugar and other drugs and recherché dyestuffs (like indigo), silk and cotton. In the course of the fourteenth and fifteenth centuries, however, the scene changed. The Mongol empire, which had enabled Italian merchants to travel personally to India and China, disintegrated. A new and aggressive Muslim power emerged, the Ottoman Turks who by the mid-fourteenth century were astraddle the Sea of Marmora and by 1453 had destroyed the Byzantine Empire. Genoese merchants were not evicted from Caffa till 1475, but in the fifteenth century their main activities were concentrated on Chios and consisted of importing alum, timber and Turkish cotton. Venice clung to her trade through Egypt and thus, at a high price, continued to monopolize the market in pepper and other spices. The two republics fought bitterly over this slowly diminishing trade.[1]

[1] Above, p. 172.

The commodities of long-distance trade

The above generalizations will be illustrated and qualified by a short consideration of some of the main commodities: the basic necessities of grain, salt, fish, timber and metals; the near-necessities of good cloth and wine; and the luxuries. One must also not forget the incessant traffic of human travellers. Something will be said later about the changing volume of trade in the period.

The existence of big towns, of long-standing in parts of the Mediterranean and more recent in the north of Europe, encouraged specialized production of grain. Much of this was grown in the areas near the big towns—in the home counties for London, in the Île de France for Paris. But much was also grown for relatively distant markets. Corn from Prussia was exported not only to countries bordering the Baltic but also to England and the Low Countries. Calabrian, Apulian and Sicilian cereals, which as we have seen were essential to the economy of Tuscany and Lombardy, were sometimes sent by sea to northern Europe, as they were for example during the great famine in 1317. Gascony, itself specializing in viticulture, depended on imported grain, mainly from England. As for cereals, those which travelled furthest and most frequently were wheat (in the Mediterranean and from English ports) and rye (exported from north Germany and Prussia).

Other foodstuffs should not be forgotten: butter, cheese and carcase meat were important, particularly where relatively rapid routes were open. But salt and salted fish were fundamental. Salt was needed for curing fish and meat, for making butter as well as for seasoning. Salt was produced in many parts of the continent in modest quantities. It could be made on any coast where fuel such as peat was available by evaporating sea water; and where there was peat which had absorbed sea water on the coast (as in Holland) this could itself be burned and the salt extracted by boiling the ashes. Some rock salt was mined. Much of the locally produced salt was foul and impure and could not compete with the finer product of the brine springs at Lüneburg or the naturally evaporated sea-salt made in the Bay of Bourgneuf, south of the estuary of the Loire. At Lüneburg, south of Lübeck, an important industry developed. The salt was sent by barge to Hamburg and Lübeck. Lüneburg salt was a basic source of Lübeck's wealth and continued to be important after the introduction into the Baltic of Bay salt, which began to be imported in significant quantities from the late fourteenth century. Bay salt was less refined than Lüneburg salt but it was cheaper, and by the fifteenth century it had come to play a dominant role in the economy of northern Europe. A Hansa convoy sailed each year to the Bay and by the end of the century English and Dutch ships were making the voyage on their own account.

The fishing grounds off the Scanian coast were the richest in Europe for herring, the best fish for preserving. The salt from Saxony or west France was used to cure the herrings which the Hansa bought from the Danish fishermen and subsequently exported through the Sound to England, the Low Countries, France, Spain and even occasionally into the Mediterranean; it was shipped east to Russia and overland into central and south Germany. The market where the salted herring was sold was at the south-west tip of Scania, at the southern end of the Sound, first at Skanör and then at Falsterbo. Here in early autumn a seasonal town was established with wooden shacks and stalls, in which each 'nation' rented its location, which was fenced off. The buying and selling of herring was the main activity, but it was also a general market. The Hansa towns, always dominant at Falsterbo, practically monopolized the scene by the end of the fifteenth century. Another product of northern waters which was traded generally was the dried cod (stockfish) of Norway, collected by Hansa merchants from Bergen.

Timber was important in both the south and north of Europe. In the Mediterranean proper, and especially in Italy, there was a chronic shortage of wood due to earlier and drastic deforestation—the work of men and their goats. Housebuilding and shipbuilding made incessant demands. Venice obtained wood for her ships from the Dolomites and Dalmatia; Genoa had to import from the foothills of the western Alps timber that had been floated down the Rhône; there was need to purchase timber from the Balkans, from the Aegean and, while the routes were open, from southern Russia by way of the Black Sea. Norwegian and Swedish timber, and later wood from Prussia and Russia, was manufactured into boats in the Hansa towns on the Baltic. Timber itself and articles manufactured from it, including boats, were also exported by Hansa shipwrights to English, Dutch and other customers who were their trade rivals; the Diet of the Hansa meeting at Lübeck in 1428 complained of this. Along with wood should be put the other products of the forest used in shipbuilding, especially pitch and tar, and the hemp which was grown in Estonia and Russia.

The rapid economic expansion of the thirteenth century had put a premium on metals, not only precious gold and silver, but iron, copper, lead and tin. By the fourteenth century international trade in these commodities had become essential, even in the case of iron which was, unlike the other ores, widely distributed in Europe. Copper and silver were mined in Saxony, the Harz mountains, the Vosges, Bohemia, Silesia and the Balkans; gold (though in small quantities) in Bohemia and Hungary. Lead ore and silver often went together, but English lead was a major export of the country and so was tin from Cornwall; bronze, an alloy of copper and tin, ensured demand for the latter. The main regions exporting iron were Styria and Carinthia, Spain and Sweden (where copper was also mined). All these mining areas had sufficient supplies of wood to smelt locally and the metal was exported in ingots or manufactured articles. By the second half of the fifteenth century another metal had joined the international trade; brass (copper and calamine) had been manufactured in the ancient world; it was once more made after calamine had been discovered in the west and south of Germany. Two other metals were also exported. Coal was mined in northern England and shipped not only to the south of the country ('sea-coal') but also to the Low Countries and France. Alum was needed in cloth manufacture. For long it had been mainly obtained from the Genoese possession of Phocaea (on the coast north-west of Smyrna) and from the interior of Turkey. In 1462 deposits were discovered at Tolfa in the Papal States. Pius II and later popes tried to place an embargo on all other sources of supply, but the importance of the Tolfa mines was assured rather by the deteriorating political situation in the eastern Mediterranean. Gold and silver had functions different from those of the base metals. There was a chronic shortage of both, but particularly of gold, all the more acute since by this time France, England and other countries had, like the Italian principalities, a gold as well as a silver coinage. We may note that considerable quantities of gold were brought across the Sahara to North African ports, secured through the 'silent trade', so-called because the barter took place at desert rendezvous where the parties did not actually meet. In the second half of the fifteenth century gold was also brought into Lisbon by Portuguese mariners sailing back from the Atlantic coast of Africa.

Cloth of all kinds was traded during this period: canvas (made from hemp) from the east of the Baltic and from northern France; linen cloth of various grades (the very best was latterly the only fabric with a market in the Far East); silk and cotton were beginning by the mid-fifteenth century to be produced in Sicily and southern Italy as well as imported through the Levant. But the international trade *par excellence* was in wool and woollen cloth, especially the very finest qualities. These were still made on a major scale at the start of the fourteenth century in two main areas: the Flemish towns, notably Bruges, Ghent and Ypres, and in many towns of north and central Italy, but above all in Florence, where there was also a very active trade in finishing cloth woven in Flanders. The raw material used in this manufacture came mainly from English sheep, especially those pastured in the moors of Yorkshire and the marshes of East Anglia, and from Spain; the main agents for supplying the Flemish as well as the Italian market were Italian merchants. In the course of the fourteenth century the pattern changed:[1] in the north cloth production shifted from Flanders to Brabant and above all to England, whose exports of wool declined but whose exports of cloth steadily rose, both of broadcloth and the lighter worsteds which had a wide distribution especially in northern Europe. These changes made for rerouting of the mordants, the alum and potash (largely made in the forests of the Baltic region), and the colouring materials, woad, madder, kermes (red), and so on, needed to finish the cloth.

The majority of simple people in this period were clothed in homespun cloth and they also normally drank local water or locally brewed ale or beer, save in the grape-growing areas where wine was cheap. It seems clear that, beginning in the towns, consumption of wine was becoming general among peasants in France in the later fourteenth century. Wine was extraordinarily widely distributed in the Middle Ages: the vine had been cultivated even in unlikely northern areas until the specialization of certain great regions enabled them to supply a higher grade product wherever it was needed. By the end of the thirteenth century this specialization had brought great prosperity to Gascony, Poitou, the Rhine area, Burgundy and the Rhône valley; though there was lively trade in wines in the Mediterranean area the bulk of wine consumed there was (as it still is) produced near at hand. Very large quantities of wine were involved in the export trade. Bordeaux exported about 25 million gallons in one year early in the fourteenth century. Figures are not available for the export of Rhine wine, largely controlled by the merchants of Cologne, but it was widely consumed in the Baltic, in England and Scotland, and formed an important commodity in Hanseatic operations.

As for the trade in obvious luxuries little need be said. The precious stuffs from the east found their way into every rich household, and so did the specialities of various European regions: amber and furs from

[1] Below, p. 389.

the countries bordering on the Baltic; *objets d'art* such as paintings from Flanders, embroidery from England, enamels from Limoges; manuscript books for church, boudoir or library; fine armour and weapons from Milan and glass from Venice.

One final aspect of international exchange must be mentioned in conclusion: the traffic in men. Granted the difficulties in transport the volume of travellers is astonishing. Many men moved great distances because of their jobs: clergy visiting the papal curia at Avignon, Florence or Rome; students going to the great universities like Paris and Bologna; soldiers looking for a paymaster; masons making for the site of a new building; Italian, German and other merchants; the galloping messengers of bankers, kings and town councils and the stately cavalcades taking high-ranking ambassadors from one court to another. In addition to these professional travellers, however, there were two other groups who augmented the traffic on certain routes—the pilgrims and the slaves. Pilgrimage now was perhaps more regular among the well-to-do, for whom it combined the pleasures of travel with the demands of devotion. It is nevertheless found among all groups in the community, even the humblest. Much pilgrimage was undertaken to local shrines, as the northern Frenchman visited Mont Saint Michel, or the midland and southern English the tomb of St Thomas of Canterbury, or the north Germans Aachen. But foreigners came to these centres as well as natives, and the holiest places, St James of Compostella, Rome and the Holy Land, attracted thousands of pilgrims. The routes were exploited by ship masters, innkeepers and couriers. Conditions in ships making for Spain or Syria were often indescribably sordid. But the ancient association of poverty, misery and pilgrimage died hard and men were prepared to undergo the rigours of long days walking or riding, or unpredictably long and dangerous voyages across the Bay of Biscay or the Mediterranean for the excitement of seeing new lands and the sensation of a concrete contact with their faith.

Slaves voyaged, we must suppose, against their will. This was a trade mainly confined at this time to the Mediterranean.[1] Italian merchants bought slaves in the Crimea from Tatar traders and sold them, not only in Muslim Alexandria (where men were needed as soldiers), but to purchasers in Italian and Spanish towns who were mostly interested in female slaves for domestic work. The Moors of Spain were widely traded in. Other sources were the peoples of the Balkans and Negroes from Guinea. At Genoa, whose merchants for long had

[1] Above, p. 75.

the biggest share in this commerce, it has been estimated that the number of slaves was over 7,000—perhaps over 10,000—in 1380, a time when the total population of the city was between 80,000 and 100,000.[1]

Commercial techniques

The economy of Europe was given a considerable degree of unity by the exchange of commodities briefly described above. It was almost united also by the penetration of Italian merchants and Italian commercial techniques: almost but not quite, for even by the end of the fifteenth century one must distinguish a region in the north of the continent where Italian practices had not yet taken root.

The remarkable advances of Italian commerce and banking belong to an earlier period. By 1300 the main lines had been established. There were, it is true, striking differences between the economic activity of the three main towns, Florence, Genoa and Venice, differences which are reflected for a time in a kind of geographical partition of international trade: in the early fourteenth century Venice was mainly concerned with trade in the eastern Mediterranean, Genoa with the Black Sea and the Crimea, Florence with northern Europe. But in each centre the organization of business tended towards a resident non-travelling capitalist, and agents in foreign countries. This had already happened in the inland cities and especially in Tuscany and in Florence, which had now completely out-distanced its rivals, Siena, Lucca and Pisa. The characteristic form of Florentine enterprise was the company.

The Florentine company was a family affair. A small group of members of a family, together with a few associates, invested money in a company (*societas*). The capital thus obtained was augmented by the acceptance of investments from others, as well as additional investments from the partners and the agents of the company. Such a company was wound up after a few years and profits and losses were distributed to its members in proportion to their share in the capital. It was then re-formed with the same or similar membership. The funds obtained from share capital and loan capital were deployed in a vast number of particular activities—trading in all manner of commodities, transfer of money from one centre to another, banking. Management lay with the senior partner, who controlled the small headquarters staff and directed the operations of factors in distant markets, in some of which permanent agents were maintained. In the fifteenth century, while factors and correspondents were still used in smaller centres, the big Florentine

[1] Heers, p. 300, n. 3.

companies had started to form subsidiary companies in the most important foreign towns. The parent body in Florence became a kind of holding company. By this time the number of Florentine *societates* was smaller than it had been a century earlier. Then a large number of firms are found: Spini, Cerchi, Frescobaldi, Bardi, Acciaiuoli, Peruzzi and others. These had mostly been overtaken by disaster by the mid-fourteenth century. This was due partly to the general recession but also to improvident management: when the Peruzzi and Bardi companies went bankrupt (1343, 1346) they had lent out, in large part to unreliable borrowers like Edward III, no less than fourteen times their share capital. By the end of the fourteenth century the restricted wealth of Florence was concentrated in fewer hands and by the mid-fifteenth the Medici out-distanced all other rivals, including the Strozzi and the Pazzi. At this stage, in the last years of the prudent management of Cosimo de' Medici, the company's enterprises may be tabulated as follows:[1]

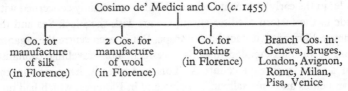

Cosimo de' Medici and Co. (*c.* 1455)

| Co. for manufacture of silk (in Florence) | 2 Cos. for manufacture of wool (in Florence) | Co. for banking (in Florence) | Branch Cos. in: Geneva, Bruges, London, Avignon, Rome, Milan, Pisa, Venice |

The Florentine companies trafficked in all commodities, but were, of course, particularly concerned with supplying the materials for the cloth industry of the city (wool, cloth, silk, dyes and chemicals) and exporting the finished product; the Medici also managed the Tolfa alum mines from 1466 to 1476. On the banking side they accepted deposits, which earned interest (6–10 per cent), and made loans. Interest charged on loans in Florence itself varied between 7 and 15 per cent; the riskier loans abroad were liable to much higher rates, 33 per cent or more. There was also profit to be had on transferring credits from one centre to another and this was an essential function of the Italian merchant, not only to effect payment for goods bought and sold but also to facilitate other money being transported: papal taxation, for instance, needed papal bankers if it was to reach its destination. This business was in the hands of a succession of Florentine houses while the papacy was at Avignon; later it was more or less a Medici monopoly until 1474.

Conditions were different in the great maritime towns of Venice and

[1] Adapted from R. de Roover, *Medici Bank*, p. 83.

Genoa. At the start of the fourteenth century partnerships tended to be limited to one voyage, the sedentary capitalist providing the funds and the travelling merchant providing the enterprise: profits were shared, with about three-quarters normally going to the capitalist. These were *commenda* contracts which gave way by the fifteenth century to contracts lasting for a period of years. The Venetian merchant now employed agents at the port of destination (sometimes members of his family) who sold exports and bought imports on a commission basis. At Genoa companies developed which, unlike those at Florence which engaged in banking, exchange and general trade, were devoted to the exploitation of a precise monopoly: taxes at Genoa were farmed by such a company; others controlled the salt trade over the Appenines, Tunisian coral, Castilian mercury and so forth.[1] Shares in these companies, which were not dominated by any one family, were freely bought and sold.

Two technical developments greatly aided the development of Italian business. During the thirteenth century there was a gradual adoption (beginning in Pisa) of arabic instead of roman numerals. The nine digits and the zero were infinitely easier to manipulate than the clumsy roman letters. In the early fourteenth century book-keeping by double entry is found: it used to be considered that this was devised first at Genoa, though claims were made also for other centres. The most authoritative view is that 'double entry developed almost simultaneously in several Italian trading centres'.[2] In any event it was a practice which speeded up business and made it possible for a merchant to tell at a glance exactly what his financial position was at any moment; it was also used as a means of control, especially in the work of branches and agencies. Professor R. de Roover points out that such an innovation was encouraged by partnership agreements (the company), by agencies in other towns and also by the credit facilities which merchants provided.

The use of credit was most extensive in banking, the feature of Italian mercantile practice which was perhaps to have the profoundest long-term consequences. The merchant banker accepted deposits, made loans and transferred funds from the account of one man on his books to the account of a second, from one client to the client of another banker, from one town to another. Here again the Florentine banks were setting

---

[1] Heers, p. 187.
[2] R. de Roover, 'Development of Accounting prior to Luca Pacioli' in *Studies in the History of Accounting*, ed. A. C. Littleton and B. S. Yamey (London, 1956), p. 115.

the pace and in particular were demonstrating the advantages of dealing in ledger settlement of debts to the northern towns where they had agents and where local money changers developed into local banks. In Bruges by the early fifteenth century there was hardly a trader or businessman of substance who did not have a bank account and who did not settle his debts by what were in effect paper transactions. The currency used in accounts was always a stable one; the problem of handling and evaluating actual coins was avoided; the effects of the perpetual shortage of specie were minimized. The operation, which at first needed the presence of the two parties, creditor and debtor, was soon conducted by written instructions, very similar to the later cheque; by the second half of the fifteenth century such a document could be endorsed by the payee in favour of a third party. These procedures clearly facilitated lending, and they were probably encouraged by the desire to avoid the sin of usury.[1] As we have seen, the Florentine merchant banks undertook massive credit transactions. In Venice the banks avoided loans to non-Venetians and functioned essentially as an adjunct to Venetian mercantile activity. Credit for small folk was also regularized at this time by increasingly stringent control over the pawnshop business by governments everywhere; in Flanders, like the rest of the north, princes and great men also raised funds from pawnbrokers. First in Italy and soon in other parts of Europe towns established official pawnbroking in *monts de piété*. Finally we should observe the emergence of institutions analogous to public banks, as opposed to the private or merchant banks. One of the first and most important of these was the *Casa di San Giorgio* at Genoa, in the early years of the fifteenth century.

The letter of exchange was used by merchants, travellers, and especially pilgrims, as a way of making money available at a distance without the risk of physically carrying it. Depending as it did ultimately on the widespread exchange of commodities, the extraordinary diffusion of the letter of exchange is good evidence of the international character of contemporary commerce. Merchants and others frequently needed to remit in this way to correspondents at a distance, with bills maturing at a given time (fixed by convention and known as 'usance'). Since these were settled in the local currency every such transaction became a slight gamble and very soon bills of exchange were being transferred without any intention of settling real debts but as a way of having a flutter in foreign currency. From this it was a logical step to using the form of these procedures, in which the element of risk made the element of

[1] Below, p. 392.

interest tolerable to the Church, for concealing usurious loans: the borrower bought his loan in one currency and repaid it later in another currency; the different exchange rates gave the lender his profit. This was known as 'dry exchange'. Thus the extensive use of bills of exchange whether for settlement of distant debts, for playing the money market, or for concealing loans at interest, was also (like the banking arrangements already referred to) a source of paper money. It is also easy to see why the merchants of the main centres—Florence, Barcelona, Bruges—needed rapid and sound news and safe, speedy, couriers.

One other technical innovation of the merchants of the later Middle Ages also deserves mention: insurance of goods in transit. The dangers of robbers, pirates and of rapacious governments, of storm at sea and fire on land, made transport a precarious affair. The trader tried to minimize risks by spreading his consignment between different convoys and different ships. But he also began to insure, especially for sea transit. The earliest surviving contracts are found in Palermo in 1350; by the fifteenth century the bigger Mediterranean ports had regular brokers and underwriters. Premiums were high for goods ventured in a round ship (*nave*), but low on the more reliable merchant galley; some Venetian merchants regarded the galley as so safe that they did not insure goods sent in this way. Commercial insurance was not developed in the north until the sixteenth century.

The north of Europe was, in general, less adapted to rapid commercial evolution than the Mediterranean. The typical merchant in Italy operated either on his own behalf, or in a company restricted largely to the family and a few associates. Even the biggest Florentine companies rarely employed more than a total of sixty or seventy men, including the partners, branch managers and staff. North of the Alps the goods traded were bulky and offered little opportunity for the making of dramatic fortunes. The typical merchant dealing in long distance trade was a member of an association of similarly occupied men, who did not depend for their success on their individual possession of capital but on a pooling of active resources. In the fourteenth century such an association was the German Hansa, and in the fifteenth the Merchant Venturers of England. These were indeed 'companies', but very different from those based on Venice or Florence with whom they did business in London or Bruges.

The Hanseatic League of towns had grown up in the thirteenth century to exercise a leadership in the Baltic and North Sea[1] which was

[1] Above, p. 122.

not merely economic but also political. Over the centuries it secured for the merchants of Lübeck, Hamburg and the other towns and districts which were members, privileged trading rights in the countries where they did business; at Bergen, London (the Steelyard), and Novgorod they had their own *enceintes*, operated their own law (in internal disputes) and had privileges in litigation with natives. They obtained rights benefiting their members by securing local debts, by covering wrecked ships, and above all through fiscal benefits. These last were especially notable in England; general privileges were most extensive in Flanders, as Hansa envoys told the English in 1386. On the basis of these protective rights the Hanseatic merchant enjoyed a favourable position in the northern countries with which he traded. Nor did he lack the advantages of collaboration. The merchant gilds of Hanseatic towns acted in the interests of their members; there were companies or gilds of men engaged in trade with particular areas—the Cologne merchants trading with England were protected by a town statute in 1324; at Lübeck the biggest association of this kind was the merchants trading in Scania (the *Schonenfahrer*); in the fifteenth century there were about ten regional groups of this kind at Lübeck and *Schonenfahrer* companies are found in eight Hanseatic towns. This is, of course, very different from the advanced company which had emerged in Italy, long-lasting, binding its associates to exclusive concern with the activities of the firm, disposing of very large amounts of capital and controlling its agents by up-to-date business methods. Nevertheless the Hanseatic merchant was employing considerable funds, and he formed temporary associations with others, often on a credit basis (guaranteed by the authority of the towns, which by 1300 had opened public registers for such transactions), although membership of such a company did not exclude a multiplicity of other similar engagements. And if he did not have branches like Italian merchant bankers, the larger and even the medium north German merchant was by the mid-fourteenth century essentially sedentary, using the offices of a factor at the foreign market.

By the start of the fourteenth century the German Hansa had all but completely monopolized the wool and cloth trade between England and Flanders, which had earlier been carried on by Flemish enterprise in the Hansa of the Seventeen Towns. But the dominant position of the German Hansa was to be challenged by English groups. For reasons which were political, not economic, English kings, and especially Edward III, heavily taxed the export of wool.[1] This involved canalizing

[1] Above, p. 130.

exports in order to control them and thus led to the fixing of markets at staple towns; by the end of the fourteenth century the English staple was at Calais. Another commercial result followed from the king's desire to anticipate his revenue from wool taxation. This he had done earlier by borrowing from Italians, who were ruined in the process. To raise comparable sums from English merchants meant negotiating with ever larger groups of them and by the 1360s it was the larger English wool merchants as a whole, the Merchants of the Staple, who gave the loans in return for a monopoly of the export trade, with the customs (which the company of the Staple farmed from the Crown) as security. Here again we have an example of the northern merchant combining in forms very different from the Italian companies, getting from public authority corporate privileges which left individuals free to organize their enterprise alone or in temporary association with others. The same is true of the later development of the Merchant Adventurers. This began as a group of merchants trading to the Low Countries, chartered in 1407 along with other groups trading to Norway and the Baltic which were incorporated at about the same time. In the event the companies trading with Norway and the Baltic never prospered and by the second half of the century the Company of Merchants Adventuring to the Low Countries came to be termed the Company of Merchant Adventurers *tout court*. The Merchant Venturers trafficked mainly in cloth and their members were predominantly the wholesalers of London.

Outside the Mediterranean there is in fact only one area where commercial enterprise assumed forms which suggest Italian models. This was in southern Germany and in the second half of the fifteenth century. In Rhenish towns like Basle and St Gall but especially in the towns in the basin of the upper Danube, Ulm, Nuremberg, Augsburg, Vienna, merchants emerged well able to employ Italian techniques of credit and exchange. The Great Company of the small town of Ravensburg had sixteen branches in Germany and abroad as well as agents elsewhere. Linen was one of the main commodities of this region. When silver mining was resumed on a bigger scale at the end of the century it provided the fortunes of new dynasties of capitalists, of whom the Fuggers and Welsers of Augsburg are the most striking. In 1487 Jacob Fugger was able to advance 23,600 florins to Archduke Sigismund of Austria followed by 150,000 in 1488. The establishment of long-lived commercial, industrial and banking houses like these puts into perspective the fugitive importance of individual merchants elsewhere in the north such as the brothers, William and Richard de la Pole in mid-fourteenth-century Hull or even Jacques Coeur (d. 1456), whose great house at Bourges survives as a reminder of his multiplicity of trading interests.

The Italian merchant was acquiring rural property at this time; it was often a surer investment than commerce in this period of recession. In the north businessmen also bought land, which was the only way of salting down funds. But possession of landed property in the north tended to drag a family into county society and continued concern for the counting house among the descendants of the successful founder of a firm revealed a pertinacity which was as yet rare.

Industrial activity

A further reason why the rich businessman's son was not impelled to follow his father's path to prosperity was the relative absence of anything comparable to modern industrial plant and equipment; the medieval manufacturer did not bequeath a factory to his family. The volume of manufactured goods which was traded from one end of Europe to the other was impressively great. But the goods that were bought and sold were made without exception by very small producers. The only big industrial enterprise, the Arsenal at Venice is, as we shall see, no exception to this rule, and the ships it made were the property of the Republic. Many of the most sought after manufactures were obviously the product of craftsmen: jewellery and the fine work of Italian goldsmiths; illuminated manuscripts or indeed manuscript books of any kind; the glass of Murano (of which mirrors were perhaps the most famous speciality at this time); the armour of the mounted soldier from Milan or Augsburg, tailormade to suit the customer. This does not mean, of course, that quantity production could not be achieved. We are told that between February and October 1380 the Venetian ambassador at Milan bought there thousands of sets of armour for his compatriots in the war against Genoa—at a time when the Visconti lords were also buying much equipment—and in 1427 two Milanese armourers responded to an urgent order by supplying in a few days the equipment for 4,000 horsemen and 200 infantrymen. In the case of the Milanese armourers we may be sure that the order was supplied partly from stock (it was safe business manufacturing armour and weapons in *quattrocento* Italy) and partly through sub-contracting the work to other masters; it was not achieved by new technical methods. But these could be developed in response to pressure. The continued urgent demand for books led to the invention of printing.[1]

[1] Above, pp. 356-8.

The almost universal unit of production was a small shop in which a master worked with one or two assistants—subordinate masters or journeymen (who had passed their apprenticeship), one or two apprentices and a man or boy or two to fetch and carry. This was even the case in the manufacture of woollen cloth at the main centres of the industry. In the early decades of the fourteenth century the Florentine chronicler Giovanni Villani reckoned that between 80,000 and 100,000 pieces of cloth were produced in the city annually, some 30,000 Florentines depending on the industry. Yet this cloth, though handled wholesale by relatively few merchants in the wealthy guild of the Calimala, was produced in a myriad of decentralized and minute enterprises. Villani estimated that there were 200 wool manufacturers (the masters being members of the wool guild, the *arte della lana*). But in fact such enterprises were usually engaged in what would now be regarded as managerial functions; the complicated work was done on the 'putting out system'—the workers worked mainly at home and owned their own simple tools. A summary of Professor de Roover's lucid account[1] will clarify the position.

1. *Preparing the wool.* The sorting and preparing of the wool were the only part of the entire process mainly done in the wool manufacturers' own premises, though even in these stages the highly trained sorter used to work for several masters and the wool was put out to be washed by separate small masters.

2. *Spinning.* This was done by countrywomen (either on the distaff or the spinning wheel), a subcontractor being responsible for delivering the wool and collecting the yarn.

3. *Warping and weaving.* These operations were performed in the houses of workers in Florence; a big firm might employ ten looms; some of the weavers were themselves small masters. Weavers were paid on piece-rates.

4. *Finishing.* Fulling (a process of beating and cleaning with fuller's earth) then followed and was undertaken by small masters who operated water driven mills on the valley streams in the vicinity of Florence. Tentering or stretching the cloth was the next operation. The tenterers rented their expensive equipment (and the halls it was kept in) from the wool guild. The remaining finishing processes— four different processes were involved—were conducted at home. Payment, as for weaving, was by the piece.

[1] *Medici Bank*, pp. 176–81. Some excellent illustrations of many of the processes in Miss Carus Wilson's chapter in *Cambridge Economic History*, II, plates II–IV.

5. *Dyeing*. This could be done in the wool, in the yarn or after the cloth was woven. Dyers were separate masters and worked for a variety of cloth manufacturers; in order to safeguard quality the latter often provided the dye-stuffs.

It will be seen that the cloth manufacturer was essentially an entrepreneur dealing largely with other masters, less wealthy than he was and less important (both in management skill and social prestige) but essentially independent. There was, in short, no vertical structure. When a big merchant and banking firm like the Medici controlled two cloth firms and one silk firm it was simply to get the profits of enterprises which were themselves conducted as to the bulk of their activities by large numbers of other individual small enterprises and isolated workers whose dependence on the firm was basically casual. In the great centres of Flanders, where an even larger proportion of the population, perhaps as much as 50 per cent, was directly employed in cloth manufacture, the picture is in essence no different, though the technical processes seem to have been in certain respects more advanced. There too the 'manufacturer' provided a host of other master craftsmen with the raw material and marketed the finished cloth. In the fourteenth and fifteenth centuries cloth manufacture gravitated more and more to the country and away from the town. The most remarkable example of this was England. But in the rural cloth industry, though the entrepreneur (such as the English clothier) was a capitalist, production was if anything organized in even smaller units than it had been in the towns of Flanders and Italy.

What has been said above with regard to the manufacture of woollen cloth applies equally to other textiles—silk and linen—made for the international market. It also applies to other industrial production which depended on imported raw materials, such as the copper-beaters at Dinant, as well as to manufacture for export based essentially on local materials, for example salt. At the Hanseatic town of Lüneburg, where some 60,000 metric tons of salt were produced from the brine springs in 1350, production was in a large number of small units—a master salter, an assistant and a furnace-boy; in fact Lübeck merchants came to own most of these installations. In mining and metallurgy small 'manorial' enterprises of four or five workers produced iron, copper, silver and coal, often at first on a cooperative basis; later, when more machinery was needed to exploit deeper seams and new processes, capitalist merchants sometimes managed larger units, though those employing more than thirty workers were rare. At Tolfa, where the alum discovered in 1460 was extracted on a large scale under licence from the popes, it is likely that only about eighty men were at work.

The largest industrial undertaking of the period was undoubtedly the Arsenal at Venice where, under state management, ships were built for the Republic. The growth of this activity is shown by the extension of the area of the Arsenal: quadrupled in the first quarter of the fourteenth century, the resulting space was practically doubled again in a further extension which was begun in 1476. Taken together, the basins, dry docks, great sheds and storehouses covered about sixty acres by 1500. The control of the entire site and its operations was vested in the Lords and Commissioners of the Arsenal, who were responsible to the superior bodies of the Senate, Great Council and the Dieci.[1] Under the Lords and Commissioners the admiral acted as a kind of general director, and under him each of the main crafts was managed by a foreman—carpenters, caulkers, mast-makers and oar-makers. All of these officials were salaried and housed by the state. The hundreds of workers employed were masters in their own right and members of the craft guilds, who worked extensively for themselves and for private shipbuilders as well as for the state. Wages in the Arsenal were in general lower than outside, but the work there was steadier and eagerly sought for in times of depression; from 1400 the carpenters had the right to work in the Arsenal. In the Arsenal were made the war galleys needed for defence (normally ten in service and ten in reserve) and also the great galleys (about twenty in the fifteenth century) leased by the state to merchants; this involved the completion of two light galleys and four or five great galleys each year. The most interesting aspects of this Venetian enterprise were the careful specialization of the site itself, which was particularly adapted to the launching, equipping and arming of the reserve fleet in a matter of hours; and the curiosity that here we are not faced with a capitalist development, for the Arsenal was financed by appropriations from the government, even if it was hoped that it might help to pay its way. Nor must the magnitude of this state shipbuilding be exaggerated. The bulk of the merchant fleet of Venice was privately built and privately owned, even if it operated on long voyages and in time of war under stringent rules laid down by the signory.

Private shipbuilding at Venice was normally financed by a company, a group of merchants who shared the cost of production and owned the resulting vessel in predetermined parts. This is found in other maritime

[1] Above, p. 120.

cities of Italy, in the Baltic towns where ships were made (the largest centres were Lübeck and Danzig) and indeed generally. It was attractive to the capitalist merchant for it enabled him to spread the risk both of construction and of trafficking with other merchants and with the investing public. But the shipbuilder himself was a small man—a master carpenter employing other masters in his own and the other necessary trades. It should, however, be added that little is known about the industry in northern Europe in this period.

One other kind of undertaking involved developments which are comparable to the state shipbuilding at the Arsenal: large-scale building operations. A great royal castle, a cathedral, even the elaborate villas of the Italian patricians or the châteaux which were beginning to rise in the Loire valley, meant assembling and controlling large numbers of craftsmen. The ambitious churches of the later Middle Ages, such as the cathedrals at Milan or Siena, grandiose and extremely expensive, were being built for decades on end, for centuries; a strategic castle, rushed up in a shorter period, presented its own problems. Here again the work was done by masters, carpenters and above all masons, who migrated to employment and who were organized by a master mason, often effectively the architect of the building, and a financial and administrative officer who was appointed by the employer, the prince, lord, town, college or chapter of the cathedral or monastery. Hundreds of workmen were involved in the bigger buildings. The corporate spirit of the skilled masons, frequently on the move but associated in 'lodges' while on the job, produced not only high standards of workmanship, but an internal cameraderie which gave their craft an international colour unlike that found in any other medieval guild. In the permanent cadres maintained by kings, such as the English office of works, an organization existed which suggests the administrative arrangements for the Arsenal. The English government is known to have spent at least £93,346 pounds on its Welsh castles between 1277 and 1339; at Harlech in mid-July of 1286 the work force totalled 944 men.[1] The building trade, at any rate that part of it working for governments and great corporations, perhaps resembles more closely its medieval predecessors than any other large-scale modern enterprise.

[1] See the extremely valuable *History of the King's Works, The Middle Ages*, by R. Allen Brown, H. M. Colvin and A. J. Taylor, 2 vols. (London, 1963), esp. pp. 1027–30.

Trends in European commerce in the later Middle Ages

The commercial activity briefly sketched in previous pages was less in volume, though in certain ways more sophisticated in technique, than it had been in the thirteenth century. The overall economic decline, touched on when demographic movement was discussed (above, pp. 31–34), naturally affected trade by reducing production and reducing consumer demand. In modern parlance the thirteenth century had been a period of economic boom; the fourteenth and fifteenth centuries endured a prolonged slump. There are, of course, exceptions to this generalization and it is perhaps fair to add that there are signs of marked recovery before 1500 in many parts of the continent. Yet the truth of the decline may be demonstrated in a number of ways.

The fiscal policy of governments has left a good many indications of the way things were moving.[1] The English customs accounts, for example, suggest that the wine imported annually from Gascony dropped from over 20,000 tuns at the start of the fourteenth century to about 6,000 tuns at the end and in the fifteenth century fluctuated around that figure. This, of course, could be, and to some extent was, due to other factors—changing habits, the importation of other wines, the consumption of beer made from hops, which begins at this time—as well as to the peculiar conditions of war which interrupted trade; nor did it necessarily involve a proportionate decline in wine production in Gascony for the wine was consumed elsewhere in France and in northern Europe. But the same decline is found in English wool and cloth exports: the former fell drastically in the early fourteenth century and continued to fall thereafter; cloth exports rose but not to an equivalent amount, and it seems difficult to explain this development in terms of changed fashions in clothes (from wool to linen and cotton).

No comparable series of customs figures are available for long periods for other parts of Europe and, if they were, they would be subject to qualification, as are the English, on two important grounds: they ignore local consumption and they ignore smuggling which certainly took place on a large scale. Other evidence is, however, in line with a contracting

[1] It is fair to remind the reader that the views here expressed have been challenged by some historians. Recent statements will be found in *Economic History Review*, new ser., 14 (1962) by R. S. Lopez and H. A. Miskimin; 16 (1964) by C. M. Cipolla, with replies by Lopez and Miskimin. The validity of English customs accounts has also been called into question. A convincing reply to such criticism is provided by E. M. Carus Wilson and Olive Coleman, *England's Export Trade 1275–1547* (Oxford, 1963), pp. 201–7.

economy. Florentine bankruptcies in the first half of the fourteenth century are paralleled by similar troubles in Florence at the end of the fifteenth century. The chronicler Villani tells us that production of cloth had dropped in the first quarter of the fourteenth century from 100,000 pieces a year to 70,000 or 80,000 and in 1378 the Ciompi demanded an annual production of 24,000, presumably more than had been produced in the years just before the revolt. In any case there seems no doubt about the drop in population and the fall in agricultural output, which has been discussed earlier.[1] A general decline does not, of course, prevent some regions prospering, as Genoa seems to have done in the mid-fifteenth century. Nor does it mean that all commodities were equally involved, for it seems certain that salt production in the Bay of Bourgneuf rose steadily in these centuries, and iron production did not decline like silver. Even in a shrinking economy fortunes could be made; though it may be felt that the total riches of Florence was smaller in the early fifteenth century than it had been a hundred years before, a few merchants were probably richer than any of their predecessors.

Part of the debate over this question has been provoked by the uneven nature of recovery as and when that took place. If commercial uncertainties made Florentine and Milanese merchants less inclined to put their money into trade and more eager to buy property in the countryside, this brought much needed capital to the rural areas of Lombardy and Tuscany, helping to turn the drop in population into a rise. Already by the end of the fifteenth century there is growing commercial activity in South Germany, where a new race of great capitalists was arising. If the Hansa was in decline after 1400, Dutch shipping was becoming more enterprising, and so was the shipping of Portugal and Castile.

With the wisdom of hindsight it is possible to discern by the end of this period the beginnings of a shift from the Mediterranean as a focal point of business to the Atlantic seaboard. This had certainly not happened by 1500. The collapse of the Mongol empire in Asia and the rise of the Ottoman Turk in the Levant had, it is true, made for significant changes in Venetian and Genoese commerce. The Genoese still concentrated on the Black Sea and Aegean but traded in the products of these areas (notably alum) and not in the commodities of the Far East. The Venetian convoys now made not for the Black Sea but for Beirut and Alexandria, but they maintained their monopoly in pepper and spices; even after the Portuguese had begun sailing direct to the East it was well into the sixteenth century before Lisbon rivalled Venice as

[1] Above, pp. 31–5.

a market for oriental goods. Italian adaptability was also displayed in other ways. The western Mediterranean to some extent supplied what had once come from the Aegean and Asia Minor. Silk came from Granada, Valencia and Calabria; sugar from southern Spain, Sicily, North Africa and Madeira; and from the same regions came dried and fresh fruits.

In the north the Hansa did not succeed, as the merchants of Genoa and Venice had done, in changing to new routes. There the story is rather of the development of Dutch and English maritime activity at the expense of the Germans in the Baltic. This is seen in the penetration of the Baltic by rival ships (in 1426 the Hanse formally but ineffectually prohibited the sale of ships to merchants outside the League). Dutch and English ships not only trafficked in the ports of the Baltic, they also challenged Hansa merchants at Bergen, in the Bay of Bourgneuf and at Lisbon. The herring fisheries of the North Sea became more important in the fifteenth century to the advantage of Scotland, Holland and England and thus intensified the decline of the Scanian fishing grounds. Cloth manufacture for export became important not only in England (as already noted) but also in Holland, taking the place formerly occupied by the industry of Flanders. All of this was reflected in the emergence of new entrepôts: London steadily grew in importance; Bristol, trading in exported cloth and imported wine, rose while South-ampton sank into insignificance. Above all, by the end of the fifteenth century Antwerp has gone far to acquiring the primacy in international trade and exchange formerly held by Bruges. The collapse of the Flemish cloth manufacture which had taken place by 1400 did not im-mediately lead to the extinction of the mercantile importance of Bruges. At Bruges in the mid-fifteenth century the Hansa was still very active, the Florentine bankers still maintained branches and it was the main northern outlet for the alum shipments of the Genoese. But then Bruges, its river silting up, gave way to Antwerp. The older centre had tried to save itself by monopoly and restriction. The new centre was freer. Its commercial controls were lighter and Brabant was not at the mercy, as Flanders was, of the rivalries and ambitions of the duke of Burgundy and the king of France. The market in cloth, in salt and eastern goods, and the market in finance moved to Antwerp and with Antwerp rose also the activity of the nearby port of Bergen-op-Zoom and, further north, of Amsterdam.

France, it may seem, was not partaking in the new opportunities opening up in Atlantic commerce. This is only partially true. Bordeaux was beginning to resume its former importance by the late fifteenth century. But the most important general development in France was linked with overland routes rather than with the western coast. From 1463 Louis XI deliberately set out to promote the fairs of Lyons— mainly at the expense of the fairs of Geneva—and the town was soon the principal market in Europe for silk, well on the way to becoming one of the great commercial and industrial towns of the sixteenth century. The king's support (exemption from taxes) was vital to the success of this development, but it should not suggest that kings uniformly supported an enlightened mercantile policy. A prosperous town was a source of loans; Louis was capable of supporting Mediter-ranean adventures which were inimical to Lyons; and he, like other sovereigns, had only a casual concern for the consequences of fiscal changes or the stability of the currency. Everywhere hope of immediate gain normally dominated attempts at the regulation of trade, although there are many traces in the urban republics, and a few in the courts of kings, of an awareness of long-term economic policy, which might be described as an early form of mercantilism. Such is one implication of a curious rhyming propaganda piece written in England in 1437, the *Libel of English Polycie*. Prompted by a precise economic crisis (a pro-hibition of English merchandise entering the Low Countries imposed by the duke of Burgundy in 1436), the author's message is the need for England to dominate the narrow seas.

> Keep then the sea about in special
> Which of England is the round wall
> As though England were likened to a city
> And the wall environ were the sea.
> Keep then the sea, that is the wall of England.[1]

Much fiercer forms of beggar-my-neighbour were played by the com-mercial towns and princes on the continent: indeed the Burgundian action of 1436 is an example.

The bonds of trade

How closely the main areas of Europe had been linked together by trade can be shown in two concrete examples. Here is a price list of articles sold in Prussia by the Teutonic Order in 1400 (prices are in Prussian

[1] *Libel*, ed. G. Warner (Oxford, 1926), p. 55. Cf. G. Holmes in *Eng. Hist. Rev.*, 76 (1961).

marks per last, equalling about two metric tons:[1]

Saffron	7,040	Hungarian iron	21
Ginger	1,040	Salt from Lüneburg	12½
Pepper	640	Herring	12
Wax	237½	Salt from Flanders	8
French wine	109½	Wismar beer	7½
Rice	80	Flour	7½
Steel	75	Wheat	7
Rhenish wine	66	Rye	5¾
Olive oil	60	Barley	4⅕
Honey	35	Potash	4¾
Butter	30		

And here is a note on the stock in trade of a fifteenth-century mercer in the small English town of Leicester:[2]

This man was at the same time draper, haberdasher, jeweller, grocer, ironmonger, saddler, and dealer in timber, furniture and hardware. Even this does not describe him adequately, for he had a small stock of wool, wool-fells and skins on hand, and he could have offered you ready-made gowns in taffeta or silk, daggers, bowstrings, harpstrings, writing paper, materials for making ink, and seeds for the vegetable garden. His resources were greatest in the drapery department, which comprised twenty different kinds of British and imported cloth; he was also well stocked with small wares, notably purses of gold cloth, belts, ribbons, skeins of Paris silk, children's stockings, silk coifs, and kerchiefs for nuns. In the way of hardware he had everything from cutlery and candelabra to coal-scuttles and horse-shoes. Provisions he had none beyond honey, raisins and salt; but the absence of any note of perishable foods . . . does not prove that they had not been included in the original stock.

Silk and raisins in Leicester, olive oil and spices in Prussia represent the end of a vast distributive effort which went far to pooling the resources of the continent.

Yet there were all manner of forces working in a contrary direction. Hostility to foreign merchants was common, even if it did not take the extreme forms of xenophobia found from time to time in London, where the Hansards and the Italians were occasionally attacked by the mob. Attempts to secure the rights of merchants to recover debts from foreign nationals by way of letters of marque led to outright piracy;

[1] Dollinger, *Hanse*, app. no. 46 (from W. Böhnke, *Der Binnenhandel des deutschen Ordens in Preussen*, 1962, pp. 51-3).

[2] S. Thrupp in *Studies in English Trade in the Fifteenth Century*, pp. 291-2.

and privateering became a kind of commercial undertaking in which honest men thought it no harm to invest. In the absence of government understanding of the matter, one basic economic problem defeated the ingenuity of even the adroitest Italian bankers—the balance of payments. It often happened that the exchange of commodities was so uneven that there were no funds in Bruges to settle accounts in Florence. The virtual cessation of papal taxation in northern Europe intensified this difficulty, especially in English–Italian trade.

Another influence on the free development of commerce was the condemnation of usury by the Church. Canonists and theologians agreed with the classical doctrine that money should not beget money, reinforced as it was by the teaching of Christ: *benefacite, et mutuum date, nihil inde sperantes* (' . . . do good and lend, hoping for nothing again', St Luke, 6: 35). The straight loan was thus theoretically debarred from earning interest. On the other hand a wide range of transactions, which in effect were interest-bearing loans, were regarded as not falling into the category of usury. Usury, in short, only arose in simple lending operations and, if the contract might involve loss or danger to the principal, interest could legally be charged. It seems likely that it was because of this doctrine that the Italian bankers elaborated bills of exchange, real and fictitious, in the way mentioned above.[1] Exchange of money, even when this concealed interest on a loan, was not regarded as usurious. Italian bankers, and business men everywhere, were in fact prepared to go to great lengths to avoid practices specifically condemned by the Church as illegal and sinful, though their massive donations to churches and charities show how guilty many of them felt about their actions. There is some evidence that regard for the forms weighed more heavily on merchants in Italy than on northern merchants or even on Italians when they were working in northern countries. The Genoese abandoned loans based on credits in the *Casa di San Giorgio* in 1466 when this was stigmatized as being usurious, although it had been a common way of raising funds for many years.[2] In England loans to the crown attracted a very high rate of interest, but this is often concealed; the crown, that is to say, undertook to repay a sum considerably larger than it actually borrowed, but it was only the higher figure which was recorded as the 'loan'.[3] The major operations of bankers and

[1] Above, pp. 377–9.
[2] J. Heers, *Gênes au XVᵉ siècle* (Paris, 1961), pp. 256–7.
[3] K. B. McFarlane, 'Loans to the Lancastrian kings: the problem of inducement', *Cambridge Historical Journal*, 9 (1947–49), pp. 57–68.

their creditors (who included many prelates as well as laity) could be brought into line with canon law in these and other ways. The loan secured on a pledge was another matter, for here the lender was not liable to lose the principal. This kind of business, money-lending on a small scale and pawnbroking, was very extensive, especially in towns of any size, and it was unequivocally a usurious activity. In Florence pawnbrokers, practically all Christians by the fourteenth century,[1] were fined heavily each year and could not join the guild of changers (*arte del cambio*), the bankers' guild. But in effect this meant that the city was licensing pawnbroking, and similar measures were taken to control pawnbrokers in other cities. The charitable *monti di pietà* charged a low rate of interest, and this was ultimately declared by Pope Leo X to be void of sin. Experience had shown that it was impossible to maintain the interest-free loan even for the poor.

These impediments to international trade, and those referred to earlier (bad communications and war) were to last long after the end of this period. What had been accomplished was, however, impressive. Communities in all parts of the continent were now regularly supplied with goods drawn from far away. Out of this extensive traffic a few great markets rose and fell and hundreds of smaller communities learned not only to enjoy the luxuries of other lands but to depend on distant sources for grain, fish, oil and dairy products. Basically most men still depended on their locality for the necessities of life, but they could in an emergency supplement local with imported supplies. And the list of necessities was getting longer.

[1] Jewish pawnbrokers were admitted to Florence by the Medici; they were by then established in other Italian towns. C. Roth, *The Jews in the Renaissance* (repr. New York, 1965), pp. 6–14.

XV

The Future: Europe and the World

In the cultural matters discussed in chapter XIII an indication was given of future developments. In the sixteenth century there was a steady assimilation over the whole continent of Italian artistic and educational programmes, and the moral values of the 'civic' humanists of Florence, as translated by the courts of Italy in the later fifteenth century, were to be acclimatized in the north. The sixteenth century was to witness not only a diaspora of Italian ideas, of Italian writers, engineers and soldiers, and a new and coherent desire on the part of non-Italians to go to the peninsula to perfect themselves as artists, scholars or gentlemen. It was also to see a scattering of Europeans over the face of the globe and colonial activity which in the end was radically to affect the history of mankind as a whole. This process was not to be accomplished for centuries, but its beginnings can be traced to this period. Venice and Genoa were, after all, deeply versed in the acquisition and exploration of colonial territories in the Mediterranean and so were the Catalans whose enterprise formed the basis of the Aragonese 'empire'. The moment wider horizons opened up there was much experience to draw on.

It is possible (and in our 'one-world' mentality it is a temptation to which historians sometimes fall) to talk of the Middle Ages, and especi-

BIBLIOGRAPHY. J. H. Parry, *The Age of Reconnaissance* (1963) replaces earlier works in English dealing with 'Discovery, exploration and settlement, 1450 to 1650': it is particularly valuable for its discussion of shipbuilding and ship design, and navigation and cartography. An exciting programme of research into Catalan and Italian colonialism before 1500 is sketched by C. Verlinden, *Précédents médiévaux de la colonie en Amérique* (Instituto Panamericano de geografía e historia, Mexico, 1954). For a brief discussion of the conventional picture held by men in this period see E. G. R. Taylor, *Ideas on the Shape, Size and Movements of the Earth* (Historical Association pamphlet 126, London, 1943) and *Mandeville's Travels*, ed. M. Letts (Hakluyt Society, 2 vols. 1952 for 1950). On the notions of Christendom and Europe, D. Hay, *Europe—The Emergence of an Idea* (Edinburgh, 1957).

ally of the later Middle Ages, as though there was frequent and fruitful contact between Europe, Asia and Africa. One can stress the travels of Marco Polo and other merchants and clergy. One can point to the regular traffic, which defeated Tatar invasions and Ottoman expansion, in spices and silk from east to west. One can instance the slow penetration into western art of grotesques and conceits which have an oriental origin, or emphasize the oriental source of some of the tales in Boccaccio and other writers. Yet when all is said and done the gulf which separated the Christian world of the Middle Ages from central Africa or the Far East was far greater than it had been in the Hellenistic period or than it was to be in centuries to come. The average world view of a literate but non-scholarly man of the fifteenth century is fairly reflected in Sir John Mandeville's *Travels*: for Europe and the Mediterranean the detail is not unreasonable, but as the traveller moves east his pages contain a fantastic amalgam of legend, much of it going back to Roman times—dog-faced men, the vegetable lamb, giants, and so on. The steady traffic in eastern commodities had done little to disperse the fog of incomprehension, though it might have done if the direct trading of the late thirteenth and early fourteenth centuries had not come to an abrupt end with the advent of the Ming dynasty in China in 1368. For most of the period the merchant in the Mediterranean was dealing with the East not directly but through a host of middlemen.

This situation was to change slowly in the late fifteenth century, notably with the activity of the Portuguese, whose mariners embarked on steady exploration in the Atlantic and down the western coast of Africa. This was made possible not merely by new and better shipping and equipment. This was of great assistance, but it must be remembered that the Norsemen had successfully navigated the North Atlantic in an earlier period, and English and other northern mariners regularly and efficiently steered the very difficult course to Iceland in the fourteenth and fifteenth centuries. What then provoked the activities associated with the Portuguese Prince Henry (1394–1460) and which have given him the soubriquet 'Navigator'? A contemporary chronicler listed his motives: to find out what lay beyond Cape Bojador, for quite practical purposes (in order to find the gold-supplying areas of West Africa); to develop new trade routes with Christian peoples; to determine the limits of Moorish political power; to evangelize among pagans; to ally with any Christian rulers (a reference to the legend of Prester John); and to 'fulfil the predictions of his horoscope'.[1] He was, in short,

[1] Parry, pp. 35–6, summarizing Azurara.

395

not interested in scientific knowledge for its own sake, but was an enlightened but otherwise fairly typical representative of an old-established Iberian tradition of trade and the crusade. It should be remembered that he played a part in the capture of the North African port of Ceuta in 1415. This is not the picture of the older textbooks, and it firmly dissociates Henry and his immediate circle from humanist influences, but it places their endeavours in a far more logical context.

Some of the Atlantic islands (Canaries, Madeiras, Azores) were already known to Iberian and Italian sailors in the fourteenth century. Under Prince Henry's patronage colonization began. The West African coast had been explored as far as Sierra Leone by his death, and the Cape Verde Islands had been discovered. More important, these achievements were beginning to pay a modest dividend. Timber came from the Madeiras and the sugar cane was introduced there from Sicily. From Africa came a little pepper, gold dust and some slaves. The next important advance came after the war between Portugal and Castile in 1476–79. The Castilians were victorious, but the Portuguese (by the treaty of Alcoçovas) retained all their overseas interests save the Canaries. Juan II of Portugal (1481–95) energetically supported further expeditions down the African coast and the most remarkable result of this was the rounding of the Cape of Good Hope by Bartolomeu Dias at the end of 1487. In July 1497 Vasco da Gama set sail on the voyage which took him to India and back.

By this time Castile had also embarked on maritime expansion. Christopher Columbus, a native of Genoa, who had failed to secure Portuguese support for a westward voyage to India or China, succeeded in getting Queen Isabella to authorize an expedition which sailed in August 1492. When he returned in March 1493 he had (as he thought) discovered the Indies; in fact he had found the islands to be called, in rectification of this error, the West Indies. Pope Alexander VI was induced to define as Castilian all territories south and west of a line one hundred leagues west of the Azores. During Columbus's second voyage in 1493–96 (which carried colonists to the West Indies) the demarcation of new lands was renegotiated between Portugal and Spain in the treaty of Tordesillas (7 June 1494). By moving the boundary between Portuguese and Spanish territory a further 270 leagues to the west this was in the end of the day to make Brazil a Portuguese dependency, though it is far from clear that this was realized at the time; what the Portuguese were anxious about was not a share of a New World but their rights in India, the commercial significance of which was not in doubt.

The full development of the Atlantic route to the East by the Portuguese and to the Americas by the Castilians lay ahead, although some of the elements in later Spanish colonization and commerce were firmly established by earlier Italian and Catalan involvement in trade and political settlement in the Mediterranean. Much that had passed for certain knowledge of the non-European world began to collapse with the early discoveries. Columbus had been convinced that on his first voyage he had reached an island of the Japanese archipelago because of an erroneous guess of Marco Polo and the serious underestimate of Ptolemy about the size of the world. Such 'science' was to be replaced by knowledge of a practical kind.

Awareness of the nature of the other continents was to affect a further feature of the later Middle Ages, the gradual abandonment of the notion of Christendom as a unifying concept. Christendom had become a self-conscious idea in the course of the eleventh century; the pope was in theory head of an area whose fundamental characteristic was its Christianity, thrown into sharp relief by the challenge of Islam. By the fifteenth century Christendom was gradually being drained of its emotional content, and in the literary sources the word Europe was making ever more frequent appearances. In the dialogue Pius II tried to conduct with Mohammed the Conqueror one would have expected the pope to use the word Christendom, but in fact it is *Europa* that is used. And not unreasonably so, for the fifteenth century, which saw the Christian Byzantine Empire disappear with the fall of Constantinople, also saw within shrinking Christendom the development of stronger national groups, of churches which looked to princes as their effective masters rather than to the pope. Equally significant, Christendom had in theory the whole world as its province. The emergence of Europe as a living concept indicated an acceptance that this was no longer practical politics.

As with overseas exploration and settlement, so with the word Europe, the late fifteenth century merely sets the scene, it does not determine the action. Christendom was to be a long time dying. Yet one may feel that the decades around 1500, which experienced an acceptance of the virtues of the active life and education for service to the community spreading from Italy, coinciding as this did with the overseas discoveries of the Portuguese and Spaniards (and of the Italians in their pay), heralded a redisposition of human resources and ambitions. To that new world 'Europe' was to contribute rather than 'Christendom'. It was, of course, a Europe which was still professedly Christian. But it was Christian in a way which already tolerated religious regionalism and which was coming to accept Christian ideals, modified by the humanist and the reformer, very different from those which had inspired St Bernard, Innocent III or St Louis.

Appendix I

NOTE ON GENERAL HISTORIES OF EUROPE
AND ATLASES

The period is surveyed in a much fuller way in a number of general works. Volumes VII and VIII of the *Cambridge Medieval History* (Cambridge, 1932, 1936) cover all areas save the Balkans and the Byzantine Empire, which are dealt with in volume IV (see Bibliography to chapter X above). The series has good bibliographies. Several chapters in the *New Cambridge Modern History*, vol. I (1957) are relevant. In Methuen's 'History of Europe' the volume by C. W. Previté-Orton, *Europe 1198–1378* (London, 1937), is better than that by W. T. Waugh, *Europe 1378–1494* (1932). The two most useful foreign surveys are French: in G. Glotz, 'Histoire Générale', vol. VI (A. Coville and R. Fawtier, Paris, 1940–41), VII (J. Calmette and E. Déprez, 1937–39), VIII (H. Pirenne, G. Cohen and H. Focillon, 1933); and in L. Halphen and P. Sagnac, 'Peuples et Civilizations', H. Pirenne and others, *La fin du moyen âge*, 2 vols. (Paris, 1931). M. P. Gilmore provides a survey of Europe from 1453 to 1517 in his *World of Humanism* (New York, 1952) and Wallace K. Ferguson a wider ranging study of *Europe in Transition 1300–1520* (Boston, 1962). Recent work by English historians in this period is reflected in *Europe in the Late Middle Ages*, ed. J. Hale, J. R. L. Highfield and B. Smalley (London, 1965).

There are no really satisfactory historical atlases currently available in English for the medieval period. Of those that are available in other languages the most useful is Westermann's *Atlas zur Weltgeschichte*, II. *Mittelalter* (Brunswick, 1956). It is imaginative and reasonably priced. For reference the best of the older atlases is still K. Spruner and T. Mencke, *Handatlas für die Geschichte des Mittelalters und der neuren Zeit* (Gotha, 1880), and there are useful maps issued for each volume of the *Cambridge Medieval History*. A modern physical map of Europe is also essential.

Appendix II

GENEALOGICAL TABLES

Note: (1) The arrangement does not necessarily place children in the order in which they were born. (2) A dotted line indicates illegitimate descent. (3) An arrow refers to another entry on the same table. Only those persons are shown who were of importance or through whom royal power descended.

Other tables will be found in the text as follows:

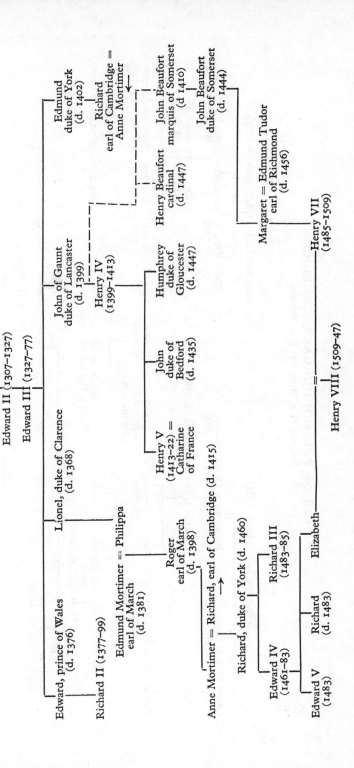

THE ENGLISH ROYAL FAMILY

(to illustrate the succession of the Lancastrians and the Yorkists)

Edward I (1272–1307)
Edward II (1307–1327)
Edward III (1327–77)

Edward, prince of Wales (d. 1376)

Richard II (1377–99)

Lionel, duke of Clarence (d. 1368)

John of Gaunt duke of Lancaster (d. 1399)

Edmund duke of York (d. 1402)

Edmund Mortimer = Philippa earl of March (d. 1381)

Henry IV (1399–1413)

Richard earl of Cambridge = Anne Mortimer

John Beaufort marquis of Somerset (d 1410)

Roger earl of March (d. 1398)

Henry V (1413–22) = Catharine of France

John duke of Bedford (d. 1435)

Humphrey duke of Gloucester (d. 1447)

Henry Beaufort cardinal (d. 1447)

John Beaufort duke of Somerset (d. 1444)

Anne Mortimer = Richard, earl of Cambridge (d. 1415)

Henry VI (1422–61)

Margaret = Edmund Tudor earl of Richmond (d. 1456)

Richard, duke of York (d. 1460)

Henry VII (1485–1509)

Edward IV (1461–83)

Richard III (1483–85)

Elizabeth

Edward V (1483)

Richard (d. 1483)

Henry VIII (1509–47)

RULERS OF POLAND, HUNGARY AND BOHEMIA

(P = Poland; H = Hungary; B = Bohemia)

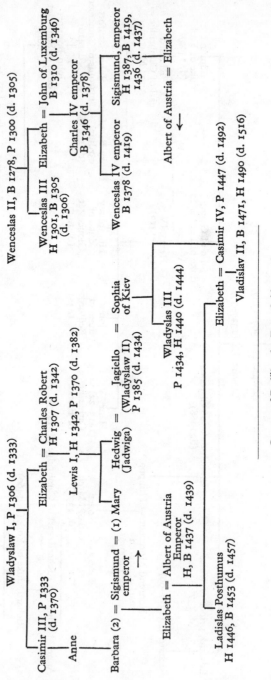

KINGS OF FRANCE

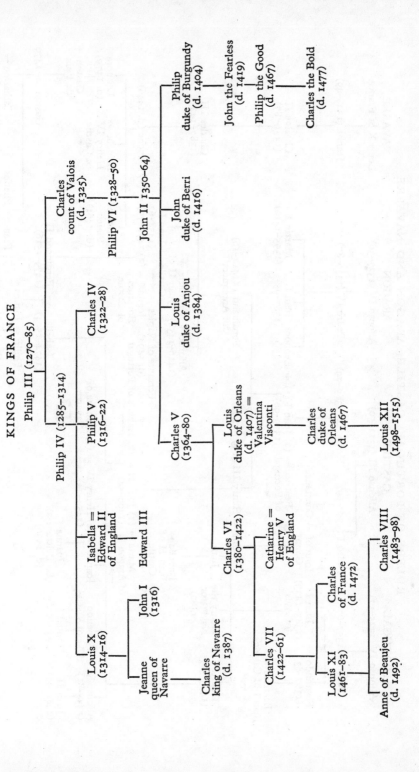

Philip III (1270–85)

Philip IV (1285–1314)

Charles count of Valois (d. 1325)

Louis X (1314–16)

Philip V (1316–22)

Charles IV (1322–28)

Isabella = Edward II of England

Philip VI (1328–50)

Edward III

John I (1316)

Jeanne queen of Navarre

Charles king of Navarre (d. 1387)

Louis duke of Anjou (d. 1384)

John II 1350–64

John duke of Berri (d. 1416)

Philip duke of Burgundy (d. 1404)

John the Fearless (d. 1419)

Philip the Good (d. 1467)

Charles the Bold (d. 1477)

Charles V (1364–80)

Louis duke of Orleans (d. 1407) = Valentina Visconti

Charles duke of Orleans (d. 1467)

Louis XII (1498–1515)

Charles VI (1380–1422)

Catharine = Henry V of England

Charles VII (1422–61)

Louis XI (1461–83)

Anne of Beaujeu (d. 1492)

Charles of France (d. 1472)

Charles VIII (1483–98)

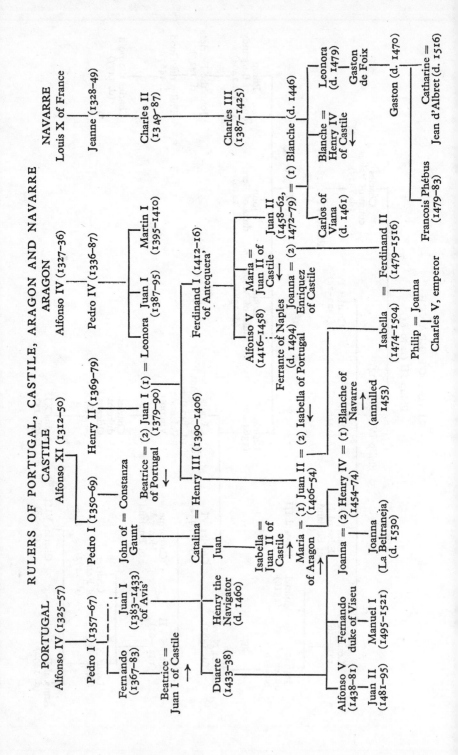

RULERS OF PORTUGAL, CASTILE, ARAGON AND NAVARRE

Index

Some additional dates and identifications are provided. Under the larger countries only the main political and administrative matters are usually indicated; other references are under the relevant topic. Names of modern authorities quoted in the text are not indexed.

Hungary, in XIV C., 212–16, 221–3;
in XV C., 41, 229, 231–40, 261
Hunyadi, John, regent of Hungary,
232–3, 236, 261, 318
Huss, John, 226, 321–2, 324–7, 330,
342
Hussites, 235–6, 288–9

Iceland, 206, 208, 395
Iconium, see Konya
Île de France, 36, 140
India, 369
Indulgences, 307–8
Industry, see Manufacture
Ingebörg of Norway, 209
Ingolstadt, 196
Innocent III, pope, 81
Innocent VI, pope, 247, 279
Innocent VIII, pope, 292, 297, 330,
344
Inns of Court, 162
Inquisition, papal, 309, 329–31;
Spanish, 152–3, 181, 320
Institoris, Henry, 331
Insurance, commercial, 363
International Gothic, 354–5
Ireland, 23, 43, 50, 95, 128, 132
Iron, 368, 371–2
Isabella, q. of Castile, 115, 150–3, 162,
320, 331, 396
Isabella, q. of Edward II, 52, 128, 138
Isabella, q. of Richard II, 155
Isabella of Bavaria, q. of Charles VI,
141
Isenburg, Dietrich of, 51
Isidore, metropolitan of Kiev, 301
Italian League, 185–6
Italy, government and politics in, 71–
77, 80–2, 85–6, 115, 117–21, 163–86;
Renaissance in, 5–6, 333, 345, 347–
354, 356–8; and exploration, 396–7
Ivan III, grand duke of Moscow, 263–
266

Jacquerie, 35–6, 38, 140
Jadwiga, see Hedwig
Jagiello, prince of Lithuania, see
Wladyslaw II
James I, k. of Scotland, 111, 135–6
James II, k. of Scotland, 136
James III, k. of Scotland, 136
James IV, k. of Scotland, 136
James of the March, St, 58, 318
Jandun, Jean de, 341
Jauer, 218, 223
Jawnuta, prince of Lithuania, 219
Jenštejn, John of, archbishop of
Prague, 225
Jerome of Prague, 325
Jerusalem, 305, 315, 374

Jesuate Order, 319n.
Jews, 21, 61, 68, 100, 140, 146, 152,
181, 306, 331–2, 393n.
Jiskra, Jan, lord of Slovakia, 233
Joan of Arc, 11, 156, 330
Joanna I, q. of Naples, 221
Joanna II, q. of Naples, 180
Joanna Enriquez, q. of Juan II of
Aragon, 150
Joanna, la Beltraneja, 150
John XXII, pope, 51n., 82, 215, 268,
271, 273, 276–7, 310, 312
John XXIII, pope, 258, 283–5, 287,
324
John V, emp., 246–8, 255, 260
John VI Cantacuzenus, emp., 246–7,
250, 252, 255
John VIII, emp., 247
John, k. of England, 24–5, 127
John II, k. of France, 98, 101, 105,
139–40, 154
John Albert, k. of Poland, 238–9
John of Luxemburg, k. of Bohemia,
182, 184, 190–1, 215, 216, 217–18,
222
John of Bridlington, St, 316
Jobst, see Moravia
John Nepomucene, St, see Pomuk
Jonas, metropolitan of Kiev and All
Russia, 301
Josas, archdeaconry of, 303, 308–9
Josquin des Prez, 356
Juan I, k. of Aragon, 149
Juan II, k. of Aragon, 148, 150–1
Juan I, k. of Castile, 150
Juan II, k. of Castile, 150
Juan I (of Avis) k. of Portugal, 151
Juan II, k. of Portugal, 151, 396
Jülich, 197, 201
Juliana of Norwich, 315
Jutland, 37, 205, 207

Kalmar, Union of, 209–10
Karl Knutsson, k. of Sweden, 210
Karlštejn, 223
Kasimov, 264
Kazan, khanate, 262–3
Kempe, Margery, 315
Kempis, Thomas à, 12, 315, 357
Kiev, 215, 230, 263–4; metropolitan
of, 264, 301 ·
Kildare, Fitzgerald earls of, 132
Kilia, 238
Kings and kingship, in W. Europe, 25,
82–8, 88–90, 161–2; in Scandinavia,
208–9; in E. Europe, 238–40; papal,
267–73, 293; in Byzantium, 244–7;
in Russia, 265–6
Kniprode, Winrich von, 204
Konřim, 234